RETHINKING THEOLOGY IN INDIA

Rethinking Theology in India

Christianity in the Twenty-first Century

Edited by
JAMES MASSEY
T.K. JOHN SJ

CENTRE FOR DALIT/SUBALTERN STUDIES

MANOHAR
2013

First Published 2013

ISBN 978-81-7304-976-7

Published by
Ajay Jain for
Manohar Publishers & Distributors
4753/23 Ansari Road, Daryaganj
New Delhi 110002

Printed by
Salasar Imaging Systems
Delhi 110035

Contents

Preface

Knowledge is a potential power source for revolutionary change. That is what the recent history of the world teaches us. When correct and adequate information is available about the condition of an individual or a group, consciousness of the sources of the manifold disabilities is awakened. Location of the root cause, agents responsible for the social malady, its spread and depth, all these are explored and secured. This necessarily inflames the sensibilities of the victim. When many members of the community, subjected to these disabilities imposed upon them by agencies outside their group come together, a heightened consciousness is the outcome. Agitations aimed at redress of the grievances and disabilities can be the next phase. Many a social movement takes their origin from such developments. Key to all social movements is knowledge and consciousness. Hence it is clear that spreading knowledge about the various aspects of the disabilities that a social group is subject to can be a significant service.

The Centre for Dalit/Subaltern Studies (CDSS) is committed to the promotion of knowledge and awareness about the actual situation of the subaltern groups now getting organized. The central focus is upon the disabilities of the Dalits in India. The Centre is aware of the large number of groups committed to the liberation of Dalits in India. CDSS is committed to contribute to this development. Organizing seminars and networking with similar groups both within the country and across the world is one of the activities of the Centre. The present volume is the result of such an international initiative.

The Centre is first of all grateful to those sections of the global human community that have been subject to multiple disabilities but now are awakened and on the move to self-empowerment. The *minjung* in Korea, the 'blacks' in the Americas, the Dalits and Tribals in India are among these sections. It is their experiences and sensibilities that are the forces behind this volume. It is with due respect and regard for their sensibilities that reflections upon them are initiated and recorded in the following pages. Therefore first and foremost it is they whom we gratefully thank on behalf of the Centre and the contributors.

The range of contributors to the volume is impressive. Their efforts to gather the materials, organize them and present them is highly commendable. It is these conscientious writers who prepared the papers that make this volume a reality for our times. We thank them for thier contribution to the Dalit awakening.

Next, we have to admit that this volume is the result of the encouragement and help received from many individuals and organizations to whom we would like to express our gratitude, particularly to the 15 contributors. We are especially thankful to the Centre for Dalit/Subaltern Studies, New Delhi for sponsoring the publication as part of its programme. We are also thankful to our colleagues Imti Jamir, Nungsang Jamir and others, who have helped in putting together and arranging the materials very carefully through its many stages. We are indebted to our publisher Ramesh Jain and his son Ajay Jain for their valuable suggestions and keen interest in this publication.

Above all we are thankful to God Almighty for giving us the strength to complete this volume, which we believe will provide further support to people of different faiths and ideologies committed to the liberation of the deprived and emergence of a genuine human community.

New Delhi EDITORS

Introduction

Why This Book?

In 1938 a seminal book entitled *Rethinking Christianity in India* was published in response to the World Missionary Conference held at Tambaram in south India. The Tambaram Conference represented the views of Christian missionaries of that time, according to which the religious traditions other than Christianity, also carry in them indicators of deep religious experiences and great moral values. But they believed that it is only in Jesus Christ that full salvation is available which humankind needs. Such a view, according to the authors of *Rethinking Christianity in India*, represents the views of some of the Christian missionaries from the West and need not be the views of the Indian Christians, who according to them, 'should think and act for themselves'. They 'demanded that Christ should be related to the great Indian religious heritage and that Christianity should assume an Indian expression in life, thought and activity'.

Ever since its publication, *Rethinking Christianity in India* has been influencing people from different spectrum of society and continues to play a major role in the ecclesiological and theological development till today.

Much has happened thereafter. Christian consciousness has been monitoring trends in the social history and registering protests and alarms raised by affected groups across history. Two cries of lament were picked up which altered the perceptions on theology, method in theology and the course of history.

The first was the cries of lamentation from Egypt. The second was the cries of lamentation from the world's deprived sections. The *minjung* in Korea, the blacks in America, the exploited workers of the world, the tribals all over the world, the slum dwellers of metropolitan cities, were noticed with more than normal attention. The most pitiful of all have been the cries of the Dalits of India because their plight was unique.

The first cries ever were from the grandchildren of Abraham who were promised prosperity and increase by Yahweh Himself but were now suffering from torments inflicted upon them by the Egyptians. Their cries reached 'the ears of Yahweh'. His response is recorded in the Bible. The re-discovery in recent times of the significance of the event led to the emergence of a new method in theology, replacing or correcting the centuries-long method tracing to St. Anselm and reaching up to Gutierrez. Yahweh and Moses were not outsiders of events, but insiders. Walking with the exiles through the desert in search of a new land and its occupation made them insiders in solidarity with the strugglers. This *experience of liberative struggle* constitutes a major component of the new method in theologizing and is to replace the method of theologians teaching from chairs in the classrooms/lecture halls, using for their resource, books from the bookshelf. The new method has to derive theology from the struggles of the deprived outside the lecture halls and libraries. The library comes only after the 'experience' of the desert or the slums. The new sprout in theology became known as the liberation theology.

The second, the cries of lament of the Dalits of India—disturbed many a sensitive and right-thinking ideologue and theologian, not to speak of Dalit activist. These were forcing a rethinking on an appropriate method of theologizing in India, to replace the existing. For it is shocking to learn that for centuries theological institutions existed and functioned in this country yet the damnable caste system and practice existed and functioned not only in the society but also in the church. It was rampant in the church at all levels—hierarchy, institutions of learning, religious houses, service centres, liturgical practices, social relations, even celebrations! How is it that theology did not take note and reflect upon?

The demand of the new theology is that the organized actions of the deprived should generate knowledge of the perverted human situation, assisted by revealed knowledge. And that knowledge should bring about change in the human social situation.

And so, the landscape of the country, i.e. social, economic, political, cultural, and religious, has been changing rapidly. People's movements including subaltern movements and human right movements, have been gaining momentum in the social sphere. The trends in Christianity too were also rapid. Theology of dialogue and its various offshoots were among the outcome. Birth of subaltern theologies is part of that trajectory and is part of the main discussion of essays of this volume.

In this book, the authors, while reviewing the developments and the emerging trends during the last seventy-five years after the concept of Rethinking Christianity in India was introduced in 1938, a revisit to theology that shapes Christianity, is attempted. It makes attempts to reconstruct by taking into consideration the many new social and theological trajectories. Here in the present volume, the Christian response represents the voice of the entire Christian community in India. The contribution in 1938 was limited to seven persons who belonged to one region of India and all were men belonging to one particular tradition of Christian faith. But the present volume carries the views of both men and women. It also carries the voices of four major disadvantaged groups namely, Dalits, Tribals, Adivasis and Women. It also carries the views of the major traditions of Christian faith, which include Roman Catholic, Ecumenical, Evangelical and Pentecostal. It also specially talks about the

'Theological and Ecclesiological Perspectives' and the entire gamut of issues of 'Relevance of Religion in the Twenty-first Century', with special emphasis on multi-faith and multi-culture response. And the last article carries an extensive discussion on 'Secular Ideologies and Theologies and Religions'. Finally the volume closes with a note from the editors on our 'Common Task for Tomorrow' which in fact represents the ongoing liberating process of the subalterns, particularly of the Dalits.

The liberative process of the Dalits or subalterns with which this book deals is not new. There have been many such movements throughout history. A careful study of the Hebrew and Christian scriptures shows that these represent the oldest of the traditions. For example, the Hebrew prophets like Jeremiah (627 BCE onward) is the most typical of such examples. His prophetic words, which he received as the Word of God, came to him either during the captivity of his community of Israelites in Babylon or during the post-captivity era. Here we have one such example, that of Dr. B.R. Ambedkar, whose liberative efforts began during the British colonial rule (1930-47) and continued during the post-independent period of India (1947-56).

However, in the case of India, Lord Mahavira (540-468 BCE) and Lord Buddha (563-483 BCE) were contemporaries of Jeremiah and other prophets, who had similar approaches to the religious, cultural and social traditions of their times. Jeremiah rejected the theology of Zion (holy temple and city based identity) and upheld the theology of Exodus (liberation), the basis of which was God's liberation of Israel from Egyptian slavery (Jeremiah 2: 4-13), and a theology which demanded, 'acting with justice and righteousness and taking care of the needy, the alien, the orphan and the widow' (Jeremiah 2: 4-13). He rejected the belief introduced by the monarchy and priestly classes, according to which God is supposed to defend the holy city of Jerusalem, where prayers were offered in the temple (1 Kings 6: 9-36; 7: 2-12; 10: 17). Lord Mahavira and Lord Buddha took the role of priests (Brahmin) and also accepted their fellowship with the people who were considered outcastes by the so-called upper caste. In the Indian context such liberative traditions continued to be upheld and sustained all through the later Indian history by many which included various Hindu Bhakti saints, Christian and missionary movements, Muslim Sufis and the teachings of Sikh Gurus. This volume, particularly Part V, deals with the theme of 'Relevance of Religion in the Twenty-first Century' and with the multi-faith and multi-cultural richness of the Indian religious traditions, which are supposed to be part of the methodologies of 'Rethinking Theology in India for the Twenty-first Century'. Here the basic truth, which the Christian and other theologians need to keep in mind, is that their theologians are able to present the God who takes the side of the poor and the oppressed, and who liberates the oppressed communities (subaltern) like the Dalits in India. This is indeed the first test of any theological expression, with its claim to present the Gospel of Jesus Christ for our times.

The present volume is divided into six parts. Part I, which contains an essay by James Massey, offers an overview of various contextual theologies. After dealing with the present status of Christianity in India, it then deals with the Indian context and offers a kind of audit of the current major theologies. It discusses in detail three streams of theologies, which have been made available in India, followed by a discussion on 'Indian Christianity of Tomorrow'. In concluding his essay the author says:

> But still we have to accept the fact that regarding active participation for fuller liberation of various oppressed communities, the Church still maintains its silence. The Indian Church should give priority to the cause of liberation of these communities. It is only through this partnership that transformation is possible.

In Part II, the case of four traditionally oppressed communities are presented in detail by four leading scholars belonging to these four sectors of Indian people. Professor A. Maria Arul Raja, a leading Jesuit scholar, deals with 'Contemporary Social

Change: Emerging Dalit Theological Sensibilities'. In his essay Prof. Raja addresses specially the organic intellectuals by saying:

> Every person claiming to be engaged in enabling the dialogue between the Dalits and the religio-cultural resources could be a Dalit or non-Dalit by birth. But what matters is that these organic intellectuals, be they from academic or ideological pulpits, have to be brought under the serious scrutiny of the hermeneutical responsibility. They have to be made accountable to the Dalit world in its struggle to annihilate the virus of caste hierarchy.

A similar tone is to be found in the essay by Wati Longchar, a scholar from Nagaland, who while discussing the uses of 'Tribal Identity and Theology', concludes his discussion on the 'vision' by saying:

> Tribal peoples affirm a people-centred church, ecumenical unity, but not a church of power, hierarchy, expansion, extension and conquest. What we envision is a church that respects, recognizes, affirms, supports, promotes, and advocates for us in our struggle for self-identification and self-determination. We envision a church that goes deeper in the tribal people's experience, not only as an *object* of study, but especially as *subject* of ecclesiological and theological elaboration.

The seniormost Christian and an Adivasi scholar, Bishop N. Minz takes over the discussion on the 'Theology and the Struggles of Adivasis/Indigenous Peoples of India' and concludes with these words:

> The theology of these churches have to change in order to be in line with the New Creation in Christ and participate in the sacrificial sufferings and pains of the displaced Adivasis with whom the displaced God, even Jesus Christ, is actively working for the survival of their Identity and for their development. This is the hope of the displaced Adivasis in India. Further steps need to be taken as per what the particular situation demands in the Adivasis communities in the mainland India.

Professor Shalini Mulackal, a Sister of the Union of Presentation Sisters, who holds a doctoral degree from Madras University, presents to us a detailed discussion on 'Women: Theology and Feminist Movements in India'. She concludes her discussion with her strong concern for the women belonging to the subaltern communities particularly of Dalit and Tribal origins by pointing out:

> Though women of Dalit origin are victims of the triple oppression their experience do not find adequate space in feminist theology at the moment. Indian Feminist Theology in the future therefore needs to take this lacunae seriously and work towards an inclusive feminist theology where voices of women from the deprived communities like Dalits and tribals find more space and attention.

If the four major sectors of Indian population are treated in the second part, in the third part, four major Christian traditions of India and their response to the concerns of Dalits, Tribals, Adivasis and Women are taken up for consideration. Fr. S. Lourdusamy, a Catholic priest and activist gives a most vivid picture of the conditions of the Dalits and Tribals within the Indian society in general and more particularly in the Roman Catholic Church. He narrates a number of recent incidents to prove his point. Some of the caste-based incidents took place in a Catholic Church in Eraaiyur of the Pondicherry diocese. About the most recent incident, he states:

> There was a caste clash on 10 March 2008 again in the same parish. Dalits demanded a separate parish. There was police firing; two persons were killed in the firing. On 11 March 2008 a peace committee meeting was held in the presence T.N. Minister Ponmudi. Archbishop of Pondicherry issued a statement for equality and peace on 1 March but still equality is not achieved.

Fr. Lourduswamy gives us full details of the ongoing efforts and programmes to improve the condition of the Dalits and Tribals in the Catholic church.

A Protestant Dalit theologian Fr. Monodeep Daniel, while discussing the response of 'Ecumenical Movements and Dalit-Adivasi Awakening', lays emphasis on the methodology of doing theology from their perspective. He says:

> In doing ecumenical theology from Dalit and Adivasi perspective we should go beyond the old ideas of federal organic unity. Instead we must see solidarity with Dalits, and Adivasis. This solidarity should also include all those who are vulnerable, rejected and isolated. Out of this

will emerge the unity of faith and fellowship among those who are united with the Dalits and Adivasis.

Simon Samuel, Principal of the largest Pentecostal seminary in India, New Theological College, Dehradun, offers a very comprehensive discussion on 'Pentecostal and Charismatic Movements and the Social Demands of the Gospel'. He asserts that:

Pentecostals maintain an ecumenical vision and advocate a non-racial, caste-crossing and caste-erasing community life. . . . For example, in Latin America the Pentecostals are playing an important political role for social transformation and empowerment of the downtrodden. It is a major focus of Pentecostal ministries in many parts of India.

Richard Howell, the General Secretary of the 'Evangelical Fellowship of India' while agreeing with the other views of this volume, lays further emphasis on 'justice' and 'power transformation'. He says that:

The transformation that Christ brings creates reconciled people who work for justice in the midst of injustice, for truthfulness in the middle of deception, and for peace in the centre of a violent society, and for integrity of creation in the context of the ravages of environmental degradation. The church must be engaged in the transformation of the world. God is the source and power of transformation.

Part V deals more directly with 'Theological and Ecclesiological Perspectives'. Roger Gaikwad, the General Secretary of the National Council of Churches in India, in his discussion on his given subject 'Ecclesiastical Perspectives', deplores the fact that the Gospel has been blunted in India, because Christian faith has

become a religion, Christianity in India has not prophetically addressed the ills of Indian society'. One such problem is the caste system. While Christians continue to affirm as in Gal 3: 28 that in Christ all discriminatory distinctions disappear, caste system remains a basic fact in the church, though one may not explicitly acknowledge it. Some churches and church-related organizations are caste-based, marriage alliances are made on caste basis; elections are fought on caste lines, inter-personal relationships are determined by caste, etc. When caste consideration still plays an important role inside church, how can Christians effectively address the caste injustice in the wider society?

How will any one answer the question raised here in his statement by Gaikwad? One possible answer is offered by Indukuri John Mohan Razu in his discussion on the theme 'Towards a Critical Theology of Risk-taking'. He defines what he means by 'risk-taking' specially in the case of any subaltern groups like the Dalits. He holds that:

The story of the cross *vis-à-vis* death and resurrection of Jesus Christ is the embodiment and assurance of abundant life for all. For the Dalits they symbolize the holistic restoration of humanity. . . . Therefore, cross and resurrection symbolize an ongoing life-affirming continuum of a theology of risk-taking. Jesus Christ is the unifier who represents the victims of risk signifying that God in Jesus actively involved in transforming those who lose while taking risk. We are reminded time and time again that we should be prepared or willing to lose life, and then only we should gain it. Therefore, a critical theology of risk-taking is clearly grounded on the dictum that 'unless the seed dies it cannot bear fruits' meaningfulness of life is not possible.

The discussion in Part V continues on the same line of the earlier sections of this volume, but now it goes beyond the Christian boundaries and goes into a look into the much discussed issue of the 'Relevance of Religion in Twenty-first Century'. Efforts are made to look into the response of multi-faith and multi-cultural dimensions of religiosity. Three scholars, Ravi Tiwari, Ashish Kumar and Atola Longkumer, articulate their views on these two broader areas. These three presentations have many common points. For example, Ravi Tiwari and Ashish Kumar conclude their discussion on the multi-faith response to the issue like of the Dalits when they say:

Finally, the multi-faith response of Dalit movement is determined by their respective religious ethos. The theory of *karma* in Hinduism . . . consider that the Dalits will continue to suffer till the effect of accumulated sin of their previous birth exhausted. However, other religious traditions which would disagree with the theory of *karma* may still find their own theory which could prevent their involvement in Dalit movement. For instance, the other worldly attitudes which is found in many religious traditions, including Christianity would claim the present suffering as momentary and would, therefore, exhort people to wait for heavenly intervention which would resolve all sufferings and problems.

Atola in her discussion on 'Demands for Social Change: A Multicultural Response' ends her reflections on a more positive note but demands that:

> The state and the communities in modern India should ensure the spirit of creative tolerance and mutual equal status of all citizens of the nation. In a simplified way, the post-modern concept of hybridity, a by-product of multiculturalism, wherein differences are accommodated respected and celebrated, need to be pursued with commitment to a common vision of equal quality of life to all the practice of multi-culturalism tempered with justice can deviate towards the goal of equal quality of life for all.

Fr. T.K. John SJ, deals with the role of 'Secular Ideologies and Theologies of Religions' in the formation of a future theology in India. He presents a challenge to the whole Christian community/church in India by addressing them:

> So if God is love and if Christ is God's love incarnate in human history, and if the church is that body of Christ and is mandated to be the light of the world and the salt of the earth, theology has to be in the service of the church. Theology has to highlight, promote and vindicate these properties as necessarily inbuilt into the community. . . . Fellowship and equality have to be experienced exercised and verified in practice, in day-to-day relationship. Conviviality, commensality, connubiality, etc., have to be actualities. But they are not yet. Caste practice is still rampant. When confronted with these is the experience of pain and resistance as well as reluctance to move away from caste-dominated living to real social egalitarianism. Theology has to facilitate their emergence in the church, and the virus has to be detected and eliminated by appropriating the divine flames poured out by the Spirit of Christ at Pentecost.

In the concluding section this volume spells out the essence of theology, which is proposed for the twenty-first century, which very clearly was the burden of 15 representative theologians and scholars who took part in the discussion on the future enterprise of theology in India in the present volume. The essence of this future theology is well expressed by the editors of this volume, in the following words:

> In other words the goal of the new theology should be for emergence of a society free from these inequities and a new co-equation has to grow. 'Together we should strive for a 'community/culture'. New relationship is to be established between the once dominated groups and dominant societies leading to mutual collaboration for riddance of the unequal relationship. The dominant groups of all cultures and communities should be invited to collaborate. . . . This new change is concretely expressed through a new culture of participation, collaboration, sharing, fellowship, togetherness, etc. It is the beginning of a new community, veritable anticipation of the reign of God on this earth inaugurated by Christ (Matthew); it is a new human and humane community.

New Delhi EDITORS

PART I

RETHINKING THEOLOGY

PART I

1

Christianity to be Renewed? Rethink Theology

JAMES MASSEY

1. Introduction: All Theologies are Contextual

The expression 'theology' is a combination of two Greek words *theos* meaning 'god' and *logia* meaning 'study'. Together therefore 'theology' means 'the study of God'. But as suggested by this definition, we hardly ever study God as an 'object'. In fact, as suggested by Rex Ambler, in theology our attempt is always to

> understand God as the source and basis and ultimate context of our human existence, and therefore as refracted in human experience and history. It is especially concerned with responses to life in the past or to-day. . . . We can call these responses 'faith' . . . but faith should then be clearly distinguished from religious beliefs and dogmas which may or may not give expression to faith. Theology could then be described as an attempt to understand the meaning of faith . . . in different and changing circumstances.[1]

The well-known Indian theologian, the late M.M. Thomas, reflects a similar viewpoint when he says, 'Living theology is the manner in which a church confesses its faith and establishes its historical existence in dialogue with its own environment'.[2] In these two statements the expressions 'ultimate context of our own human existence' and 'our environment' are very important, because these give us a clue to consider theological expressions as the product of a context or an environment. In other words, we can also say that every expression of theology is contextual by which an attempt is made to understand 'the meaning of faith' as such. The living example of this contention can be seen in the first four books (Gospels) of the Second Testament (New) in which four different authors have made attempts to present the understanding of their faith in Jesus Christ's works to different readerships that was placed in different contexts of life. With this in mind we can conclude that there is nothing as 'universal context' and that the context not only varies from place to place and country to country but also continues to change with the time. Likewise 'theology' would also differ in every context and according to each 'environment'. This amply explains why today we are having so many expressions of theology in the world.

As is well known, the traditional missionary theology was rooted in the Pietists' theological understanding of the Christian faith. This theological expression was born in response to the Christian faith that was being followed during the medieval period in Europe, particularly in Germany, where the Christian church was completely under the control of the rich feudal lords. The ordinary people there lived in an extreme dehumanized state.[3] Even the sacraments like the Holy Communion and Baptism could not keep the Christians together.[4] The pastors and bishops also behaved accordingly and considered themselves *sahibs* (Lords).[5] It was in such a context that Pietists' theology came into being. Naturally therefore, this theological expression addressed the concerns of the rich and the dominants, laying particular emphasis on the second or new birth, personal holiness and otherworldliness.[6]

The centre of the Pietistic contextual theology was at the University of Halle in Germany, where most of the Protestant missionary groups were trained later. Among them were Ziegenbalg, Pentschau and Schwartz, who formed the first group of missionaries who came to India. These early missionaries introduced the Pietistic understanding of Christian faith to our country. They were subsequently followed by more such missionary groups who invariably had direct or indirect link with the Halle Centre of Pietistic Theology.[7] An interesting point that needs to be noted here is that though the Pietistic theological expression was a response to the context of the rich and dominants in Germany, yet it was passed on to the poor masses of Indian Christians. This understanding of Christian faith has left an indelible imprint on Christians in India—particularly the Protestant Christians—which they passed on from one generation to the next, and which carries on till today.

What I want to emphasize here is that right from the beginning the understanding of Christian faith that was given to the followers in India was devoid of any contextual relevance. Having realized this we must now see what we can do about it. For this we have to first appreciate that in our country the 'context' is not static, but is constantly changing. This is due to many factors at work in our society, but more importantly it is the caste-based social order that keeps our 'context' in a state of flux. The Indian caste-based social order is not the same today what it was before Independence or even earlier when the caste groups like Vaishya or Shudra had no right to education. Again, it was during that period of our history that the so-called untouchables or outcaste communities (who address themselves today as Dalits) had no right even to call themselves as human beings. But today, in the post-Independence period, such a situation or 'context' stands changed (at least legally). At the same time other factors are added in the Indian context, like 'globalization', which has adversely affected the context of the victims of the old caste-based social order of our society. For any theology therefore, to be relevant to the Indian context, it becomes imperative that the caste factor is properly taken care of. Christianity in India equally gets affected by this context, which actually brings an added challenge to all groups of Indian theologians to respond to this changed context. The process in this direction is already on, but not in full swing. The various theological responses today include that of Dalits, Tribals, Women and Adivasis. We will be looking into these in detail in Section 4 of this article, because before that we need to deal with other important areas of the topic at hand. The remaining discussion of this article will be followed under the following heads:

- The Present Status of Christianity
- Scanning the Indian Context
- Audit of Theologies
- The Three Streams of Theology
- Indian Christianity of the Future
- Conclusion

Every theological expression has to pass two tests, which are based on the two divine interventions the details of which are in the Bible. According to the first intervention 'God takes the side of the oppressed' (Ex. 3: 7-9). The story of the First Testament (Old) centres on this theme. The second divine intervention has the message that 'God liberates the oppressed' (LK 4: 18-19), and it is the core of the theme of the Second Testament (New). The Gospel message, delineating these two divine truths, has to be the spirit behind all theological expressions, irrespective of the contexts they are drawn from. It is such theological expressions which we shall be considering in this as well as in other essays of the present volume with the hope that they will help in forming the base for 'Reshaping Christianity for the India of Tomorrow'.

2. The Present Status of Christianity

Today the need to reshape Christianity for India of the future becomes urgent because of two major reasons: *one*, the declining number of Christians in our country, and *two*, the 'identity crisis' that most Indian Christians face today. Let us first take a look at these two reasons in detail.

2.1 *Declining Number of Christians*

According to the census carried out in 2001, the total population of India was 1,028,610,328, out of which 24,080,016 (i.e. aprox. 2.34 per cent) were Christians. But compared to this the total population of India according to the census carried out twenty years ago, in 1981, was 666,287,849, out of which the number of Christians were 16,185,447 (i.e. approx. 2.42 per cent). On further analysing these figures region-wise an interesting fact emerges: while the 1981 census showed that 10,599,159 or 65 per cent of the Christians lived in the four southern states and union territories, according to the 2001 census their number was 12,182,080 or 50.59 per cent of the total Christian population of India. Likewise, the figures of 1981 census showed that in the north-eastern states the member of Christian population was 2,219,153 or 14 per cent, while the 2001 census gave this figure as 6,258,396 or 25.99 per cent. The remaining 23.42 per cent Christians, i.e. approx. 5,639,540, lived in the north, central, eastern and western regions of India.[8]

The figures given in the two censuses can also be viewed against the geographical areas covered by the regions. The total area of all the Indian states and union territories is 3,280,483 sq. km, out of which the southern states and union territories is 6,42,255 sq. km (that is about 25 per cent of the total land) where 65 per cent of Christians lived in 1981, which declined to 50.59 per cent by 2001. The north-eastern states cover 176,576 sq. km (i.e. about 6 per cent of the total land) where 14 per cent of Christians lived in 1981 which grew to 25.99 per cent in 2001. The remaining states and union territories of the north India, covers 74 per cent of the country's territory, where only

21 per cent Christians lived in 1981 and by 2001 this percentage came to 23.42.

On analysing the available figures we see a growth in Christian population only in the north-eastern states which is inhabited mostly by the tribals; the growth to some extent can also be seen in the two states of Jharkhand and Chhattisgarh where mostly Adivasis live. In central and eastern states of Orissa and Madhya Pradesh also a substantial increase of Christians can be seen because in these states there are large pockets populated by Adivasis. In the rest of the north India, as well as in the three southern states of Karnataka, Kerala and Tamil Nadu, growth of Christian population is either normal or less than normal. The worst decline of Christian population is in Andhra Pradesh, where in 1981 the Christians were 1,433,329; in 1991 their number came down to 1,216,348, and in 2001 it came down further to 1,181,917.

Some of us may doubt the authenticity of these figures and say that these do not correspond to the ground realities. They may be right in some cases, but they cannot decry these figures altogether. For example, we know that in states like Andhra Pradesh where the Christian population is on the decline, the number of Dalit Christians is much higher than given. Then, in Andhra Pradesh as well as in some northern states there are cases where people follow dual-religious membership (Christianity and Hinduism) or have returned to the old fold. Be it as it may, the overall picture that emerges before us from these figures is certainly not very encouraging. We cannot deny the fact that in states where a large majority of Christians are Dalits, their number is either declining or is static. In fact, this issue should not be viewed with blinkers on, but in a larger perspective because it is linked up with the whole issue of 'justice' and 'human rights' or 'constitutional rights' and the response of the Christians in India. It is here that the whole issue of the need of reshaping Christianity in India comes to the forefront.

2.2 *Indian Christianity with Identity Crisis*

Besides the constantly declining number of the Christians in our country today, the other reason which directly relates to them is the 'identity crisis' which stares at them. While the Christian community is generally considered to be the best service provider in the country, particularly in the areas of education and health, it remains by and large the 'community of the poor' because the fact is that the large majority of the members of the Christian community belongs to the marginalized communities of the Dalits, Adivasis, Tribals or Other Backward Classes (OBC) and other weaker sections of our society. The 'elitist' myth about the Indian Christians gets easily shattered when we look at the related statistical figures and care to go through some of the insightful views expressed by the Christian groups and their various bodies.

According to one rough estimate, about 15,000,000 out of a total of 25,000,000 Christians in the country are Dalits. But if we add here the number of Christians of Tribal, Adivasi and OBC origin, this number gets very high. It will become more than 80 per cent. But in spite of this naked reality, the Christians continue to project their 'elitist' image or identity. The final report of the Inculturation Commission and Conclusions of the Jesuit Conference of India (1978) has been very explicit about the image or identity of Jesuits (a most important Roman Catholic Order), when it says:

> The society's massive investment of men and resources in the educational apostolate in India makes it inevitable that the Jesuit image is mainly derived from our men in education and from our educational institutions. A large urban thrust doubtless characterizes Jesuit educational service in the country; its favoured medium of instruction is English, and the sector of the human community served by it is comparatively the more privileged one. Whether we like it or not, all these factors combine not only to project an elitist image, values of the 'upper ten' to the point of successfully obscuring truly evangelical values while uprooting and alienating us from the values of the majority of our people.[9]

The same truth is also recognized by the Church of North India (a major Protestant Church). In one of the reports of the CNI Synodical Programme 'Towards an Understanding of Mission' (1993); it says:

Despite the majority of the membership of the Church consisting of the marginalized, it has been primarily serving the interest of the elite and upper ten per cent through the educational, medical and other institutions. . . . The Church also generally reflects the culture and values of the dominant systems.[10]

It is interesting to note that what the above two Indian Christian Church traditions have realized now, Dr B.R. Ambedkar had realized about 60-70 years before them, and stated the same very clearly in his essay 'The Condition of the Convert'. But his challenge went unheeded. Dr. Ambedkar wrote:

It is necessary to bear in mind that the Indian Christians are drawn chiefly from the Untouchables and, to a much less extent, from low ranking Shudra castes. The social services of Missionaries must, therefore, be judged in the light of the needs of these classes. What are those needs? The services rendered by the Missionaries in the fields of education and medical relief are beyond the ken of the Indian Christians. They mostly benefit the high caste Hindus. . . . If this is so then the money and energy spent by the Christian missionaries on education and medical relief is misapplied and do not help the Indian Christians. The Indian Christians need two things. The first thing they want is safeguarding of their civil liberties. The second thing they want is ways and means for their economic upliftment.[11]

What these views and statements confirm is the irony that exists, both theologically as well as sociologically, within the Indian church, and consequently with her members. Indian church is 'the church of the poor and marginalized', but both she and the Christian community continue to present their 'elitist' image in every possible way. This contradiction is responsible for the crisis of Christian identity with which they are living today. As a result, the Indian church has failed to make any meaningful impact on the poor in general, and on the Indian Christians in particular. She has also failed to fulfil their needs, still less fulfil her own faith commitment. This therefore, provides another major reason why Christianity in India needs reshaping today by way of reconsidering her theological stance.

The climax of the identity crisis can be observed from the most recent (2011) case history which shows how gravely it has damaged our community, and how deeply the cancer of caste has afflicted our church.

The wrinkles on S. Royappan's face are a result of the advancing age, but the ridges and furrows in them tell a story of humiliation of this Dalit Christian, as also of others like him. Royappan, 82, was a bonded labourer, or a *padiyaal,* in Thachur village in Tamil Nadu's Kancheepuram district, but it is his 'bond' with the Roman Catholic Church in the village that remains vivid in his memory.

The 175-year-old Arockiya Matha (Our Lady of Health) Church has a chequered history. The most recent additions in that may have the potential to be a turning point for Dalit Christians in the village. It concerned the burials of two Dalit Christians in the cemetery attached to the Church which was opposed vehemently by the upper-caste Reddiar Christians. They claimed that the cemetery was meant only for *their* dead. The behaviour of the Reddiars failed to unnerve Royappan for the time being because in his time he had seen worse.

An eerie silence pervades Thachur as most of the men of Reddiar families stayed away from the village for several days fearing police action. The Dalits in the village succeeded in overcoming the stiff resistance from the Reddiars; they asserted their right twice in January when they buried the brother of a Dalit priest and a Dalit farm worker in the cemetery. The priest's brother Velankanni had died of natural causes, but the farm worker Rajendran was murdered and his body was retrieved from the lake in the village.

The full import of the development in Thachur, a predominantly Christian village about 80 km from Chennai, can be understood only by delving into the past.

Though the church building was constructed in 1922, the village is considered to be one of the oldest parishes in the State because the first Christians here arrived in 1836. The parish was then under the Pondicherry-Cuddalore Diocese. In 1969 it came under the Madras-Mylapore Diocese, and later was moved to the Chengalpattu Diocese which was created in 2002.

The population comprises of Reddiars, who migrated from Andhra Pradesh, and the Dalits which included Adi Dravidars and Arunthathiars. Though almost all of them are Christian converts, a sharp division existed between the two communities right from the beginning on the basis of their socio-economic disparity. *Varna-vyavastha* (caste hierarchy), which is deeply rooted in Hinduism, has been absorbed by the converts and this has deepened the hiatus.

Fr John Suresh, a priest who is also the director of the Chengalpattu Rural Development Society, said the cross-shaped church enabled the upper-caste Christians to occupy the centre, while the sides were earmarked for the Adi Dravidars and the Arunthathiars. The administration of the parish had been under the control of a team of *dharmakartas* (trustees) belonging to the Reddiar caste. The Dalits were denied a role even in the day-to-day affairs of the church, not to speak of its administration. They were not allowed even to take the role of readers or lectors at Mass. They challenged this decades-old discrimination in the 1990s. The protracted legal battle resulted in the closure of the church for over 10 years, until a path-breaking tripartite agreement was reached in November 2006.

In spite of that agreement caste discrimination continues in the church which could be seen in the above incidents. The village has three cemeteries, one for each group. The one inside the church complex is claimed by the Reddiars, while the other two groups have theirs on the outskirts of the village.[12]

This case history reveals the naked truth about the crisis of identity of Indian Christianity in the present century. It also establishes a definite need for its reshaping for a better tomorrow.

3. Scanning the Indian Context

It is indeed unfortunate that the Indian Christians have failed miserably to get rid of the shackles of the caste-system which has so powerfully gripped our society at large. The incident cited above in which the powerful section of the 'caste' Christians did not allow the Dalit members of the church to bring their dead for burial in the cemetery is not unique. Many such incidents take place almost everyday throughout the country. This certainly shows that it is not only the theology of our faith but the iron-hand of the caste based social order that is deeply rooted in the Indian society, which also gives the present shape to Indian Christianity. We will therefore do well to review briefly this caste-based social order before we take a look into the theological responses and the future form of Christianity in India. So in this section I will first try to explain 'different communities in the Indian context'; and then, discuss the role of caste-based social order in our life.

3.1 *Various Faces of Indian Communities*

In general, when we talk about the people who belong to the lowest rung on the social scale we tend to cover their identity by using generalized expressions like 'people', 'public' or 'the poor'. But at the outset we must understand that these people are not a faceless mass of living beings. Their identity emerges once we go through the report of the Mandal Commission. These people are spread across the country living a life of degradation for centuries without any foreseeable future. What is surprising is that these people are not Hindus only; every religion in our country has its share of this destitute population. Together they are 82.42 per cent of the total population. The report of the Mandal Commission gives their statistical break-up as follows: Scheduled Castes (15.05), Scheduled Tribes (7.51), Muslims (other than STs 0.02) (11.19), Christians (other than STs 0.44) (2.16), Sikhs (other than SCs & STs 0.22) (1.67), Buddhists (other than STs 0.03) (0.67), Jains (0.47) and Hindu OBCs (43.70). Among non-Hindu religions 8.40 per cent are OBC and among Muslims and Christians more than 75 per cent are either from SC or ST origin, which leave behind Muslims and Christians from various dominant castes origin between 20 and 25 per cent (about 4 per cent of the total population) and after deducting this percentage from 82.42 per cent, we will be still left with 78-80 per cent population, which can be considered the oppressed communities in India. These include Other

Backward Classes, Scheduled Castes, Scheduled Tribes and Religious Minorities.

The Mandal Commission also helps us to understand the contextual aspects of these oppressed communities of our country. The main factor responsible for their oppression is the caste based social order, which according to this report is

> transfixed for over 3000 years, had far-reaching effects on the growth and development of various castes and communities. For instance, as executive custodians of higher knowledge, the Brahmins developed into a highly cultivated community with special flair for intellectual pursuits. On the other hand, Shudras (OBC and also SC and ST) being continuously subjected to all sorts of social, educational, cultural and economic deprivation, acquired all the unattractive traits of an unlettered rustic.[13]

In fact, because of the caste system the burden of this oppression gets hitched on an individual by birth itself, because the kind of job or income sources that is available to him/her are already fixed through this system. The report of the first Scheduled Castes Commissioner (1951) very clearly says:

> Caste in Hindu society is still the most powerful factor in determining a man's dignity, calling or profession. Such a rigid caste system is not found anywhere else outside India. All such professions involve handling of the so-called dirty jobs like tanning and skinning of hides, manufacture of leather goods, sweeping of streets, scavenging etc. allotted to some castes, also known as Harijans. . . .[14]

So, while dealing with the caste system the historicity of its yoke on the oppressed mass cannot be ignored because it is this factor which denies them any outlet to come out of the captivity of this system. This factor is important which unfortunately even the social scientists (including economists) of today have ignored altogether.

3.2 *Caste-based Social Order*

Let us now take a look and see how this caste based social order works in the Indian society. First and foremost, we should be aware that in the Indian society, life is strictly structured and controlled on the basis of caste of a person. As an individual, no person—high or low—has any role in the system; nor has s/he any place in it shorn of her/his caste. This reality of the system looms large on every individual's life the moment s/he is born. Consequently, his/her individual rights as a human being (or human rights) do not find any place in this social order. Caste or *varna* specifically defines the limits for every individual.

In the beginning, this social order recognized only four communities or castes, which included: Brahmins (priests), Kshatriyas (warriors), Vaishyas (traders), and Shudras (servants). But later another group called Panchama was added to the original four. This fifth group was constituted to include outcastes; they were condemned as 'untouchables' and were not given any rights within the society.

There are three basic principles on which the caste-based social order stands.[15] The *first* principle is *the principle of graded inequality*, which is the 'fundamental principle' of this order. This order does not only divide the society horizontally into thousands of castes or sub-castes or communities, but it divides it vertically too. According to it, Brahmins are placed at the top, next comes the Kshatriyas, followed by the Vaishyas. Below the Vaishyas are placed the Shudras. The Panchams are given the last place. Having thus divided the society the creators of the caste-based social order tried to give authenticity to the system by explaining it in terms of Divine order of things. They proclaimed that the first four divisions were created from different parts of the Divine body and so their identity should remain separate and distinct. In this way, besides the social and legal dimension, the system was given a spiritual and moral dimension also. There is no sphere of human life, which is not regulated by this principle of graded inequality.

The *second* principle is *fixity of occupations*. According to this principle, Brahmins were assigned the job of teaching and research; Kshatriyas were to protect the state and fight for it; the Vaishyas were to look after the trade and the economics of the society; Shudras were given the job to serve the first three groups. The point to be remembered here is that every member of the community had to follow the work assigned to his or her community. There was no scope for individual choice. In fact, punishments were given to any member of a community who went against this principle.

The *third* principle of the caste based social order is the *fixation of people within their respective communities* according to which the community status or caste status of every person was decided by birth and not by one's ability.

Before moving on to the next section of this article, one question about the caste based social order which needs our attention is whether what has been discussed here are the things of the past or they are applicable even today? The answer to this can be had from L.M. Shrikant's Report on the *Commissions for Scheduled Caste and Scheduled Tribes for the Period Ending 31 December 1951*, which opens with these words: 'The Caste in Hindu society is still the most powerful factor in determining a man's dignity, calling or profession. Such a rigid caste-system is not found anywhere else outside India'.[16] Shrikant's words stress that what was true in the past about our existing social order, is still true even after the Independence of our country.

Another Commission's Report (well known as the Mandal Commission), which was ready in 1980, made public in 1990, has devoted two full chapters on the same issue. The Report has the following to say about the Indian social order:

> Even if the caste model described by us represents an ideal State, yet it does not negate the fact that caste system has been the most enduring basis of social organization in India. Or that, it has divided the Indian society into a large number of hierarchically arranged high and low castes or, that, the lower castes have suffered crippling social handicaps for centuries as a result of a low caste status. Similarly, despite all the modifications that caste has undergone over the ages and specially after Independence, changes in the caste system are representative more of shifts in emphasis than any material alteration in its basic structure.[17]

So, we have seen that the Indian social order is deeply rooted in the *varna* system and because of the rigidity of this system, even today there is practically no material alteration in its basic structure. This means that no radical structural change has taken place in the life of any community/communities in India. Is there any way to deal with this problem which has not only affected negatively the lives of all the people of India (including the Christians) for centuries now, but has also proved a huge impediment in establishing a just and humane society where all human beings will enjoy equal dignity. It is to seek an answer to this that we need to look to the theological responses that have come down to us from the Indian Christians themselves.

4. Audit of Theologies

While attempting theology either at the global level or at the local level, we are bound to come face to face with different realities of our times. This means through theology we are to experience the presence of the Ultimate Divine Reality (i.e. God) in our different contexts. In other words, the processes of doing theology according to each context will enable human beings to face global as well as local contextual problems. Many efforts by noted theologians have already been made in this direction all over the world; they tried to search the meaning of their faith in each situation at the time of crisis.

Out of the numerous responses available to us from the past and the present, let us focus here only on those that are most relevant to us with regard to India's contextual reality today as discussed earlier. The principles and methodological approaches of these will certainly help us in formulating our theological responses as part of the process of reshaping Indian Christianity for tomorrow.

4.1 *Traditional and/Competing Theologies*

Much has been written about the traditional theologies, particularly the Pietistic expression of theology, which was generally followed by various missionary groups and about which we have already made reference in the introductory section of this article. This approach to theology in many ways was the result of the European Christian Reformation movement. By the middle of the twentieth century the situation started changing. The Europeans who had moved to a new situation in North America started the process of theologizing from the perspective of Americans which was different from that of the Europeans. For example, in Herbert W. Richardson's work *Theology for a New World* (1967) the concern was the development related issues that propped up during that time, such as professional management, computer technologies, urbanization and struggle for a world community. For this changed context, he felt that traditional theology was outmoded because, 'redemption is neither the principle nor the sole concern of Christianity' he argued and explained that 'the primary purpose of God in the incarnation and the indwelling of the Spirit is sanctification, a purpose that is not contingent upon the occurrence of sin'.[18] Calling America as the 'center of the modern revolution' Richardson asserts the need for a theology in this new American context, making clear how the American Christianity and European Christianity stood on two different planes in their theological understanding of the Christian faith. He points out these differences in following words:

> It can fully and gladly use secular therapeutics. So it is not merely by chance that American Christianity, the child of the Puritans of the radical reformation, has consistently affirmed and used psychotherapy, technology, social reform, and political action as adjuncts to the gospel. And it is not merely by chance that European Christianity still tends to interpret the increasing scientific control over the various therapeutic processes as a threat to God and to religion. In these two different attitudes towards the modern world the practical differences between a theology of sanctification and a theology of redemption are seen.[19]

Professor Richardson's work can be taken as one of the excellent attempts towards the formation of an 'American Theology'; but it cannot be taken as a 'theology' for the entire modern world because majority of us are living today in a multi-religious, multi-ethnic, multi-cultural contexts. Added to these factors is the factor of multi-castes which is a very grim reality of the Indian context.

After Richardson's book came out, there appeared a number of important works that helped theologians of different backgrounds to develop various methodologies of theologizing. In spite of the limitation of the scope of this article, I shall like to refer here to two of these theologies of non-Indian context in which attempt is made to search for the meaning of Christian faith at the global and the local level. Both these works—Rex Ambler's *Global Theology* and John Reader's *Local Theology*—belong to the English context.

As we have seen in the beginning of this article, Ambler considers theology as that which helps in understanding God 'as the source and basis and ultimate context of our human existence'.[20] He focused in his work upon the issues like poverty, environmental pollution, threat of nuclear war and human responsibility in relation with God. He tries to find the solution to these issues in the messages of the Hebrew prophets who spoke about 'a new world' that was coming 'where justice and peace will prevail, but only if we seize the opportunity before us to bring it about'.[21] According to Ambler 'The main thrust of the prophetic traditions is that the future is placed in our hands, to be realized as a covenant relationship with God'.[22] As a Christian theologian, I think Ambler scores a valid point, but I am doubtful if other fellow Dalits belonging to different faiths will accept his claim on 'global theology'. However, his closing statement is certainly noteworthy which says: 'Real faith takes responsibility. It also faces the possibility of failure, but without despair. Tragedy for us is not the last word. We find meaning and hope in knowing what is possible for us humans and our earth and devoting ourselves to it, whatever the outcome.'[23]

A number of theologians today are of the view that traditional Christian theological approaches are bound to be rigid and inflexible because they offer universal or 'centralized' theological solutions for every problem, and with these local communities do not easily get tuned. Reader belongs to this school of thought. He believes that a theology cannot be universal in form, because as a matter of fact theology is the result of a dialogue between the church and a community, and it helps the community to think theologically about the issues that confront them in their everyday life. In other words, it is the solution to the local problems that are generally sought by a community in theological works. That is the reason, Reader asserts, that a theology cannot be universal in form. Following this lead, he advocates for a separate theology for the people on the margin of the society. 'Theology for those on the margins needs to have a different format to the traditional one now taught at universities and training institutions.'[24] This will 'create an environment within which people could begin to express more openly and confidently the various dimensions of their religious experiences'.[25] This point can be very relevant for Indian theologians who intend to 'rethink' theology for India of tomorrow.

Some theologians from North America and Europe have recently given us a theological expression which they call 'Public Theology'. To appreciate their approach let us now refer to two books: (1) *Globalization and Grace* by Max L. Stackhouse (particularly Chapter two on 'The Approach to Public Theology', and (2) *Asian Public Theology* by Felix Wilfred. Stackhouse is one of the strong proponents of Public theology. Almost rejecting all the contextual theologies as 'belonging to the experience of particular sub-communities', such as 'Afro-American theology in USA, feminists and/or women's theology around the world, Dalit and Tribal theology in India, Minjung theology in Korea, Coconut theology in Pacific Islands, etc.', Stackhouse labels these as '"civil religion" of a particular class, caste, or cultural group'. Among his other concerns in this regard, the major one is about 'the caustic interpretations of the faith by those anti-globalization ecumenical voices who have theologically absolutized certain models of liberationist thought and Marxist social analysis'.[26] In his assessment, however, what Stackhouse does not appreciate is that these contextual theologies do not claim to be absolute or universal. Through issues that relate only to their context they try to understand the Ultimate Divine Reality (i.e. God) in their theology. With that the scope of contextual/local theology ends. To counter these theologies, however, Stackhouse upholds the idea of 'public theology'. Rooted in the classic Western Christian traditions, public theology, according to Stackhouse, initially developed in America and later was adopted by Europe. He claims that public theology is based upon 'a new public' which is beyond 'the local contextualizationism of many current analyses' and has 'potential capacity to address the issues posed by globalization'.[27] Through this theology Stackhouse sees Christian thoughts taking the form of the universal in various local contexts, ultimately affecting 'the emergence of a potentially global civil society'.[28]

It is indeed difficult to ignore the irony behind the claim of public theology that Stackhouse puts forward. On the one hand he criticizes contextual theologies for being tied to local contexts that inhibits them to look beyond and appeal globally, while on the other hand he is hopeful that public theology can be helpful in the emergence of a potentially global civil society even though the brief history of its idea shows that it is after all a part of the theologies that emerged out of the European and American contexts.[29] Also he accepts that it is basically a Christian public theology.[30]

In his book at one place Stackhouse defines the difference between 'public theology' and 'political theology'. He says, '"public theology" tends to adopt a social theory of politics, and political theology inclines to a political view of society'.[31] This observation brings us to the topic of 'Asian Public Theology'. The most recent work on Asian public theology is by Felix Wilfred by the same name. Generally speaking, Wilfred goes with the views of Stackhouse, but in a number of places he makes definitive departures from him. He begins his discussion with an opening statement about Asian public theology 'in which the accent will be stronger on the "public" than on theology. The focus will be on the issues and questions that affect the people and society of Asia and which need to be addressed urgently. . . . Asian Public Theology will be one that will be inherently interreligious in nature.' According to him there are four crucial areas of public context—political, social, cultural and economic, etc., delving into which 'will pave the way for shaping a distinctly Asian Public Theology'.[32] In spite of this approach, it is interesting to note that he is not interested in entering into the area of politics while doing this specific theology. Even when he says that Asian Public Theology 'will deal only with public sphere' he is quick to add that 'it may not touch upon the burning questions and issues affecting the poor in Asia'. Like Stackhouse he also hesitates to enter into the actual 'political questions' as part of the public share.[33] Fr. Wilfred actually worked with a number of presuppositions, which include: (1) that all religions do have a role in public life, (2) that in Asia 'all theology will be inherently Public Theology', (3) that in Public Theology 'we address and interpret the truths of faith in such a way that they became meaningful to people around us', and (4) that Asian Public Theology besides its 'functional role' related to region, can play a 'performative role' in the society.[34]

After a long general introduction Wilfred takes up almost all those issues and concerns in his book which theologians from various subalterns groups like Dalits, Tribals and Women are dealing with. His main discussion is based upon the re-interpretation of Christianity in relation to the issues that confront the people of Asia in general. But for this he maintains an interreligious approach throughout which proves very much in tune with the disposition of the people of Asia. This is very clear in the concluding statement which he made at the end of his work:

> The various public questions in Asia we deal in this book have also shown the avenues for religious traditions to make their contribution. It is important then that public theologies be developed in the various

religious traditions and there be continuing dialogue and exchange among theologies. Christian theology is challenged to become truly a partner among the various public theologies of the continent sharing the same historical, social, political and cultural situation and turn into a force of transformation for justice and peace, and for harmony with the entire creation.[35]

Introducing the old paradigm of inter-faith dialogue once again, Wilfred insists on an emphasis on public issues closing with the slogan of 'justice and peace'; at the same time, he is careful not to touch 'the burning questions and issues affecting the poor of Asia'. We can trace the origins of public theology (as put forward by Stackhouse) from the old Christian traditions of thc northern countries; similarly Wilfred is leading us to the dominant religious traditions of India and Asia. We will come back to some of those concerns later in the discussion.

4.2 *Liberating Theologies*

So far we have discussed theologies that claim either to cover the entire world or a part of it. But the 'people', 'community', 'public' that these theologies talk about do not cover the entire spectrum of the society. The underbelly of the society, which is constituted of the oppressed and destitute people, is not covered by them. In this section therefore, we shall discuss only those theologies that focus on the neglected sections of the society. Together these theologies not only have a common historical base to operate, but they also have a common goal, which is the total liberation of the people. That is why these are called 'liberating theologies'. These are bold expressions of the oppressed people who are trying to understand the scriptures from their angle, and therefore, are willing to take risk while dealing with the issues related to religion (spiritual), economics (including globalization, cultural including various . . . ideology-based nationalism), politics, poverty and human development, etc., in its entirety. In the process these expressions also unmask the 'masked section' of the community. I shall refer here to five such expressions: Japan-born 'Theology of the Pain of God'; the South American born 'Liberation Theology'; the United States and South Africa-born 'Black Theology'; Korea-born 'Minjung Theology'; and Philippines-born 'Theology of Struggle'. We will deal separately with 'Indian Contextual and Liberating Theologies' in Section 4.3.

One of the earliest works of Liberating Theology came from Kazoh Kitamori of Japan after Second World War under the title "Theology of the Pain of God". Originally written in Japanese it was published in 1946. Later on it was translated into English in 1965 and the first edition in English appeared in 1966. But before that it had gone into five editions between 1946 and 1958 in Japanese. In the preface to the first Japanese edition Kazoh Kitamori stresses the fact that till the end of the nineteenth century, Christian theology had been mainly the product of Western Christianity which was 'Greek' in its approach because it used the Greek thought form to 'transmit the message of the Gospel'. He questions this and says:

> Greek theology, seeking to transmit the message of the Bible, performed this function in its own way; however, precisely for this reason, it created a problem. If this is correct, is it not legitimate for Japanese theology as a non-Western theology be freed from the particularity of Greek theology and to approach from a fresh point of view?[36]

In answer to this question, was written this first non-Western theology during the twentieth century. Even after sixty-five years the question continues to recur whenever attempts are made in the Southern part of the globe to enter into the process of doing theology from non-Western perspectives. In his preface to the second edition (1947) came another important statement from the author: 'In the conclusion of this book, I wrote that the theology of the Pain of God must remain "outside the gate, outside the city". But today I find myself, with surprise and perplexity, watching the theology of the Pain of God drawn "inside the gate, into the heart of the city".'[37]

According to John W. Taylor, the General Secretary of

Church Ministry Society, 'One may guess that the agony of Hiroshima lies in the background of Kitamori's theology. But his insights are born out of the long Buddhist traditions rather than from any particular experience of pain.'[38] Perhaps the views of Taylor were biased by his concern that Hiroshima's tragedy was created by the Western world, because Kitamori is very much concerned with the context or situation created by Second World War while doing this theology. In his preface to the third edition (1951) he clearly states:

The divisions of the world are becoming sharper and sharper in recent years. The recklessly torn situation of World War II, during which time this book was written, appear to have become worse. We must deal with the situation point blank. We must proclaim again, and in a most radical way, the straightforward theme of this book: 'God embracing completely those who should not be embraced—that is, "God in Pain"!'[39]

Kitamori makes his stand still more clear in the preface to the fifth edition (1958): 'The starting point of theology of the pain of God was to stand "outside" the universal—general, following Jesus who suffered "outside the gate" (Heb. 13: 12).' He did agree that 'the task of theology is to serve the universal church', but at the same time he cautioned that: 'Theology becomes dogma when recognized by the universal church.'[40] However, as far as his 'Theology of Pain of God' is concerned, he gave a very strong and clear basis of both biblical and also his Japanese context. About the former he says: 'The Pain of God means that the love of God had conquered the wrath of God in the midst of the historical world deserving his wrath. Thus the pain of God must necessarily enter the historical plane as a person.' This is the truth recorded in Romans 8:3.[41] He therefore, relates the Christ event experience by using a Japanese word *tsurasa*, which he says is 'the basic principle in Japanese tragedy'; 'it is realized when one suffers and dies or makes his beloved son suffer and die, for the sake of loving and making others live'.[42] But in the later part of his work, he also concedes that according to the Japanese meaning it is only one side of the whole truth, because love should also include 'loving the unlovable, the unworthy and even the enemy' which is encompassed by God's Love.[43]

Finally, about his theological expression he is honest when he says that 'The Theology of the Pain of God, if true to itself, must retain this characteristic of being "outside". It should never become a so-called "dominant" theology'.[44] We shall see in the course of our discussion in this and the next section that what Kazoh Kitamori had said about the theology of pain, should apply to all the other 'liberative theological expressions'. But before doing that it may be good to refer to another Japanese theologian Kosuke Koyama, who was based in northern Thailand and came out with other very powerful Thailand based contextual theological expressions. Koyama gives the entire credit for his Water-buffalo Theology to his audience in the local churches. He says, 'It is not I, but my audiences, who determine this approach of "theology from below". Truth of "self-emptying" ('*Jesus Christ who emptied himself*', Phil. 2:5-7) in the incarnate state means, to me, beginning my sermon with "sticky-rice" and "cock-fighting" even preaching to my people, farmers of Thailand.'[45] Koyama believed that theology from below, showed the right way of taking the Gospel message to a particular historical context: 'Contextualization of theology is something more than taking the historical and cultural context seriously; it is letting theology speak in and through that context.'[46] We will be referring again to Koyama's work later in our discussion, but first let us take a look at other liberating theologies.

Among the Latin American theologians, perhaps the first theologian who has helped in understanding the role of human history in the construction of a theological expression is Gustavo Gutierrez. I am referring here to his well-known work *A Theology of Liberation* which was first published in 1971 in Spanish and later in 1973 in English. In the beginning of his work, Gutierrez, while re-reading the well-known Biblical text says:

In the first place, charity has been fruitfully re-discovered as the centre of the Christian life. This has led to a more Biblical view of the faith as an act of trust, a going out of one's self, a commitment to God and neighbour . . . , Love is the nourishment and the fullness of faith, the gift of one self to the other, and invariably to others. This is the foundation of the praxis of Christians, of its active presence in history. According to the Bible, faith is the total response of man to God, who saves through Love.[47]

Gutierrez is not saying here anything new, but only drawing our attention to the two greatest commandments of Christian faith, namely—'Love the Lord your God with all your heart, soul, mind and chose thy neighbours as thyself.' These two commandments according to our Lord was the greatest among all the commandments found in the Bible (Mark 12: 28-31). Both the application and implementation of these greatest commandments of Christian faith took place in the human history, which actually gives the wholeness of faith as a response to God. Gutierrez calls this process of Christian faith, functioning through the human history, 'historical praxis'. To make his point more clear Gutierrez discusses historical praxis much in detail saying: 'The Christian community professes a faith which works through charity. It at least ought to be real charity—action and commitment to the service of men. Theology is reflection of a critical attitude.'[48] History as mentioned earlier has been divided into two, one dealing with the issues of the Other World and the other dealing with the issues of this world. But Gutierrez in this regard says:

There are not two histories, one profane and one sacred. . . . Rather only one human destiny, irreversibly assumed by Christ, the Lord of history. His redemption work embraces all the dimensions of existence and brings them to their fullness. The history of salvation is the very heart of human history.[49]

Gutierrez's point about oneness of history is very important for any Liberating theology, if it is going to attack the old captivity on the psyche of various oppressed groups by the traditional theological expressions.

Like Gutierrez, James H. Cone in his essay 'Black Theology and Black Liberation' has equally upheld the role of history in the construction of Black theology. In fact, he is more aggressive while discussing about the black people's history. He says:

Black history has arisen to establish an authentic black past. Unlike European immigrants who came to America seeking escape from unjust tyranny, African presence was not by choice: we came as bondsmen, chained in ships. It was the slave-experience that shaped our memory of this land. . . . Unfortunately, our slavery was not limited to physical bondage. Added to physical domination was the mental enslavement of black people—the internalization of the values of slave-masters. We were required to deny our African past and affirm those European values responsible for our enslavement. At the worst, this means accepting the slave-condition as ordained by God. . . .[50]

How is the black history related to black theology? To this Cone's answer is:

Black history is recovering a past deliberately destroyed by slave-masters, an attempt to revive old survival symbols and create new ones. Black power attempts to shape our present economic, social and political existence according to those actions that destroy the oppressor's hold on black flesh. Black theology places our past and present actions toward black liberation in a theological context, seeking to destroy alien gods and create value structures according to the God of black freedom.[51]

A leading Korean theologian Kim Yong-Bock in his work *Messiah and Minjung* while describing the Minjung (i.e. ordinary masses of people) as the subjects of history, says:

The discovery of the Minjung led not only to the realization that it is the Minjung who are the perceiving subjects of real historical experiences, but also to the understanding that the Minjung are the subjects in the making of history. They bear the historical burdens to sustain human societies. They work, they cultivate and they serve. . . . The sustenance of human life, the creative process in cultural life, the transforming dynamics of the social and political processes are fundamentally based upon the endurance and suffering sacrifice of the Minjung. Therefore, their suffering becomes the foundation of the society, and they sustain the ups and downs of the historical processes. In this sense, they are the subjects of history.[52]

The reality of Minjung as a subject of history is important for any oppressed community, because this realization is the first step towards regaining lost human dignity of any historically oppressed community.

The people of the Philippines have also gone through a very painful and oppressive historical experience. Eleazat S. Fernandez in his *Towards a Theology of Struggle,* while going through the process of construction of a Filipino expression of theology which he has named 'Theology of Struggle', begins with re-reading of his history, but from the perspective of his oppressed people. In this regard he says:

> My reading claims to be a reading from below—from the experience of those whose history has long been muted. It is a reading derived from the experiences of those who are daily threatened by another kind of trinity: the absence of breakfast, lunch and dinner.[53]

According to him: 'The history of the Filipino people is a history of struggle against the negative forces, both within and without, that continue to abort the people's cherished dreams'. About the Filipino people's struggle Fernandez says, 'The struggle is the struggle of the whole people, some of whom may not profess the Christian belief . . . Christians must learn to work with those with whom they do not agree on everything, but agree on something that is vital'. He elaborates further saying,

> Out of the involvement of Christians in the struggle of the whole Filipino people, the theology of struggle has struggled to be born. From this womb of struggle it came to see the first light of day and from its cradle it has been nurtured. Born in and out of the struggle, it has no life apart from this struggle; it has taken shape in and out of the struggle; and it cannot be properly understood, apart from this struggle. It has basic pre-suppositions, shape and content; all bear the indelible work of this involvement in the wider struggle.[54]

Here in this statement lies a challenge for the Christians who, unlike the Filipino Christians, are a very small minority. So it becomes more pertinent for us as Christians to get involved in the wider struggle of the oppressed, to be partners in the making of our common history, which ultimately will be the womb from which the required liberating theologies will be born.

4.3 *Indian Contextual Liberating Theologies*

The 'context' of Indian liberating theological expressions differs from other liberating theologies, because besides historical oppression it has also to deal with the element of 'caste' that is ingrained in our society and about which we have already discussed earlier in Section 4.2 of this article. There are four expressions of contextual liberating theologies from India, which are: Dalit theology, Tribal theology, Adivasi theology and Feminist theology. Except the Tribal theology, the context of the other three has a close link with the 'caste' element. Divisions within the tribal theology are based on 'tribalism' which is part of their context. Only difference is that the 'caste' element has religious sanction, whereas the tribal divisions are free from that element. Instead of going into details of these theologies, we will be limiting our discussion here to the nature of these four contextual theologies, by making reference to a couple of pioneer works of each expression, as we have done in the case of other liberating theologies.

We will begin our discussion with the 'Dalit theology', the process of Dalit theology began in 1981 with Arvind Nirmal's address, which he delivered as a valedictory address to the Carey Society of the United Theological College, Bangalore under the title 'Towards a Shudra Theology'. Shudra is the fourth group in the caste-hierarchy, and other term 'Harijan' was used by Mahatma Gandhi for the 'Dalits', but both were not accepted by the Dalits, therefore later the expression 'Dalit' was used as prefix with the expression 'theology' and this is how we got today the term 'Dalit theology'.[55]

A considerable work has been done in this area since Arvind

Nirmal's address in 1981. Here we shall refer to three most comprehensive works that can give us information about Dalit theology. These are: *Towards a Dalit Theology* edited by Late M.E. Prabhakar (1988),[56] *Indigenous People: Dalits—Dalit Issues in Today's Theological Debate* edited by James Massey (1994)[57] and *Frontiers of Dalit Theology* edited by V. Devasahayam (1997).[58] One other important early work is *Emerging Dalit Theology* edited by Xavier Irudayaraj S.J. (1990).[59]

M.E. Prabhakar has summed up the following three factors responsible for the emergence of Dalit theology:

(i) Dalit theology has been conceived in the context of the struggle against casteism and aspirations for social justice, both in the church and society.

(ii) The principles and practices of caste are rooted in the religious-philosophical-theological traditions of the dominant Hindu culture. The theory of *varna* (ritual ranking) provides the doctrinal basis for hierarchy and discrimination between *jatis* or castes (functional groups) and exclusion of certain 'impure' castes as untouchables and outcastes. The critique of this system of inequality has to be theological.

(iii) The insensitivity of the church and Indian Christian theology to Dalit concerns and the deeper dimensions of their struggle and aspirations for fuller humanity, despite the majority of Christians being of Dalit origin, makes imperative the formulation of a Christian Dalit theology, with a universal appeal.[60]

About the goal of Dalit theology, Arvind Nirmal wrote in one of his early essay that,

> For a Christian Dalit theology it cannot be simply the giving of the rights, the reservation and privileges. The goal is the realization of our full humanness or conversely, our full divinity, the ideal of the *Imago Dei* (the Image of God) in us. To use another Biblical metaphor, our goal is the 'glorious liberty of the children of God.[61]

In one of my own essays on 'Roots and Vision of Dalit Theology', I have spelt out the overall role of Dalit theology in the following words:

> Dalit theology has to create the possibility of full liberation or salvation, based upon the Christ event of redemption, which will not only stop with freeing the Dalits from the oppressive structures, but will go further to achieve the salvation for the whole people of God, including their oppressors. And in this way Dalit theology will enable the Dalits to become an instrument of establishing a just society.[62]

The second expression of India's liberating theology comes from the tribal context of north-east India. The tribal theologians call it 'Tribal theology'. The pioneer tribal theologian, the late Renthy Keitzar, in the opening statement of his essay 'A Contextual Christian Theology' had defined the source and scope of Tribal theology saying:

> In order to develop a contextual Christian theology for North East India we have to make use of all resources of socio-biblical studies and socio-religious backgrounds of the people of North East India. The Christian message has to be expressed in socio-cultural, traditional, and liturgical thought patterns of the people. The gospel must be interpreted within the content of our cultures, then only it will be meaningful.[63]

Because north-east India comprises seven Indian states that have a number of tribes, sub-tribes and communities, a considerable difference within the people living there is quite visible in spite of some degree of homogeneity. All the tribes differ from one another and have their own identities. This factor becomes very important while formulating the Christian theology for north-east India, and every theologian while working on different expression of theologies must keep the requirement of such a wide scope in mind. Renthy Keitzar explains that 'Assamese Christian theology—similar to Sanskrit context, a Khasi Christian theology, a Mizo Christian theology, a Naga Christian theology and so on may be developed in relevance to each socio-cultural context.'[64] A later younger theologian Wati Longchar while agreeing with Keitzar about the contextual aspect of Tribal theology tried to elaborate its aims:

> Like the Dalit and Minjung theologies, the tribal/indigenous theology is a contextual theology, a theology from 'below' and 'underside of history'. It aims to liberate them from their inferiority complex, from oppression and discrimination by attempting to rediscover the liberative theology in their cultures and religion, and by reinterpreting the Bible and Christian tradition from the perspective of the people. Hence, the focus and goal of the tribal/indigenous theology is liberation and transformation.[65]

Bishop Nirmal Minz represents the first generation of Indian Christian thinkers and the key pioneer of Tribal-Adivasi theology. He saw a close historical link between the Adivasi and the Dalits; about this he says: 'Tribe is an administrative concept. The Tribals do not call themselves "Tribal". They call themselves "Adivasis" or Mundas, Oraons, Bhils, Gonds, Nagas, Mizos, Todas, etc. The historical changes of "Dalit" and "Tribal" reveal to us the inner dynamics of their context.'[66] Bishop in his essay 'Dalit-Tribal: A Search for Common Ideology', did not use the expression 'theology'; instead, he replaced it with 'ideology'. He says:

> The primal form of common ideology is the liberation *motif* of the indigenous people. They have to liberate themselves from the inferiority complex, from the oppression and discrimination by the dominant people around them in India. Liberation has its social, economic, cultural and political dimensions. In the process of working for their own liberation they should work for the liberation of the oppressors and the exploited also.[67]

In the foreword to Rev. Abhay Kerketta's book *Adivasi Theology*, Bishop Minz gives the basis and direction which future Adivasi theology needs to take. 'Any Christian theology relevant for Jharkhand Adivasi should address the perennial issues of alienation and displacement adversely affecting their history—their geo-political and cultural identity'.[68]

Abhay Kerketta, a young Adivasi theologian, is well-versed in the contexts of the other available theological expressions about which he has discussed in his work *Adivasi Theology: Towards a Relevant Christian Theology for the Jharkhand Adivasi*. He explains the term 'adivasi' as 'original settlers' and says that 'their context/situation is different'.[69] Therefore various other theological expressions are not relevant to the Adivasi context. About Western theology and liberation theology born in the Latin American context, he says that,

> The present Western theology with a dogmatic nature has failed to address the existent issues and challenges of the Adivasi society. Liberation theologies already challenged the Western theology, but still it has great impact on Jharkhandi Adivasi. However, the theologies of liberation worked out by Gutierrez, Sobrino, and Bonino are also not easily transferable due to our very different historical and socio-political situation.[70]

Therefore he concludes:

> Theological reading of the Jharkhandi Adivasis context proceeds to situate the emergence of Adivasi Theology. The Adivasis' experience of struggle involved reconstructing a relevant Adivasi theology with a new perception, perspective and understanding. Adivasis' struggle is the struggle of the whole Adivasis people for self-determination and liberation as well as the struggle for self-determination of the various Adivasi communities within one particular context. Their struggle is for equality, justice, integration of creation and peace.[71]

The other most important expression of theology from India is the Indian women/feminist theology. I am referring here to the works of two most prominent women thinkers/theologians of today—Ruth Manorama and the late Rev. Prasanna Kumari Samuel. Ruth Manorama is the leading Dalit women activist, and a creative lay thinker. In her statement, which came as part of her 'personal theological reflection on Dalit women's situation' (1988) she says:

> As I perceive and understand Dalit theology, it cannot negate the participation and the 'humanity of women' since Dalit women constitute

half the population in the church in India. In my understanding, any theology denying women's questions/concerns in the ingredients of making theology is unwholesome and unholy.

Theologizing, as one understands it, is a political task which should lead to transformation of any oppressive situation. It should empower the weak, the vulnerable and the oppressed, socially, economically and politically. It demands distribution of power, not only sharing. I dream that these aspects should become a reality, in the day-to-day life and struggles of Dalit women for their liberation.[72]

Ruth's views are very clear about the concern of women, specially the Dalit women, in the construction of Dalit theology. Very close to the views of Ruth are the views of Prasanna Kumari Samuel who leads us systematically to understand the nature and role of feminists/women theology. Here again we are referring to two important statements from Samuel, which will clear this point. The first statement reads as:

It is in this line, Indian feminists desire to construct a theological method to study theology, from an abstract classical theology to a women's experiences based feminist theology of life, a paradigm shift. More precisely, feminist theology of life draws heavily on the social experiences of women—their discrimination, their invisibility, their being silenced, oppressed, excluded and subjugated reality—in a male-dominated, patriarchal churches and societies.

Further, most Indian feminists do not focus on caste based oppression on women as they are not yet prepared to dismantle it. By recognizing this fact, and by fostering alternative visions of feminism including human relations, Indian feminism can more effectively challenge historically-entrenched and varied patriarchies of caste both within the church and the society.[73]

Samuel's second important statement for the purpose of this paper is:

At the heart of women's theology and research is the goal, even more the obligation, to act and bring about change in the conditions of women. They openly address persistent gendered practices and expectations and evolve visible possibilities and alternatives. By and large, feminists world over are committed to the dual vision of research as to (i) promote the welfare of women and (ii) further social science knowledge giving voice to the voiceless women through narrative, or a retelling of their stories, both to empower them and to learn from their experiences. Explicitly or implicitly, creating social change to better women's status appears to be a theme across much of feminist thought.[74]

About the existing theological expressions Samuel pointed out that our present 'Theological concepts are a proof of socially conditioned patriarchal thought—patterns that have emerged from male chauvinistic perspectives.'[75] She welcomed the emergence of Dalit theology, but even this expression, she added, 'failed to pay resolute attention to Dalit women and their struggles for life, though unquestionably, they are the most oppressed of all human races in India'.[76]

5. Three Streams of Theologies

In the introduction reference has been made to the theological expression rooted in Pietistic Christian traditions of Europe which came to India with various early missionary groups. In this way the traditional Pietistic theology became responsible for shaping the present form of Indian Christianity, and laid the foundation of the first stream of theology in our country. Like Pietistic theology, this stream of theology was also based on Greek thought form and had no bearing whatsoever to the soil it was planted in. We have seen that Kazoh Kitamori even went to the extent of referring to it as 'Western theology' or 'Greek theology' (see Section 4.2). However, this first stream of theology was upheld by the International Missionary Council at Tambaram, Madras (India) which met in 1938. As an outcome of the Tambaram Council meeting, a published document came out entitled *The World Mission of the Church*. To counter this, a group of Indian thinkers came forward to respond with another document entitled *Rethinking Christianity in India* which laid the foundation of the second stream of theology in our country. Later this stream came to be known as the Indian Christian theology. This expression of theology had its roots in classical Hinduism, and it continued to dominate the ecumenical circle, especially among the Urban Christian elites, till the end of the 1970s of the last century. During the 1980s came the reaction to both these dominant theological expressions from the underside of the society, as a result of which we have a third stream of Subaltern Indian theologies today. This stream comprises: Dalit theology, Tribal theology, Adivasi theology and Feminist/Women theology. We have already discussed these in Section 4.3. The subaltern Indian theologies are influenced to some extent by other liberating theologies around the globe that originated mostly in the non-Western world. For our purpose here let us now take a comprehensive view of these three streams of theology in our country.

5.1 *The World Mission of the Church*

The meeting of the International Missionary Council of 1938 at Tambaram, Madras, was actually the follow up of the World Missionary Conference of Edinburgh in 1910 and was held to carry on the agenda of that World Conference further.[77] In that meeting was rooted the first stream of Christian theological thinking. This point becomes clear from the faith statement of the Council, part of which reads as follows: 'For those that are without Christ the true Church yearns with love of its Master Lord. It goes first to them with the evangel of His grace'.[78] What the World Council of Missionaries intends to say becomes further clear in its message to the 'Non-Christian Religions':

> Jesus Christ alone is adequate for the world's need. Therefore, we want to bear witness to Him in the entire world. There are many non-Christian religions that claim the allegiance of large multitudes. We see and readily recognize that in them are to be found values of deep religious experiences and great moral achievements. Yet we are bold enough to call men out from them to the feet of Christ. We do so because we believe that in Him alone is the full salvation which man needs.[79]

It was expected that even in missionary run-educational institutions, a Christian teacher should 'by personal contact with their pupils lead them into the fullness of the Christian life'.[80]

The thinking Indian Christians could not accept either the agenda or the approach laid down by the Council. In truth they did not find much in this report of the International Missionary Council, except its only agenda—to win the world and India for Christ. As a result they responded to it by another document which is being discussed in the next sub-section.

5.2 *Rethinking Christianity in India*

It was a group of Indian thinkers (mostly lay persons) who gave us a most creative and classic document, which later on went to become the foundation of the second stream of theology and which Indian Christians could claim that it belonged to them. *Rethinking Christianity in India* came as a response to the 'findings and recommendations of the International Missionary Council'. This document became the basis of what some call 'indigenous theology', and others call 'enculturation' of Christian faith. It also helped to start an inter-faith dialogue movement in India, and ecumenical movements in other parts of the world. This paper is also inspired by this document. However, in this section I shall be making reference to a few of those sections of this work which deal with the theological aspects only.

All the seven contributors to *Rethinking Christianity in India* were Indians. They were G.V. Job, P. Chenahiah, V. Chakkarai, D.M. Devasahayam, S. Jesudasan, Eddy Asirvatham and A.N. Sudarisanan. Out of them three were theologically trained and the remaining four were laypersons; but they were also highly qualified in their own fields. Their intent behind this document was made clear by the editors of the work in the Preface:

> That the Indian Church should think and act for itself, and make Christianity an indigenous movement has been a burden on the minds of the great men who brought the Gospel to the land as well as of those

who accepted it. This urge has also come from Indian *bhaktas* and lovers of Christ outside the church, who have repeatedly demanded that Christ should be related to the great Indian religious heritage and that Christianity should assume an Indian expression of life, thought and activity.[81]

About the place of Jesus in the Indian multi-religious and multi-cultural setup, they noted that

> In Europe and other Christian countries, Christians see Jesus only. In the unique situation in India which determines the status and influence of Christianity, we see Jesus in the company of other founders of religion or saviours of men—Buddha, Rama, Krishna. . . . In India these religions are in numbers and influence such as to compel mutual attention and respect. The life and destiny of Christians has to be studied in this vital context.[82]

They saw a Christian convert in double bondage, therefore they said:

> The emancipation from double bondage, namely to the traditions of Hinduism on the one hand and to the traditions of Christianity on the other, gives him the freedom to study the question of the meaning and significance of Jesus untrammeled by the doctrine and dogma and seek in the living forces of Hinduism a positive key to the still inaccessible riches in Jesus.[83]

As for their faith in Jesus, they added, 'The Jesus of the Gospel transcends the measure of man. We try to make Him the every man. He presents us a harmonial picture of God man—not merely hyphenated God-Man.'[84] What they further added completed their understanding of Christian faith in their fuller understanding:

> Christ however sought to establish a new universe with a new cosmic energy—the Holy Spirit. . . . He (*a Christian*) is a new creation and not a prolongation or perfection of the old creation. The Holy Spirit is the new cosmic energy; the Kingdom of God, the new order; the children of God, the new type that Christ has inaugurated. The Gospel is that God in Jesus has made a new creation. Christianity has been a failure because we made a new religion of it instead of a new creation.[85]

The group behind the *Rethinking Christianity in India* also had an advice for the theological education in India:

> Theological institutions should be completely over-hauled, both in regard to the syllabus or study and to the discipline and life of students under training. They should learn more of Indian philosophy and Religion and less of Western theology. They should be taught plain living so that any talent capacity that there may be in them for high thinking may be drawn out. Above all they should learn the art of silence and meditation, an art which can only be communicated and not taught.[86]

5.3 *Christian Participation in Nation-building*

The document under consideration is a post-Independence document, and it came as a Christian response to and their participation in the whole issue of nation-building. But this document is equally important from the perspective of theology. It is so because in all the sections—related to political, economic, social and cultural life of the people of the newly-freed nation—this document reflects Christian views. Some of the theological issues are also discussed in the 'epilogue' which can be taken as a starting point of the third stream of theologies in our country. So here I will be referring to a few relevant passages, containing the seeds of a paradigm shift from the missionary theological understanding and Indian theological understanding of Christian faith towards 'contextual and liberating' understanding of Christian faith. For example, while stressing on 'Christian participation in political life', it directly refers to the Pietistic doctrinal basis about which it says: 'They interpret the Gospel in purely spiritual, other-worldly, or individualistic terms and forget that it is the message of Christ's salvation to whole of life, including, that is, our organized life together.'[87] The document also makes it clear that the church/Christian community 'and its local manifestation, the Christian congregation, share the sociological features of the natural social structure in which they live'.[88]

One of the most important points that *Christian Participa-*

tion in Nation-building brings forth is the relationship of the Christian faith to that of a local culture. 'Culture is an area of human life which comes under the universal Lordship of Christ!' Therefore, the document suggests three things for the Church/Christian community:

Firstly, to acknowledge Christ's presence in the cultural renaissance of India. . . . Secondly, to make an evaluation of India's cultural renaissance. Evidences of Christ's activity are to be found in man's cultural creativeness. . . . Thirdly, to present the crucified and Risen Christ as the source of power that redeem cultures from the powers that do violence to the essential humanity of man and set up walls of partition among them.

The document also adds:

Christians have no ready-made culture to offer to India. The Gospel is not identical with any culture. No doubt, Western culture is more informed by the Christian faith and understanding that may alter cultures; but it should not be forgotten that even where its ethos is most Christians it is the result of the operation of the Gospel on decidedly non-Christian cultural traditions. The same power is available to us in India, and the distinctive service of the Indian church to the development of cultural foundations for the new life of India lies in its being a channel for the transforming power of the Gospel.[89]

On the question of caste-based division, the document says,

Caste, casteism and communalism, as well as class and class rigidity exist in the Christian community in large measure. The Indian Christians are to a great extent still conditioned by their social life by certain traditional cultural patterns of thought, and living or alternatively swept off by some of the modern currents of thought and Westernisation. Both of them contain elements contrary to the Christian faith, and inimical to the Christian fellowship.[90]

To deal with this situation the document suggests:

The Christian congregation in any city or village, therefore, has a responsibility for the total community—*basti, chawl, mohalla, village* or *cheri* wherever it is placed. The responsibility includes not only a concern for each person as a child of God, but also a duty to help transform all human situation, so that they may more adequately reflect the purpose of God.[91]

In these lines the issues referred to are related to Dalits, particularly Dalit Christians, who are made to live in the segregated parts of the village, town and cities like *basti, cheri* and presently *harijan basti*, for over three millennia. So a Biblical, as well as theological, reminder comes to the church/Christian community, when it says: 'Human dignity, therefore, is ultimately derived from the fact that he is a "brother for whom Christ died". The "least one" among men, the poorest, the lowliest and the lost, has infinite worth because of what God had done in Christ for him'. The document *Christian Participation in Nation-Building* came out in 1960, when the terms 'Dalit', 'Tribal' and 'Adivasi' were hardly in use, otherwise these terms would have been used here in these passages while expressing these thoughts.

The document ends with a message, which contains in it some of the theological issues, which are directly related to the Gospel-based nature and mission of the Christian church/ Christianity in India. As we will be referring to some of these theological issues in the discussion in our next section on 'Indian Christianity of Tomorrow', here we will close this part with the opening paragraph of this statement, which reads:

> There is basic need for the church to understand and assess the social and cosmic characters of the redemption of Jesus Christ. Without a theological renewal at this level, the awakening of the church to social responsibility will be impossible, and even if it were possible, the social mission of the church's will remain an extra instead of becoming an integral part of the Churches mission. Two theological affirmations are important in this connection . . . (i) Jesus Christ is Lord and Saviour of all creation; (2) The Church's Social Mission is Integral to the Total Life and Mission of the Church.[92]

The challenge to realize this theological affirmation brings us to the next section.

6. Indian Christianity of Tomorrow

Since theology or our theological understanding of Christian faith is the key towards reshaping Christianity for the India of tomorrow, we shall delve deeper into the subject in this section. For this purpose I shall divide the discussion in three parts. Part one shall take note of the summary of the factors related to the present form of Christianity; in the second part, shall ensue the discussion on the kind of Christian church or Christianity that one can foresee in future; and in the third part, we shall discuss the issue of 'Rethinking Theology'.

6.1 *Major Factors Responsible for the Present form of Christianity*

In our discussion on Sections 1 and 2 of this article, besides referring to our views that all the theologies are contextual, we had also looked into the present status of Christianity and factors responsible for its present form. The first and the major factor that we considered was the theological understanding of Christian faith. Today the average Christian is having Pietistic outlook towards life, which has the dual perception of 'personal holiness' and 'other world' central to it. In India, Christian faith that was based on this outlook was passed on by various missionary groups who came here. Then this was carried forward from generation to generation by Indian Christian leaders of various denominations. The issues related to 'this world' were their prime concern.

The second major factor for the present condition of the church/Christian community is adherence to the deep rooted evil of caste in the life of the church. The issue of caste is related also to the issue of 'justice' and this has become the primary cause for the declining number of Christians in India. As a matter of fact, in India caste and theology are closely related to one another—even to the point of helping one another to deepen the problem of Indian Christianity as such. Let me explain this point by referring to some of the historical facts related to Indian Christianity. I shall take the examples of three major Christian traditions, namely Syrian Orthodox, Roman Catholic and the Protestants.

Syrian Christians generally claim that they are in Kerala from the first century; but there are historical evidences that different groups of Syrian Christians came from the Middle East. Once they reached India, they were not only welcomed by the Hindu kings but were granted charter of privileges also, and taken into the services of the local kingdoms. These privileges were also enjoyed by the members of the caste Hindus. As a result, the Syrian Christians started behaving like the so-called upper caste Hindus and looked down upon those belonging to the lower caste. C.P. Mathai and M.M. Thomas endorse this in their book: 'There was also a very unfortunate aspect of them, namely that the community, being thus recognized as a high caste, came to look down upon the lower castes and imbibed more or less the same attitude towards them as that of the high caste'.[93]

The first Roman Catholic missionary to come to India was Francis Xavier who arrived in October 1542 and preached mainly among the Dalits.[94] But Roberto de Nobili who followed him in 1606, totally changed the missionary approach of Francis Xavier. In order to gain converts from the so-called upper caste Hindus, he declared himself a high caste,[95] and even introduced separate priests for upper and lower caste Christians.[96] These efforts of Nobili brought much fruit, but it proved to be negative also: 'A divided Church resulted. On the one hand, were Brahmin Christians, on the other hand, Pariah Christians (*Dalit*)'.[97]

The Protestant missionaries, Ziegenbalg, Plutschan and Schwartz were the products of the Pietistic school of theology of the University of Halle. They arrived in south India during 1706. About their mission work we get a view from one of their disciples Christian David, a student at Bishop College, Kolkata, who gave a testimony before Bishop Heber in 1823. When Bishop Heber asked Christian David's views about caste among the Christians of South India, his answer was summarized by an English Church historian in these words:

> First, with regard to the nature of Caste it was declared by Christian David, that it was among the natives of Southern India, "purely a worldly idea". . . . From the days of Ziegenbalg downwards they had wont to sit at church in two separate divisions, and had communicated separately at the Lord's table, drinking out of the same cup, but high-caste converts drinking first.[98]

So this is how the different denominations of church in India let Christianity embrace the evil of caste in its fold. On the one hand, it tried to promote the theological understanding of Christian faith traditions, while on the other it allowed caste to be part of the Christian life. Unfortunately this dichotomy continues in the church even to this day as can be seen in the case of Thachur Church, which is cited in Section 2.2. To overcome this, the authors of *Rethinking Christianity in India* make two good suggestions: first that the Indian theological students 'should learn more of Indian philosophy and Religion and less of Western theology';[99] and second that the Christian converts in India need 'emancipation from double bondage, namely from the tradition of Hinduism on the one hand, and the tradition of Christianity on the other'.[100]

Even authors belonging to other faiths have showed concern about the future of Indian Christians because of caste related issues infesting it. For example, in the case of Dalit Christians, Dr B.R. Ambedkar points out that because of 'the mental make-up' of Indian Christians there is 'a complex absence of any urge to break his bonds with the past'. He also adds that it is 'very rare of an untouchable becoming Christian because of a positive discontent from the Hindu religious teachings. The result is that Christianity became only an addendum to his old faith'.[101] About the future of Indian Christians, Nirad C. Chaudhuri is more vocal in predicting it by saying:

> The wealthy and well-placed among them will become merged in the anglicized Hindu upper middle class, with only a difference of

faith, which nobody including themselves will take very seriously. On the other hand the majority of Indian Christians, that is, those who are poor and already depressed socially, will become something like inferior castes in Hindu society.[102]

In situations of such gravity we have to agree with the authors of *Christian Participation in Nation-Building* when they declare that: 'Without a theological renewal at this level, the awakening of the Church to social responsibility will be impossible'.[103]

6.2 *Christianity Ought to be 'of the Poor'*

Earlier in Section 2, while discussing the present status of Christianity in our country, two observations were made: (1) the declining number of Christians, which we consider is related directly to the question of 'justice' and 'human rights'; and (2) the contradiction in Christian identity due to existing Christian traditions which ultimately resulted in crisis that the Christians in India are facing. Let us take a look at the second observation here to assess the ground reality before we get on with the discussion on rethinking theology for our need today.

Indian Christians are basically a 'community of the poor' because more than 90 per cent of its membership comprises of Dalits, Tribals, Adivasis and Women. But in spite of this the church in India continues to present an 'elitist image' or 'elitist identity' of itself. This is the contradiction in which the church in India has been living. It is because of this primarily that she has failed to make any impact on the poor and marginalized, and thus fulfil her own faith commitment. To uncover this truth convincingly to the members of the church is the role of theology/theologies, if the authentic, contextual and liberating nature of the church is to be maintained. Much discussion about this identity-crisis of Indian Christianity/church has been going on for the last three to four decades, particularly in the Roman Catholic circle as well as in the ecumenical circles. In his inaugural address to the Fathers of the Second Vatican Council, Holy Father Pope John XXIII had said that the church

> . . . ought to contribute/help in the diffusion of the social and communitarian content which is immanent/inheritance to authentic Christianity in its entirety: only in this manner can the church present herself as the church for all peoples (universal) and, above all, as the *Church of the Poor.*[104]

Taking a cue from the Holy Father, recently some discussion ensued with regard to the likely name for the church that would correspond with its nature as the *Church of the Poor* or *for all Peoples*, because many church people found it difficult to accept this as common name for the entire church. During the discussion proposals came to name it as the 'Church in solidarity with the Poor' or 'Church's solidarity with the poor' or 'Church's preferential option for the poor'. But the Southern countries pointed out that these alternatives seem to have emerged out of the experience of the Western churches, where poor people do not outnumber the others as church members. As far as the churches in the Southern countries are concerned, they felt, the expression *Church of the Poor* is most apt.[105]

The name *Church for the Poor* can be endorsed for Indian context too, because it is very near to the reality. However, the identity of the Indian church can also be expressed by calling it 'Church for the Subaltern communities', because a large majority of the membership of the church comes from Dalits, Tribals, OBC and other weaker sections of the society. According to one rough estimate about 12,000,000 out of a total of 20,000,000 Christians in the country are Dalits alone (based upon 1991 census). But if we add to it the number of Tribal-Christians, OBC-Christians and women members, this number will be very high percentage-wise. It will be more than 80 per cent. But instead of letting the question of identity of Indian church be decided by the number of the majority we have to be more careful. With that in view the best option with us, both theologically as well as sociologically, would be to call it the 'church of the marginalized' or the *Church of the Poor*.

The underlying reason behind this elitist image or identity of the church is the traditional theological understanding of

Christian faith. But structurally also, it seems, the church has inherited her present form from the Christendom model of the church, which came about at the time of Constantine the Great (AD 280-337). The Christendom model of the church was based upon the image of the Roman Empire. It is through the adoption of this model that the church got accommodated by the state power, which offered her patronizing relationship in return for this. In return the church also legitimized the power of the State. It is through this adoption that the authorities (leaders) of the church started imitating the day-to-day life of the empire and started considering themselves the princes of the church: they dressed themselves in imperial robes, sat on elaborate thrones, and were careful in keeping their social position in the church.[106] As this model was imitated by other churches, so also it was followed by Indian church. It is this model which is being followed by her even today, and which inhibits her from becoming the Church of the Poor. Therefore, unless a structural change in the life of the Indian church is brought about, it is going to be very difficult for her to return to her original subaltern roots and play the role which has been assigned to her by the Founder Lord Jesus Christ.

However, church of the poor does not mean a church exclusively for them. It actually means a church for all the peoples of God, but with a definite preference for the Dalits, tribals, OBCs, women, and other marginalized groups of the society. It means a church in solidarity with them, after the example of her Founder Lord Jesus Christ. The Church of the Poor is supposed to follow the life of the prophet-servant, as was lived by her Lord. Here I will like to quote from the statement made by Bishop Julio X. Labyen OCD, in which he has summed up one of the main outcomes of the Asian Bishops' historic meeting of 1970 dealing with the theme 'Church of the Poor'. Bishop Labyen writes:

> The Asian Bishops in their first historic meeting in 1970 in Manila—a meeting that was presided over by Pope Paul VI himself declared that

"we feel that God is calling the churches in Asia to become the *Church of the Poor*". This was the conclusion of their observation that two-thirds of the world's population resides in Asia, and that the majority of these peoples are poor. The Church cannot, therefore, put up islands of affluence in the midst of a sea of misery and poverty. Hence, the call of God to the Church in Asia to become the Church of the Poor.[107]

This definitely hints at structural change within the church on one hand by getting itself rid of 'Christiandom model', and on the other getting transformed itself to become the 'Church of the Poor' after her faith commitment. Our key understanding of the Christian community/church is that Jesus himself is the real church, who suffered 'outside the gate' (Heb. 13: 12). It is this that Kazoh Kitamori reminds us while talking about his 'theology of the Pain of God'. According to him this Pain 'takes place in the church, which is the body of Christ'.[108] 'The church inherited the Pain of God and became the symbol of the Pain of God'.[109] Explaining his stance he says, 'God embracing completely those who should not be embraced' makes Him 'God in Pain'![110] This is what the Christian community/church in Asia or India is supposed to embrace—'outcastes', 'untouchables' including Dalits, Tribals, Adivasis and Women, who are victims and are suffering for centuries under the burden of the caste based and oppressive social order.

The authors of *Christian Participation in Nation Building* make the same point when they define a church in these words:

The church has traditionally been defined as a people, a congregation, created by God around the Word and the Sacrament, with an essential order. This definition of the church as a people of God among the peoples of the world receives new depth in the light of the church's awakening to her social responsibility.[111]

There are other problems which the Indian Christianity needs to consider before it gets reshaped and established in India. The authors of *Rethinking Christianity in India* make us aware of this:

Indian Christianity which has to establish itself as a religious force in the country cannot afford to take any step that will not carry her forward as an evangelistic agency. But it may be admitted that construction of Indian Christianity itself demands attention to the problem of Western denominationalism.[112]

Again, making an important theological point, they said:

> Christ however sought to establish a new universe with a cosmic energy —the Holy Spirit. . . . In this sense, Christianity is not a religion. . . . The Holy Spirit is the new cosmic energy; the Kingdom of God, the new Order; the children of God, the new type that Christ has inaugurated. The Gospel is that God in Jesus has made a new creation. Christianity has been a failure because we made a new religion of it instead of a new creation.[113]

6.3 *Rethinking/Relevant Theology*

In the course of this paper we have seen that three streams of theology—Traditional theology, Indian Christian theology and Indian Contextual theology—run concurrently for the theologians of our country. All these are different in perspective and form because of the context each deals with. We have also seen that with time, traditional theology that came from the West became the major area of study under the name 'Systematic theology' in our country. The other stream called Indian Christian theology was based mainly on Indian philosophical thought and was the product of Indian intellectuals. Both these theological expressions centred on the study of God or Brahman, having in their mind the Greek connotation of the expression 'theology', as the science of pure being or God. Both these systems of theology have very little to do directly with human history. The theologians of the first stream believed that there are two histories, namely sacred and human (profane); and for the theologians of the second stream history as such, has no meaning. According to the Indian classical Hindu religion it is irrelevant to consider history, as it is generally understood. Hindu philosophy talks of history as a cycle, which moves on, from one great age or *yuga* to another until at last the wheel turns full cycle and it returns to the beginning. So according to this view, history is not linear; it has no concept with either purpose or progress.

Because human history is the bedrock of the Indian contextual theology (third stream), it should not be presumed that it came up as a counter-theology to the other two traditional theologies that ignore human history. Indian contextual theology has come into existence independently, and today much social thinking is being assimilated in formulating this stream of theology, enabling its theological expression to deal with the life issues of those Indian communities that have been the victims of our caste-based social order for so long. In the same way, it will be a serious fault in thinking that the Indian contextual theology could be replaced with any of the liberation theologies that we find around us. Some Indian theologians have tried to commit exactly the same mistake with abortive results: for example, their attempt to mix elements of South American Liberation theology with that of Indian contextual and liberating theology almost hijacked the latter. No doubt all the liberation theologies have a common theme—as suggested by the name itself—and identical goal, which is *liberation for all*. But the actual history, social milieu and issues, racial elements, ideological basis of almost every people differ, and with that shall very naturally differ every people's theology and the idiom of its expression. For example, our African brothers and sisters in North America were uprooted from their native place and taken there by force; they did not come of their choice. The South Americans had gone through extreme economic oppression, though their oppressors belonged to their own stock. As a result of this, the Liberation theology of South America which centres on the economic problems differs from the Black theology of North America which focused on colour, cultural and social trauma and slave-master relationship based oppression. Likewise, the Korean based Minjung theology is the outcome of ordinary people's pain, their frustrations, their agonies and their sufferings, along with their hopes, aspirations and struggle. The

'Theology of Struggle' of the Philippinos is based on the sufferings of the politically colonized people.

However, when we talk about Indian contextual liberating theology—based on the experiences of Dalits or Tribals or Adivasis—the situation changes immediately. In the course of their history, the Indian oppressed communities have lost most of what they had: they lost not only their land, culture, language, religion, political/social rights, but also their history, and along with it their dignity and self-esteem. No other community in the world has undergone such intense oppression. Then the story of their oppression is also much too long as compared to any other known group. For them everything has to begin anew. Their opponents, who as colonizers came at different stages of history, have become the masters today of not only the resources that once belonged to them, they even enslaved them and became their 'owner' as well. This historical context is enough to assure that the Indian contextual and liberating theologies cannot be clubbed with any other traditional or liberation theologies.

What I want to stress on in particular is the element of relevance of theology to the people it is trying to address. When we are considering the traditional theologies, or even liberating theologies, for their application to the Indian context, the question of their relevance to the people—the Dalits, Tribals, Adivasis and Women—should be uppermost in our mind. Because most of the theologies ignore this, the theologians of the Indian contextual and liberating theologies begin with showing their 'suspicion' about both their form and content. In one of my earlier articles I have said:

> This is the reality to which up till now we Indian Christians and others, as thinkers and converts, have tried to respond. Certain responses to this reality have given birth to a theology known as 'Indian Christian theology' which, however, is not really relevant to the living situations of the majority of Indian Christians. When I say "it is not relevant", I mean that it has not been based on or drawn from the experiences of the majority of the people (i.e., between 80 per cent to 90 per cent). . . . What these poor village Christians are searching for even today is

how to earn their daily bread, how to overcome their life situation of oppression, poverty, suffering, injustice, illiteracy, and denial of identity. Now, Indian Christian theology or any other theology has failed, and continues to ignore these issues, which for the majority of Christians and most other Indians, are questions of survival. Here I do not propose the rejecting of the known expressions of Indian Christian theology or question its usefulness. All I am saying is that we have to work out another expression of Indian Christian theology which should be relevant to the living situation of the vast majority of people in their widely dissimilar regions.[114]

Similar views, but in a more positive sense are expressed by the late Renthy Keitzar, while expressing the need for a relevant expression of theology for the tribals of north-east India:

> This is to be noted, however, that Western theologies such as Calvinism, Evangelicalism, Fundamentalism, Puritanism, and so on have been derived from their own cultural and historical background or situations. These have come out of their contexts in response to their contemporary realities. Similarly, Christian theology in North East India must emerge from the contemporary cultural realities. Some of the problems we are confronting today in North East India are identity crisis, tribalism, insurgency, cultural revival, spiritism, social change, political corruption, bribery, cheating, injustice, and the influence of Indian (Hindu) ideas. In our theologization we must bear these problems in mind.[115]

Bishop Nirmal Minz in his foreword to *Adivasi Theology* also expressed the similar views while establishing the need for an Adivasi theology. He makes two most important points. He agrees about the usefulness of various existing theologies, including contextual and liberating theologies, but also adds: 'But the basic problem remains because the life situation of the Jharkhandi Adivasis is radically different from all these theological formulations'. Therefore, 'A Relevant Christian Theology means and demands a paradigm shift. . . . Any Christian theology has to be relevant for Jharkhandi Adivasis; it should address the perennial issues of alienation and displacement adversely affecting their history—their geo-political and cultural identity.'[116]

The late Prasanna Kumari Samuel in her work *Dalit Women's Experiences: A Theological Iimperative for Indian Feminist Theology* laid a continuing emphasis on 'a paradigm shift' while making her point clear for those theologians who claim their theologies are not 'definitions, but descriptions'. She says:

> If theology is not definitions and doctrines why then women are continued to be discriminated even among Third World Theological circles? It is this question that needs to be addressed. Male chauvinism is much worse in Indian church institutions when compared to secular institutions, about their attitude to women. This reality in church institutions reveals the need for recovery by the oppressed of their authentic selves as a crucial concern—in this case the Dalit women. The nation's history based on caste, its religious traditions and various other forces in the pretext of culture and tradition, denied women in general, Dalit women in particular of their true selves resulting in muting them of their dignity and identity; this necessitates creation of space for Dalit women to speak differently.[117]

Such is the Indian women's context which the Indian Feminist theologians themselves are addressing and which the traditional theologies or the liberating theologies have failed to do.

7. Conclusion

It is true that the acceptance from the church and even from the academic world comes slowly for such ventures. The Liberation theology of Latin America had to face the same challenge and it was only during 1986 that it was accepted as valid theology by the Vatican. However, for the Indian contextual and liberating theologies the acceptance came in a very short period of two decades. Today the Indian Contextual and Liberating theologies have become part of the core curriculum of the Bachelor of Theology of the Senate of Serampore College (University), and are also being taught in other Catholic institutions. It is true that response of the Indian churches to these expressions is slow, but during the last one decade it has been gaining momentum. The best example is that of the *Dalit Bible Commentary*. The churches, including their heads, both Protestant and Roman Catholic, have shown keen interest, while participating in various release functions in Delhi, Bangalore, Chennai, Kolkata, Vijayawada, Pune and Vellore. The active participation came from the heads of Roman Catholic, Church of South India, Church of North India, Lutheran Church and others. But still we have to accept the fact that regarding active participation for fuller liberation of various oppressed communities the churches still maintain their silence. The Indian church should give sincere priority to the cause of liberation of these communities. It is only through this partnership that transformation is possible. The role of the Catholic institutions, and of Serampore College University, with regard to *Dalit Bible Commentary* is indeed positive step in this direction. It is hoped that with the introduction of new contextual curriculum by the Senate of the Serampore College and various Catholic seminaries the future response of priests, pastors and bishops will be different.

NOTES

1. Rex Ambler, *Global Theology: The Meaning of Faith in the Present World Crisis*, London: SCM, 1990, p. 9.
2. R.H.S. Boyd, *An Introduction to Indian Christian Theology*, Foreword, Madras: CLS, 1979 (rpt.), p. v.
3. John Weborg, *Pietisma: The Fire of God Which Flames in the Heart of Germany*, in Protestant Spiritual Traditions, ed. Frank C. Senn, New York: Paulist Press, 1986, pp. 185, 186 (top).
4. Ibid., p. 186 (bottom).
5. Ibid.
6. Quoted in Stephen Charles Neill and Hans-Ruedi Weber, *The Layman in Christian History*, London: SCM Press, 1963, p. 162.
7. Ibid., p. 210 (bottom).
8. See for Detail Information:
   (a) *Census of India* 1981, Paper 4 of 1981 Household Population by Religion of head of Household, P. Padmanabha of the Indian Administrative Service Registrar General & Census Commissioner, India, New Delhi, 1984, pp. 4-22.

(b) *Census of India 2001*, the First Report of Religion Data, Jayant Kumar Banthia, Registrar General & Census Commissioner, India, 2A Mansingh Road, New Delhi, 2001, pp. xxvii, xxxiii.

9. J. Aixala, *Jesuit Formation and Inculturation in India Today*, Anand: Gujarat Sahitya Prakash, 1978, p. 17.
10. CNI Synodical Programme—'Towards a Holistic Understanding of Mission Consultation', in *Church: A Community in Mission for Justice, Peace and Integrity of Creation* (15-17 November 1993), a Report, New Delhi.
11. Dr Babasaheb Ambedkar, *Writings and Speeches*, vol. 5, Bombay: Education Department, Government of Maharashtra, 1989, pp. 452-3.
12. *Frontline*, 25 February 2011, vol. 28, no. 4, pp. 38, 39.
13. *The Mandal Commission 1980*, op. cit., p. 21.
14. L.M. Shrikant, *Report of the Commissioner for Scheduled Castes and Scheduled Tribes for the Period ending 31st December 1951*, p. 1 (top).
15. Ibid., pp. 111-15.
16. Ibid., p. 1.
17. *Reservation for Backward Classes, Mandal Commission Report of the Backward Classes Commission, 1980* (along with Introduction), Delhi: Akalank Publications, 1990, p. 23.
18. Herbert W. Richardson, *Theology for a New World*, London: SCM Press, 1968, p. 158.
19. Ibid., pp. 158-9.
20. Rex Ambler, *Global Theology: The Meaning of Faith in the Present World Crisis*, London: SCM Press, 190, p. 9.
21. Ibid., p. 68.
22. Ibid., p. 81.
23. Ibid., p. 83.
24. John Reader, *Local Theology*, Church and Community in Dialogue, London: SPCK, 1994, p. 93.
25. Ibid., p. 99.
26. Max L. Stackhouse, *Globalization and Grace*, New York, London: Continuum, 2007, p. 5.
27. Ibid., p. 77.
28. Ibid., p. 78.
29. Ibid., pp. 86-95.
30. Ibid., p. 116.
31. Ibid., p. 102.

32. Felix Wilfred, *Asian Public Theology, Critical Concerns in Challenging Times*, Delhi: ISPCK, 2010, pp. xi-xii.
33. Ibid., p. xx.
34. Ibid., pp. xxii-xxiv.
35. Ibid., p. 326.
36. Kitamori Kazoh: *Theology of the Pain of God*, London: SCM, 1966, p. 8.
37. Ibid., 9.
38. Ibid., see Back Cover for Dr John W. Taylor's comments.
39. Ibid., p. 12.
40. Ibid., p. 15.
41. Ibid., p. 34.
42. Ibid., p. 135.
43. Ibid., p. 138.
44. Ibid., p. 150.
45. Kosake Koyama, *Waterbuffalo Theology*, New York: Orbis Book, 1974, Preface, p. viii.
46. Ibid., p. 21.
47. Gustavo Gutierrez, *A Theology of Liberation: Huston Politics and Salvation*, New York: Orbis Books, 1973, pp. 6, 7.
48. Ibid., p. 11.
49. Ibid., p. 153.
50. James H. Cone, 'Black Theology and Black Liberation', in *Black Theology: The South African Voice*, ed. Basil Moore, London: C. Hurst & Company, 1973, p. 174.
51. Ibid., p. 52.
52. Kim Young-Bock, *Messiah and Minjung: Christian Solidarity with the People for New Life*, Hong Kong: CCA, 1992, p. 5.
53. Eleasar S. Fernandez, *Towards a Theology of Struggle*, New York: Orbis Books, 1994, p. 7.
54. Ibid.
55. M.E. Prabhakar (ed.), *Towards a Dalit Theology*, Delhi: ISPCK, 1988, pp. 65, 66.
56. Ibid.
57. James Massey (ed.), *Indigenous People: Dalits, Dalit Issues in Today's Theological Debate*, Delhi: ISPCK, 1994.
58. V. Devasahayam (ed.), *Frontiers of Theology*, Madras/Delhi: ISPCK/Gurukul, 1997.
59. Xavier S.J. Irudayaraj (ed.), *Emergency Dalit Theology*, Madras: Jesuit Theological Secretariate, 1990.

60. Prabhakar (ed.), op. cit., p. 2.
61. Ibid., p. 146.
62. James Massey, *Introducing Dalit Theology*, New Delhi: CDS, 2004, p. 27.
63. Ranthy Keitzar, *In Search of a Relevant Gospel Message*, Guwahati: CLC, 1995, p. 66.
64. Ibid., p. 69.
65. Ibid., pp. 8, 9.
66. Nirmal Minz, 'Dalit Tribal: A Search for Common Ideology', in *Indigenous People: Dalits*, ed. James Massey, op. cit., p. 136.
67. Ibid., p. 142.
68. Christ Sumit Abhay Kerketta, *Adivasi Theology, Towards a Relevant Christian Theology for the Jharkhandi Adivasis*, Ranchi: ATCR/ GTC, 2009, p. xii (Foreword).
69. Ibid., p. 1.
70. Ibid., pp. 2, 3.
71. Ibid., p. 122.
72. Ruth Manorama, *Dalit Women: The Thrice Alienated*, in 'Towards a Dalit Theology', ed. M.E. Prabhakar, op. cit., p. 149.
73. Prasanna Kumari Samuel, *Dalit Women's Experiences: A Theological Imperative for Indian Feminist Theology*, Chennai: Gurukul, 2009, p. 3.
74. Ibid., 31.
75. Ibid., p. 2.
76. Ibid., p. 17.
77. *The World Mission of the Church, Findings and Recommendations of the International Missionary Council*, Tambaram, Madras, India, 12 to 29 December 1938, London and New York: International Missionary Council, 1939, p. 5.
78. Ibid., p. 15.
79. Ibid., p. 20.
80. Ibid., p. 74.
81. J.V. Job et al., *Rethinking Christianity in India*, Madras, 1938, p. iii (Preface).
82. Ibid., p .47.
83. Ibid., p. 49.
84. Ibid., p. 53.
85. Ibid., pp. 54, 55.
86. Ibid., p. 39.

87. P.D. Devanandan and M.M. Thomas (eds.), *Christian Participation in Nation-Building*, Bangalore: NCCI & CISRS, 1960, p. 48.
88. Ibid., p. 227.
89. Ibid., pp. 268.
90. Ibid., p. 235.
91. Ibid., p. 228.
92. Ibid., p. 270.
93. C.P. Mathew and M.M. Thomas, *The Indian Churches of Saint Thomas*, Delhi: ISPCK, 1967, p. 22.
94. Joseph Thekkedath, *History of Christianity in India*, vol. II, Bangalore: CHAI, 1967, pp. 22, 23.
95. John William Kaye, *Christianity in India*, London: Smith-Elder, 1859, p. 30.
96. David Jenks, *Six Great Missionaries of the Sixteenth-Seventeenth Century*, London: A.R. Mowbray, 1930, p. 127.
97. William B. Anderson and Charles R. Watson, *Far North in India*, Philadelphia: Board of Foreign Missions of the United Presbyterian Church of North America, 1911, p. 146.
98. Kaye, op. cit., pp. 252, 253.
99. Job et al., op. cit., p. 39.
100. Ibid., p. 49.
101. James Massey, *Dr B.R. Ambedkar: A Study in Just Society*, New Delhi: Manohar & CDS, p. 60.
102. Nirad C. Chaudhuri, *The Continent of Circe*, Bombay: Jaico Publishing House, 1983, p. 304.
103. Devanandan and Thomas (eds), op. cit., p. 290.
104. Quoted in Julio X. Labayen, *Revolution and the Church of the Poor*, Quezen City, Philippines: Claretian Publications, 1995, p. 32.
105. See for detailed discussion in: Ninan, The Rt. Rev. Dr A. George: *The Poor and Poverty in India in Church and Society*, ed. Rajendra K. Sail & Akshay Sail, Mumbai: BUILD and RCDRC, 2001, p. 249.
106. Labayen, op. cit., pp. 52ff.
107. Ibid., pp. 32-3.
108. Kitamori, op. cit., p. 104.
109. Ibid., p. 67.
110. Ibid., p. 12.
111. Devanandan and Thomas (eds), op. cit., p. 304.
112. Job et al., op. cit., p. 157.

113. Ibid., pp. 54, 55.
114. Prabhakar (ed), op. cit., pp. 58, 59.
115. Keitzar, op. cit., pp. 66, 67.
116. Kerketta, op. cit., p. xii (Foreword).
117. Samuel, op. cit., p. 133.

PART II

TERRAINS

2

Negotiating with Contemporary Social Change: Emerging Dalit Theological Sensibilities

A. MARIA ARUL RAJA

Multi-pronged Hegemonic Violence of Casteism

Indian soil has its specific configuration of structural violence sustained by both caste and class based systems. The vast majority of the population still reels under grinding operation of the most retrogressive feudal system. It is under the grip of a high poverty index, a relatively high rate of illiteracy, landlordism including absentee landlordism, suicide of farmers, bonded labourers, child labour, severe forms of patriarchy, crude and obscurantist forms of religiosity, etc. These manifestations of the feudal system sustain themselves in mutuality with the caste system, which is a typically Indian form of feudalism. The workings of the caste system have changed their modality in urban areas. But in the rural agrarian setting, they continue to manifest themselves in their raw brutality.

By and large Indic sensibilities have embraced a hierarchical and inegalitarian structure of the society as a natural way of life. It is legitimized by religious myths and ethical traditions claimed to be of divine origin. Whenever we probe into casual brutality and organized violence unleashed against Dalits, Adivasis, Muslims, or Christians, we identify that the roots of the malady lead to the deep-seated belief that the superior human has the birth right to dehumanize the other humans deemed to be 'inferior'.

Endless cycles of violence is perpetrated in the form of atrocities upon the subaltern classes of people in post-Independent India.[1]

> [S]ince the early 1970s, the activism of groups who call themselves Dalits have been the other central element in these confrontations. . . . Such militant 'Dalit' groups were therefore stigmatized on two counts at once. They were reviled as 'Naxalite' insurgents fomenting sedition and criminality, and at the same time as enemies of caste order (*Dharma*) to be fought by the righteous 'caste Hindu' with the weapons of the community and moral mandate.[2]

We find here a simultaneous process of subaltern activism and the counter-strategy of hegemonic forces to demonize them as politically violent and culturally abominable. This is a typical strategy the dominant forces of which keep playing in the hierarchical society of India. The open communal clashes seem to be the strategies for sustaining 'the will to hegemonise' a society, and retain its power over a society.

An honour code is an ideology of stratification that emerges from and leads to a particular kind of social structure. It is a moralistic legitimization of the stratification. In fact 'societies with an honour culture are notorious for their level of violence, and even more for their pervasive atmosphere of threat and insecurity'.[3] In the caste-ridden culture of South Asia, this stratification is built upon the understanding of the violent and hence powerful over those supposedly non-violent and hence powerless. In other words, toughness or roughness is made as the organizing principle of the stratification. And here, any wild or mild aggression initiated to combat the 'dishonour' purportedly caused by the lower strata is justified with the aim of establishing and perpetuating the traditional social hierarchy. And even any mild assertion against such aggression is counted as 'grossly violent'. In the context of caste conflicts we could identify some of the features of violence triggered by the perception of violation of the honour code as indicated below:

Violence related to Perception of Violation of Honour Code in Caste Conflicts

Initiated by the Dominating Groups	Responded to by the Subaltern Groups
• An aggressively pro-active one • Motivated by seeking elite status • Inegalitarian move to raise oneself above others • By and large an interference process	• An assertively reactionary one • Motivated by fear and lack of security • Egalitarian self-help security enforcement • By and large an avoidance process

In spite of the self-proclamation of India as a secular and democratic state, the SCs/STs suffer from institutional hatred. The Dalits have been internationalizing that casteism is worse than racism. There is a culture of hatred expressed through violent behaviour against Dalits as inherently and irretrievably inferior. And not only through hate speech but hate behaviour expressed through violent actions and deeds directed against the community and the backward classes with the intent of asserting their imaginary natural inferiority or the superiority or domination of other groups, the casteism is sought to be perpetuated.[4]

By linking achievement, status and merit with caste, the SC/STs are made to internalize inferiority. Perpetuation of social stereotypes of inferiority leads to feelings of self-hatred, humiliation and isolation and affects achievement. It could be understood as the system of domination perpetuated through violence deliberately causing avoidable deprivation of basic human needs through inegalitarian distribution of resources. This subtle and invisible form of violence, embedded in social structures, is made to appear to be unquestionably normal and natural. Eventually it is promoted as a moral and divine order. It is never visibly noticed like direct violence causing skull breaking or bloodshed. But with the institutional backup, it keeps on systematically producing untold suffering and slow deaths[5] through denial of opportunities for health, hygiene, home, food, water, and franchise.[6]

> The term *structural violence* has been used to designate people who experience violence (and violation) owing to extreme poverty. . . . The World Health Organization (1995) estimates that 20 per cent of the world's population lives in extreme poverty. Authors writing about this population, especially ethnographers, use the phrase 'the violence of everyday life' to indicate the violence such structural deprivation does to people.[7]

Here we refer to the violence inherent in a system: not only direct physical violence, but also the more subtle forms of coercion that sustain relations of domination and exploitation, including the threat of violence.[8] Casteism, untouchability, patriarchy, racism, discrimination based on birth or merit are some of the structural forms of violence of day-to-day life. Such oppressive systems are maintained through the means and mechanisms of violence. Ultimately they lead to deep lying conflicts based on power relations, dynamics of resource-sharing, negotiation of identities, and so on.

Resurgence of Dalit Theologies

Dalit theologies are as old as the oppression of the Dalits and as young as the assertion of the Dalits. They may not have been systematically articulated through the printed pages of renowned publications by learned scholars. But they have all along been writ large on the multivalent articulations subtly or vociferously expressed through the day-to-day Dalit struggles. Such expressions seeking to cherish glimpses of abundant life in limited space amidst conflicts could be ranging from silent protests to consensual collaboration or from violent outbursts to weapons of the weak. Those claiming to theologize and articulate from Dalit perspectives have to be alert with their antennas.

No doubt, the Dalits are on the receiving end of the direct, structural, or symbolic violence imposed upon them by socio-cultural structures and armed forces with or without the implicit and explicit approval of the ruling elite and state apparatus.[9] And obviously in the contemporary Indian scenario, discourses on violence and non-violence are quite rampant in all walks of life both in the public realm and private realm. They are articulated by the perpetrators, pro-violence groups, victims, anti-violence groups, or altruistic observers. By and large, in theoretical texts or theological literature claiming to speak for and on behalf of the Dalits, we come across articulation of the Dalit, non-Dalit, pro-Dalit, and anti-Dalit subjects who may or may not share the Dalit socio-cultural location. Quite often, those not walking with the Dalits tend to use such discourses as a vehicle for their own ends.[10]

From the ongoing search into Dalit theologies, we could locate some of the theological sensibilities, emerging from Dalit religio-cultural soil seeking to negotiate with the contemporary trends of social changes. Though not exhaustively, a few of them could be articulated as follows:

Methodological Refinement

- Spirit of self-critique
- Normativity from within

Awareness of Inadequacies

- Advanced critical historicity
- Away from ideological imprisonment

Expected Outcome

- Habitual resources to exploration into new resources
- Theologian-centred to people-centred

Methodological Refinement

The methodological refinement for doing Dalit theologies has to be gradually attended to with the emerging social awareness on the ecological sensibilities, feminist insights, and the growing role of the civil society.

Spirit of Self-critique

Against this background, all the existing Dalit theological attempts have to be further empowered by the spirit of self-critique. The rising consciousness of the ecological crisis in terms of alienation of the Dalits from the natural resources like water and land triggered by the profit-centred developmentalism urgently invites Dalit theologies to go beyond mere anthropocentrism. One has to be acutely aware of the fact that mere anthropocentrism does not lead Dalit theologies to the next level of emancipatory models. At the same time the feminist discourses are sharply awakening the Dalit theologies from deliberately or inadvertently falling into the rut of ignoring the feminine face of Dalits and Dalitization of women. The expanded space growingly claimed by the civil society piercingly brings to notice how both the private and public aspects of the human society is affected by the virus of corruption as a customized way of normal life. The cry for inclusion at all walks of life in every conflict situation is also feebly heard from the defeated-yet-assertive people like the Dalits, immigrants, indigenous peoples, women labourers, and the victims of child labour.

With all these trends of social changes, Dalit theologies have to go beyond the borders of mere anthropocentrism. And accordingly, the Dalit discourses have to be evolved on the foundational commitment of enabling the Dalits to keep on becoming co-born with Mother Nature and co-creators with Creator God while continuing to be co-workers with other humans. The cry of the children and women labouring to survive at the bottom of the society's caste hierarchy has to occupy the centrestage of the exploration of Dalit theologies. In this era of the Right to Information Act (RTI) from top to bottom, the active agents of corruption at all levels are sought to be exposed by the weak but committed minority of the powerless civil society. This has to challenge those Dalits who were the beneficiaries of Dalit theological discourses and who tend to settle down with their existing privileges without further committing themselves for Dalit emancipation. If so, the cultures of accumulation, addiction, or fragmentation as practised by the hegemonic oppressors is/are to be replaced with the cultures of democratization, recovery, and community building. The Dalit leaders cannot be exempted from this process of creating new cultures of accountability and transparency in the private and public spaces of the society. With this spirit of self-critique, the 'Dalit-only-model-of-emancipation' has to give way to 'open-minded-Dalit-discourses' with uncompromising inclusion of all types of victims of multifaceted hierarchies based on gender, colour, language, region, ethnicity, nationality, or religion. By no means, the agenda of the radical inclusive approach can ever be given up by Dalit theologies.

Normativity from Within

One is aware that the Dalit theological search is not merely for understanding but for transformation. It seeks to journey away from the present order of discriminatory caste hierarchy and asymmetry of power to a new order of egalitarianism and democratization of power. As a contextualized hermeneutical exploration with the social option for promoting the political agenda of the Dalits, it seeks to enable them to emancipate themselves from the clutches of untouchability. Its orientations could never be elitist, authoritarian and individualistic but subaltern, participatory and communitarian.[11]

The interpretative key of the Dalit theological orientations is at once the 'rejection' and the 'affirmation'; the rejection of exclusion (the imposed identity) and the affirmation of inclusion (the identity of being co-human with other humans). This is the foundational norm of the critical principle of the Dalit hermeneutics. This foundation is built upon the Dalit narrative experience of being the victims, becoming the subjects and believing in building up a casteless human community. That is why any allegation against Dalit interpretation as mere 'subjective activity' becomes baselessly redundant. In effect, Dalit pursuit of the agenda of becoming co-humans with other humans becomes the foundation of their interpretative orientation. It does not engage itself in the pretension of scientific objectivity. It is not an excavation into the world of antiquity. Rather it is a future-oriented search.

Dalit consciousness has the necessity of bringing together 'hermeneutics, social theory, and the search for a transcendental dimension which will allow a psycho-social critique of societies and traditions which is not merely contextually internal to them'.[12] It claims self-esteem on the one hand, and owns up its legitimate anger on the other. That is why Dalit theological articulation tends to become more socio-critical (actual conflicts) than socio-pragmatic (apparent harmony). That does not mean that Dalit theologies are bent on indulging in 'enemy-making'. In fact, Dalits are convinced that every form of dehumanization of the other is ultimately the dehumanization of oneself.[13] That is why it is a Dalit contribution to the whole of the human community. And hence Dalit theological pursuit should become the birthright of every human person.

Brahminism is the worldview that upholds that the untouchables with their permanent pollution have no rights but only duties and responsibilities. Indian heritagist reading seeks to identify the supreme values embedded particularly from classical texts like the Vedas, Upanishads, *Bhagavad Gita*, Dharmashastras or Puranas from the Indian soil and other texts like the Koran and Bible. While doing so, they tend to uphold the so-called supremacy of classical Indian categories or Semitic and Hellenistic expressions. But on the other hand, Dalit theologies intuitively opt for the direction of deploying the stories of such classical texts and traditions 'in ways that would guarantee their relevance and poignancy'.[14] And consequently, the sacred texts need not be assumed always to be the deposit of the 'holy' word to be defended. Complex philological intricacies may not occupy the primacy of place. Rather, the thread-line of stories and discourses from such texts will be the central characteristic of Dalit interpretation. By its foundational orientation, Dalit theologies are to be free from 'excessive textualism, disparagement of both major and popular religions, and homogenization of the poor'.[15] And so, every claim of supremacy based on sacredness, tradition, or textualization may not find a privileged position in the Dalit theologies. The normativity of leading the Dalits to effectively to struggle against the practices of untouchability and casteism have to be reflected in the locus theologicus, theological questions, tools of analysis, and praxical orientation of the Dalit theologies.

Awareness of Inadequacies

In continuity with the spirit of self-critique, the existing Dalit theologies need not be ashamed of openly acknowledging and expressing its current inadequacies. These are the opportunities for stepping up the critical historicity and transcending the habitual ideological sites.

Advanced Critical Historicity

Mere ethnographic explanations or political interpretations, or moralistic exhortations do not lead us to a comprehensive understanding of the impact of violence upon the Dalits. Nor are they adequate in offering adequate explanations on the response of the Dalits ranging from mild resistance up to assertive confrontation. By and large, discourses on non-violence articulated in the name of constructing peace end up in overtly or covertly supporting the continuous perpetuation of the hegemony of the dominant and betray the Dalit hopes of constructing a caste-free society. Dalit engagement with their life struggles can never be adequately served by soulless legal documents. In fact, discourses on the virtues of non-violence seem to transform 'a matrix of real historical experiences' into 'a matrix of abstract legality', thereby 'detaching an experience from its living context'.[16] The same thing could be said of exegetical or theological documents.

Gramsci[17] recognized that 'subalternity' refers to the situation in which one 'powerless' class becomes subjected to the decisions of the 'powerful' another. The term connotes the 'non-hegemonic groups or classes'.[18] And hence 'subalternity' cannot be explained from the location of hegemonic powers but from the dusty soil of being silenced and subordinated. If the discussions on violence or non-violence are divested of the down-to-earth subaltern experience, the subaltern person/group is reduced to be an object (objects) of high handed humanism of those upholding non-violence or the armed hegemonizers advocating violence. In both of these hegemonic orientations, the subaltern subjectivity is repressed, their inner voice is muffled and their outer voice is silenced. And hence, the positive documents on subaltern insurgency are neither available nor accessible to the public. The only sources of information are texts or commentaries on subaltern counterinsurgency produced by elite documentation.

But from the Dalit resources from the oral memory or written texts systematically or unsystematically preserved or abandoned have to be deployed for getting to know their critical historicity. For instance, quite often a-historical and trans-situational explanations portraying the trajectories of violence will not be adequate for protecting the Dalits from the grip of violence. Rather, historical and micro-level explanations from the ground reality of the perspectives of the most affected people in the situations of conflicts and violence could help us to grapple with violence along with the subalterns groups. And if discourses on violence in the context of the life struggles of the Dalits have to be adequately comprehensive, they have to grapple with the following three components:

- existing asymmetry of power relations between conflicting groups
- relational anthropology actually lived out or envisaged
- critical appraisal of concrete historical situation.

The following snap-shot portrays how each of the micro-level situations (for instance of violence) has to be interpreted with critical historical discernment undertaken from the point of view of the Dalits defeated by the denial of power and of space to be treated as co-humans in any society.

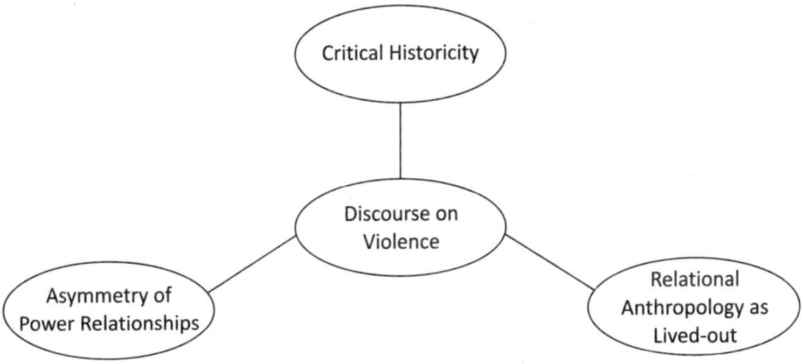

Away from Ideological Imprisonment

Dalit theologies have the necessity of being well informed of the multiple literary theories and strategies in the act of addressing the contemporary Dalit readers in their respective contexts. They could eclectically incorporate the idioms of historical, literary, social, anthropological, psychological or other schools of human thought. But there is a clear shift from the basis of these theories or methodologies to the basis of the Dalit subjectivity.[19] In other words, Dalit subjectivity has to be activated by the subjectivity of the other types of victims projected through the texts of local or other cultural soils towards a new possibility of emancipatory movement from the present order. If so, the emerging Dalit theological insights could effectively address the needs of their emancipatory efforts.

Every act of interpretation of the past text should take a lead from and towards the contemporary politico-historical and socio-cultural contexts.[20] In this process, the religio-cultural experience of the first and the successive readers should help the present readers to creatively expand the imagination of new possibilities and alternatives in the current context.[21] The primary task of Dalit theologies is to identify the transformative (performative) aspects of the texts. For achieving this, various methods of discovering the (significative) meaning of the texts (oral and written) are to be deployed from the world of scholarship professionally handling them. The role of the Dalit theologians is to create an appropriate atmosphere for Dalit subjectivity to be activated in dialogue with the subjectivity of the other subalterns.

The ethical option of the Dalit theologies is the advocacy of enabling the Dalits, as subjects of their own history, to move ahead from the existing disorder towards a new world with better possibilities. The reality of Dalit emancipation is a matter of dynamic tension between the 'already' and the 'not-yet'. The vision of Dalit liberation has to be tangibly enfleshed here and now, as well as the subject matter of contemplation through memory.

In this process Dalit theologies have to be constantly in dialogue with the wide spectrum of ideological sites of classical Marxism, neo-Marxian, Marxist-Leninism or eco-Feminism and with belief systems of theosophy, Advaita, Dvaita, monotheism, polytheism, or atheism. Getting bogged down with a single belief system or set of ideological tools may not be very helpful for comprehending the complex layers of Dalit consciousness. It will be dangerous for the Dalit theologies to be imprisoned by a set of fixated ideological tools and belief systems.

Expected Outcome

With the spirit of risk-taking for venturing into new avenues of struggle, Dalits could reap the fruits of engaging themselves with new resources for theological dialogue. And progressively they could grow as people-centred articulation in the actual site of struggles rather than the theologian-centred academic discourses.

Habitual Resources to Exploration into New Resources

There might be a tendency to settle down with theological dialogues with habitual religio-cultural resources. New discourses on Dalit emancipation have to explore into the new resources in their on-going theological ventures. 'A faith-filled reading of the signs of the times is cognitive (beliefs), affective (trusts), and effective (deeds).'[22] 'Action without critical reflection and even without gratuitous contemplation is disastrous activism. And theory or introspection in the absence of collective social action is escapist idealism or wishful thinking.'[23] If so, all pedagogies deployed for the purpose of initiating the culture of theologizing have to be revamped from the perspectives of the complex sensibilities of the Dalits. Some dimensions that need to find a place in these explorations could be spelt out as follows:

- Basic and advanced familiarity with the Indian Constitution
- Basic legal and human rights education
- In-depth probe into native resources like Dhammapada, *Granth Sahib*, Ambedkar, Ramabai, Rama Samy Periyar, Ayyankali, Kabir Das, Ayodhidas Pandithar, Mahatma Phule, Savitribai Phule, Narayana Guru, Meenakshi Moon and others.
- Dalit women's concerns and challenges and Dalit movements.
- Skill and capacity building training to handle conflict situation and to face the challenges of life and livelihood.

Genuine process of theologizing may romanticize neither the traditions of the cultural soil of the people concerned nor the classical religio-cultural traditions. The anti-life elements found both in the culture of the people and that of the expressions of the religiosity would be identified to be eliminated. The interpretative agenda of any serious theologizing attempt has to seriously grapple with the people's ground reality of the complex worldviews, textures of religio-cultural location, expectations emerging from the conflicting consciousness, and the intertextual ways of constructing the utopias. If theologizing exercises impose themselves on people's native sensibilities as the privileged discourses claiming absolute power with unquestionable authority, then they cease to be a liberative tool for them.

Theologian-centred to People-centred

It is a matter of fact that the agency of the theologian is coloured by his/her own socio-cultural location. The implicit or explicit prejudices operative in such locations determine his/her way of objectification of the reality of the people and their context. Whatever are the theologian's actual identity and the fabric of the personality tempered both by nature and nurture, his/her ethical stand and commitment has to be adequately made explicit in the process of accompanying Dalits.

The people, whose problems of life and death are grappled with, are the central agents in any act of theologizing. The stories of successes and defeats told by the people in their own words are the foundation upon which the real questions of conflict-ridden situations emerge. Not all these subaltern articulation may hit the headlines of the media world.[24] Rather they are drowned under the commotional clamour of the celebrities projected by the market forces. The theologians have to plough through such jungles of elite prejudices before rightly identifying the actual voice of the oppressed people. The agency of the people, with its interior movements and cultural location has to be incorporated into the theologians' inner world with a sense of solidarity. The complex web of their intertextual religio-cultural resources is the vast reservoir very much to be deployed in the process of the generation of meaning. Any gratuitous offer of readymade solutions and meanings from theologians' own religio-cultural resources, very often, becomes an odd misfit.

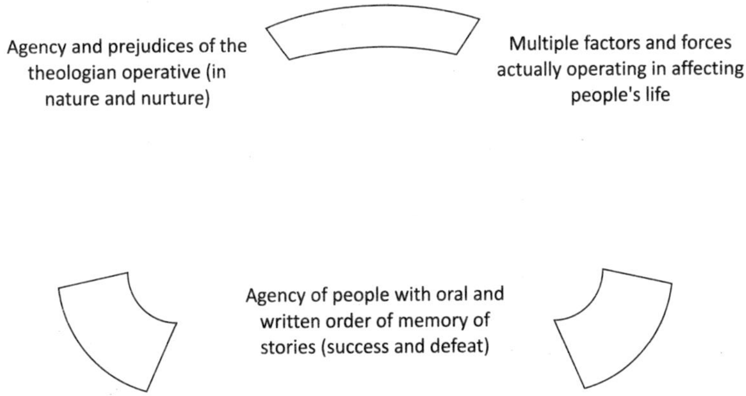

Growing as Credible Dalit Theologians

The ongoing process of victimization of the Dalits leads them to develop an ever-growing culture of self-assertion. As agents of their own destiny, they deconstruct the meta-narratives of various systems of hegemony (caste, gender, colour, ethnic and linguistic dominance). Further, they seek to construct their own alternative discourses in claiming their cultural identities and political space in their respective socio-cultural location. Upon these conflict-ridden and hope-generating contexts, the 'organic theologizers' are challenged by the complex sensibilities and interior movements of the multi-layered consciousness of the Dalit world. With the sense of empathetic accompaniment with them, these theologizers will attempt at locating liberative energies and the enslaving factors from the active and operative Dalit meaning systems (mythos, ethos, and logos).

- The questions emerging from the life-experience of the silenced Dalits (as victims, subjects, and community-building community) are analytically sharpened by the tools provided by human sciences with an interdisciplinary approach.
- These sharpened questions, in dialogue with the active and operative meaning systems, will be articulated in terms of crucial and critical queries along the lines of theological questions with constructive transformative agenda.
- Such theological questions are the dialogical partners with the life-affirming streams found in the religio-cultural world of the Dalits as well as other subalterns like underprivileged women, victims of violent migration, excluded indigenous people or blacks. The platform of such a dialogue is open to the religio-cultural world of the oral traditions, classical traditions as well as of secular ideologies.
- The process of dialogue between the liberation-seeking life questions and the liberation-oriented cultural energies will result in the evolution of the newer possibilities for further encountering the life-situations.

Every person claiming to be engaged in enabling the dialogue between the Dalits and the religio-cultural resources could be a Dalit or non-Dalit by birth. But what matters is that these organic intellectuals, be it from the academia or ideological pulpits, have to be brought under the serious scrutiny of the hermeneutical responsibility. They have to be made accountable to the Dalit world in its struggles to annihilate the virus of caste hierarchy. The salient features of such accountability to Dalit emancipation could be enlisted as follows:

- An ongoing attempt on the part of the organic intellectuals is to identify and enter into the web of the inter-textual layers of Dalit consciousness. It has to be undertaken with intense and sustained proximity with the people.
- An empathetic journey of solidarity into the Dalit world has to be undertaken by them. It entails deep insights into their native symbolic universe.

- They need to further dwell upon their linguistic world with narrative patterns and poetic outbursts. The dynamics of their oral articulation and communication, historical perceptions through genealogies, myths and folklore, is to be recognized. The animating dimensions of rituals and performing arts, traditional modes of encountering joys and sorrows, and the psycho-social complexities operative in the human-made atrocious situations are to be grappled with.
- The complex process of Dalit identity-formation, both at the individual and collective levels, is to be perceptively located amidst imposed identities by the caste powers overtly or covertly perpetuating the practice of un-touchability.
- An overall familiarity, if not scholarly, with the diverse ways of interpreting God, revelation, enlightenment, salvation, spirituality, or ethics from Dalit perspectives with advocacy positions has to be in order. This is to avoid methodological dogmatism and doctrinal fundamentalism.
- Traversing through the intra-Dalit world and the world of religio-cultural resources does not suffice here. The inner world and the interior movements of the third pole, i.e., the so-called organic theologians has to be correctly identified. Their mindset, pre-understanding, and the texture of consciousness formed by their formal education and their upbringing also play an important role in any of their attempts at theologizing. And hence the progressive or regressive map of their ideological leanings is also to be unveiled in this very process.
- Their attitude towards the Dalits and their outlook towards the classical texts or the popular oral texts have to be openly manifested. Consciously chosen ideological sites and interpretative strategies are to be explicitly articulated.
- Care should be taken to become acutely aware of the original agenda of such organic theologians whether they are closely accompanying the Dalits in their struggles or not.
- No doubt, the subject(s) of Dalit interpretation of the Bible is none other than the flesh-and blood person(s) from among

Dalits, and not primarily the organic intellectuals. At the most, they could play the role of the mid-wife empathetically enabling the 'Dalit delivery of new meanings' in dialogue with the religio-cultural resources.

NOTES

1. Cf. Susan Bayly, 'Caste Wars and the Mandate of Violence', in Susan Bayly, *Caste, Society and Politics in India: From the Eighteenth Century to the Modern Age*, Cambridge: Cambridge University Press, 2002, p. 345.
2. Ibid., pp. 348-9.
3. Randall Collins, *Violence: A Micro-sociological Theory*, Princeton and Oxford: Princeton University Press, 2008, p. 230.
4. Ambrose Pinto, *Mainstream*, vol. XLVII, no. 15, 28 March 2011. http://www.mainstreamweekly.net/article1258.html
5. Stefan Bucher, 'Globalisation and Structural Violence'. Jonathan E. Lynch and Gary Wheeler (eds.), *Cultures of Violence*, papers from the Fifth Global Conference, Oxford: Interdisciplinary Press, 2007, pp. 9-10.
6. Arthur Kleinmann, 'The Violences of Everyday Life: The Multiple Forms and Dynamics of Social Violence', in Veena Das et al. (eds.), *Violence and Subjectivity*, New Delhi: Oxford University Press, 2008, p. 227.
7. Ibid.
8. Slavoj Zizek, *Violence: Six Sideways Reflections*, New York: Picador, 2008, pp. 2, 9.
9. Cf. Human Rights Watch, 'Violence Against "Untouchables" Growing, Says Report', *Human Rights Watch Press Release* (April 1999), http://indianterrorism.bravepages.com/violenceagainstdalits.html
10. Cf. Gayatri Spivak, 'Can the Subaltern Speak?', in Nelson and Larry Grossberg (eds.), *Marxism and the Interpretation of Culture*, Urbana: University of Illinois Press, 1988, pp. 271-313. *A Critique of Postcolonial Reason: Towards History of the Vanishing Present*, Cambridge: Harvard University Press, 1999.
11. Cf. Pablo Richard, 'Hermeneutics of Liberation: Theoretical Grounding for the Communitarian Reading of the Bible', in Fernando F. Segovia and Mary Ann Tolbert (eds.), *Teaching the*

Bible: The Discourses and Politics of Biblical Pedagogy, Maryknoll: Orbis, 1998, p. 273.

12. Cf. Anthony C. Thiselton, *New Horizons in Hermeneutics*, Grand Rapids: Zondervan, 1992, p. 404.
13. Rosemary Radford Ruether, *Sexism and God-talk: Towards a Feminist Theology*, London: SCM, 1983, p. 231.
14. Vincent L. Wimbush, 'A Meeting of World: African Americans and the Bible', in Fernando F. Segovia and Mary Ann Tolbert (eds.), *Teaching the Bible: The Discourses and Politics of Biblical Pedagogy*, New York: Orbis, 1998, p. 192.
15. Cf. R.S. Sugirtharajah, *Poscolonial Criticism and Biblical Interpretation*, New York: Oxford University Press, 2002, p. 103.
16. Ranajit Guha, 'Chandra's Death', in Ranajit Guha (ed.), *Subaltern Studies V: Writings on South Asian History and Society*, Delhi: Oxford University Press, 1987, pp. 135-65, esp. p. 140.
17. Cf. Antonio Gramsci, *Selections from the Prison Notebooks*, ed. Quintin Hoare and Geoffrey Nowell Smith, New York: International Publishers, 1971.
18. Stephen Morton, *Gayatri Chakravorty Spivak*, New York: Routledge, 2002, p. 48.
19. The complex world of the interior world of Dalits with all its conflicting layers of consciousness is referred to here. It could be individual or communitarian or both. The same holds good in Feminist, Tribal, Black, Burakumin, Minjung or other hermeneutical attempts at social transformation.
20. These could be concretely the problems of life or death often articulated in the form of questions emerging from real life-situations.
21. Cf. B. Lonergan, *Method in Theology*, London: Darton, Longman & Dodd, 1972.
22. Peter Henriot, 'Social Discernment and the Pastoral Circle', in Frans Wijsen, Peter Henriot and Rodrigo Mejia (eds.), *The Pastoral Cycle Revisited: A Critical Quest for Truth and Transformation*, Maryknoll: Orbis, 2005, p. 25.
23. Juan José Luna, 'The Pastoral Circle: A Strategy for Justice and Peace', in Frans Wijsen, Peter Henriot and Rodrigo Mejia (eds.), *The Pastoral Cycle Revisited: A Critical Quest for Truth and Transformation*, Maryknoll: Orbis, 2005, p. 27.
24. For instance, the invasion of the US empire into Iraq is presented as the just war against terrorism in the mainline media. The alleged

racist attack on Shilpa Shetty, an Indian actress in the *Big Brother* television show in London was given wide coverage both by the Indian and the British media. But the rape of a Dalit girl and her mother by higher caste people was blacked out by the Indian media until Dalit rage burnt down a train.

3

Tribal Identity and Theology

WATI LONGCHAR

Tribal Identity

These voices of tribal people against development activities in Nandigram, Singur and in many other places reflect the identity of the tribal people in India.

> *When the mountain disappears, what will be our identity?*
> *If we leave our ancestral village, what will be our culture and spiritual identity?*
> *If you do not allow us to cultivate, what will we eat? Do you want our children to die?*
> *If you do not allow us to fish, how can we send our children to school?*
> *If you do not allow us to practice shifting cultivation, what will be our religion and identity—our religion and identity are centred on the soil! How can we worship God?*
> *If you do not allow us cultivate, what will we do the whole day?*
> *When all the trees have been cut down, where will be the home of the animals and birds?*
> *When all the waters are polluted, what will we drink? Do we have to buy water?*
> *When all the air is unsafe to breathe, can we buy air?*

Land, forest, river, mountains and entire cosmic universe are inseparably related to tribal identity. Contrary to the colonizers' description of the land as 'wilderness' or `empty space', the land is our temple (cathedral), our university, our hospital, our market, the vast hall where we congregate and celebrate, our parent, our life. It is in the land that we worship, we heal the sick, educate our children, and feed our people. The loss of land and the destruction of tribal peoples environment is an affront to our identities, the loss of our spirituality and our self-determining existence. If the land is lost, the family, clan and village and the tribe's identity too will be lost. A person who is not deeply rooted in the land cannot become a good citizen. He/she is like a stranger without an identity and a home.

Even the Sacred Power is understood in relation to land/space. For example, the Aos and Sangtams of Nagaland call their Supreme Being, *Lijaba*. *Li* means 'land' and *jaba* means 'real'. It means the Supreme Being is 'the real soil'. Sometimes people call the Supreme Being *Lizaba*. *Li* means 'soil' and *zaba* means 'enter', meaning 'the one who enters or indwells into the soil'. People believed that the Supreme Being enters into the soil with the seeds and rises again along with the crops. Thus, the blooming flower, bearing of fruits and rice signifies the presence of the Creator. The Sacred Power is present in every iota of creation and the whole creation becomes the manifestation of the Creator. For tribals, there is no concept of the Creator without the land; the land and the Creator are inseparably related. The Creator dwells not only in human persons, but also dwells in the soil.

The land/space is also understood as the symbol of unity of all living creatures, the spirit(s) and of the Creator. The land is the basis that enables them to co-exist with other living beings, their ancestors and the Creator. The land is the foundation of unity and their identity.

Tribal people intimately move along with the soil cycle and surrounding environment. All the festivals and religious activities of the people are centred on the soil cycle. When the land and surrounding environment are destroyed, people experience a vacuum; the rhythm of life is seriously jeopardized. The whole universe is also perceived as a religious universe. Rocks and boulders, trees and rivers are not just empty objects, but religious objects; the voices and songs of animals speak of a religious language; the eclipse of the sun and of the moon are not simply a silent phenomenon of nature, it speaks to the community that observes it, often warning of an impending danger and misfortune. It is in this milieu that people experience history and time. Thus, the concept of history and time is inseparably interlinked and rooted in the soil.

Unlike other great religions of the world, tribal religion does not have any founder(s) or reformer(s) or guide(s) nor do people dance and sing adoring a divine historical person(s). They too have traditions of divine births and manifestations, but they are not worshipped. They have priests, officiating elders, diviners and other famous men and women in the body of beliefs, and mythologies which are respected and which form an integral part of their religious milieu, but they are neither worshipped nor adored as divine representatives. Instead, people dance and sing along with the cycle of land. A peculiar feature of tribal religion is that the whole religious system, ceremonies, rituals, festivals and dances are all centred and deeply rooted on the land itself.

The British and Tribal Identity

The coming of the British affected all areas of life in tribal society. The British with the introduction of a new political process, economic system, communication network of roads, post and telegraphs, telephones, wireless and radio, books, journals, newspapers and cinemas contributed to intensifying this erosion of tribal identity. Some of the major changes brought in by the British were:

(a) With the introduction of a unified political system, the British brought a wider nation state political dimension to the whole of tribal society. The customary laws and customs which were very much geared towards the protection of nature as well as community as a whole were replaced by the new laws developed either in the West or in other parts of India. It led to the erosion of traditional customary laws and customs. Consequently, the tribals were slowly alienated from the earth and community centred laws and customs. In addition, the villages who in their history had never been subjected to foreign rule, suddenly found themselves without much political power.

(b) Traditionally, the tribals lived and worked with the soil. It was the soil that gave them not only identiy, but also sustenance. However, through the introduction of money economy, people were forced to opt for the non-traditional avenues of work, that is, work which was unrelated to the soil, and to work for money in all sorts of employment. This new economy introduced the concept of time as a commodity to be sold and bought; it involved also earning and spending money with all the inherent dangers, temptations, difficulties and risks that go with it. Therefore, the money economy alienated the tribals from soil-centred works.

(c) For the tribals, the village is the centre of the community. It is the village that gives the individual an identity. However, with the emergence of urban places and the introduction of communication and business enterprise, the core of the tribal community, that is, village polity gradually disintegrated. This threatened both community and individual identity. It provided opportunities for wider interaction with other tribal groups, but led to the emergence of many new social problems hitherto unknown or non-existent.

(d) The tribals' contact with outsiders and Western people brought new tools. Gradually, people began to acquire factory made goods and things for improving amenities for living and for personal security. As a result, people slowly discarded those things and goods which were directly produced from the soil and replaced them with factory made goods. For example, the wooden and bamboo cups, plates and other utensils were replaced by manufactured goods made from aluminium. Lanterns and kerosene oil lamps gradually drove out the reed torches. Flint stone fire-making was replaced by manufactured matches.[1] All these goods alienated the people from the closeness to the earth.

Christianity and Tribal Identity

The Christian missionaries were the first people to come and work for the liberation of the tribals in India. Along with Christianity a new worldview made up of Western culture, politics, science, technology, medicines, schools and literature were brought to the tribals. Needless to say, the Christian missionaries brought about the greatest revolution in the tribal society.

The theology that they brought to the tribal was deeply rooted in and shaped by the Enlightenment rationality. There nature is seen in terms of mere utility. The scientific method of reductionism took the mystery out of their theology. People began to perceive that there is nothing amazing about the world; it is merely a sum-total of many material components and energies. Humans are able to understand, predict, and control everything related to the world; we are separated from, and masters of, the earth. Natural resources are given value only in so far as they are useful for the development of science and technology. We see three theological perceptions quite contrary to the tribal view of life which contributed to the neglect of earth-centred spirituality and identity.

(a) *Hierarchical structure of creation:* Christianity brought a structure of hierarchy. People began to see society, human community and even Christian ministry within hierarchical order. The most problematic one is the explanation of land and God's creation within this hierarchical structure.

God, the Creator, in the beginning, simultaneously created a hierarchy of creatures, ordered according to their degree of perfection. There are perfect and imperfect beings. The imperfect being are created to serve the needs of more noble beings, for instance, plants draw their nutrients from the earth, animals feed on plants and these in turn serve human use. Therefore, lifeless beings exist for the sake of living beings, plants for animals and animals for humans. The other non-human creatures are protected, preserved, sustained by God to serve human needs. This theology gives justification for manipulation and exploitation of other segments of God's creation. In this understanding how do we perceive God's revelation in creation?

(b) *Anthropocentric View of Creation:* Christianity gave a notion that humanity is the point of reference for everything. The whole creation of God exists for the benefit of humans. The ultimate purpose of creation is for the service and benefit of humans. God is not known through His creation, but only through Christ. Salvation history begins from the incarnation of Jesus Christ, but not from the creation. For the sake of election, nature is sustained, protected and upheld. Creation is merely a 'show place'. It has no history, not redeemed, but merely used.

(c) *Heaven and Hell:* Christianity brought an understanding that this world is not our world. The evangelicals came with a strong emphasis on 'the Second Coming of Christ'. They believed that this world is coming to an end, all materials will be destroyed, but only those who believe in Christ will be saved. Only the soul will live eternally. This kind of teaching made many people to think that this world is not our home. If this world is not our home and perishable, why should we take care of it!

The colonial power and Christian missions (no matter from which denominations or missionary societies they came from) considered themselves 'superior' in terms of religion, race, economy and culture and they consistently maintained an exclusive and negative attitude towards the traditional religions and cultures. They considered the 'others' as primitive, uncultured, uncivilized and savages. 'Their description of the people ranges from people with no culture to inferior culture, lifestyles and ways of life. Their religion was derided as demonic, superstitious and evil.'[2] The people's characters and virtues also came under serious negative attitude and they were held at the lowest esteem.[3] This superiority value system justified slavery system, colonialism, war, domination and replacement of native culture by the white culture and saw cultural conversion prerequisite to conversion to Christianity. Such an ideology was grounded in the beliefs of modernity, Christianity and rapid industrial advancement. The colonized people, like the Tribals and Dalits, who have been suffering under the caste system further led to internalization of native inferiority and the idealization of the white culture and religion. Even today many people think that their own religion, economy and culture are inferior and backward. Hence, 'conversion' was justified. The process of conversion had, George Tinker[4] noted, four cultural disorientations:

First, the converts were separated from their home community and relatives in new communal enclosures; that is, the native persons were removed from their former mode of existence. For example, the first sign of conversion was cutting of man's hair like the white man. Then both men and women were required to change their clothing.

Second, once converted and relocated in the mission compound or in a new village, the converts were permanently proscribed from rethinking their conversion and returning to their own homes. In some context, the missionaries had military assistance at hand to hunt down fugitives and return them to their missions for discipline.

Third, converts were committed to a rigorous regimen of work to support the mission, the missionaries and their obligation to the military government.

Fourth, converts gave up all aspects of self-governance to live under the strict and authoritarian governance of the missionary priests.

Furthermore, the perception of cultural and intellectual superiority motivated missionaries to promote Western scientific rationality informed by the European enlightenment. This campaign for a new rationality against the traditional wisdom of the natives was conceived as a civilizational imperative and carried out with utmost earnestness. The new scientific rationality was presented as the only norm for growth and prosperity.[5] Mission schools were used as instrument for civilizing local people and integrating tribal people into imperial/colonial structures.[6] Gangmumei Kamei also observed that modern education was 'designed to inculcate European liberal ideas, literature, and science in the Indian mind, and to produce educated persons who could be conveniently employed to run the colonial administration'.[7] Even if the missionaries did not consider themselves agents of colonial powers, they participated, wittingly or not, in advancing the colonial project.

This wrong notion and control over the education process, medical practice, reduction of languages into written form and the production of the first literary texts, introduction of new housing, hygiene, clothing, time, history led to complete disorientation of traditional cultural structures of existence that give a people a sense of holistic and communal integrity. No longer did the life of the people revolved around the soil-centred culture, but revolved around church services, prayer meetings, revival camps, Christian Endeavour, etc. This process contributed to the loss of identity and spirituality rooted in the soil.

Tribal Theological Vision

The song[8] below reflects what should the nature, goal and identity of tribal theology:

We will not leave our village, or our jungles, or our mother-earth.
We will not give up our fight.
They built dams drown villages and built factories.
They cut down forests, dug out mines and built sanctuaries.
Without water, land and forest where do we go?
Oh, God of development, we pray, tell us how to save our lives?
Dry is the Jamuna River, the Narmada River and the Suvarnrekha River.
Ganga River is a dirty drain, Krishna River-but a black line!
You may drink your colas and bottled water, how shall we quench our thirst with such polluted water?
Were our ancestors fools that they conserved the forest?
Made the land so green, made rivers flow like honey?
Your greed has charred the land and looted its greenery!
The fish are dead, the birds have flown, who knows where?
The minister has become industry's broker, snatched away our lands!
Armed battalions protect them!
The officer is king and the contractor is millionaire!
Our village is their colony!
Unite and break the silence!
Fisherfolk, dalits and adivasis (indigenous people) unite!
From fields and mines arise! Sound the nagara!
Listen, people of the country, struggle is the only way out!

Land is the tribal people's identity and life. The land is God's given gift to all humanity. It is our life and mother. This is the slogan of the indigenous people in Asia, South America, Africa, North America and Europe.

Tribal theology has to relate radically with totality of God's creation. It should aim to restore their self-identity and dignity by creatively engaging on the Gospel and culture in their struggle for social, economic, religious, cultural, political and ecological justice. Methodologically speaking, the point of departure of tribal theology from the other contextual theologies is that, the tribal theology seeks liberation from the perspective of 'land' because it is the land that sustains and nourishes people and give them an identity. Human liberation will be void and empty without affirming the integrity of the goodness of land and its resources. Liberation without land is not liberation. It will lead to slavery and destruction. Therefore, the land and its resources that sustain and nourish all beings and give them an identity and selfhood is not merely a justice issue to be set alongside other justice concerns. It is the foundation of history, existence and identity.[9] Poverty, war, oppression, ethnic conflict and identity problems cannot be understood or solved without relating to integrity of creation/land. Justice to creation/land becomes very central to liberation and human dignity and fullness of life.

When all the trees have been cut down,
When all the animals have been hunted,
When all the waters are polluted,
When all the air is unsafe to breathe,
Only then will you discover you cannot eat money.[10]

That is why doing justice to 'land' is the starting point of the tribal people's theology and their search for liberation. Commitment and dedication to the harmony of creation/land springs forth in love, nurture, care and acceptance. This methodological priority of justice to land is essential not only because of their 'earth-centred' worldview and tradition, but because of our contemporary ecological crisis, misuse of resources, market culture, war for oil and survival crisis of many people. This methodological priority of doing justice to totality of creation is the primary departure of the tribal theology from the other contextual theologies.

Our Theological Perspective

No person or community can have monopoly over theology. To express our knowledge of God in one's own way is the inherent right of all human being. We can apprehend God by what he has done to our fore-parents even before the arrival of Christianity and is doing for the people in the concrete historical context. Therefore, we are called to articulate our faith journey with God and community in our own way.

Biblical Testimony of Creation

The tribal communities recognize several 'scriptures', including oral traditions to acknowledge God. The Bible is the book of tribal people. It speaks of people's relationship in society, cultivation, animals, nature and encounter with the Divine power in their search for liberation. The Hebrew Bible starts with the creation of heaven and earth, and then moves on to creation account of humanity as created from the ground/land, that humanity is created in God's image and that each race and nation was assigned a space in God's world (Deut 32: 8). The land, from whose womb humanity was formed (Gen. 2:7), is also viewed by the Bible as really alive. It is not a mass of dead matter, but a living, pulsating organism. From our land-centred lenses, the mountains and hills and trees do sing and clap their hands. These are not mere metaphors or poetry. The land or the whole creation is alive, and it is so intimately weaved with the lives and struggles of the indigenous communities that the former groans in travail (Romans 8: 19, 22) whenever we, the people of the land, suffer displacement, alienation, exploitation, exile and persecution. The New Testament Gospel, too, proclaims how central the redemption of the margins is in the divine economy. Jesus always located his ministry within the farming or fishing context and worldview. Jesus' language, metaphors, symbols are drawn from day-to-day experience of the farmers, fisherfolks and their struggle for justice against the empire. In other words, the Judeo-Christian gospel of the reign of God is an affirmative of our tribal worldview and spirituality that constructs our understanding of who we are and what we struggle for.

God in Creation

Creation is the first act of God's revelation. God cannot be perceived without water, wind, trees, vegetations, sky, light, darkness, animals, human creatures. In this first God's act of revelation, God revealed himself/herself as *co-creator* with earth. The most striking aspect in this first act of God's revelation is 'God is present in creation'. The presence of God makes this earth sacred. That is why God entered into covenant relationship with all creatures. There are many stories, myths, parables, and even fairy tales of how the Sacred Power and the land sustain life together. How 'the whole earth is full of God's glory' (Isa. 6: 1-3). People always conceive of God-world very much attached to them in their everyday life. Totem, taboos and other customary laws tied them together as one whole. To perceive God detached from creation/earth or mere transcendental being who controls life from above is not the biblical faith. We believe in God because God as the creator is present and continues to work with the land, river, sea to give life and hope. This affirmation is the foundation for life. The major problem in theology is faith articulation of human history.

Liberation and Integrity of Creation

The Bible is the book that affirms life from destruction. The most striking one in the Bible is the institution of Sabbath and Jubilee. Jubilee, in the Biblical tradition, is an invitation to participate in the dreams and designs of the Divine to recreate relations among living beings through restoration and renewal of history. Jubilee epitomizes the hope for an eschatological possibility in historical terms, creating systems that are free from the possibilities of exploitation and oppression. Ancient seers introduced the concept of Jubilee through the principles of economic, political and social justice within cosmic framework which inherently negates marginalization of any living beings. To actualize this vision, God revealed himself/herself as the liberator in the Exodus episode. More precisely, God is revealed as the God of liberation of the oppressed. 'I am Yahweh your God, who has brought you out of the land of Egypt, out of the house of slavery' (Ex. 20: 2; Deut. 5: 6). Israel as a people came to know God as liberator through the exodus. By delivering the people of Israel from Egyptian bondage and inaugurating the covenant on the basis of that historical event, God is revealed as the God of the oppressed, involved in their history, liberating them from human bondage. In the exodus episode, God took the side of the oppressed community; the people who have been denied the human dignity and earth's resources.

The Nazareth manifesto of Jesus reaffirmed liberation by proclaiming the Year of the Lord's favour. Jesus reiterated the importance of Jubilee tradition for liberation (Luke 4: 18ff.). The proclamation of the Year of the Lord is a message of liberty to those who have lost their land, personhood or status that they could return to their former position and ancestral land; both the rich and poor, master and servant, the empowered and the weak and even nature itself were all to return to their original. The conflict with Satan and the powers of this world, the condemnation of the rich, the insistence that the kingdom of God is for the poor, and the location of his ministry among the poor for liberation threatened the oppressors which cost Jesus crucifixion. In the absence of a reorganization of life prescribed by the values of Jubilee, a just community is only an empty word. The spirituality of Jesus is martyrdom and that is why it is a 'costly discipleship'. The resurrection conveys hope in God. That is why Jesus becomes the symbol of struggle for justice for indigenous people. To fight and resist against the new empire of global market, anti-people development activities of the present time is justified and it is the Divine mandate to participate in God's liberative act in history.

Our Ecclesial Vision

The church is a house of prayer for all nations, races and language. There are no barriers and discrimination in the house of God. The indigenous people, women and persons with disabilities are all invited to celebrate and share their gifts for common good.

We need to understand the household of God on the basis of the richness of God's creation. This is expressed in the plurality of his creation. Attempts to exclude other forms of expression are denial of God's richness. No culture, no community is excluded from this God's structure of creation. All are unique in their own ways and, therefore, no one has the right to dominate and suppress the other. Life is protected and it can grow to its fullness only by affirming to the beauty of diversity.

Christian missionaries have done immense work for the liberation of indigenous people. Recognizing their genuine interest in the well-being of the oppressed people and commitment to bring the people to the gospel message of salvation, many oppressed people converted to Christian faith searching for a more dignified life. While acknowledging many dedicated and selfless works rendered by the missionaries, we also recognize that the church has been an ally or agent of empires in the marginalization, oppression, exploitation and even obliteration of tribal people's communities. It became the Trojan horse of empires, and to this day continues to be an instrument of subjugation of indigenous people's communities. The church has consistently played her role as the cultural partisan in our colonization, consistently breaking our will to resist subjugation and domination, and tragically standing in silence in the face of the destruction of our habitat, our livelihood and culture.

Tribal peoples affirm a people-centred church, ecumenical unity but not a church of power, hierarchy, expansion, extension and conquest. What we envision is a church that respects, recognizes, affirms, supports, promotes, advocates for us in our struggle for self-identification and self-determination. We envision a church that goes deeper in the tribal peoples' experience, not only as object of study but especially as *subject* of ecclesiological and theological elaboration.

NOTES

1. W.C. Smith, *The Ao Naga Tribes of Assam*, London: Macmillan, 1928, p. 182.
2. Yangkahao Vashum, 'Revisiting Tribal/Indigenous Theology and Its Theological Methodology', a paper presented at consultation on 'Revisiting Tribal and Dalit Theologies and Their Theological, Methodologies', New Delhi: Centre for Dalit/Subaltern Studies, from 14-16 March 2008, p. 8.
3. Ibid.
4. George E. Tinker, *Missionary Conquest: The Gospel and Native American Cultural Genocide*, Minneapolis: Fortress Press, 1993, pp. 48-9.
5. M.P. Joseph, 'Be Witness to Life: Towards a People's Concept of Mission', in *Re-routing Mission: Towards a People's Concept of Mission and Diakonia*, Tiruvalla: CCA-URM, 2004, p. 11.
6. Ward Churchill observed that 'since schooling was brought to non-Europeans as part of empire . . . it was integrated into the effort to bring indigenous peoples into imperial/colonial structures.' See his book *Since Predator Came*, Colorado: Aigis Publications, 1995, p. 245.
7. Pounglau Gangmei, *Ethnicity and Social Change: An Anthology of Essays*, Lilong, 2002, p. 138.
8. This is a song composed by Bhagwan Maaji, leader of Adivasi struggle against bauxite mining in Kashipur. Lyrics by Meghnath with the support of Sunil Minj and Vinod Kumar.
9. For this insight, I owe a deep gratitude to Prof. George Tinker's article on 'American Indian and the Art of the Land' which appeared in *Voices From the Third World*, vol. XIV/2 (1981) and 'Spirituality and Native American Personhood: Sovereignty & Solidarity', in K. Abraham and B. Mbuy (eds.), *Spirituality of the Third World*, Orbis Books, 1994, pp. 127-8.
10. See Max Eidger, 'Indigenous People: Spirituality and Peace', a concept paper presented at Asia Pacific Alliance of YMCAs and Interfaith Cooperation Forum, 19-24 October 2007.

4

Theology and the Struggle of Adivasis/Indigenous People of India

NIRMAL MINZ

Introduction

India is proud of maintaining unity in its vast diversities of religions, languages, cultures/ideologies and also peoples and races. There are Adi people and Jati people in our motherland. In between Adi and Jati people there are the Tibeto-Burman people in the north-east and the Muslim communities in the mainland. Since our main concern is with the Adivasis we shall make only passing references to the north-east tribals as and when necessary.

We maintain that Adivasis and Dalits belong to the same original Adi communities of ancient India. The Aryan invasion of India, approximately in 3500-2500 BC, was responsible for the bifurcation of the Adivasis and Dalit communities separately. Dalits are that section of Adi people who were captured and who accepted the subjugation of Aryan invaders. Thousands of years of life under subjugation led them to forget their language and cultural values. They are treated now as an appendage to the Jati people's hierarchy. But we must mention here that the Dalits are seriously searching for their original identity and Adivasis wish them great success in their sacred search of their true identity. It is hoped that they will overcome many socio-religious, socio-economic and political odds on their way and come to terms with their Adi identity. Adivasis escaped Aryan subjugation and receded to remote jungles maintaining their language, culture, socio-political and economic organizations. They kept their idea of human equality, cooperation, consensus in decision-making process. They lived very close to nature finding many clues to organize and live as human beings learning from the laws of nature. In course of time through thousands of years of history they spread out in different parts forming separate communities but never accepted the *jati pratha* (tradition) of the dominant society.[1]

Identification of Adivasis by Clarifying Some Key Terms

The terms 'tribe', 'indigenous people' and 'Adivasis' need clarification. Tribes and Scheduled Tribes are widely used in social science literature and government documents. The 'People of India Project' enlists 461 tribal communities in India.[2] These will include the north-east tribals also. To many social scientists and government officials, this term has an administrative meaning. 'The question of tribes in India is closely linked with administrative and political considerations'.[3] There is a debate for and against regarding the existence of indigenous people in India. Those against, argue on the basis of historical uncertainty of a cut-off point clearly separating the Adi people from the *jati* people (Ghurye 1963, S.C. Dubey 1977, Beteille 1998, Hernann 1957, B.S. Guha, N.K. Bose and others are in this camp). The supporters for the existence of indigenous people in India are few. Among them Ray 1973, B.K. Roy Burman, Kumar Suresh Singh, one term director of Anthropological Survey of India, and Virginius Xaxa are the outstanding scholars. In seminars and their writings these scholars have clearly maintained that tribes are the indigenous people of India. They are called Adivasis in Hindi. Among them, B.K. Roy Burman has maintained. 'The use of the term Indigenous People to refer to the tribal people is defended on yet another ground . . . their Indigenous identity can not be brushed away by juxtaposition of non-meaningful occurrences in space and time in systemic terms.'[4] (Roy Burman 1992: 24), this is quoted by Xaxa.

This establishes the fact that tribes, indigenous people, and Adivasis are descriptions of the self same reality, the Adi people in India. Adivasis/Tribes/Indigenous People of India are spread all over in the mainland. But they are located and identified as Anusuchit Jan Jati in nine states and in some small pockets in other states in south India. Tribes live in the 5th Scheduled Areas of India with special constitutional provisions for protecting and developing them according to their own genius. These states are Himachal Pradesh—the Kenaur and other tribes. (2) Gujarat—Bhils. (3) Maharastra—Bhils and Gonds, and Warlis. (4) Madhya Pradesh—Gonds, Kol and others. (5) Chhattisgarh —Gonds, Oraons. (6) Orissa—Konds, Kuvi, Sauras, Oraons. (7) Jharkhand—Munda, Santhal, Ho, Kharias, Oraon (Kurukh), Malto, Pahadiya, Ashur, Korwa, Kishan. (8) Andhra Pradesh—Koyas, Chenchus. (9) West Bengal—Rajbansis, Oraon, Munda, Santhal and others.

Besides these major areas, there are tribes/indigenous people/Adivasis in Nilgiri Hills—the Todas, Kotas and others. Wynad district in Kerala—the Pannyan and others, the Gadabas. The 5th Scheduled Area are partially Excluded Areas as per constitutional provisions and notifications of the Government of India.[5]

Two important points need our serious considerations

(1) Tribe/indigenous people/Adivasis is a generic term and not a term for administrative and political consideration only. An Adivasi of India is an Adivasi wherever he or she lives. There is no question of scheduling him/her. So Anusuchit Jan Jati is a cultural term of an assimilation process. Adi-

vasi is an Adi people and cannot make himself or herself as Jati people. This concept must be revised in future by the Government of India. A Munda community member is a Munda wherever he/she goes. A vast majority of the Kurukh, Munda, Santhal tribes/indigenous people/Adivasis are in Assam. Since Assam is not a Scheduled Area, they are deprived of all the rights and privileges available to them from the Government of India. An amendment to this concept is urgently needed.

(2) The existence of the indigenous people in India, is established by some scholars and thinkers in our country, yet it is doubtful if the Government of India accepts this concept of indigenous people as it is understood and used in the international fora. The Government of India is still guided by 'melting pot' theory of the social scientists and has continually denied the existence of indigenous people in India. The acceptance of the existence has legal, political and social implications in it. All the UNO conventions on indigenous people's questions accept the special rights of self-determination of the indigenous people all over the world. In fact the Declaration of Indigenous People Rights in New York . . . is a challenge to the Government of India.[6] At the international levels, the government agrees on the letters and spirits of these conventions. But they have to be ratified by the Government of India in order to implement them in our land. This technicality has to be observed both at the international and domestic levels of policies regarding the tribes/indigenous people/Adivasis in India.

The foregoing discussions on Adivasi identity shows that the Adivasis are pushed around and they are experiencing the threat of their very existence, let alone their identity, as indigenous people. Such a situation has given rise to an Adivasi consciousness in India. This consciousness is building up in the entire 5th Scheduled Areas and beyond in our country. Adivasi consciousness and articulation of the indigenous people's status is not so much about whether they are original inhabitants of India as about the fact that they have no power whatsoever over anything (land, forest, river resources) that are in the territory they inhabit. This is despite being the original inhabitants of India in relation to the others. The consciousness and its articulation are basically an expression of the yearning to have or to establish a special relation with the territory in which they live. It is the same kind of yearning that the various dominant communities of India, articulated before Independence or after Independence.[7] In a sense there is an Adivasi Bharat in India. The Supreme Court judgement on 'Nandabai 25 years of age belonging to the Bhil Tribe' upholds that the 8 per cent tribals/ Adivasis are original inhabitants of India.[8]

Adivasis under the Governments and Rulers Assisted by Social Scientists

We take the liberty of accepting the historical cut-off point of Indus Valley civilization and the invasion of Aryans as about 3500-2500 BC. Thereafter Adivasis began to live as defeated people in India. India's checkered history of rulers and kingdoms make it very difficult to say anything positive about the life of Adivasi people during Aryan rule and Mughal periods. This is an area of research for Adivasi scholars and friends of the Adivasis. Only the glimpse of their life is found in the Vedas and Puranas, *Ramayana* and *Mahabharata*. These Adivasis have been described as Dasyus, Vanaras, Kols and Kiratas. The Adi people as a whole are Panchamas (fifth castes) in the caste hierarchy of the Jati People.

In *Shivpurana* it is said,

अय: पात्रे पय: पानम
शाल पात्रे च भोजनम
शयन खजूरी पात्रे
झारखंड इति विधियते

This is the description of the life of Adivasis in Jharkhand region. A free English translation is as under:

In earthen wares they drink water and milk,
sal leaves are their plates to eat food,
on date/palm leaves' mat they sleep,
this is the custom and culture of Jharkhand Adivasis.

Rev. C. Hans thinks that for about 1,400 years Aryans ruled in different parts of India till the coming of the Mughals in the sixteenth century. Mughal rule came to end after the *dewani* of Bengal and Bihar (Orissa) in 1756 and finally established the British Raj after the Battle of Plassey. The British colonial period, roughly from 1756 to 1947 has recorded accounts about the Adivasis of India. During this period social science, particularly anthropology, became quite popular. Anthropologists and sociologists studied Adivasi communities all over India. Their findings were the basis of government dealings with Adivasis.

British colonial government officers and the government as a whole found the Adivasis (the aboriginal tribes, primitive tribes, the indigenous people) as something different from the dominant society in India. They identified the Adivasis and differentiated them from other general population around them. The government officials studied the Adivasi communities in different parts of India like E.T. Dalton's, *The Ethnology of Bengal,* W.G. Archer's work on the Kurukh language, and culture and others. The Western scholars produced marvellous works. Verrier Elwin, Stephen Fuchs,[8] and others made major contribution to the study of Tribes/Adivasis communities in central and north-east India. In Ranchi S.C. Roy, published the *Man in India* magazine and his monumental works—*The Mundas and their Country* (1912), *The Oraons of Chhotanagpur* (1920), *The Kharias* and other publication brought many new insights into the life and cultures of Adivasis in north-central region.

The British government developed an idea and understanding of the identity of Adivasis both in the north-east and mainland India. In 1919, and later in 1935-6, the excluded and partially excluded areas concepts were promoted. Excluded areas are in north-east India. The partially excluded areas are in the rest of India as we have already mentioned above. The basic idea of the 5th Schedule (Partially Excluded Area) is that the Government of India Acts will not be applied directly in the 5th Scheduled areas. The governor in consultation with the Tribes Advisory Council will consider them if these Acts and central laws may disturb the life and customs and cultures of Adivasis, then these laws had to be duly remolded and made suitable to Adivasis and then sent back to the President for his/her assent. After this these Acts and laws will be notified by the governor to be implemented in the 5th Scheduled areas. This arrangement was accepted by the Government of India after Independence and the President of India notified it in 1950.[9] In the meantime Chhotanagpur Tenancy Act 1908, Santal Pargana Tenancy Act 1769, and Wilkinson's Rule in Kolhan country were introduced for the safety and security of Adivasi lands, forests and other immovable properties. Non-Adivasis had no right over Adivasi land according to the 5th Schedule legal provision.

The social scientists, particularly the anthropologists, have been used as advisors to the government at different levels on Adivasi matters. At the early stage of Government of India, Pandit Nehru took advice from scholars like Verrier Elwin in dealing with Tribes/Adivasis in India. Nehru's Panchsheel is the result of this consultation. It is true that the British colonial government and the Government of India also took advice from the social scientists, particularly the anthropologists. But these anthropologists also realized their limitations. Foreign scholars know their limitation, and the Indian scholars with very few exception were influenced by the biased attitude and understanding of the Jati people with regard to the Adivasis in India. The leading scholars express the limitation of their contribution to the welfare and development of the Adivasis. Karlison says,

> I believe that the collective experience of the collective Indigenous movement shared in forums like the WGIP sessions, can be useful.

There is no blueprint for indigenous sovereignty, and as far as I can see assisting to right to self-determination need not imply the exclusion of non-indigenous ethnic others, but can as well facilitate a peaceful 'inclusive' alternative. In this process of formulating justifiable indigenous futures, the concerned anthropologist could have a role as critical interlocutor and a partner in dialogue.[10]

This humble suggestion will apply in our Indian situation very much.

Having said all these, let us come to the ground realities that affected the Adivasi identity and development during the British colonial government and the Government of India after the Independence. It is true that the British government and the social scientist during that period did do service to the Adivasis by establishing the Excluded Areas and partially excluded Areas in north-east India and in the mainland. Legal protection was given to save the identity of the Adivasis. But the British government machineries and the administrative tools did a great deal of damage to the life and identity of the Adivasis/indigenous people in the mainland. First, the police system reached even to the interior village through its 'chaukidars'. He was made the official informant about the situations and occurrences in the village to the police station (thana). The headman of Adivasi villages—the Munda, Majhi, Mahto and others were displaced from their administrative and legal authority granted by the customary laws of the communities. This damaged the village administration, traditionally managed for thousands of years.

Second, colonial government carried on the survey settlements of the land and forest properties of 5th Schedule areas. Individual members were granted land rights with a *patta*. The community ownership of land and forests in Adivasi villages was transferred to individuals. This created problems and litigation increased in villages. Peace and goodwill were disturbed and the entire community feeling, fellowship and sharing of goods and services began to deteriorate in Adivasi society. Third, the education system introduced by the colonial government cut the Adivasis in the mainland from their socio-cultural roots; English medium of education served the colonial government purpose. Adivasis could not get education through their mother tongues and socio-cultural values among Adivasis got completely diluted and infected with foreign and outside cultural influences through education. Lack of education through mother tongue even at the primary level has far-reaching consequences in the life and experience of the Adivasis. Individualism and self-seeking, greed and competition have completely overshadowed the universal human values widely practiced in Adivasi society like community feeling and fellowship, cooperation with others in everyday life and sharing ones belongings in society according to the need. These values were maintained as honesty and integrity in dealings with each other. These human values have almost disappeared from our Adivasi social life. Fourth, and finally the colonial government used the members of Jati people to carry on their local levels of administration. Brahmins, Kshatriyas and Vaishya Jati people were appointed below the district levels of administration, police, revenue collectors, and lower officers in administration. This unfortunate step taken or method of administration adopted by the colonial government became a major source of oppression, suppression and displacement of Adivasis from their home and hearth.

On top of all, these *thekedars* were allowed to go into the interior, taking the management of villages according to their own will. These greedy businessmen tried to grab lands from the Adivasis and Adivasi women were sexually exploited. Therefore socio-economic exploitation was openly carried on under the umbrella of the colonial government.

Now let us come to the period of Independence. The Government of India under the leadership of Pandit Jawaharlal Nehru declared the policy of developing a socialistic pattern of society in India with an idea of socio-economic and political equality to be granted and practised in the country. Pandit Nehru had his Panchsheel as a basic vision to deal with Adivasis in India. As per the five points of Panchsheel:

1. People should develop along the lines of their own genius and we should avoid imposing anything on them. We should try to encourage in every way their traditional arts and cultures.
2. Tribal rights in land and forests should be respected.
3. We should try to train and build-up a team of their own people to do the work of administration and development. Some technical personnel from outside will, no doubt, be needed especially in the beginning. But we should avoid introducing too many outsiders into tribal territory.
4. We should not over administer these areas or overwhelm them with a multiplicity of schemes, we should rather work through and not in rivalry to their own social and cultural institution.
5. We should judge results not by statistics or the amount of money spent but by the quality of human character that is involved.

(Quoted from *Tribal Awakening*, ed. M.M. Thomas and Richard Taylor, CISRS, Bangalore 1965, p. 19.)

If in actuality, the government had carried on the same Panchsheel policy to deal with Adivasis, we are sure, that the Adivasi life today would have been quite different. But we all know that the Government of India slowly deviated from the original vision of the development of India. To be honest to Pandit Nehru, we must mention that he was not against industries. In fact, it was Nehru's idea that led to the establishment of Heavy Engineering Corporation, at Ranchi with Russian collaboration. We may see a sort of contradiction here in the period of Nehru, Sardar Patel, and other architects of freedom. Slowly and surely the country's economy took a turn during Prime Minister Narasimha Rao and Finance Minister, and Manmohan Singh's time. Liberalization as a basic principle of economic policy was adopted in which capitalism in its modern sense was adopted and there sprang up the corporate houses to deal with mining and Industries in our country. This change in economic policy has done more harm than good to the Adivasis of mainland India. Unfortunately or fortunately all the numerous resources—iron, coal, bauxite, uranium, manganese, silver, gold are found in the 5th Scheduled Areas of India. The major forest areas are also in this region.

The government of Independent and democratic India was led by greed and benefit motives more than by people's welfare. President of India notification in 1950 with respect to the 5th Scheduled Areas (Partially Excluded Areas) constitutional provisions for the protection and development of Adivasi identity were somehow completely neglected. In utter violation and complete disregard for the 5th Scheduled Areas the Congress government in the early period, and later the Bharatiya Janata Party (BJP) and many regional political parties like the Jharkhand Mukti Morcha and Jharkhand Vikas Morcha and others, cared the least to implement the 5th Scheduled Areas constitutional provisions from 1950-2011. Out of the nine states with 5th Scheduled Areas, not even one governor of these states cared to be responsible to the Adivasi People in his tenure by taking adequate cognizance of the 5th Scheduled Areas provision and attempt to implement them. No national or regional political party cared to look into the 5th Scheduled Areas constitutional provisions in doing their political work among the Adivasis. It is tragic that for more than 63 years of Independence Adivasi life has been deteriorating and disintegrating in present-day India. It is all the more tragic to think that Adivasi elite groups also did not care to raise this issue early enough before things really got bad. But better late than never, the Adivasi community leaders and some intellectuals among them have begun raising the Adivasi issue in the light of 5th Scheduled constitutional provision now.

Already Adivasis are displaced from home and hearth due to mining operation and setting up of various industries and big dam constructions for the benefit of other people than the Adivasis of 5th Scheduled Areas. Adivasi land alienation has gone on for decades without any break. Adivasis are now a displaced people from their own ancestral land, forest and public places, like Masna, and others. The paradox is that Adivasis are displaced from lands and the people from Jati Society have moved into their place. As such the demography of the 5th Scheduled Areas is rapidly changing and this is creating new problems for the 5th Scheduled Areas. In Jharkhand there was 56 per cent Adivasi population in 1952 and today in 2011, the census people are trying to say that Adivasi People's population is only 20 to 22 per cent. There are census mistakes also granting that even with let us say 30 per cent. Adivasi population at present in Jharkhand is quite staggering, and particularly with 13 districts full and 3 more districts partially out of 24 districts in Jharkhand state are 5th Scheduled Areas.

The remedy to all this is to implement 5th Scheduled Areas provisions rigorously and make up the loss sustained by the Adivasi People so far. Mahatma Gandhi launched Satyagraha movement to drive out the British from India; Adivasis have already launched 'Nyayagraha Andolan' to chase out the unwanted population from the 5th Scheduled Areas in mainland India. All Adivasis are uniting to take this *andolan* to its final destination in future under the leadership of Akhil Bharatiya Adivasi Mahasabha.[11]

To conclude this part we turn over again to the ordeals and voices of indigenous people (Adivasi) of Asia and India. Listen to what they have to say about their condition,

> We the participants of the Asia Indigenous and Tribal Peoples consultation on Empowerment of Indigenous Tribal Peoples for self-rule held on 2-4 March 2005 in Srimanta Sankeradeva Kalakaritra Panjabasi, Guwahati, Assam, address widely the serious deterioting situations and problems placed by Indigenous and Tribal People (Adivasis) in most of the Asian nation. They feel and fully realise that the Indigenous and Tribal Peoples (Adivasis) are the most disadvantaged groups in the society despite the considerable efforts that have been made during the last several decades for their protection and development.[12]

India has much to share with others in this respect. The representatives gathered at New Delhi in Talkatora Indoor Stadium between 28-30 March 2011 made the following remarks in their official written presentation.

> Deprival of these resources and our empowerment through deforestation and displacement and the attack on our livelihood has caused a major crisis in our total life. We are forced to give up much of what once belonged to us . . . our very identity is centered on these resources and we would like to maintain it since that is part of our self-respect and human right.[13]

We have already made passing suggestions of some remedial measures in the previous pages. The need of the hour is a limited and concerted effort by all Indigenous and Tribal (Adivasi) communities in India is needed to struggle and fight for their God given identity as a people differentiated from the Jati people in our country. God has a great purpose for the betterment of our social and human existence in the Indian sub-comment in future.

Struggles of Indigenous People (Adivasis)

Western nations' political and economic power expansions have created a worldwide situation of struggles of indigenous people (Adivasis) all over. There is a general movement to protect the identity of the indigenous people in different non-Western countries of the world. The reporting in the meetings of UNO Working Group of Indigenous and Tribal People each year has provided data of struggles in different countries of the world.

Adivasi struggle for survival and identity is a part of this worldwide movement. As there are different situations in different countries, so there are differences in the nature and impacts of these struggles. We have already indicated that there is little or no historical records and data of Adivasi struggles during the Aryan and Mughal rules. Only from British colonial period we have data of Adivasi struggles in mainland India. We admit our weaknesses in not being able to present here about Adivasi struggles during British Colonial period 1765-1957 from all 5th Scheduled Areas states. We will present only a few examples of these struggles from greater Jharkhand, West Bengal, Chhattisgarh, Orissa and Andhra Pradesh. Adivasi struggles are movements which have been labelled as *vidrohas* (rebellion) in some documents. The struggles of Adivasis are:

(i) The Chero Andolan 1795-1800. The Cheros were the ruling Adivasi community in the Palamau area of Chhotanagpur. They opposed and fought against the British invasion. The British used military power to suppress and subjugate them.

(ii) Similarly there were Munda Vidroh in 1797, Chuar Vidroh in 1798, Bhumi Vidroh in 1798-9. These are different Adivasi communities in greater Jharkhand areas. The Kol Vidroh took place between 1820-36. The Ho Adivasi community in Jharkhand is one of the most forward groups to resist any inroads by outsiders in their region. Their country is called the Kolhan region of southern Jharkhand at present only east and west Singhbhum districts are in Kolhan though originally it included a very wide area in this region. This was quite a strong and wide Adivasi movement (*vidroh*) against the British. Battles between Adivasis with their traditional bows and arrows and axes and lathis on one side and the modern shootings by guns on the other by the British. British official—Wilkinson met the defeated people and he formulated a self-governing rule for Kolhan which is called Wilkinson Rule, empowering the Adivasis to self-rule according to their socio-political and economic systems up to certain levels from the village upwards.

(iii) There are two more important Adivasi struggles for their safety and identity against the British colonial power.

First, the Safa Hor movement of the Santhals. The British invasion into Santhal Pargana was widely opposed by the villagers. But ultimately Sidhu-Kanhu and Chand-Bhairov —four Santhal brothers took the lead and pitched a bitter battle against the British. In the un-approacheble region with rough terrains like jungle and rivers, the Santhals were able to drive the British army away. For some time this situation continued but finally the British reconciled with the Santhals. This Santhal Vidroh took place in 1855-6 before the 'sepoy mutiny' of 1857. As a result of this struggle the Santhal Pargana Tenancy Act of 1867-8 was enacted giving rights to control the land system in Santhal Pargana region.

Finally we must mention here the Birsa Munda Andolan from 1895-1900 in Munda country (present Khunti district) of Jharkhand. Already there were struggles going on in this region. With Birsa Munda, this movement against the British took a countrywide turn. Birsa Munda a youngman of 25 had prepared himself to lead his people to fight against the British power which had disturbed the Munda village system by leasing villages to the *thekedars* (Sikhs and Moslem). These intruders had begun molesting the Munda women also. Birsa Munda was called by Singh Bonga (Supreme God) to go and save his community of people. He collected young and old and inspired them to fight with their traditional arms and ammunitions against the British and the zamindars also. According to Birsa Munda these intruders had to be driven away from the Munda country. Birsa travelled far and wide and invited his neighbour, the Oraon (Kurukh), the Hos and others to join him in this life and death struggle for safety and security of the Adivasis in this region. People in thousands gathered around him, the final battle look place in Dumbari Hills east of Khunti in 1900. The British government used its military power and crushed the crowd of Adivasis gathered on this hill. Hundreds even thousands of Adivasi were killed, Birsa was finally captured and jailed in Ranchi. He died in Ranchi Jail in 1900. As a result of Birsa Andolan and final defeat of Adivasis in Dumbari hills, the government was moved to do something for the safety of land of Adivasis in this region. Chhotanagpur Tenancy Act was passed in 1908 which restricted the sale of Adivasi land to the Adivasis alone, and not to any non-Adivasi.

(iv) In Andhra Pradesh there was the Rampa Revolution led by the Koya tribes of the Telangana region against the British in 1879.

These examples of Adivasi struggle against British colonial power had the innate will of the Adivasi to fight for their safety and distinct identity. It was sure that without these and other struggles (*vidrohas*) led by the Adivasis against the intruders the Adivasis could not have survived and kept their identities through the British period in Indian history.[14]

There is another angle to the Adivasis' struggle for survival.

These Adivasi leaders saw the external enemy as the British government but they also saw the internal enemy within their own society. The evil of alcohol was weakening their society. They fought against this internal evil also. Birsa Munda, for instance, forbade people to drink Haria Daru and organized a society of Birsaites in his country. The Birsaites do not consume alcohol at all and wear white clothes be it *dhotis* or *saris*.

The Safa Hor of the Santhal Pargana also gave up drinking and began to lead a pure life. They recognized the evils of alcohol in their society.

Among the Oraons (Kurukh), Jatra Oraon of Bisunpur thana led a movement called the Tana Bhagat Andolan. He completely gave up drinking and all kinds of worship to *devi devatas* and led people to worship the supreme God Dharmas only. They too wear white *dhotis* and *saris* in their daily life. These Tana Bhagats fought against the British and zamindars saying that the land they occupied was not given by any king or zamindar or the British government but the land was given by God and therefore they gave up paying land tax and also lending support to Mahatma Gandhi during the freedom struggle. Later they met Gandhiji in 1940 at the Ramgarh Congress and supported Gandhiji.[15]

Adivasi Struggles in Independent India (Democratic Republic of People of India 1947-50)

A radical change was expected in Independent India. British India had been under foreign colonial rule. Independent India had its own constitution and was declared Republic on 26 January 1950. It was a government of the people, for the people and by the people being administered by their representatives both in state legislature (the MLAs) and at the centre by the members of both the houses of parliament, the Lok Sabha and Rajya Sabha. It now had a president, a prime minister, cabinet ministers and a central and state administrative machinery to implement the laws and constitutional provisions.

The constitution provided the right to education in the mother tongue for all major/minor language communities in India. In the 6th and 5th Scheduled Areas (Excluded and Partially Excluded Areas) constitutional provisions were accepted for the protection and development of the tribes (Adivasis) of the mainland and tribes of north-east India.

Linguistic states were carved out according to major languages of India—Tamil, Telugu, Kannada, Malayalam, Marathi, Gujarati, Rajasthani, Hindi, Bangla, Odia and few others in the north-western region, Kashmir, Himachal Pradesh, Madhya Pradesh and centrally administered areas like Goa, Pondicherry, Daman & Diu and others.

Tribal (Adivasi) languages and their regional population were tagged with Assam in the north-east, and Bihar and Madhya Pradesh, and others in the mainland.

This situation challenged the tribes (Adivasis) as they were kept under an internal colonial political situation in Independent India.

In Jharkhand region there was already an Adivasi Mahasabha, a socio-political movement for the separate existence and identity of the Adivasi of Jharkhand region. The Naga, Khasi, Mizo movements for their regional identity were launched after the Independence of India and finally all of them have their own states with Excluded Area Provision of the constitution. We won't comment on the latter developments as our focus is on the mainland Adivasis of India.

The Adivasi Mahasabha later became the Jharkhand Party, a purely political concern focused on Adivasi struggles in this region. In 1956, State Boundary Reorganization Commission visited Jharkhand. Unfortunately the Adivasis missed the bus. Their leader Shri Jaipal Singh Munda did not appear before the commission and place demand for a Jharkhand state. Small groups met the commission but their presentation could not impress and convince the commission for the creation of a separate state for Jharkhand for the safety and security of Adivasi identity in free India.

So the struggle continued. This author was a student of university at that time and so had the privilege of witnessing the struggles of the Adivasi leaders and their participation in the events and activities of their movement. Ultimately the Jharkhand Party merged with the Indian National Congress in 1963 with future promises for Adivasi welfare and development. Jaipal Singh and others were promised seats in the central and Bihar state governments. All these promises flopped as the Adivasi were badly cheated. In 1972 Sibu Soren, a young reformist and social worker, emerged as a political leader and he launched Jharkhand Mukti Morcha, a regional political party, to continue the Adivasi's struggles for their existence, identity and development. His leadership also did not deliver the expected good. Other political parties paid lip service to help the Adivasis in their struggles. But all in vain. Finally as we know the BJP-led NDA government came to power in the Centre. This was dominated by businessmen also. This government granted Jharkhand the 15 districts of Chhotanagpur and Santhal Parganas of southern Bihar. The Jharkhand state was formed in 2000 when Adivasi struggle was at its lowest ebb. The Adivasis were at the time disorganized. The BJP formed the Jharkhand state government and the state became a grazing ground for people from outside.

Other groups are still struggling against the ruthless violation of the 5th Scheduled Areas constitutional provision by all the governments at the centre as well as at the state levels. General laws passed by the centre are being used to rule and govern the 5th Scheduled Areas also. During the last sixty-three years of Independent India Adivasis are desperately trying to save their social, cultural, and political identities in the Jharkhand region.

There were some minor movements after the formation of the Jharkhand state in 2000. For instance, Jharkhand Jan Adhikar Manch for defining Jharkhandis with a cut-off point, so that local people from Jharkhand and certainly the Adivasis could get advantage. Then the Jharkhand Jan Adhikar Morcha was launched in 2003-4. And finally Salkhan Murmu has launched a Jharkhand Desum Party to struggle for the safeguard of Adivasi interest in this region.

This question of 5th Scheduled Areas constitutional provisions reached all-time high when Akhil Bharatiya Adivasi Maha Sabha was organized on 11 November 2008, at Ranchi. The Maha Sabha is working on issues around 5th Scheduled Areas provision and has launched the 'Nyayagraha Andolan' to drive out all unwanted people and programmes which are against the interest of Adivasi community, its identity and development in free India.

The Adivasis in Jharkhand feel that there is a subtle conspiracy on the part of the government and corporate houses to displace Adivasis from the 5th Scheduled Areas and make this area an industrial and business hub in the future.

Innate self-inspired struggle, both in British colonial period and Independent India under internal colonial rule, have gone through ups and downs but with minimum violence. These struggles have achieved some of their objectives and there are others yet to be achieved. This is true particularly in free India and Adivasis are in an internal colonial rule situation. This is accentuated due to the non-implementation of the 5th Scheduled Area constitutional provisions for the protection and promotion of Adivasi socio-economic, political-cultural identities in India. We have yet another spell of Adivasi struggles inspired and guided by foreign sources. They are the Naxalite and Maoist struggles against the statecraft and injustices perpetrated in Tribal areas. It is very difficult to assess the impact of Adivasi struggles led by the Naxalite and Maobadi ideologies. The country is threatened by this internal conflict in our society. This conflict has torn the Adivasi society into pieces, particularly in Lalgarh area of West Bengal and Bastar region of Chhattisgarh state. Here are few views by leading authors, thinkers and intellectuals in our country. The following statements do explain the rising popularity of Naxalite and Maoist movement. Brahmdeo Sharma and Digvijay Singh, former SC-ST commissioner and the former chief minister of Madhya Pradesh respectively, do reiterate that violation of the 5th Scheduled Area constitutional provision is the central reason for agitation and violence in the Adivasi region in the mainland.[16] Various other authors are also of the opinion that there is a gross injustice done from all corners of dominant Indian society to the Adivasi communities in India. Ira Jha, born and brought up in Bastar narrates that Bastar Adivasis had accepted the Naxals and Maobadis as their 'Dada' (bodyguard, protector). These Dadas have freed the Adivasis from the police atrocities and they have been able to save the jungle from the Government of Chhattisgarh and their *thekedars*.[17] Even Mahashweta Devi, noted writer and activist, also holds the Government of West Bengal responsible for the bloodbath in Lalgarh (Midnapur) in West Bengal.[18] And finally Arun Tripathi the editor of वर्तिका (*Vartika*) in the article 'Maobadi or Adivasi' contends,

> due to injustice perpetrated by the Government and alter future of development programmes in Adivasi communities all over India has

led the Adivasis to turn their back from the democratic Government and turned their face to the Maobadi and joined their movements by taking up arms in their hand. (Free translation of Hindi version)[19]

After reading the above, we are again led to believe that the present state of affairs of our central and state governments in the 5th Scheduled Areas is responsible for the unrest and violence among Adivasi communities led by Naxalites and Maobadis. These are struggles, but not of the nature we have described above. This is not for preservation of Adivasi identity and their development. But it appears that Adivasis are drawn into the whirlpool of Naxalite and Maobadi movement to change the entire statecraft of Indian administration and economy. Whereas the Adivasi struggles are for implementing the constitutional provisions made in the 5th Scheduled Areas of India and other details for the protection and development of Adivasi communities in India.

Theology and Struggle of the Adivasis/ Indigenous People of India

An International Ecumenical Peace convocation was held in Kingston, Jamaica in May 2011 where Rt. Rev. Ofelia Ortega, president of WCC, H.E. Metropolitan Hilariun of Volokomask and Paul Oestreicher as the keynote speakers were present with 1,000 participants from more than 100 countries. Reverend Olav Fykee Tvert, general secretary of WCC, moderated the sessions. The keynote speaker appealed participation of all organizations and involvement of all disciplines of knowledge in the attempt to establish peace in our present world. He mentioned theology also as a discipline of knowledge in course of mentioning other disciplines. To quote him, 'Every discipline will be involved—law, politics, international relations, economics, sociology, gender studies, personal and social psychology and last, and for us, not the least, theology, the way we interpret the will of God'.[12] It is interesting to note that theology here is defined as interpreting the will of God. For our purposes here we take this understanding of theology seriously as it does try to speak to the context and content of our subject. The 'we' represents the Christians all over the world. It is very well understood that theology is interpreted by the believing community and/or its representatives as theologians. Let us accept that the believing community, the Church, is the agent to interpret the will of God in our world. To be more specific this interpretation of the will of God is meant for the people of this world. Here the task is to pin down the issue by saying that the theology that we mean is the theology which will express the will of God for the struggling Adivasis/indigenous people of India. To take a shortcut we discover that the will of God for all people is expressed in these words, 'As I live, says the Lord God, I have no pleasure in the death of the wicked, but that the wicked turn from his way from and live; turn back from your evil ways; for why will you die, house of Israel? (Ezekiel 33: 11).[13] The New Testament teaches that will of God is that people should know the truth and the truth will make them free. In this context truth is Jesus Christ Himself. Therefore knowing truth means knowing and believing in Jesus Christ as the redeemer of this world.

The Adivasis are the most disadvantaged group of people in this world and particularly in India. There are believers, Christian communities, among the Adivasis of India. Taking Adivasis as a people separately, there might be about 5 per cent of Adivasi Christians in our country. If we include north-east tribes also in this category then a greater percentage of Christians are found in India. Therefore as we have already seen before Christian communities among the Adivasi People will interpret the will of God as they struggle for their identity and existence in this country.

Paul Oestriecher has tried to interpret for us the history of Western Christianity. After King Constantine's acceptance of Christianity, the church became a symbol of political power. As we continue through the medieval and modern period the matter becomes more complicated as the kings and political heads of states take leading role in the life and work of the church. Yes, in modern political states the church and state is separate for convenience's sake but the political and economic form of the world has made inroads into the church/churches we know today. Let us briefly look at the churches in India. The Syrian Church of Malabar (Kerala) group is in the upper caste camp. And all the later converts from the lower caste/out caste are belonging to the lower strata of Indian society. The Adivasi and Dalit Christians have no place in the caste social structure of Indian society. But the self-understanding of these Christians and the churches are different. They are the products of the missions from Europe, England, and America. And most of these missions were promoted by the colonial government of the West. Therefore there is a peculiar self-understanding of Adivasi and Dalit Christians in certain quarters. After 2nd Vatican Council Roman Catholic Church has taken a turn towards becoming an Indigenous Peoples Church, they have decidedly taken steps to be the Church of the Poor. But among all the protestant and evangelical churches there are as many ideas of this self-understanding as there are denominations and sects. The Roman Catholics in general are pro-*status quo* and therefore, they cannot serve the people with their own ideas and programmes. To be the Church of the Poor finally ends up with a lip service as the church goes by the ideas and programmes of the party in power at the centre or at the states in India. This situation makes it very difficult for us to apply theology as 'interpreting the will of God for the struggling Adivasis in India. Two factors: the *jati pratha* (caste tradition) and the denominational differences in the Christian churches have made the situation worse for our task of 'interpreting the will of God' for the struggling Adivasis in our country. On top of these mighty events there are some evils of the west which have found their place in the churches among us. Western democracy as the will of the majority making decisions for the whole country and people has been accepted in our churches as sacred. This principle of majority democracy has damaged the image of the church very badly. Church is the body of Jesus Christ and therefore the principle of consensus as decision-making process should be accepted. This is what the Adivasi communities have practised all through the ages and they could save their existence and identity even in the midst of all waves of political social powers that have come and gone in this country. But today under the majority democracy the situation has become quite unmanageable. Individual freedom and majority power in decision-making has corrupted the church also, as it was done to Indian society. Therefore we have to find out a way through this jungle to interpret the will of God for the struggling Adivasis of India today.

For interpreting the will of God for the struggling Adivasi people in India, relevantly and meaningfully, the following steps seem necessary. First, that the present theological thinking and practices of the churches in Adivasi regions have to change radically. Bishop A.S. Hembrom has dealt with this issue in comprehensive details in his paper presented in an ecumenical gathering of Christians a couple of year's ago about the irrelevance of theology for this world's life and some concrete suggestion for change.[14] The Christian Mission and ministry in Adivasi Christian communities must change from only heavenly concerns and religious celebrations to a meaningful Christian life to be lived, here on earth serving the people in their need in the society around us. The life and ministry of Jesus meeting the needs of people and freeing them from bondages of different kinds and calling them to be community of love and concern for all around them should be our model. Gospel as Good News is for here and now as much as for the life after. And for this he suggests that since the churches in the Adivasi region have taken Adivasi people as their base, the mission of the church must be geared towards *lokhit* (public/peoples' welfare).[15]

Second interpreting God's will among the struggling Adivasis is a call to the church from God. This call must be materialized in the writings and actions of those few who have heard this call in the church/churches of Adivasi regions of mainland India.

While describing the Adivasi struggle we have mentioned that the Adivasi leaders heard the call of the Almighty (High God) to take a stand to protect and promote the Adivasi communities from the onslaughts of the colonial political, economic, and cultural powers. They organized and gathered Adivasi armies to fight against the enemy. They used their traditional arms (bow and arrow, axes) and in some instances the British forces were forced to retreat from the region. In other cases the Adivasis were crushed by superior military and political powers and the Adivasis were subjugated under the colonial political powers. This served their purpose in the history of Adivasis in India. They were recognized as different and differentiated races/people and communities in India, other than the Jati people of India. Adivasis are the Adi people with different social, cultural and even political life as against the Aryan system.

But more than anything else these Adivasi leaders who led their people to protect themselves from the enemies, also saw the need of reconstructing, reforming and renewing their communities for their existence and identity in the changing modern world. Some evil customs and practices which are detrimental to sound human growth like drinking, believing in evil spirit, and some inhuman, social practices have to be abandoned in order to exist and maintain Adivasi identity in the modern world. Socio-cultural changes for the better was accepted and initiated by the Adivasi communities in the greater Jharkhand region.

To conclude it must be clear that *hinsa* (taking up arms and fighting), for Adivasi existence and identity cannot bear good fruit at present and in future also. Violence begets violence and there has been no human progress and gain through violent methods, and it must not be used for maintaining the existence and promoting the identity of the Adivasis in India.

The key issue in this age of 'survival of the fittest' is what can promote the theology of 'survival of the weakest' (Adivasis) today and in the days to come?

Survival of the fittest always functions with the power of violence. Without violence the process of survival of the fittest cannot continue. We have already proposed to avoid/give up the road through violence for Adivasi cause. The way of love, tolerance prolonged sufferings are the expressions of God's will for the Adivasi people in India. It is a different, difficult and very hard way.

A relevant theology must address the struggle of the Adivasis in the 'Internal colonial' situation in India. This internal colonial situation is quite subtle and invisible in some sense. The Constitution of India is meant for the protection of the existence and identity of Adivasi communities in India. The 5th Scheduled Areas and the constitutional provisions are quite sufficient in some sense for the existence, identity and development of the Adivasis in nine states of India. But the Adivasi people themselves are extremely distracted from the main issue and the whole administrative system of the Government of India is looking the other way. The administrative machinery is not willing to implement the provisions of the 5th Scheduled Areas. The political parties have no interest in the Adivasi issue. The social activists and non-government organizations including the church are continuing with their self-interest and self-centred and greed-based economic programmes and projects, and, a selfless and painful participation in the struggles and sufferings of the Adivasis has become almost impossible to come out from this self-centredness.

The 'displaced' Adivasi community has almost no place/socio-cultural space to be rehabilitated in this country. Here we are in need of a theology that will make sense to the displaced Adivasis.

Only a displaced God can meet the aspirations of the displaced Adivasis in India and the indigenous people in the world. The cry of the Adivasis has reached the throne of God in heaven. He has displaced Himself and come down to this created world to meet the weakest among the people. And this displaced God has appeared as Jesus of Nazareth. He has taken up the task of rehabilitating the socially, culturally and religiously displaced communities. In this mission of saving the weakest, he has taken the form of a suffering servant of God. He participates in the pains and sufferings of the Adivasi people. And by sheer love for the weakest, Jesus of Nazareth, suffered crucifixion and the Risen Lord has entered the Adivasi communities in India. By faith and trust in Him a new creation has taken place in this region and in other parts of India. All those who have paid faithful allegiance to this suffering servant Jesus of Nazareth crucified and Risen Lord, are incorporated into His body of believers. The will of God for the Adivasis in India is to become a new people with the Holy Spirit as the new energy to form a new order in society for the rehabilitation of the Adivasis. This new creation is within the created world around us with its own principles and dynamics of life—Interdependence with persons, communities, natural world and the spiritual world in which there is acceptance of each other and enabling peoples and communities to live in harmony with each other. In this process of new creation the Adivasis see themselves as accepted partners where their alienation is negated and a spiritual dynamic, of acceptance of the unacceptable Adivasis is extended in and through the name Jesus Christ as the suffering servant of God in the midst of this world.

The churches as we find them today have to enter into this mystery of the displaced God in Jesus Christ and *janhit* (peoples welfare), with the people of the 'New Creation' in Jesus. The theology of these churches have to change in order to be in line with those New Creation in Christ and participate in the sacrificial sufferings and pains of the displaced Adivasis with whom the displaced God, even Jesus Christ is actively working out ways for the survival identity and development of the Adivasis together with all other New Creation in Christ all over the world. This is the hope of future for the displaced Adivasis in India.

NOTES

1. Virginuis Xaxa, 'Tribes as Indigenous People of India', in *Ordeals and Voices of Indigenous and Tribal People of India*, ed. Joseph Bara, souvenir, Guwahati, 2005, p. 14. In this book Professor Xaxa emphatically says that the Adivasis never accepted the administrative structure of the larger society and were not part of the social organization and worldview. Whereas these Dalits who were subjugated accepted the social organization and worldview of the Jati people.
2. Ibid., p. 1.
3. Ibid., p. 19.
4. Ibid., p. 13.
5. 5th Scheduled Areas constitutional provisions and Notification.
    (i) Government of India Act 1935, Chapter V Excluded and partially excluded Areas.
    (ii) Reform office Notification New Delhi, 19 March 1936, Scheduled Part I. Excluded Areas, Scheduled Part II. Partially Excluded Areas.
    (iii) The Scheduled Area (Part of State) Order, 1950.
    C.O.G. – In exercise of the power confessed upon by sub-paragraph (1) of the paragraph 6 of the 5th Schedule of the Constitution of India. The President is pleased to make the following order, namely (1) the order may be called Scheduled Areas (Part of State) order 1950 (Appendix III).
    (iv) The Gazette of India Extraordinary published by Authority No. 180 New Delhi Wednesday the 11 April 2007. Chaitra 21, 1929 (This document enlists the 5th Scheduled Areas of Jharkhand).
6. Declaration of Indigenous People's Rights, New York.
7. Xaxa, op. cit.
8. Supreme Court Judgement Adivasis Areas, *Raviwar*, 10-16 July 2011, New Delhi, p. 20.
9. This quotation is taken from a Hindi paper presented by Rev. Cyril Hans in a seminar of common leadership formation held on 13-14 June 2011 at Ranchi, p. 1.

10. As in fn. 5.
11. Xaxa, op. cit., p. 41.
12. All India Adivasi Mahasabha was organized on 11 November 2008, at Ranchi and it is slowly spreading in West Bengal, Chhattisgarh and other states.
13. Xaxa, op. cit., p. 262.
14. 'Ordeals and Voices of Indigenous and Tribal People's/Adivasis', Talkatora Indoor Stadium, New Delhi, 28-30 March 2011 excerpt from ICITP Report, p. 30.
15. Adivasi 'Vidroh'.
16. Adivasi Reform movements and struggles.
17. *Vartika* (Maobadi or Adivasi), ed. Mahasweta Devi and Arun Kumar Tripathi, New Delhi: Vani Prakashan, 2010, pp. 15-16.
18. Ira Jha, 'Bastar Ka Dard to Samjho' (Understand the Pain of Bastar), *Vartika*, p. 17.
19. Mahasweta Devi, 'Lalgarh Ke Liye Sarkar Jimmevar' (Government is Responsible for Lalgarh Incident), *Vartika*, p. 65.
20. Arun Tripathi, *Vartika*, Editorial, p. 2.
21. *Peoples' Reporter*, vol. 24, issue 10, Mumbai, 25 May-10 June 2011, p. 5 column 5, para 5.
22. Ezekiel 33:11, Revised standard version.
23. Bishop A.S. Hemrom, An ecumenical consultation on Adivasi issues held on 23 July 2007, S.D.C. Purulia Road, Ranchi (unpublished paper) in Hindi.
24. Ibid., pp. 6-7.

5

Women: Theology and Feminist Movements in India

SHALINI MULACKAL

Introduction

It is an obvious fact that most women and girls are not treated as full human beings, equal in worth and dignity to men and boys neither in the church nor in the society in spite of the progress humanity has made in all walks of life. As a result, a vast majority of Indian women continue to be victims of various atrocities perpetrated against them. Glancing through any newspaper any day will bear witness to this fact. Moreover women are denied their full humanity by denying them the right to participate and contribute in the domestic and public spheres on par with men. The reasons for such discriminations and denials are many. In spite of this hard reality faced by women, majority of men and women either look with suspicion or are indifferent to feminism, feminist concerns, feminist theology, feminist movement or women's movement in India. Some even have an aversion to anything concerning feminism and look with scorn on those who call themselves as feminists. Some feel that 'feminism' is an imported idea from the West and it is bound to break families here as it is supposed to have done in the West. Others argue that there cannot be equality between men and women, which is the fundamental demand of feminism, since women are biologically different from men.

But what do feminists mean by equality? When feminists talk about equality, they affirm that men and women are equal in worth and dignity and that equal opportunities to be left open for both to develop their potentialities to the maximum. Further, the specific biological roles which women are called to play are to be recognized as equal in value to that of the role the men are called to play. For most feminists, equality is not identity of treatment and roles but more of self-realization, freedom to direct one's life, and availability of equal opportunities to develop oneself.[1] Equality envisages relationships that are mutual between men and women and not hierarchical or dependent. Various liberative movements of women aim at the restructuring of gender relationships in view of creating a more humane society for all.[2]

For the past couple of decades, people who call themselves as feminists gradually realized that religions too play a role in legitimizing certain prejudices and biases against women. As a result religions too contribute towards the oppressive situation of women prevalent in any society. Since patriarchal roots are present in almost all religions, a critical look at these and their respective scriptures is imperative if we want to create an egalitarian society. At the same time feminists are aware that religions do provide sources to counter such oppressive situation of women. In this paper I intend to focus on Christianity and see how, as Christians, we need to look at the present situation of women in India. Do we have sufficient resources within our tradition to work for the liberation of women? Further, I want to explore whether working for the empowerment of women and creating a gender-just society and church is a Gospel imperative or not.

Contextual theologies today consider the *context* as a very important source of doing theology, in addition to scripture and tradition. I believe that the aim of doing any contextual theology is to bring about liberation or transformation, both at the individual and societal levels. As the word indicates, there are many contextual theologies already existing, like the Black theology, the Tribal theology or the Dalit theology. Feminist theology too comes under contextual theologies where the oppressive context of women becomes the locus of doing theology. In order to judge whether feminist theology is relevant for our context, it is necessary to examine some salient features of Feminist theology. But before taking that up, it is pertinent to look at the Indian scenario and see the status of women even after 65 years of self-rule and governance.

Multilayered Oppression

Recently a three-month old baby girl, Neha Afreen was mercilessly beaten up by her father for being born a girl child. She died in a hospital in Bangalore a few days later.[3] The female child is still an unwelcome intrusion in many homes. Many even prevent her entry into this world through selective female foeticide. Millions of female foetuses are aborted every year in our country. The census of 2011 bears witness to this brutal fact. Though there is marginal improvement in the sex ratio from 933 to 940 per 1,000 males in the general category, the Child Sex Ratio (CSR) fell from 927 in 2001 to 914 in 2011. What is alarming is that the CSR fell far more sharply in villages in comparison to urban areas in the last decade as per the 2011 census. This is due to the rampant use of prenatal sex determination technology in rural areas. If this trend continues, by 2050 there will be around two crore of men in India who will not get a bride.[4]

A girl is often referred to as *paraya dhan* (somebody else's property) in most Hindi speaking areas of our country and a boy as *apana dhan* (one's own property). Son-preference is rather widespread. Educated and uneducated, moneyed and the poor, resident Indians and the NRIs are all infected by this 'disease' without exception. Women devaluation is manifested at multiple sites and in various combinations. In a sense it is ingrained in the body, mind and psyche of every Indian woman without exception. Our society functions in a way that keeps the male as the norm, resulting in an automatic devaluation of women at every level. Atrocities, violence, discriminations, and the like practised against women and girls are expressive of their devalued status in the society. Not a single day passes without the newspapers reporting some crime or the other committed against women.[5] National Crime Records Bureau data shows that a total of 1,95,856; 2,03,804; and 2,13,585 cases of crime against women were registered during the years 2008, 2009 and 2010 respectively.

Women experience manifold oppressions within the family. There exists discrimination in terms of work allocation,[6] food, leisure and rest, health care, and education.[7] Moreover, there is severe lack of freedom for women. They are secluded, often not allowed any other social contacts outside the four walls of the house. They hardly have any voice in the decision-making process. They experience domestic violence ranging from verbal abuse, mental torture, deprivation of food and money, denial of permission to meet friends and relatives, to beatings and physical torture. The available statistics say the true story. For instance, the National Family Health Survey III (2005-6) data shows that in the 15-49 age group, 35.4 per cent of all women and 40 per cent of married women have experienced physical or sexual violence and 6.7 per cent experienced both physical and sexual forms of domestic violence.[8] Often a woman has no control over her body and sexuality. Her body is considered as the 'property' of her husband.

There was a shocking incident reported last year where a minor girl was sexually exploited by over 100 men including her own father. In another case, an alcoholic husband 'loaned' his wife to a friend for Rs. 15,000.[9] Selling of women's bodies takes place both in the sex industry and outside. A sophisticated form of selling women's bodies takes place in and through the advertising agencies and companies. Their bodies are used either in full or by part in order to sell various products. The mass media projects women as sex objects, models of physical beauty, and victims of violence, powerless, homebound, docile and sexy.

Apart from the explicit and open gender discrimination, one can also observe the hidden face of gender discrimination that exists in our society. Verbal and non-verbal gestures often belittle girls/women both at home and outside. The burdening of girl's/women's bodies with multiple roles/tasks[10] results in irreparable damage to their health and psyche. Often the day-to-day representations and programmes provide visibility and voice to men while women are kept invisible and silent. The suffering and condemnation endured by victims of rape and trafficking, unwed mothers and widows cause lifelong psychological harm. There are traditions and norms that deny women decision-making right or freedom of choice in the day-to-day affairs and social mobility,[11] and on areas of great significance in their life.[12] All these limit the space women have to function as makers of their own destiny. The increasing incidence of mental illness, especially depression, which women suffer, is a result of overt and hidden acts of abuse they undergo.[13]

The Heterogeneous Nature of Women Devaluation

The devaluation, oppression and denial of rights are not uniform among different groups of women in India. Approximately around 16 per cent of the Indian population come from Dalit origins. Dalit women experience triple oppression due to their caste, class and gender. In a survey conducted among the Catholic Dalit women in Tiruvallur district, Tamil Nadu, 21 per cent of the respondents said that they experienced deprivation because they were girls. 10 per cent experienced rejection as their parents used to scold them just because they were born as girls.[14] 'To be a Dalit woman is a great calamity in Indian society', says Kumud Pawde.[15] The conversation I had with Sumathi, a thirty-eight year old married woman echoes similar sentiments. When she was asked whether she ever complained to God for creating her as a Dalit woman she said,

> Yes, so many times. You see Jesus suffered only three hours on the cross. Do you know how many 'three hours' I have finished so far! I often ask God why God created me as a woman. God could have created me as a small worm, a small bird or any other small creature, so that I could have been swallowed up by other animals![16]

A few years back two Dalit widows in Dhanbad were forced to swallow human excreta by the villagers who blamed them for being responsible for an outbreak of chicken pox.[17] In another incident, a teenaged Dalit girl was set on fire in her house in Bamanpur village, Kanpur for resisting a rape bid.[18] Kalavati, a middle-aged widow from a backward community has been forced to wear a garland made of shoes and paraded naked with her face blackened on the streets of a Jharkhand village, as she dared to enter a Kali temple.[19] In Bihar two Dalit women were gang raped at Lakhanpur Sonedipi village.[20] All the above atrocities are symptomatic of how devalued Dalit women are in this country.

Causes of Oppression and Devaluation

Various factors contribute towards the present situation of women. Some of these can be traced to socio-economic, religio-cultural, psycho-political spheres. Over and above, patriarchal values and attitudes seem to have penetrated deep into almost all structures and systems of our society. Many prejudices against women are due to this internal colonization of men and women by the patriarchal value system. The patriarchal system has inculcated many unquestioned assumptions such as 'woman is weaker than man', 'woman is inferior to man', 'Woman is the property of man', etc., into the society. The value systems implicit therein and communicated through social conditioning make women accept their ascribed inferior status in society. It is this mental process which is at the root of socio-economic exploitation of women. Religion too is used as a powerful weapon to sustain and perpetuate anti-women practices. Almost all scriptures, including the Bible, are used to keep women in a subservient condition.

For women all over the world, patriarchy has become the most important analytical model for understanding the situation of women. It is an organization of society which is based on a false relationship, i.e. on domination. This system hampers the development of all people, especially women, it stands on several connected pillars—racism, sexism, classism, militarism, and ecological destruction.[21] In spite of the progress India has made in many areas including higher rate of literacy and education, our society continues to be under the grip of patriarchy to a large extent. The culture of patriarchy consists of all those ideas, norms, traditions, beliefs and values that uphold men and downgrade women. Women are still considered to be biologically, intellectually and spiritually inferior to men in spite of the fact that a considerable number of women today have entered the public domain.[22] The ideas and beliefs about women's inferiority and men's superiority are transmitted from one generation to the next, from one cultural group to another through language, gestures and postures and audio visual images and symbols. Further, in a patriarchal social order all social structures and institutions are based on non-participation or peripheral participation of women in decision-making and governance in the family and society which includes the public sphere of economy, polity, education, media, religion and civil society.[23]

Through the process of gendering or socialization, boys and girls are formed to manifest the characteristics assigned to them by society.[24] Men and women who are products of patriarchy in turn become the vehicles of patriarchy. In modern society, mass media channels such as newspapers, magazines, films, film songs, television programmes and advertisements, play a major role in transmitting stereotyped notions and beliefs about women and men. Often without understanding this process of patriarchal genderization and internalization of patriarchy, women are blamed for sustaining patriarchy, through son-preference, gender discrimination in homes and communities. They are blamed as being the worst enemy of women. This is another game or strategy of patriarchy, the strategy of blaming the victim who has been turned into a perpetrator of gender discrimination.[25]

Religion is often used as a weapon to reinforce the subjugation of women. When we look at Hinduism we see that during the Vedic Age there were eminent female scholars, poets and teachers.[26] But by the time of the lawgivers the literate woman had become almost an anathema. Manu decreed that women had no right to study the Vedas. According to *Manusmriti* a woman must not be independent at any stage of her life. In the *Bhagavad Gita* women are lumped together with sinners, slaves and outcasts.

> They had come to be regarded as intrinsically evil, spiritually contaminate, poisoning by their very presence, and obstacles to salvation. . . . Women, according to the texts, are the root of all evil and suffering. Behind even the most innocent exterior there is a raging passion of lust, since they are beings of insatiable sexual appetite.[27]

Islam strongly advocates the *purdah* system. The Koran explicitly stresses the superiority of men over women. 'And they (women) have rights similar to those (of men) over them in kindness, and men are a degree above them' (2: 228). And again, 'Men are in charge of women, because Allah hath made the one of them to excel the other . . .' (4: 34). Men and women are not held to be socially equal by Islam. Down to the present time, for example, the evidence of two women is considered equivalent to that of one man in countries with Islamic law. Women are not socially independent in Islam, but legally need a man to act on their behalf. A woman's share of inherited property is less. Under Islamic law, she inherits half of what the male members of the family receive.

When it comes to the question of women and how they are portrayed in Biblical texts, theological articulations, Christianity too is not very different from other religious traditions. Feminist analysis points out that the Christian churches and theologies perpetuate women's inferiority through their institutional inequalities and theological justifications of women's innate differences from men.[28] Christian ethics impede the development of self-assertion and autonomy of women by making them internalize certain 'feminine' passive attitudes like meekness, humility, submission, self-sacrifice, self-denying love, etc.[29] Since women cannot be ordained as ministerial priests in the Catholic church, they are denied the full participation in ecclestial life. Christian faith affirms that women are created in the image and likeness of God, redeemed in and through Jesus Christ, and they are sanctified by the Holy Spirit. Yet this basic affirmation of the Bible is not actualized in the reality of the church life. On the contrary, women are forced to accept their inferior status within the church. The Biblical and theological portrayal of women in a subordinate position reinforces in women as well as in men the value systems of a patriarchal society.

Historical studies and hermeneutical discussions have amply demonstrated that theology is a culturally and historically conditioned endeavour. Not only theology but also the revelation of God in Scripture is expressed in human language and shares culturally conditioned concepts and problems. Feminists have pointed out time and again that scripture as well as theology is rooted in a patriarchal-sexist culture and shares its biases and prejudices. Moreover scripture and theology express truth in a sexist language and images and participate in the myth of their patriarchal-sexist society and culture.[30] Radical feminists point out that the Christian past and present, and not only its records, victimized women. 'Tradition is a source not only of truth but also untruth, repression, and domination. Christian traditions and theologies in fact stimulated and perpetuated violence, alienation, and oppression.'[31]

Responses to Women's Oppressive Situation

Since women suffer multilayered oppression, the response to this situation requires a multi-pronged approach. Depending on the type of analysis a particular group makes of the oppressive situation, the response too becomes diversified. For instance, Marxist feminists trace the oppression of women to their economic dependency on men. Therefore they work towards the economic empowerment of women. The liberal feminists work towards attaining equal opportunities for women in every field since they trace the oppression to the unequal treatment of men and women in the society. In a similar way social feminists work for the social empowerment of women. Religious feminists try to reinterpret their respective scriptures and theological articulations in such a way as to affirm the full humanity of women. It is important at this juncture to have a glimpse of the women's movement in India and what they have been able to achieve in the past decades towards the empowerment of women in India.

Women's Movement in India

Women's movement in India is rich and vibrant which has taken different forms in different parts of the country. Many of the positive initiatives of the state have been taken as a result of forceful arguments of the women's movement in the country.[32] Women activists play a crucial role in publicizing women's issues and lobbying for changes. Much of women's earlier engagements were born as part of popular struggles. For example, the women *satyagrahis* who defied the police during the British Raj, or the peasant women fighting for land reform did not emerge from a strictly feminist consciousness. But these attempts did help in politicizing women and to some extent to feminize the polity.

The first wave of contemporary women's movement can be traced back to the pre-Independence period. Women were part of the freedom movement both as volunteers and leaders.

Women set up the Prayag Mahila Samiti way back in 1909. Later many organizations like the Women's Indian Association (WIA) 1917, the National Council of Indian Women (NCIW) 1926 and All India Women's Conference (AIWC) 1927 began as voices against women's oppression. Even the issue of women's franchise was first raised in 1817, during the freedom movement.[33] Recalling her life as a Telengana activist in the late 1940s, Dayani Priyamvada describes that moment thus: 'When we left home and stepped out, braving all this, we did so in the faith that there was a good future, a fine society coming in which all of us would live really well. We dreamt that in families there would be no such thing as women bending before men.'[34]

The second wave of women's movement started in the late 1960s till the mid-1980s. This era saw the emergence of widespread grassroot movements all over India. The emphasis at this time was more on economic and social rights of women. On the whole five themes have dominated this post-Independence women's movement: the struggle for legal reforms; the struggle against violence; the struggle for political participation and social reform; and the struggle to change ways of seeing.[35] Way back in 1931, it was women like Muthulakshmi Reddy of the AIWC who had proposed a resolution urging that a measure to 'amend the present state of Hindu Law relating to women to make it equitable' be taken. Later this was introduced as the Hindu Code Bill in the Constituent Assembly of 1948 and eventually passed in a staggered fashion and the Hindu Marriage Act of 1955, the Hindu Succession Act, the Hindu Adoption and Maintenance Act and the Hindu Minority and Guardianship Act, all of 1956, became the laws of the land. In fact, most of the legislation concerning women from the 1970s onward was a response to mass campaigns of protest by women's movement.[36]

The Mathura Rape Case was something of a watershed in the Indian women's movement. Besides creating awareness about society's hypocrisy and the state's tacit collusion with them, it did bring home to women the need to organize themselves. As a result many women's organizations came up in different parts of the country like Mumbai's Forum against the Oppression of Women set up in January 1980, and Saheli in Delhi, founded as a counselling unit for women in distress. The Stri Mukti Andolan Sampark Samiti of Maharashtra was the collective of 30 women's groups who collected 10,000 signatures on a petition calling for the reviewing of the Mathura Rape Case. Similarly, in the south groups like Stree Shakti Sanghatana of Hyderabad and Vimochana of Bangalore filed an appeal in the Rameeza Bee Rape Case and were granted for the first time, the *locus standi* to move a court in a rape trial. The Chhatra Yuva Sangharsh Vahini of Bodh Gaya was a rural based women's organization which struggled for land rights for women. Later they also took up the issue of wife-beating.

A third wave emerged in late 1980s linking women's issues with environment. They focused more on alternative strategies of development. The Chipko (to hug) movement came about through a process of awareness building in the early 1970s. Twenty-seven women of Rani village in the Chamoli district of then Uttar Pradesh resorted to hugging trees that grew in the local forest to prevent them from being axed by timber contractors. For the past couple of decades, under the leadership of Medha Patkar, the Narmada Bachao Andolan is struggling against a certain model of development which displaces whole communities and puts their future in peril.

The 1974 Status of Women Committee Report not only urged the setting up of statutory women's *panchayats* at the grassroots but also encouraged many Indian scholars to study women's situation more closely. Women's studies have contributed greatly in critically examining society for its sexist and patriarchal biases. Further, they present a powerful critique of patriarchy and its manifestations especially in gender relations in our society. Women's studies try to transform the perceptions and attitudes of people and to inspire their involvement in women's struggles and movements. Women's studies further aim at making women visible in history. They challenge mainstream historiography which ignored women's contribution in different spheres of society and public life, economists who have omitted women's unpaid work from official records, and sociologists who talked about women only in relation to marriage, family and kinship. Women's studies are the 'intellectual arm' of the women's movement.[37]

Thus, women's movements in India are dynamic in character and strength. They have intervened in every significant field, be it women's education, food security, shelter, violence against women, management of natural resources, legal rights or economic and political opportunities for women. Women's movements have significantly contributed to the transformation of society and Indian mentality. It has also influenced certain government policies. At the same time one cannot be complacent.

There are also serious weaknesses found in women's movements in India. Some groups do more harm by reinforcing traditional understanding of women and sex roles. To a great extent, women's movements remained middle class and urban based. There is much competition, fragmentation and even division among women's groups. Many women's groups are dependent on subsidies from the government or are dependent on foreign funds. Today women's movements stand dispersed and it lacks a clear orientation, direction and organization. A well organized movement is the need of the hour.

Feminist Theology

For women with a feminist consciousness and who are followers of Jesus Christ, articulating the Christian understanding of God, the world, the humans, etc., from the standpoint of women is pertinent for affirming the full humanity of women. Such articulations are termed as feminist theology. In other words, feminist theology is not a separate 'ladies' theology. It is not primarily a reflection on 'feminine' themes in theology or a sub-category of theology. Rather it arises from a recognition that traditional theology had been done primarily by males. Women, until recently have been excluded from this study. As a result, traditional theology suffered from an androcentric and misogynist bias. Feminist theology arises as a critical response to this bias in the tradition. It is a recently recognized type of theological reflection. It is theology from women's perspective, arising from their particular experiences. In this process of theologizing, feminist theologians ask critical questions with respect to all endeavours of doing theology. It looks at a wide range of themes in Christian theology and the language that used to discuss them. It invites the readers to rejoice in the diversity of voices in today's theological landscape. It shows how theology done by the whole body of Christ cannot ignore the human bodies of women and men if it wants to be true to Christ incarnate.

There are many feminist theologies. In the 1970s and 1980s, the work of Black American and Latin American theologians made clear that there were indeed different 'worlds' within the one world. Doing theology has to take place where people live and advocate issues that arise from their particular lives. Liberation theologians for instance, advocated a change in perspective which requires the theologians to ask how justice can be done through theology and through the life of the church. Feminist theologians on the other hand argued that something else was missing from the agenda of theology: theology overlooked the existence and the lives of *women*. They also made clear many of the ways that this sacred discipline had been used as an instrument to silence and oppress women. Not only women's experience denigrated or excluded as a source of theological reflection, but women were forced to assume a 'male' perspective if they wanted to be involved in the task of doing theology.

Feminist theology questions some of the premises of conventional theology which did not permit the full humanity of women. It questions the patriarchal appropriation of scriptures and traditions and the distortions that have entered into the theological, liturgical (hymns and prayers) and canonical sources. It also questions the biological essentialism which leads to the prioritization of the mother and wife roles of women to the exclusion of her other roles and responsibilities in the society. In addition, Feminist theologians have sought to unearth the dimensions of theology that have elements of liberation. They criticize the perceptions that see women's role as being complementary to men's; concentration of leadership or decision-making roles in the hands of men and the allocation of roles in church-based institutions where women are given the subordinate roles or are the lowly paid workers. In short, feminist theology seeks to end the marginalization, discrimination and exclusion to which women have been subjected to in the church and in the society at large.

Theology from a feminist perspective requires critical analysis and constructive *re-reading and re-writing* that involves a commitment to transformation. Feminist theologians analyse the situation of women in the church and society, past and present. Critical analysis is concerned with all texts, not only theological texts but all aspects of life, as they create and shape the situation of women. As a second step, feminist theologians develop new ways of reading the history of the church and all theological texts from the perspective of women. Therefore feminist theology can be defined as 'the critical, contextual, constructive, and creative re-reading and re-writing of Christian theology. It regards women—their bodies, perspectives, and experiences—as relevant to the agenda of Christian theologians and advocates them as subjects of theological discourses and as full citizens of the church.'[38] Feminist theology aims at the transformation of theological concepts, methods, language, and imagery into a more holistic theology as a means and an expression of the struggle for liberation.[39]

A feminist way of doing theology involves an awareness of the ambivalence that many of the symbols and texts within the Christian tradition create for women. It implies an ability to respond to this ambivalence, not by discarding the key symbols of Christianity altogether, but by identifying dis-empowering readings of them and constructing and proposing new readings that advocate the full humanity of women. Feminist theologians are in constant dialogue with the Christian tradition. This dialogue can take a variety of forms. Some try to reconcile Christianity and feminism by arguing that Christianity, read in the right way, advocates equality and justice in the same fashion as feminism does (Leonard Swidler, Denise Lardner Carmody). Other feminist theologians advocate a radically new reading of Christian theology. This new reading understands women's experiences and the full humanity of women as the criterion by which all theology has to be judged (Rosemary Radford Ruether and Elisabeth Schussler Fiorenza). Fiorenza argues that the Bible can no longer be understood as the authoritative source for women, as an archetype of Christian belief, but must rather be seen as a resource for women's struggle for liberation. The ultimate criterion by which any tradition or text is to be judged according to Ruether is whether or not it promotes the full humanity of women and thereby advocates women's struggle for liberation from male oppression.

Feminist theology takes the oppressive situation of women as its starting point. Being interdisciplinary in its approach, it unearths the factors that contribute to the negation of women's full humanity, equality and dignity. It also makes a faith reflection on the reality of women's experiences with the aim of taking steps that will restore women's dignity and rights. Keeping in line with this general trend, Indian feminist theology too begins with the oppressive and exploitative situation of Indian women in its multiple dimensions. On the whole, majority of Indian women are seen as valueless, faceless and voiceless. This experience of devaluation is not uniform but varies from group to group. For instance, a Dalit woman is devalued much more than a caste woman or a tribal woman, a non-literate woman more than an educated and employed woman, a widowed or barren woman is devalued much more than a married woman with a son, an elderly woman is devalued more than a young woman and so on. Within the church too, married women seem to be devalued more than the 'religious' women.

Scriptural and Theological Foundations

In the context of women's experience of oppression and devaluation, feminist theologians engage with the key sources of Christian theology—scripture, the history of Christian thought, and traditional approaches to doing theology. Feminist theology is concerned with reading and interpreting the scripture and the Christian tradition in the light of women's experiences. The aim of such re-reading is to uncover women's absences as well as to discover women's presence throughout the history of the Christian church and in those texts the Christian church considers relevant and normative.

Having explored the salient characteristics of feminist theology, we now look at the Bible to find whether we have sufficient basis there for working towards the liberation of women. The Bible, both the Old and the New Testament, is the foundational document of our Christian faith. This faith document unfortunately contains patriarchal elements since it was written in a patriarchal culture of the time. Because of this, the Bible has been used to legitimize certain discriminatory practices against women even to this day. However, the Bible also contains critiques of patriarchy. Keeping this aside, if one looks at the Bible closely, one can see a strong emphasis on liberation and salvation throughout the Bible beginning with the exodus event which was the foundational event for the Israelites. In fact, Jewish faith was based on this experience of liberation from the bondage of slavery in Egypt.

Liberation theology has called our attention to this liberative thrust of the Bible. On the whole, the Bible proclaims a message of liberation, a message of hope, for any group that is under bondage. Yahweh said to Moses, 'I have seen the miserable state of my people in Egypt. I have heard their appeal to be free of their slave-drivers. Yes, I am well aware of their sufferings. I mean to deliver them . . .' (Ex 3: 7-8). Can Yahweh, the God of tenderness and compassion (Ex 34: 6) who heard the cry of the Israelites in Egypt, turn a deaf ear to the cry of women in distress in different parts of our country? God's desire to free the oppressed is seen at different times and in different circumstances throughout human history. The whole of prophetic literature is loud and clear about the same intention of God. For instance, Yahweh speaks through the prophet Isaiah saying, 'Take your wrong doing out of my sight. Cease to do evil. Learn to do good, search for justice, help the oppressed, be just to the orphan, plead for the widow' (Is 1: 17). Again through the prophet Amos Yahweh declares, 'I hate and despise your feasts. . . . I reject your oblations. . . . But let justice flow like water, and integrity like an unfailing stream' (Amos 5: 21-4). God made known God's preferential love and care for the weak and the oppressed, the widows and orphans throughout the Bible and it reaches a climax when God sent Jesus into our midst with the same message.

The central message of Jesus was about the Reign of God. Jesus through his words and deeds gave expression to this reality. He began his ministry saying, 'The time has come and the kingdom of God is close at hand. Repent, and believe in the Good News' (Mk 1: 15). In order to become partakers and collaborators of God's reign, the first condition is *metanoia* or repentance, a turning away from all that is against the design God has for humanity. And God's plan is nothing but fullness of life for all (Jn 10: 10). Wherever this life is negated, diminished, violated, it is God's purpose for humanity that is being thwarted. God created human beings in his own image and likeness, male and female, and entrusted them with the responsibility of taking care of the earth and all that is in it (Gen 1: 26-7). Wherever this God given dignity, equality and co-responsibility are denied for women, there is a deliberate distortion of God's intentions for humanity. And the only way to believe in the Good news proclaimed by Jesus is to come to that realization that I, as an individual, am part of the sinful structures that oppress and deny life for many, especially the women in this country.

In the Gospel of Luke, Jesus, quoting prophet Isaiah, declares his mission as preaching good news to the poor and liberty to the captives (Lk 4: 16-19). Jesus came to liberate us from all that binds humanity. Through his words and deeds he revealed that God desires freedom, justice, equality and fullness of humanity for all. The church, the body of Christ, is entrusted with the same mission of furthering the reign which Jesus inaugurated and lived it through his words and deeds. As followers of Jesus each Christian is invited to the same work of Jesus. It is to build a society where the values associated with the reign of God such as equality, fellowship, peace, love, forgiveness, freedom, etc., are given concrete expressions in all the structures and systems of society and the church.

Anyone who is a genuine follower of Jesus cannot ignore God's preferential option for the poor and God's desire for justice in the world. The present situation of women in the church and in society indicates that women are denied justice, dignity and equality at various levels. Working for gender-justice therefore is a Gospel imperative for every Christian as long as women are victims of injustice and violence. The synod of 1971 acknowledges that working for justice indeed is a new form of evangelization.

WOMAN CREATED IN THE IMAGE OF GOD

In the book of Genesis we read, 'God created man in his image, in the image of God he created him, male and female he created them' (Gen 1: 27). Human beings are male and female, which underscores sexual bi-polarity as an essential part of being human. Individual human beings exist as man and woman, equal in dignity, called to be in communion, created as such by God in accord with his design. In the Hebrew thought, it was the whole human person who was the image of God, the whole race, both male and female. This unique Israelite idea conveys that all persons occupy a pre-eminent place in the created world. Unlike myths that showed human persons as slaves of God, here they were representatives of and witnesses to God's power and love toward all creation. Both man and woman share this responsibility and this greatness. Both bring God's touch to the world. Therefore anything that goes against this God-given dignity of woman needs to be countered at all costs.

WOMEN IN THE BIBLE

Though the Bible gives images of women who were victims of a patriarchal culture, it does not stop there. There are many instances where the Bible critiques patriarchy which confines women just to wives' and mothers' roles. We come across some powerful narratives in the Old Testament which call our attention to how women and men were created as equal partners in the divine plan; how God intervened on the side of the victimized, in the case of Hagar (Gen 21: 8-21), in the case of Susannah (Daniel 13), in the case of Hannah (1 Sam 1); how women have played pivotal and dynamic roles in the case of Moses' birth (the midwives, Shiprah and Puah, Moses' mother and sister, the Pharaoh's daughter); how they have been lawgivers and rulers in the case of Deborah, Judith and Esther. There are also women who played key roles in salvation history like Sarah or Ruth, women as prophetesses and leaders, industrious women, women missionaries, evangelists, social workers and supporters. And in the New Testament, Mary, the simple Galilean woman plays a unique role in bringing about the historical presence of Jesus through her fiat.

The Bible speaks of powerful personalities like Deborah who played the role of a charismatic leader in Israelite society. She was the wife of Lappidoth. She served as a prophet and judge, sitting under a certain palm-tree between Ramah and Bethel in the hill-country of Ephraim. She proved to be a fearless leader and a motivator giving courage to break against mighty foes and led her people to victory (Judges 4). Moreover, the people of Israel celebrated their victories through the songs of their women who came out in joy with their dances and songs. It was like a liturgical celebration. We still remember and make use of Miriam's (Ex 15: 21) and Deborah's songs (Judges 5). There are other women like Hannah (1 Sam 2: 1-10) and Judith (Judith 16: 1-17) who praised God and interpreted God's action in history through their songs. Mary's song of Magnificat continues that same tradition (Lk 1: 46-55).

In the New Testament, Jesus gave great importance to women to the extent of going contrary to the usual Jewish traditions. He took note of the poor widow (Mk 12: 41-4), reached out in compassion to the widow who lost her only son (Lk 7: 11-17), allowed an 'impure woman' to touch him by brushing aside the Mosaic law that declared women impure during menstruation and child birth (Mt 9: 20-2), entered into an intimate dialogue with the Samaritan woman (Jn 4), heard the plea of the Syro-Phoenician woman (Mk 7: 24-30), accepted the hospitality of Martha and Mary (Lk 10: 38-42), allowed women to minister to him and to his disciples (Lk 8: 1-3), befriended Mary Magdalene (Jn 20: 1-18) and felt compassion for the women of Jerusalem (Lk 23: 27-32). While most of the apostles 'forsook him and fled', Mary and other women stood by him even at the cross (Jn 19: 25-7). Mary Magdalena was one of the first to meet the risen Christ, the first to carry the message of resurrection to the rest of the disciples.

Situating the teachings and actions of Christ in the context of Palestinian Judaism, we see how the evangelists not only highlight Jesus' concern for women, but also his radical re-defining of their place and role in their society. In a culture where women were seen only in relation to men, Christ not only liberated them from their oppressive traditions but upheld their dignity. Moreover, Jesus used the life-experiences of women to explain the mystery of God's reign and God's forgiving love. For instance, Jesus compares the mystery of God's reign to a woman mixing the yeast with flour (Mt 13: 33) and a woman experiencing birth pangs (Jn 16: 21). The woman who searches for the lost coin (Lk 15: 8-10), in fact symbolizes God who is in search of sinners.

St. Paul reiterates the baptismal equality of men and women in Gal.3:28 and continues to refer to many exemplary women. The early Christian community was sustained by the deep faith of women who shared in the apostolic ministry. We find women extremely active in the missionary effort for sharing the Good News, as deacons (Rom 16: 1; Tim 3: 11), prophets (1 Cor 11: 5, 14: 34-6; Lk 2: 36-8; Acts 21: 9), presiders, fellow workers (Rom 16: 3; Phil 4: 3), preachers and evangelists (Rom 16: 6, 12). In Paul's long list of greetings, women feature prominently. He mentions, for example, Prisca, Mary, Junia, Typhosa, Typhaena, Persis, and Julia. Prisca risked her life for the Good News. Mary worked hard. Junia served as an apostle. Typhaena, Typhosa, and Persis laboured without counting the cost. Phoebe carried the letter to the Romans.

WOMEN IN CHURCH TEACHINGS

The Catholic church too has made numerous declarations concerning the equality and relationship between women and men at different times. Pope John XXIII reflected the concern of the church for women in his encyclical saying, 'Since women are becoming ever more conscious of their human dignity, they will not tolerate being treated as mere material instruments, but demand rights befitting a human person both in domestic and in a public life'. And again 'Man and woman are called to work in a relationship of equality towards the attainment of universal good' (*Pacem In Terris* No. 41). The second Vatican Council on various occasions dared to wipe aside the many layers of patriarchal dominance of the church in order to give concrete expression to the egalitarian message of Jesus. For example, Vatican II in its Pastoral Constitution, condemns any form of discrimination when it says, 'Every type of discrimination, whether social or cultural, whether based on sex, race, colour, social condition, language or religion, is to be overcome and eradicated as contrary to God's intent' (*Gaudium Et Spes*, 1965, no. 29). Moreover, it gives a few glimpses of models of a collaborative church where gender justice can be put in place.

Pope John Paul II in his Apostolic letter, *Mulieris Dignitatem*, on the dignity and vocation of women, affirms the 'essential equality of men and women since both of them—the woman as much as man—are created in the image and likeness of God'. He further states, 'Both of them (man and woman) are equally capable of receiving the outpouring of the divine truth and love in the Holy Spirit. Both receive His salvific and sanctifying 'visits'. Further, Pope John Paul II in His appeal to Ecclesial communities, States and international institutions, urged everyone to make every effort to ensure that women regain full respect for their dignity and role; to make effective and intelligent campaign for the promotion of women, concentrating on all areas of women's life; to examine the past with courage, to work in a convincing manner so that the widest possible space be opened to women in the economy, politics and in the life of the church.[40]

Conclusion

The strong emphasis on social justice and liberation in the Bible and Jesus' proclamation of the Reign of God urges every Christian to further God's reign. In a situation of oppression and discrimination that women experience, it is the Gospel imperative that the church as a community and each baptized Christian work towards establishing a society which is gender just and gives space for women to develop their full humanity as intended by the Creator God. Feminist theology came into existence in order to respond to the oppressive situation of women both in the church and society. Over the past few decades feminist theology has made a considerable impact on the way of theologizing and the interpretation of scriptures. Though women of Dalit origins are victims of triple oppressions, their experiences do not find adequate space in feminist theology at the moment. Indian feminist theology in the future therefore needs to take this lack seriously and work towards an inclusive feminist theology where voices of women from the deprived communities like Dalits and tribals find more space and attention. Indian feminist theology also needs to take cognizance of the many grassroots women movements in the country and join hands with them in creating a safe space for women where they can live in harmony with the rest of creation.

NOTES

1. See Leelamma Devasia and V.V. Devasia, 'Women in India: Equality, Social Justice and Development,' Indian Social Institute, New Delhi, 1990, pp. 3-4.
2. John Desrochers, 'The Women's Movement', in John Desrochers, Bastiaan Wielenga and Vibhuti Patel (eds.), *Social Movements Towards a Perspective,* Bangalore: Centre for Social Action, 1991, p. 122.
3. See *The Pioneer,* New Delhi, 12 April 2012, p. 7.
4. See K.C. George, 'No More Daughters', in *Indian Currents,* vol. XXIV, issue no. 09 (20-6 February 2012): 26-9.
5. For instance *The Hindustan Times* reports the following: Pregnant woman raped in Bihar by two employees of a government hospital, 8/4/2008; 'Call centre staff molested'—A young girl returning home with her colleague was pulled inside a car and molested by a group of six men in Delhi, 31/3/2008; 'Uproar in Bihar assembly over thrashing of woman'—The opposition created an uproar in the Bihar assembly over an incident in which a woman was mercilessly beaten and her head tonsured in Adalchak Dumaria village, 28/3/2008. *The Times of India* reports the following: 23 year-old woman gang raped in Pune; Kolkata teacher molests school girl; 14-year-old raped by minor friend; dowry angle to death—20/2/2008; Husband, in-laws detained in dowry death case—24/2/2008; Doctors rape minor in Bihar—21/2/08; 19-year-old alleges rape by cleric—27/3/08; Drugged, raped and left to die —14/3/08; Man held for using nude

photos to blackmail—26/3/08; Man agrees to buy wife back to save her from flesh trade—30/3/08; Orissa speaker faces sexual abuse charge—27/3/08.

6. Among agricultural labourers in Tamil Nadu, it was found that while men's work hours was 10, it was 16 hours or more for women and while men took bath daily, women could bathe only once a week.
7. In this connection the noted economist Amartya Sen speaks about the many faces of gender inequality in India. He identifies seven gender inequalities, namely, mortality inequality, natality inequality, basic facility inequality, special opportunity inequality, professional inequality, ownership inequality and household inequality. See Amartya Sen, 'Many Faces of Gender Inequality', *Frontline*, November 2001.
8. See, Aarti, 'Women in Unsafe Mode', in *Indian Currents*, vol. XXIV, no. 10 (27 February–4 March 2012): 30-1.
9. Ibid.
10. For instance, housework, marital duties, child bearing, employment, community building work, caring of the elderly and sick.
11. For example, even to meet relatives and friends the woman needs husband's permission.
12. For example, marriage time, marriage partner, number and spacing of children, education, work, use of one's income/earnings, etc.
13. See Rita Noronha, 'Empowerment of Women in the Church and Society,' in *VJTR*, vol. 72, no. 6 (June 2008): 402-47.
14. Thresiamma Thomas, 'Women and Rituals: A Critical Inquiry into the Religio-Cultural Practices of Catholic Women of Dalit Origin in Tiruvallur Dist., Tamil Nadu', Doctoral thesis submitted to the University of Madras, Chennai, under the guidance of Felix Wilfred, August 2007, pp. 73-4.
15. Kumud Pawde, 'The Position of Dalit Women in Indian Society', in James Massey, ed., *Indigenous People: Dalits, Dalit Issues in Today's Theological Debate*, Delhi: ISPCK, 1994, p. 143.
16. In personal communication with Sumathi, from Tirupassur—18/2/2006.
17. See *The Times of India*, 7/4/2008.
18. See ibid., 4/4/2008.
19. See ibid., 5/4/2008.
20. See ibid., 5/2/2008.

21. See Jana Opocenska, 'Feminist Theology', *Indian Journal of Theology*, 37/2, (1995): 40-6 at 43.
22. There are four women chief ministers besides having a woman as the president of the ruling party. There are women serving as CEOs, top bureaucrats, ministers, professionals, etc.
23. See Noronha, op. cit., pp. 402-47.
24. Indian society has different socialization for girls and boys, making boys masculine and aggressive, while girls are socialized to become docile and self-sacrificing. Such socializing harms both the groups.
25. See Noronha, op. cit., pp. 402-47.
26. Benjamin Walker, *Hindu World: Encyclopedic Survey of Hinduism*, vol. II, New Delhi: Munshiram Manoharlal, 1968, p. 603.
27. Ibid., p. 604.
28. Georgia Masters Keightley in one of her articles examines contemporary feminist scholarship on issues in theological anthropology and explores traditional interpretations of woman's nature, the long standing tendency to justify woman's social inferiority on the grounds of her 'natural' inferiority and the complete oversight of the area of woman's experience. See Georgia Masters Keightley, 'The Challenges of Feminist Theology', *Horizons* 14/2 (1987): 262-282.
29. See Elisabeth Schussler Fiorenza, 'Feminist Theology as Critical Theology', in *Theological Studies*, 36/4 (December 1975): 608.
30. Ibid., p. 611.
31. Ibid., p. 612.
32. See Meena Anand (ed.), *Dalit Women: Fear and Discrimination*, Delhi: Isha Books, 2005, p. 159.
33. See Bharti Chhibber, Women's Movements and Struggle for Equality through Socio-Political and Legal Reforms', in *Women's Link*, vol. 14, no. 3 (2008): 42-8 at 43.
34. 'We were Making History, an Oral Account', quoted by Pamela Philipose, 'Fighting for Change: Fifty Years of the Women's Movement', in Shanta Serbjeet Singh and Jyoti Sabharwal (eds.), *The Fiftieth Milestone: A Feminine Critique*, New Delhi: Sterling, 1998, pp. 49-50.
35. Pamela Philipose, 'Fighting for Change: Fifty Years of the Women's Movement', p. 51.
36. Ibid., p. 52.
37. John Desrochers, 'The Women's Movement', p. 123.

38. Natalie K. Watson, *Feminist Theology,* Grand Rapids, Michigan/ Cambridge, U.K.: William B. Eerdmans Publishing Company, 2003, p. 2.
39. Ibid., p. 3.
40. Pope John Paul II, *Letter to Women,* no. 6.

PART III

CHRISTIANITY IN INDIA: AN APPRAISAL

6

Catholic Church and Dalit-Tribal Movements in India

S. LOURDUSWAMY

Dalits in India

The caste system survived for centuries because the religious leaders transmitted this false theory through the Hindu scriptures to the common people and attributed the caste system to divine ordinance. Any violation of this system individually or collectively, was tantamount to breaking the divine law. Painstakingly, every dimension of caste was included in the scriptures. The caste system having thus been sanctioned by scriptures came to be accepted even by the outcastes themselves.

Untouchability has been practised in the Hindu society for almost three millennia. Various reasons are given justifying the practice. The main causes were the obsession of the Brahmins to maintain purity and to avoid being polluted. Endogamy is the essence of the caste system. Brahmins introduced an elaborate system to preserve their purity. They married among themselves and if they had sexual relations with a woman of a lower caste like the Kshatriyas, Vaishyas or Shudras, the progeny was not entitled to the privileges. In order to maintain the purity all relations with lower castes were proscribed.

Those who opposed the Brahminic religion or rebelled against the caste system were branded as untouchables and thrown out of the society. Initially, *Dasas* and *Nagas* who opposed the Aryan invaders were looked down upon as inferior people because they had been vanquished. *Dasas* in ancient Sanskrit, language of the Brahmins, meant slaves, when they had been completely subjugated.

Some theories of the Origin of Dalits were expressed by sociologists E.R. Leach, in *The Aspects of Caste in India, Cylone, Northwest Pakistan*, L. Dumont in *Homo Hierarchicus*, and G.S. Ghurye in *Race and Caste*. These included (i) unclean menial occupation, (ii) impure, (iii) intermixture of the four *varnas*, (iv) social ostracism due to mixed marriage between Brahmin women and Shudra males, (v) subjugation after military defeat of invaders; (vi) economic exploitation and (vii) religious sanction by upper caste, etc.

Though untouchability was related to the caste system this system came to be prectised in a later period, probably AD 200-700. Manu codified and defined Untouchability in *Manusmriti* (Manu's Code) AD 200-700 which is followed by the people with religious sanction. Manu's Code had been sanctified by religious scriptures later. *Manusmriti* (10: 51, 52) describes the wretched status as 'chandalas and sapakas (should be) outside the village; they should be deprived of dishes, their property (consists of) dogs and asses. Their cloth (should be) the garments of dead and their ornaments (should be) of iron and their food should be in broken dishes and they must wander about.' Later Dr B.R. Ambedkar burnt this Manu code and stressed that annihilation of the shastras, which uphold caste system, will abolish the caste system. The epics (Puranas), *Ramayana* and *Maha-bharata* narrate the stories of Sambuka and Eklavya to justify the *varna* system and its prescribed duties. Sambuka, a Shudra, was killed by Rama for doing *tapasya* (penance and meditation) which was the *dharma* of the Brahmins. Eklavya, a Dalit boy (indigenous) lost his right thumb for his skill in archery, which is assigned to the Kshatriya caste. These events portray how low castes were deprived of their human rights. The *Bhagavad Gita* also confirms that the caste system was created by God. Each caste group should fulfil their duties prescribed to them. The oppression has been continued in the Gupta period, to the Mughal period (AD 700-1700), British period (AD 1700-1947) and post-Independence period.

Dalit Movements

The history of the caste system in India is a record of a perpetual social tension and revolt against the prevailing social code. Buddhism denied the Vedic literature as divine revelation and refused to accept the social order on the basis of the caste system. Buddhism was destroyed by Hindu leaders by accommodation and Buddha was regarded as the *avatar* of Vishnu. Jainism and Vaisnavism also rejected the caste divisions. The *bhakti* poets stressed on equality and brotherhood. Guru Nanak, the founder of Sikhism rejected the caste order and established the organized fellowship (*sangat*). The Impact of Christianity and Islam was great and played a great role in the social change for equality.

Mahatma Jyotiba Phule created a forum called 'Satya Sodhak Samaj', to wipe out untouchability through a united struggle of the Shudras and the Ati-Shudras. Dr B.R. Ambedkar, the redeemer of Dalits, sacrificed his whole life for an equal society. He wrote several landmark books against caste oppression and his slogan was 'Educate, agitate and unite' the people against caste system. As a protest against untouchability and caste divisions in Hinduism he embraced Buddhism. Narayana Guru and Iyyankali in Kerala, Iyothidhasar, Rettaimalai Srinivasan, E.V.R. Periyar in Tamil Nadu, and several other leaders all over India fought against caste oppression and formed peoples movements against the system.

Though the caste system is a rigid stratification of social groups, due to emerging Sanskritization, Westernization and modernization there is mobility among the castes. The process of social change has begun. Education has brought socio-economic and cultural mobility in several areas. Constitutional safeguards, legal protection like SC/ST prevention of atrocities act are shielding them. Reservation privileges are paving way for development. Dalits are conscious of their rights and identity and assert their human dignity and equality. They are determined to regain their lost identity and make attempts to become a powerful community. In modern India Ambedkar movements, Dalit liberation movements, SC/ST employees unions and various other associations reject the unjust Brahminical order and assert their rights for liberation and empowerment.

Dalit Christian Liberation movement (DCLM), Christian Dalit Liberation Movement (CDLM) of Tamil Nadu, Karnataka Dalit Christians Federation, Kerala Dalit Christian Mahasabha, United Christian Movement of Equal Rights of Andhra Pradesh and other movements in north India also assert their equal rights in the church. They struggle to restore the image of God in them and others.

Plight of Dalit Christians

The Christian population of India in 2001 was

Total Catholic	18 million
Total Christian	24 million
Total Dalit Christian	16 million

According to the caste system that prevailed in Indian society throughout these last 3,000 years, the Dalits have been considered to be so low that they are outside all castes. Even in these modern times, they are treated as untouchables by many. Having undergone 3,000 years of slavery and discrimination, the Dalits find it nearly impossible to get out of this terrible trauma. The general situation of untouchables is miserable but it is all the more wretched in the case of those untouchables who have become Christians because they now suffer severe discrimination in two ways—in the society and as well as in the church.

Social Problems

Dalit Christians continue to live in the same segregated place, the 'Cheri, colony or slum', even two generations after becoming Christians instead of being relocated to somewhere better. They continue to work in the villages for low wages for their masters, enduring their tyranny, abuse, beatings and killings. Their wives and daughters face molestation, rape and burning of huts and killing of their children by the upper caste. Except for the wrong records in the revenue offices, a Dalit remains a Dalit in every sense of the word ethnically, lineally, racially, socially, economically, culturally, vocationally, geographically, relationally, contextually, and emotionally.

Actually, a Dalit encounters more torture and persecution now because he or she is a Christian Dalit. The masters of the Dalit cannot accept the idea of a Dalit rising into anything that can attempt to end their eternal slavery. Dalits as well as Dalit Christians are being attacked by the upper castes without any difference.

> The change of religion did not always succeed in eliminating castes. The converts carried with them their castes and occupations to the new religions. The result has been that even among Sikhs, Muslims and Christians, casteism prevails in varying degrees in practice, their preaching notwithstanding. Casteism has thus been the bane of entire Indian society, the difference in its rigidity being of a degree varying from religion to religion.
>
> (Art. 400, Mandal Case Judgment, vol. 6, no. 9, 30 November 1992, *Judgment Today*).

Psychological Problems

The Dalit Christians also suffer from very low self-image. This is due to generations of exploitation and oppression resulting in total subjugation of the Dalits. Deprivation of their human dignity leads them to a resignation to their plight, even accepting dehumanization as unchangeable and legitimizing their own existence because of the myths and beliefs foisted on them by the dominant caste culture. It leads the Dalits to a lack of self-understanding and self-respect of themselves.

None of the problems can be taken in isolation. The socio-cultural aspect, economic-political condition and personal community struggle of the Dalit Christians themselves have been taken together to understand their reality. The problems of the Dalit Christians can be classified broadly into objective and subjective factors. The objective factors are social discrimination, economic dependence, low educational level, low occupational status, absence of political support, legal disabilities, and discrimination in the church, etc. The subjective factors are the divisions and discriminations among the Dalit Christians, low self-image such as the unwillingness to change their social approach, indifference to the Dalit problem, etc., are also the causes of the condition and problems of the Dalits.

Educational Problems

The lack of economic resources for Dalit Christians is one of the main reasons for their poor literacy. The upper caste attitude towards the Dalit Christians and the low self-image of themselves are due to their poor education. The report of the Backward Class Commission of Tamil Nadu (1970) reports the following on the Dalit converts to Christianity: Chattanathan Commission Report, vol. II, p. 21.

> While there may be progress in the field of elementary education, the converts have not made much progress in the field of high school or college education as their Hindu brothers. The same spirit or renaissance which animates the Hindu Scheduled Castes has not spread to the Christian sections and that due to the absence of employment opportunities similar to those reserved for Scheduled Castes, there was no great temptation for the converts to go into higher education. It is claimed that they have not been able to make any headway to government and they stand now where the Scheduled Castes stood years ago.

Political Problems (Denial of Dalit Human Rights)

The President was empowered by Article 341(1) to extend benefits to the Scheduled Castes and races eligible for reservation and in this he is expected to enlist the castes only, not the religions. In contradiction to Article 341, he promulgated the (Schedule Caste) Order 1950 stating in Para 3 'notwithstanding anything contained in Para 2, no person who professes a religion different from Hinduism shall be deemed to be a member of the Scheduled Caste'. The order is communal and anti-constitutional because it brings in religion as a base for extending reservation. It goes against the Constitution Article nos. 15/4, 46, 330, 341, where caste factor was given as the criterion for the extension of reservation benefits.

The parliament has rectified this lacuna arising out of para 3 of the order by amending the Constitution (Schedule Caste) Order 1950 and included Dalits of Sikh religion in 1956 and Dalit Buddhists in 1990. However, Christians of Scheduled Caste origins were not included. This discrimination deprives the Christian Dalits to seek civil protection and safeguards provided for all Dalits under the Civil Rights Act 1955, Untouchability Offenses Act 1979 and Prevention of Atrocities Act 1989. This is a blatant violation and denial of the human rights of the citizen under our constitution as well as under Article 18 of the Universal Declaration of Human Rights of the UNO to which India is a signatory.

The Christian churches in India have been fighting against this unjust discrimination since the Independence of our country. Many commissions appointed by the Government of India have studied the actual situation of Dalit Christians and have concluded that the Dalit Christians suffer the same economic and social disabilities as the other Dalits. The commissions have highlighted the fact that the Dalit Christians are 'twice discriminated', both by the state and by the church. The commissions have also recommended that they are outside all castes. Even in these modern times, the elite and even the ordinary people treat them as untouchables.

But the Government of India has not taken these recommendations seriously. For the last fifteen years, the Christian communities have been appealing to the government to include the Dalit Christians in the Scheduled Caste list in order to restore their legitimate rights as assured by the Constitution. Many non-violent rallies, demonstrations and hunger strikes have been carried out to press the government to render justice. On different occasions, many delegations of different churches have met successive Presidents of India, prime ministers and other politicians to plead on behalf of the Dalit Christians. All politicians acknowledge that injustice is being done against the Dalit Christians. These politicians have made sugar-coated promises to the Dalit Christians in order to win their votes; but once in power, they have denied their rights for the sole reason that they practice Christianity, which is said to be a foreign religion. Another lame and fallacious excuse offered by the politicians is that there is no system of caste in Christianity, and therefore, the Dalit Christians cannot be suffering caste discrimination.

Catholic Church and Caste

One of the apostles of Jesus, St Thomas brought Christianity to India in the year AD 52. He preached the Gospel in Kerala and the southern part of India. The Christians were called St Thomas Christians. Christianity grew in Kerala by immigration and inter-marriage among themselves. The converts were from upper caste in Kerala. They had relationship with Mesopotamia and Syria and Chaldean Syrian Church or Syro Malabar Church. The early history of Syrian Christian Church is very scanty and several areas still remain obscure. It was the only church existing in India till the arrival of the Portuguese in 1498.

Entry of the Caste System

The Diocese of Goa was established in 1534. The Portuguese missionaries focused only on upper caste conversions believing that inferior castes would follow later. Jesuit Francis Xavier arrived in Goa in 1542 and preached in the costal areas. Mass conversions occurred on the Coromandal coast. A large number of Paravas and Mukkuvans were converted in 1535-44. These Roman Catholics followed Latin rites. This was the beginning of Dalit conversions. Jesuit Robert De Nobili came to India in 1602 and established the Roman Catholic Madurai Mission close on his heads came the great Missionaries John De Britho and Joseph Constantine Beschi who contributed a lot towards growth of the church in the seventeenth and the eighteenth centuries in India. Jesuit Missionary Robert De Nobili changed this missionary policy and followed Malabar Rite, alongwith Hindu upper caste symbols. It included acceptance of the smearing of ash or sandalwood paste on the forehead and use of Brahminical sacred thread, etc. He restricted his evangelization only to Brahmins and believed in top to bottom conversion. He was the cause for entry of the caste system into the church. He accepted the caste system of the upper caste converts. He not only introduced Dalit distinction between high caste and low caste but also separate churches. He went to the extent of dividing missionaries into Brahmin *sannyasis* who ministered to high castes and Pandaraga swamis who ministerd to the Dalits. They were following the policy of adaptation and viewing caste not as a religious factor but as a social factor within the caste system. Thus caste system entered the church from time of the early Madurai Mission.

The Society of Jesus was abolished in 1773 by Pope Clement XIV. Congregatio de Propaganda Fide (Congregation of the Evangelization of Peoples) offered the Malabar Mission (south India) to the Missionary Society of Paris (Missions Etageres de Paris) abbreviated as MEP, in 1776. Later the name of Malabar Mission was changed into the Pondicherry Mission. It was affected by the French Revolution. Mgr. Hebert the first Bishop of Pondicherry, Mgr. Bonnard and Mgr. Laouchan contributed a lot towards Dalit conversions to Christianity in the nineteenth century. Mass conversion of Dalits happened in the nineteenth and twentieth century.

MOTIVES BEHIND DALIT CONVERSION

- To regain dignity and equality
- To follow God of love and compassion
- To gain upward mobility by getting education and economic privileges
- To find solidarity in times of sufferings
- To liberate themselves from oppression.

Above all it was to realize a life of happiness here on this earth and eternal happiness promised by Lord Jesus. The struggle for realizing the above-mentioned visions is found in every stage of the history of the church in India.

In 1599 Archbishop Alexis Dom Menezes of Goa convened the Synod of Diamper in Kerala. He brought the St. Thomas Christians under Padraodo rule and made radical reforms in the church. The Malabar Rite which was following Hindu symbols and caste characteristics was suppressed and all were made to follow the Roman Catholic church. When Jesuit Missionary Robert De Nobili, the head of the Madurai Mission, introduced the Malabarian Rite again in this Mission in the seventeenth century, the Archbishop of Goa who quelled such measures among Syrian Christians, wanted to suppress such Brahmin culture, upper caste symbols and discrimination in the Roman Catholic Church, referred the matter to Rome. Robert De Nobili also appealed for the continuation of the Malabarian Rite. Thus the response of the Pope in the form of a papal Bull in 1623.

Prevalence of Caste Discrimination in the Church

The Bull of Pope Gregory XV, 'Bulla Romanae Sedis Antistes', dated 31 January 1623, accedes to the requests of the missionaries to accommodate certain caste practices and customs of the new converts. The Pope was granting this permission only as a provisional and conditional measure. It was given to the Madurai Mission as a response to the demand of Robert De Nobili

The Bull agreed to tolerate the continuance of certain traditional customs considering the difficulties encountered by the Brahmin converts if they were obliged to abandon external signs (such as sacred thread, sandal, ablutions). The Bull agreed to tolerate them since these external rites could be interpreted as signs of nobility and function (nobilities official) and also to express that the church was empathetic towards human sensibilities. However, the Bull put a condition for which a permission that the new converts avoided all dangers of superstition and showed real charity and respect towards people of obscure condition, which presumably was a reference to the Dalits. This document shows the prevalence of the caste mentality among the converts. The Pope warns the high caste Christians about their caste pride.

The Synod of Pondicherry in 1844 was convoked to foster harmony between the Dalit Christians and the caste Christians, who wanted to have a partition in the church to separate them from the Dalits. A statement was issued for equality but church attendance was boycotted till the order was restored.

In church history, one can study how the caste difference and practices have permeated even into the Christian community. For example on 15 January 1925, the Dalits Christians of Tiruchirapalli sent a memorandum to Bishop Alexius Maria Henry Lepierier, Vicar Apostolic for India, enumerating the demands of the dominant castes and the discriminations that they suffer. It states:

> The absurdity of their pretensions to enforce their distinctions of caste against us in the house of God is only matched by the arrogance with which they put them forward . . . (1) that we should forever be segregated as untouchables in the House of God, (2) that Holy Communion should be distributed to them, first and that when they have all been served, then and then only the officiating priest should carry the Sacrament to us (3) that our children under no circumstances,

be admitted in St Joseph's College Catholic Boarding House, the Convents. . . . the Holy Redeemer's School, the Seminaries and other institutions. As Catholics we demand our Catholic privilege for equal treatment in the House of God and for equal education facilities.

(H. GRAFE, *History of Christianity in India*)

The results of the research conducted by Antony Raj SJ, the president of DCLM, reveal the following discriminatory practices in the Catholic and Protestant churches in Tamil Nadu as existing in some parishes (Antony Raj, *Discrimination against Dalit Christians in Tamil Nadu*, pp. 223-4).

1. The construction of two chapels, one is for the non-Dalits and other for the Dalits. In some parishes liturgical services are conducted separately.
2. Separate seating arrangements are made within the same chapel. Dalits are usually seated in the two aisles of the Church. Even if there are benches or chairs, the Dalits are asked to take their seats on the floor.
3. The existence of two separate cemeteries and two separate hearses to carry the dead bodies are found.
4. Two separate queues are formed to receive the sacred body of Christ. In some places Dalits are asked to receive communion only after the non-Dalits.
5. It is forbidden to be an altar boy or lector at the sacred liturgy.
6. The non-Dalits restrict the Corpus Christi procession, Palm Sunday procession, and other processions only to their streets.
7. Dalits are not invited to participate in the washing of feet ceremony during Maundy Thursdays.
8. For fear of equal participation in the celebration of the parish patron saint, the parish council decides not to ask any contribution from the Dalits.
9. The feast of the village patron saint is celebrated separately.

The report of the Archbishop M. Arokiasamy (Chairman of the Scheduled Caste/Scheduled Tribe Commission) in the CBCI (1989) substantiates these discriminations against the Dalit Christians. He states:

In Tamilnadu, in the predominantly Christian villages, the Harijan colony or *cheri* is distinct and separate from the upper caste settlement, with all the civic municipal amenities, such as the hospital and school, being located in the area of caste Christians. The church in the village is cruciform (cross shaped) as in most parts of Tamilnadu and Harijan Christians are in some places required to confine themselves to one wing of the house of God. CSCO are not allowed to assist the priest or read scriptural passages during Mass and not allowed to enter the sanctuary. They are also denied participation in the church choir, when sacraments such as baptism, confirmation and marriage are being administered, the CSCO have to receive them only after the upper caste Christians have been administered the sacraments. And they are being discriminated even in death, for CSCO are allotted their own cemeteries or a different corner of the main cemetery. In some places a wall separates the CSCOs. (Most Rev. M. Arokiasamy 'Caste and Conversion' Report to G.B. of CBCI, 1989, p. 53)

The Pulaya Christians, who are poor and belong to the labour class, are often ignored and not treated equally within the Christian community. Bishop Arokiasamy stated, 'In certain dioceses of Central and South Kerala, there are pockets of Pulayas who because of their low caste origins are considered to be inferior. The Church hierarchy ignores their very existence. M. Arokiasamy, *Caste and Conversion*. Reports of the General Meeting of the CBCI, 1989, p. 53; see *Times of India* (Bengaluru, 17 September 1989).

In Andhra, as much as 90 per cent of the Protestants and 75 per cent of the Catholics are Dalits. Among them, the majority belong to the Mala and Madiga communities. The caste differences and the discriminations against the Dalit Christians by the high castes, Reddies and Kammas, is much the same as the Hindu Dalits.

In 1985, there was a Court verdict upholding the 80 year-old practice of a separate graveyard for Dalit Christians of Trichy in Tamil Nadu. But till today a wall separates the Dalit and upper caste graves.

K.K. Pudur village in Maduranthugam taluk, Chengalpattu district, 60 km away from Chennai, has a Christian population of 2,500 and among them 1,500 are Dalit Christians and the rest belong to Reddy and Naidu upper caste. Dalit Christians have been oppressed by upper caste Christians for the past 200 years, who did not give them their due place in the church and in the graveyard. Caste clash among Christians occurred on 5 July 1994 at K.K. Pudur as they were preparing for the celebration of the patron feast of St. Joseph. A police case was filed at Maduranthagam under PCR 687/94. 147. 15 148, 374, 323, 336, 452 and 307, IPC: 84. People from both sides were imprisoned and the church remained closed for 6 months.

UNTOUCHABILITY IN ERAIYUR, PONDICHERRY ARCHDIOCESE

On 15 February 1999 the funeral of a Dalit priest Fr. A.C. Irudaynathan's mother was not allowed to pass through the main street to the church by the Vanniyar Catholics. In Eraiyur of Pondicherry Archdiocese's there are separate graveyards for Dalits and caste people. Since the funereal procession led by Archbishop Michael Augustine, was prevented to go through the main street there was turmoil in Eraiyur of the Pondicherry diocese. There was a caste clash again on 10 March 2008 again at the same parish. Dalits demanded a separate parish for themselves. There was police firing and two persons were killed in the firing. On 11 March 2008 a peace committee meeting was held in the presence of T.N. minister Ponmudi. The Archbishop of Pondicherry issued a statement for equality and peace on 18 March but still equality remains a dream.

CASTE WAR CONTINUES AT THATCHOOR

Thatchoor village is located in Maduranthagam taluk, in the Kanjeepuram district of Tamil Nadu. Tamil and Telugu Catholics are residing in the same village. On 1 May 1997, there was a caste clash between the Telugu Reddiyar Catholics and Dalit Catholics due to deprivation of the equal rights to Dalit Christians in the matters of different places in the church, participation in the feast preparation, car procession to Dalit areas, etc. It resulted in the closing down of the church. A case was filed (O. S. 214/95, O.S. 66/96, O.S. 108/97, O.S. 473/97, O.S. 410/99) in Maduranthagam Sessions Court. On 2 May 2005 there was a peace committee meeting in the presence of the District Collector and the church but still the caste problem continues.

Though caste discrimination is prevalent among the Christian community, the official church has been constantly appealing to the community for brotherhood and equality in the church.

Agitation of People's Movements Against Untouchablity

Dalit Christians has been fighting against the oppression. It was a spontaneous action. There were a few Dalit Christians movements such as the South India Dalit Christian Federation, Christian Dalit Liberation Movement, Social Action Movement, Dalit Christian Liberation Movement (DCLM), United Christian Movement for Human Rights (AP), Dalit Christian Mahasakha (Kerala), National and Regional SC/ST commissions, etc., organizing agitations against discrimination and demand for equality and human dignity.

Given below is a year-wise list of the agitation:

1831: Paraiyar revolution at Pondicherry
1869: Dalit agitation at Uthamanur, Madurai district.
1880: Dalit and Udayar caste clash at the church, Pudur Madurai
1884: Synod of Pondicherry to abolish caste discrimination in the church of Pondicherry, lead by Archbishop Clement Bonnand.
1898: Dalit protest in Sivakasi.
1907: Dalit agitation against oppression in Poondy, Kumbakonam
1921: Mylapore Archbishop Rebiro Castro circular for abolition of caste discrimination.

1922: Hunger strike for equal rights in the church of Kumbakonam.

1925: Dalit agitation against caste discrimination in the Cathedral Church of Trichy.

1933: South Indian Bishops' circular on abolition of caste practice in the church.

1936: Dalit Christian rally and convention at Kumbakonam.

1937: Bishop Leonard of Trichy diocese breaking the wall of division of caste in the church.

1944: Caste clash at the church of Varadarajanpet.

1953: Caste clash and bloodshed at Athippakkam parish church, Pondicherry diocese.

1985: Court judgement against Dalit agitation for breaking the dividing wall between Dalit and other castes in the Trichy diocese cemetery.

1990: Dalit students protest against caste oppression at St. Joseph's College, Tiruchirapalli.

1994: Dalit and caste Reddys clash in the church of K.K. Pudur, Chengelpet Diocese. A case was filed and the church remained closed for six years.

1997: Dalit agitation against oppression of caste Reddys at Thatchur Parish, Chengelpet Diocese. A criminal case was filed and the church remaind closed for eight years.

1999: Dalit protest against the denial of a common graveyard to bury the mother of a Dalit priest at Eraiyur.

2003: Dalit agitation against untouchability in Pulavanbadi, Vellore Diocese.

2008: Dalit boycott liturgy and separate parish demand at Eraiyur against the practice of untouchability. Pondicherry Archbishop and Tamil Nadu minister Ponmudi made a joint declaration of establishing equality in the church.

The Church and the Development of Dalits

Statements, resolutions and action plans were proposed in the General Body Meetings of Catholic Bishops Conference of India

(CBCI) for equality and Empowerment of Dalits.

Given below are excerpts from the statement of CBCI General Body Meetings:

CBCI General Body Meeting at Tiruchirapalli 4–14 January 1982

STATEMENT ON CASTE

The Catholic Bishop's Conference of India at its general body meeting in Tiruchirapalli in January 1982, considered the question of caste and its baneful effects both on society at large as also within the church. Notwithstanding all these efforts, much remains to be done within the church and outside particularly in the eradication of what is known as the 'caste mentality' which often finds expression in actions that are manifestly unchristian and even affects, in some areas, the sphere of religious practices. The tensions arising from the caste mentality are not confined to the oppression of the lower castes by those of the higher castes but are also found within the castes themselves.

We state categorically that caste, with its consequential effect of discrimination and 'caste mentality', has no place in Christianity. It is, in fact, a denial of Christianity because it is inhuman. It violates the God-given dignity and equality of human beings. God created man in his own image and likeness. He accepts and loves every human being without distinction. He so loved the world that He sent His only Son, Jesus Christ, who became fully man and died to save all men. 'In Christ Jesus you are all sons of God . . . there is neither Jew or Greek . . . neither slave nor free. . . . For you are all one in Christ Jesus' (Gal 3, 26-8). Thus, human dignity and respect are due to every person and any denial of it is a sin against God and man. It is an outright denial of the Fatherhood of God, which in practice renders meaningless the brotherhood of man.

General Body Meeting of CBCI Kottayam, April 1988

The Bishops of India gathered at St.Thomas Apostolic Seminary in Kottayam, Kerala from 13-22 April 1988 and proposed and unanimously passed the following resolutions:

- It is resolved to inform the Government of India that the Christians of Scheduled Castes origin suffer from extreme social, educational and economic backwardness arising out of the traditional practice of untouchability.
- It is further resolved to request the Government of India to take early steps to suitably amend para 3 of the Constitution (Scheduled Castes) Order 1950 to include the Christians of Scheduled Castes origin in the list of Scheduled Castes.

CBCI Meeting at Varanasi 21-8 March 1998

The church in India particularly in recent years has been actively involved in denouncing caste system and discrimination against the Dalits. Further, it has taken positive measures for their development. However, we have to admit that the situation still remains a serious concern. The prevalence of the caste system, not only in society but also in some parts of the church in India even at the close of the twentieth century, is a matter of shame and disgrace to all of us. It is a cause of sorrow and expression of our inability to live our Christian faith adequately. It is not only a denial of human dignity and equality but is also against the fundamental teaching of Christ who was a friend of the outcastes of His time, and freely mixed with them. He came to tell mankind that we are all brothers and sisters having God as our common Father. The core of the Gospel consists in this perfect reconciliation and fellowship. The early Christians manifested their faith in Christ by being a community of love without discrimination of any member based on race, language or economic or social status. If our Christian communities are divided and discriminated on the basis of caste we cannot affirm in truthfulness that the Gospel has touched our life, and that we are the disciples of Christ even if we celebrate our worship devoutly and proclaim our faith correctly. What India needs is precisely this witness of Christian love. Our evangelizing mission loses its efficacy if our Christian communities forget this image which is specific to Christianity, for Jesus said 'By this everyone will know that you are my disciples, if you have love for one another' (John 13, 35). Hence, discrimination against anybody on the basis of caste is a sin against God and humanity. This needs to be proclaimed from the house tops so that the caste system will be removed from the Christian community totally as part of our preparation for Yesu Krist Jayanti 2000.

ACTION PROGRAMME

After listening to what the spirit was telling them the bishops recommended the following measures to be implemented in all dioceses:

- First of all there needs to be a faith-based vision that enables us to see Jesus in the poor, the Dalits and the tribals so that there is a change in our attitude towards them. This must become evident to them in our policies and practices and day-to-day interactions.
- Non-formal education to conscientize, train, organize and empower the poor. The Dalits and the tribals must be given top priority in our social apostolate.
- The church must take a clear stand against caste discrimination and declare it a sin. This must be taught in catechism and homilies and any form of discrimination must be completely stopped, wherever it exists, be it among the priests, in religious communities, in practices of selection of candidates for priesthood and religious life and in the sphere of administration. We propose this as a goal to be set in motion power-

fully and immediately so that we can present to the Lord and proclaim to the world that we are a fully reconciled and transformed Christian community at the dawn of the third millennium.

- Our liturgy should challenge us to build relationships as members of one family, and foster fellowship and solidarity, leading to active concern and equality. There should be no sign of any discrimination in places of worship, cemeteries, etc. Our liturgy should also challenge us to face the realities of the world with a sense of mission. The World of God that we celebrate should become a life-giving event for the world. Our celebrations of popular devotions such as novenas and prayer sessions should have a mission thrust.
- Our institutional services must cater increasingly to the poor and there must be reservations both in admission and in employment for the Dalits and Tribals.
- Following the example of the first Christians who shared generously with the poor, we should make personal and institutional sacrifices, whatever they may cost us, for the poor, the Dalits and the Tribals of today. Only then will we become truly the Church of the Poor. This is the New Way of Being Church that we want to usher in as we enter the third millennium.

Concerted efforts made by the church in India to uplift the oppressed Dalit Christian Community at various levels have given us a ray of hope. Regional and national Bishops' councils and conferences have declared the dignity and equality of Dalit Christians and have repeatedly condemned the practice of untouchability and discrimination as sin and have appealed to the Christian community to live in equality and brotherhood. The implementation of the 10-point programme for empowerment, and formation of leadership at different levels include intensive coaching for employment, training eligible candidates for Indian Administrative Services to commit themselves to the development of the oppressed and to a relentless struggle to demand equal rights to Dalit Christians from the government. Many students who have been trained by the Commission for SC/ST/OBC have been secured administrative and managerial jobs in the states.

10-Point Programme of TNBC

Tamil Nadu Bishop's Council and Tamil Nadu CRI declared this 10-point programmes at the General Body Meeting, at Vellore, on January 1990, for the Empowerment of Christians of Scheduled Caste Origin (CSCO).

1. In places of worship and burial grounds, Christians of Scheduled Castes origin (CSCO) should be treated with equality and there should be no discrimination.
2. Opportunities should be created in the diocese to enable CSCO to join seminaries, convents and religious congregations in large numbers.
3. In order to create leadership in their ranks, CSCO should be encouraged to become members of parish councils, parish finance committees, diocesan pastoral councils, multi-purpose social service societies and other church-related organizations, and entrusted with responsible positions.
4. In matters of admission to Catholic Teacher Training and Industrial Schools, preference should be given to the students belonging to CSCO.
5. Special coaching classes should be conducted to improve the educational standards of the students who are weak in their studies to enable them to improve their performance.
6. Preference should be given to CSCO in matters of appointment in the educational institutions, social service societies and other church-sponsored organizations and projects.
7. In the Diocesan Social Service Societies, developmental projects should be exclusively designed to promote the economic development of the CSCO and members of these

should be chosen to involve actively in the execution of such projects and in the training programmes connected therewith.

8. To encourage higher education, particularly technical and professional education among CSCOs, the diocesan and religious congregations should jointly create a scholarship fund as a source of encouragement to deserving students.
9. A SC/ST/SC Commission should be created in each diocese immediately to monitor the programme meant for these people.
10. In the CSCO struggle to obtain their rights and privilege from the central and state governments, the church in India should actively support their programme in this regard.

History of Struggle for Equal Rights

Constitution (Scheduled Caste) Order 1950 para 3 denies all constitutional rights of Dalit Christians. The Christian community have made several concerted efforts to obtain constitutional rights for Dalit Christians in India. Important events in the history of the struggle are given below:

24.10.1950: Shri G.X. Francis, President of Catholic Regional Committee of Nagpur, submitted a Memorandum to the Prime Minister Jawaharlal Nehru.

09.05.1985: Hunger strike by 2,000 people under Shri Sitaram Kesari (leadership of Bishop of Vellore Bishop Michael Augustin).

24.09.1988: A mammoth rally and *Dharmika Manadu* was organized by the church in Trichy, Tamil Nadu. Seven lakh people from all over Tamil Nadu assembled to demand extension of reservation to Christians of Scheduled Caste Origin. Ministers and members of the parliament addressed the participants, assuring to introduce the required bill in the parliament.

17.09.1990: Rally in Delhi with a delegation led by Archbishop Arokiasamy and Saral Chatterji who met Prime Minister V.P. Singh and apprised him of the plight of Christians of Scheduled Caste Origin.

May 1992: 200 Hon'ble Members of Parliament of all parties in a memorandum to the Hon'ble Prime Minister were pleased to extend statutory benefits to Christians of Scheduled Caste Origin.

10.10.1992: 8 judges out of 9 in the Mandal Case judgement have clearly stated that the Scheduled Castes carry with them all levels of caste and other disabilities even after conversion, and that the caste doesn't change with change of religion and so there should be no denial of reservations on the basis of religion.

13.08.1993: Shri V. Narayanasamy moved a Private Member Bill for the amendment of the Constitution (Scheduled Caste) in order to include Christians. The Private Member Bill moved by Narayanasamy was debated in the Rajya Sabha for eight months. The house had fruitful discussion on 13 August, 27 August, 17 December 1993, 4 and 18 March 1994.

23.08.1994: Central government published Gazette Order declaring 27 per cent job reservation for OBC (Other Backward Classes) including Scheduled Caste converts to Christianity. (No. 12011/68/93-BCC(C) 10 September 1993.)

18.11.1995: Justice-demanding programmes seeking equal rights to Dalit Christians were inaugurated at New Delhi with a solemn prayer service followed by relay fasting. The prayer service was led by Mother Teresa. The Relay Fasting was continued by Christian leaders. The media, both national and international, gave wide coverage to all these events.

21.11.1995: Closure of Christian educational institutions all over the country, as part of the on-going struggle was a grand success. 20,000 Christian schools and 240 colleges remained closed on that day expressing solidarity with the justice-seeking programmes. The nationwide closure of the education institutions had a great impact and millions came to know about the injustice to the Dalit Christians and the need for a speedy solution.

A National Coordination Committee for Dalit Christian Bishops, composed of representatives from the CBCI, National Council for Churches in India and other church related organization was formed to continue the struggle for equal rights and strengthen the confidence of the Christian community. Archbishop Alan de Lastic (CBCI), Raja Rathinam (NCCI), Fr. S. Lourduswamy (CBCI commission for SC, ST, BC), Rev. Karam Mashi, Dr. James Massey (DSP), and Bro. Jose Danial (AICUMER) were office-bearers of NCCDC.

12.03.1996: Introduction of the Amendment Bill and its defeat: The government's belated move to introduce a bill for reservation for Dalit Christians was not allowed by Lok Sabha speaker due to the procedural lapse in introducing the bill. He turned down the government's request to introduce the bill as it had not fulfilled the stipulated conditions.

20.03.96: The Ordinance proposed and rejected by the president: Constitution (Scheduled Caste) Amendment Ordinance, 1996. The President declined to promulgate the Scheduled Caste Ordinance

Amendment 1996 on the ground of constitutional propriety, stating that it might not stand the test of constitutional propriety at this juncture of the impending Lok Sabha polls.

03.10.1998: Mammoth human rights rally to demand equal rights to Dalits Christians. 5,000 youths, sporting black bands, coming from every nook and corner of India along with Religious Heads, Christian and Dalit leaders, staged a rally on 3 October 1998 in the nation's capital demanding the long pending Constitutional Rights for Dalit Christians.

16-02-2004 : The Centre for Public Interest Litigation, a body headed by the illustrious advocates Shanti Bhushan, Prashant Bhushan, etc., came forward to file a writ petition in Supreme Court for extension of Scheduled Caste rights to SC converts to Christianity. The discussion was held in the CBCI Centre. The Commission provided all the materials. The booklet written by Rev. Fr. S. Lourdusamy *Equal Rights to all Dalits* (with special reference to Dalit Christians) was given to them for the historical knowledge of relentless struggle for equal rights.

02-04-2005: A CBCI and NCDC delegation met Hon'ble Prime Minister Manmohan Singh and forcefully demanded equality for Dalit Christians.

13-04-2007: At a rally and public meeting held at Jantar Mantar. CPI Party Secretary D. Raja, CPM Party Leader Brinda Karat, Mohammed Madani MP and other ministers participated and gave assurance of support.

15.05.2007: National Commission for Religious and Minorities for Extension of Scheduled Caste Society to Christian and Muslims of Scheduled Caste origin submitted its report to the Prime Minister under the chairmanship of Justice Ranganath Misra, with the following recommendations:

1. Scheduled Caste people converted to any religion should be considered as Scheduled Caste only.
2. Change of religion does not change socio-educational status of an SC.
3. Constitution (Schedule Caste) order 1950, para 3 should be deleted to extend SC status to all SC people.

03.09.2007: A memorandum from various party leaders including Smt Mayavati, Ram Vilas Paswan, and Thiru Ma Valavan was submitted to the Prime Minister Manmohan Singh.

14.03.2008: A public meeting held in Delhi. Archbishop A.M. Chinnappa, Archbishop Peter Fernando, Bishop Neethinathan, former secretary of CBCI SC/ST Commission and more than 5,000 people along with all the party leaders except from BJP demanded justice to Dalit Christians and Dalit Muslims.

24.02.2009: A mammoth rally and a huge public meeting were held in Delhi for equal rights to Dalit Christians and Dalit Muslims.

2010: CBCI, NCCI, NCBC and all the regional commissions for SC jointly organized various demonstrations to implement the recommendation of Justice Misra Commission by extending Scheduled Caste status to Dalit Christians and Dalit Muslims.

2011: A huge rally starting from Ramlila Ground to Jantar Mantar, Delhi with 15,000 people and a mega public meeting was held and important political party leaders addressed the gathering. This demonstration focused on exerting pressure on the Government of India to render justice without delay. Congress party was accused of cheating the Christian community for the past sixty years by the act of denial of equal rights to Dalit Christians.

The Response of the Government

The successive governments have been giving assurances in and outside of the parliament to extent the statutory benefits to the Dalit Christians but they have not fulfilled it. Congress government has the moral duty to redress the long pending grievance of the Christian community in India because the unjust Constitutional SC Order of 1950 was promulgated during the Congress rule and amendment bill 1996 to include Dalit Christians in SC list was brought before parliament by the same Congress government. Even after the recommendation of Justice Ranganath Misra Commission (2007), UPA government is not willing either to respond positively to Supreme Court or render Justice by amending the order.

Tribal Movements in India

The Adivasis in south Bihar, Orissa, West Bengal, Madhya Pradesh, etc., united and fought for a separate state for Adivasis. The peoples movement succeeded in getting Jharkhand state under the movement/party Jharkhand Mukti Morcha (JMM). They declared the ownership of 'water and land and forest' and organized agitations against displacement and exploitation by aliens.

The tribal people in India have a similar historical and cultural experience as that of the Dalits. History has shown that this section of people has been treated as third class citizens. Many of the rights have been denied to them and they continue to face injustice in the form of social discrimination, oppression and economic deprivation. The tribal people of India who are referred to as Adivasis are actually the original inhabitants of this country. The Sanskrit word *adivasi* comes from *adi* meaning original or primitive and *vas*, meaning dweller or inhabitant. Therefore the tribal people as per history, are the indigenous people of India.

Thus being deprived of their indigenous identity, the tribal people in India have always been treated as outsiders with no right over their land. Many of their lands have been forcibly taken away by the state for mega projects like steel plants, hydroelectric projects or national parks. The Amendment of the Land Acquisition Act in 1984 has only empowered the state and private sectors to acquire land more easily (Kujur 2006: 256). This sort of political and economic oppression has led to the emergence of Naxalities among the tribals. But the government has deliberately denied this issue and termed it as a 'law and order problem'. Many tribal youths are recruited to fight against their own brothers and sisters (Kujur 2006: 258).

In recent years we see the rise of many subaltern groups like the Dalits, the tribals, bonded labourers, women's groups, etc. The tribals are becoming aware of the injustice done to them and they are organizing themselves to fight for justice and to redress the inequitable situation (Pinto 2006: 127).

North-east India is located in the far eastern corner of India bordering Myanmar in the east, China and Bhutan in the north, and Bangaladesh in the south. North-east India comprises seven states, often known as the seven-sister states which are home to large indigenous/tribal communities that comprise several tribes and ethnic groups with their own languages, ways of life and histories. The hill-tribes consist of various groups of the Mizo-Kuki-Chin family, Nagas, Khasis, Garos and Arunachalis and reside in the states of Mizoram, Tripura, Nagaland, Manipur, Meghalaya and Arunachal Pradesh respectively. Orissa, Bihar, Andhra Pradesh especially, most of them either belong to the Munda-speaking family or Dravidian-speaking family.

On the basis of geographical location, the tribals of north-east India can be broadly divided into two categories—hill tribes and plain tribes. Various tribes, such as the Mizo, Kuki, Chin family live in Mizoram, Manipur and Tripura. The Nagas in Nagaland and Manipur; the Arunachalis in Arunachal Pradesh, the Khasis in Meghalaya and the Garos in Meghalaya and Assam. Most of the hill tribals were Christianized in the twentieth century.

The people's movement for their right is seen in all the states of north-east India. In order to fight for their rights and to protect their land, culture and identity, the whole of north-east India is today engulfed by people's resistance movements. Some of these are given below:

1. *Naga National Council (NNC):* It is a powerful full-fledged apex political body and was formed at Wokha on 2 February 1946 and it gained political power.
2. *Mizo National Front (MNF):* The freedom movement of the tribals of Mizoram gained momentum with the emergence of the MNF in the 1960s and declared independence of Mizoram and an armed revolt was carried on.
3. *People's Liberation Army (PLA):* There are more than twenty groups of people's movements in the State of Manipur. Among them the prominent ones are the PLA, the United National Liberation Front (UNLF), the People's Revolutionary Front of Kangelipak (PREP AK), the Kuki National Front (KNF) the Kuki National Army (KNA), the Zoumi Revolutionary Army (ZRA), etc.
4. *United Liberation Front of Asom (ULFA):* In Assam the indigenous people have been reduced to a minority due to the influx of immigrants from Bangladesh. The presence of the immigrants pose a serious threat to the cultural, religious, political and economic life of the people of Assam. As a result, people's movements started with the All Assam Students Union agitation in the late 1970s. After some years, in 1979, a political movement known as the United Liberation Front of Asom (ULFA) emerged to fight for the independence of Assam through armed revolution.

5. *Tripura Upojati Samity (TUJS):* In order to protect their identity the tribals formed the Tripura Upojati Samity (TUJS) on 16 January 1967, leading to the formation of the Tripura National Volunteers (TNV).
6. *United Liberation Volunteers of Arunachal Pradesh (ULVA):* With the formation of ULVA, Arunachal Pradesh has also joined the freedom movement in the region. This has emerged due to the threat caused by the influx of Chakma refugees from Bangladesh.
7. *Achik Liberation Matgnik Army (ALMA):* This movement spearheaded by Garo youths has a big following in the state of Meghalaya. The other groups are the Federation of Khasi-Jaintia and Garo People (FKJGP) and Hynniepwtrep Achik Liberation Council (HALC), which are also actively engaged in resistance activities.

Problems of Tribals

The problems of tribals of today are mainly the product of the attitude and policy of the dominant group towards the minority tribal/indigenous people. As a result they suffered discrimination, exploitation and alienation. Their rights to live as human beings in freedom were not recognized by the invaders. The policy of isolation was applied by the Britishers towards the tribals which were supposedly intended to protect them from the interference of the non-tribals in their affairs. But the policy to protect them did not guarantee the actual protection of their cultural identity and rights in their existing situations.

The process of modernization has brought drastic and rapid social changes to the tribals. A sudden breakdown in the traditional system has been created through the onset of modernity. This has led to the situation of dependency in technical, engineering and business fields. The migrants get better opportunity to work because of their training and skills or pattern of work behaviour in the new economic enterprises.

The local people deprived by the outsiders in the field of economy, is another factor of unrest in this region. The region is rich in minerals and other forest products which supply materials for the development of other regions.

The tribal people in India have been denied their due identity. Since the invasion of the Aryans in 1500 BC, the tribal people in India have been broken. They occupy the fifth place in the caste hierarchy and they are often treated as less than humans.

Tribal groups have often been victims of division among themselves. Tribal communities in India have from time to time been displaced from their habitat. Many tribal people in India have been deprived of their rightful resources, land and habitat. The tibal people in India have always become victims of inappropriate exposure to the outside world. The tribal people of India who are referred to as Adivasis are actually the original inhabitants of this county. The Indian Constitution drafted by Hindu high castes, have deliberately erased the term 'indigenous' and replaced it with 'Scheduled Tribes'.

Thus being deprived of their indigenous identity, the tribal people of India have always been treated as outsiders with no rights over their own land. Many of their lands have been forcibly taken away by the state for mega projects like steel plants, hydroelectric dams or national parks.

In recent years we see the rise of many subaltern groups like the Dalits, the bonded labourers, women groups, etc. The tribals too are becoming aware of the injustices done to them and are organizing themselves to fight for justice and to redress the inequitable situation.

The Church and Tribal Development

JHARKHAND

Some of the clans Munda, Oraon, Khadia, etc., were converted by missionaries. They were empowered by education. Ecclesiastical leadership was gained by the Adivasis of the Jharkhand region. They have become liberators to their own people. They were made Christians by Belgium Jesuit missionaries. Fr. Livens, a Jesuit, was responsible for the entire development of this region. In this span of hundred years of Christianity in Jharkhand, miraculous developments were realized by the church.

NORTH-EAST INDIA

Christianity came to north-east India sometime in the middle and later part of the nineteenth century. The first Christian missionaries were affiliated with the American Baptist Missions and the Welsh Presbyterian Missions. While the Baptist missionaries worked upon the Nagas, Kukis, Assamese and Garos, the Presbyterian mission concentrated upon the Mizos of Mizoram and the Khasis of Meghalaya. Today, with the exception of the Assamese and Meiteis of Manipur, almost all the hills-tribal communities have embraced Christianity. The predominant Christian community in north-east India continues to be the Baptists and Presbyterians, although there are other churches such as the Roman Catholics and Seventh Day Adventists. In recent years Evangelical churches and Pentecostals, also known as the charismatic movements, have begun to establish a presence in the region.

Social Development

For the tribals, prior to the coming of Christianity, land as a commodity that could be sold, was not just strange but unthinkable. But today land is no longer regarded as a life-sustaining entity. Land and her natural resources have become commercial entities. The inalienable land has become a mere piece of land to be sold and bought. People are moving to the towns and the tribals' good ways of living in corporate harmony with nature are slowly eroding. Sustainability is challenged. Theology of land must be developed in tribal theology.

Political Development

Political unrest among the indigenous people of north-east India is no more a closed topic. But the church still finds it comfortable to stay away from the political aspirations of the people. Many of the churches prefer to remain conversionists and not liberationists which would take the concerns of this worldly matter for the total liberation of the people. To the tribal mind church and politics are separate bodies that should not be brought together.

Women Development

The androcentric interpretation of the Bible also causes a serious challenge to the liberation of the indigenous women. Tribal women who enjoy more freedom than their counterpart of other cultural orientation like the Hindus and Muslims have also received the Western interpretation of the Bible that seems to justify the subjugation of tribal women. Therefore, Christianity has further marginalized the tribal women. Tribal women must read the Bible not from the Western perspective but from their own experiential point of view to find liberative messages from the Bible.

Action Plans for the Empowerment of Dalits/Tribals

After having analysed the life situation and problem, and root causes of the problem the people and the leaders proposed the following action plans to be implemented by all the sections of the church of the society for the empowerment of Dalits and Tribals.

Education for Empowerment

Education is an effective instrument for the empowerment of Dalits/Tribals and weaker sections and it is readily available in the church. CBCI and CRI have been committed to make it available to the target group in their statements. Therefore CBCI and CRI should make provision for free education up to higher-secondary level in the Catholic educational institutions and provide scholarship for professional education to the poor Dalits/Tribals. A report regarding implementation of this educational programme has to be presented to either regional or national commission for SC/ST/BC every year.

Equality in the Community

As it is condemned in successive statements the discrimination based on caste is shameful and a sin against humanity and God, every member of the church is urged to make use of all the opportunities, and resources, such as liturgy, pastoral, social programmes to build-up equality and brotherhood in the church and in the society.

Equal Justice in the Church

Dalits are a majority in the church but the participation of the community in the administrative bodies, church-related councils, commissions, societies, priestly and religious life is less than 5 per cent. Therefore well-planned and intensive action should be taken by Diocesan and CRI authorities to offer participation in all the levels, including priestly, religious and ecclesiastical leadership according to the size of the population.

Equal Rights from Government

Dalit converts to Christianity were declared as Other Backward Classes (OBC) in most of the states in India and they are provided statutory and non-statutory benefits but Scheduled Caste status is needed to avail due fundamental and constitutional rights for their protection and promotion. Hence nationwide indefinite agitations and demonstration should be undertaken by the church as immediate step to pressurize the government to render Justice.

Structure for Facilitation

Even though the problem of the Dalit/Tribal is a burning issue in India as a whole, the SC/ST commissions do not function in many dioceses. Hence, it is essential that each diocese should establish as well as activate the commission with financial assistance. Besides, the regional Bishops' councils could insist on the establishment and functioning of the regional level SC/ST commissions. This will enable a greater collaboration as well as execution at the national level, towards the empowerment of the marginalized people.

Dalits/Tribal Theology

Existing Indian Christian theology is expression of mostly upper caste converts to Christianity without reference to Dalit sufferings and liberation. Brahmabarudh Upadhyaya, Sadhu Sundarsingh, Narayan Vaman Tilak, etc., were not from Dalit families. They were theologians on the basis of Brahminical scriptures and culture, whereas Dalit theology should evolve from Dalit historical context of bondage and struggle for liberation.

Though it is influenced by the liberation theology and black theology, it is a reflection of suffering death and resurrection of Jesus and God's liberative action in history for the integral salvation of the oppressed.

THERE IS NEED FOR DALIT THEOLOGY

- To inspire society and church for total eradication of caste system.
- To conscientize Dalits about their dehumanized situation and enable them to regain divine image.

- To motivate the Christian community for involving themselves in the struggle for social change and a just society.
- To urge non-Dalits in the church and society for restoration of their humanity by abandoning inhuman treatment of Dalits.
- To bring total liberation/salvation based on Christ the event of redemption to both oppressed and oppressors.
- To be an instrument in establishing the Kingdom of God.

TRIBAL THEOLOGY

Anything that alienates, anything that oppresses and marginalizes, anything that exploits and discriminates on the ground of caste, class, race or gender must be taken into account in our theological articulation. The futile attitude that we must continue preaching the gospel and let God take care of the historical process is a misrepresentation of the gospel. Tribal hermeneutics must take into consideration the experiences and sufferings of its people in its theological articulation with a strong commitment to liberate the people from biases, and from alienation and injustice meted out to them. Tribals must therefore seriously consider constructing a Tribalist Liberation Theology.

The Role of Different Sections of the Church

BISHOPS

- To ensure equality and brotherhood in the church.
- To urge the Christian community to implement the action plans.
- To facilitate Dalit vocations to priesthood and religious life.
- To establish SC/ST commissions with full infrastructure.
- To make 'Dalit theology/Tribal theology incorporated in the syllabus of the seminaries.

- To establish centres for the study of the theology of the oppressed.

PRIESTS

- To involve themselves in the liberation and empowerment of Dalits, the oppressed people.
- To motivate the people through liturgy, preaching and action for equality and justice.
- To establish a small Christian community based on equality and brotherhood.

RELIGIOUS

- To adopt Dalit/Tribal villages as their mission area and engage in the development of the depressed.
- To follow the policy of reservation in education and employment.
- To help the poor and weak students through special coaching and remedial classes.
- To utilize education and personal power for the empowerment of Dalits.

PEOPLE (LAITY)

- To organize themselves as a 'people's movement' which is self-reliant and sustainable by their own contribution for realizing the vision of empowerment.
- To encourage inter-caste marriages for eradication of caste discrimination.
- To uplift the weaker sections of the community by sharing their resources.
- To build-up selfless and committed leadership for social transformation.

REFERENCES

Baxla, Z., 'The Adivasi Identity in Assam', in *Mission Today*, vol. 8, no. 1, 2006, pp. 21-9.

Cummings, Charles, *Eco-Spiritualtiy*, New York: Paulist Press, 1991.

Dr. Babasaheb Ambedkar, Writings and Speeches, vol. 5, *Untouchables and Untouchability Social-Political-Religious*, Education Department, Government of Maharashtra, 1989.

Kananaikil, Jose, *Constitutional Provisions for the Scheduled Castes*, New Delhi: ISI, 1st pub. 1984, rpt. 1986.

———, *Christians of Scheduled Caste Origin*, New Delhi: ISI, 1st pub. 1983, rpt. 1986.

Kujur, J.M., 'An Adivasi Assessment of UPA's Two Years in Power', in *Social Action*, vol. 56, no. 3, 2006, pp. 250-63.

Lafrenez, Jean (in French), *Precis d Histoise de la Mission de Pondicherry*, p. 22, Imprimarie de 1a Mission, 1953.

Longchar, W., *An Exploration of Tribal Theology*, Jorhat: Tribal Study Centre, 1997.

Lourduswamy, S., *Towards Empowerment of Dalit Christians*, New Delhi, 1st edn., October 2000.

Lourduswamy, S. and James Massey, *A Demand for Equal Rights to Dalit Christians*, New Delhi, 1999.

Mandal Commission Report 10.36, 12.14.

Massey, James, *Emerging Political Scenario in Indian and Christian Response*, Delhi, 1999.

———, *Roots of Dalit History, Christian Theology and Spirituality*, Delhi: ISPCK, 1996.

Pinto, J. Prasad, 'Mission in the North Indian Context', in J. Mattam and J. Valiamangalam (eds.), *Emerging Indian Missiology: Context and Concept*, Delhi: FOIM/ISPCK, pp. 121-46.

Syiemlieh, David R., 'The Future of the Hills of North-east India 1928-1941: Some British Views', in B. Datta Ray and S.P Agrawal (eds.), *Reorganisation of North-east India since 1947*, New Delhi: Concept Publishing Company, 1996, pp. 24-36.

Wesley, A. Kumar, 'Towards a Comprehensive Theological Enterprise: A Subaltern (Tribal Dalit) Perspective', in *Asia Journal of Theology*, vol. 20, no. 1, 2006, pp. 17-35.

Zelliot, Eleanor, *From Untouchable to Dalit: Essays on the Ambedkar Movement*, New Delhi: Manohar, 1992, 2nd rev. edn. 1996, rpt. 2010.

7

Ecumenical Movements and Dalit-Adivasi Awakening

MONODEEP DANIEL

Introduction

Before the commencement of the ecumenical movement in the twentieth century, the idea of unity has had a long history. However, the difference in the attempts made for it in previous centuries *vis-à-vis* the twentieth century is this: earlier the Christian unity was knotted with political interest of the monarch whereas in present times it is a voluntary effort for the advantage of the people. We will see that the endeavour for Christian unity comes out in four ways: 1. Political unity of Christendom, 2. Inspirational unity of mission agency, 3. Organic unity of established agencies and churches and, 4. Unity of people for their emancipation. Except for the last, none of the above endeavours had people's interest at centre. But first let us study the ideas associated with the term 'ecumenical'.

Like the term 'catholic', the term 'ecumenical' is also very old, for instance, the head of the orthodox Christians in Constantinople (now Istanbul) is called the ecumenical patriarch. Before we discuss the various issues related to this topic here, we will do well to recall the various nuances of this term:

1. *Oikomene* refers to the whole inhabited world, i.e. 'all people everywhere' [Acts 17.30].
2. It referred to the whole of Roman Empire under the Caesars, i.e. 'all world' [Luke 2.1].
3. It referred to the whole church especially within the Roman Empire, i.e. the Ecumenical Councils.
4. It meant a theological category of a universal validity, i.e. the statements of belief are called 'ecumenical creeds'.
5. In its present sense it refers to the unity and relation between two or more Christian denominations.
6. It is an expression used since 1937 to underscore an awareness of a world Christian fellowship.

Fundamentally, in the 'ecumenical' category, we can tag all that is valuable to enhance global and national unity.[1] Moreover ecumenism as a movement of unity is still evolving, but in the Indian context it has a distinct flavour. This will come to light in our discussion under two major subheadings: The Dalit Awakening and the Adivasi Awakening. The question before us is: do these awakenings give us fresh insights for doing ecumenism in India? The answer is 'yes'. These awakenings have brought to the centre the interest of the disadvantaged communities to reinforce egalitarianism. However, before we take up this discussion we will give a brief overview of the ecumenical movement in India.

Attempts and Failures

The Western missionaries succeeded in spreading Christianity in large parts of India within a hundred years, but they also gave us the fragmented church of the West. Not only the church was divided into Catholic and Protestant camps but the Protestants were further split-up into numerous streams. This contradicted Christ's desire of unity of his disciples (John 17.11). Nonetheless, down the history, various attempts were made to unite the church. Ecumenical movement is one such attempt in the modern times. Interestingly, the schemes of union can be classified into six: 1. spiritual union, 2. union in cooperation, 3. intercommunion, 4. federal union, 5. corporate union and 6. organic union.[2] To study these schemes of union in detail is not our purpose here but these will be reflected in the unfolding of the key idea of this chapter, namely, the unity of people has superseded the union of institutional churches. But first let us bring to the fore the major historical attempts made to forge Christian unity.

Political Unity of Christendom

In the earlier centuries the church unity was for the sake of political cohesion. Consequently, the decisions once reached at the ecumenical councils were imposed on all with the help of the state. For instance, in the famous Council of Nicaea convened by the Roman Emperor in June CE 325 he dominated. Here more than 220 bishops gathered who took stand against Arian which was articulated in the Nicene creed. This is how it standardized its belief of Christ:

> Eternally begotten of the Father
> God from God
> Light from Light
> true God from true God
> begotten not made,
> one in being with the Father.

This Christology came to be regarded as official.[3] The aim was to forge unity by imposing this and other decisions of the Nicene Council on the whole church. Similarly, the initiative of Pope Leo III in CE 800 who crowned Charlemagne as emperor of the Holy Roman Empire to unite Christians in Christendom is also a model of unity. Interestingly, this Empire which was centred on Germany and included European Christian countries lasted till 1806. Another glaring Indian example of unity is the Syro-Latin controversy associated with the Synod of Diamper (or Udayamperoor) convened on 20 June 1599 where unity was imposed by using the force of the Portugal state. The aim was to unite the Syrians with the Roman Catholics. In such attempts to impose unity on the Christian populace, primarily the interest of the rulers and the church, rather than of the people, was served. In the long run these attempts failed to unite the Christians. However, the modern ecumenical movement does not seek to impose the wish of a church that is wedded-to-State; rather it seeks reconciliation between the differing Christian factions through dialogue, fellowship and mission.

Inspirational Unity of Mission Agencies

This type of unity was popularized in the colonial era of nineteenth and twentieth century to strengthen the mission venture. The Indian ecumenical movement was part of this process which started with the World Missionary Conference in Edinburgh, in 1910. The Indian representative in the ecumenical movement was Bishop V.S. Azariah of Dornakal (1875-1945). His significance at this point is to recall his acquaintance with Dr B.R. Ambedkar (1891-1956), a nationalist and Dalit leader. In 1937 at the Edinburgh meeting Bishop Azariah shared Dr Ambedkar's view with the delegates. This is what he said in his speech,

> A leader of the Depressed Class in India said to me that his people had decided to give up Hinduism and were considering what religion they should accept as likely to give them a fuller and higher life. 'When Christianity is mentioned', he said, 'they remind me of the many divisions within the Christian Church. We are united in Hinduism, they say and we shall become divided in Christianity. And, Sir', he said, 'I had no answer to give.' And need I say I had no answer to give either? . . .[4]

It is evident from this excerpt that the church's divided condition was known to Indian leaders. In their view this was neither helpful nor exemplary. Some missionaries who strongly felt this gave impetus to the ecumenical movement in the Protestant circles. We can mark 1914 as the beginning of this movement in India when the National Missionary Council was established. Various mission agencies and churches become associated with this body. In 1923 it was renamed as the National Christian Council of India. After the emergence of new independent countries like Pakistan, India, Bangladesh, Burma (now Myanmar) and Sri Lanka, each country formed its own national council. Accordingly the National Christian Council of India was renamed as the National Council of Churches in India (NCCI) in 1979, with its headquarters at Nagpur.

Endeavours towards unity are visible in independent churches too which have come together to be associated under the umbrella of the Evangelical Fellowship of India (EFI).[5]

Organic Unity of Established Agencies and Churches

Admittedly, the ecumenical movement did succeed in the organic union of churches in India. There were three unions of significance: first was the United Church of Northern India (UCNI) in 1924,[6] second was the Church of South India (CSI) in 1947 and the third was the Church of North India (CNI) in 1970. The Mar Thoma Church (MTC) was a unique case in the ecumenical endeavours which came into being in 1889. Deeply influenced by the Anglicans due to the Church Missionary Society's intervention, it stepped out from the Syrian tradition. Led by Abraham Malpan (1796-1846) this section adopted the Evangelical principles.[7] He translated the liturgy in Malayalam to celebrate the *Holy Qurbana* and revised it on the principles of reformation but he kept it rooted in the Eastern tradition of St. Thomas. The MTC was accepted in the wider communion with Canterbury and is in full communion with CNI and CSI. Later in 2004 the Communion of Churches (CCI) was formed by three churches, namely CNI, CSI and MTC. This national body is a corporate union.

Unity of People

The point of this discussion is to underscore the fact that the majority of church members belong to the Dalit and Adivasi communities. Therefore unity in the organized life of the Christian community should be helpful to create solidarity and consolidation for action in the interest of these people.

Fundamentally the attempts at Christian unity were aimed to make either Christian governments strong or to make institutional church influential or mission agencies succeed. The people, whether Christians or of other faiths or no faiths, were perceived as objects for state or church benevolence, but as we progress into the twenty-first century this will change. The people will be the subjects not objects. The Dalit and Adivasi will be the subjects of their history, church and society. It will be their history, not the history of a country or institutional church or important personalities. Similarly, the unity will be of the people not of the institutional churches or mission agencies. This change has come due to awakening among the Dalit and Adivasi communities in India.

Dalit Awakening

Dalit awakening in the contemporary sense started with the foundation of the Satya Shodhak Samaj and its founder was Mahatma Jotirao Phule (1827-90). His views were partially contemporaneous with Raja Rammohun Roy (1772-1833) of Bengal, but the difference between the two was that Roy, unlike Phule, did not discard the caste system.[8] Mahatma Phule not only detected the caste system as the source of inequality but he viewed it as an instrument to enslave people. In his times the power of the priest and prince both converged in the Brahmin. This especially was true of central India. This is what Phule wrote:

> The Bhats invented an elaborate system of caste-distinction . . . condemning some to the lowest rung and some to a slightly higher rung.

Thus they permanently made them into their protégés and by means of the powerful weapon of the iniquitous castes-system drove a permanent wedge among the shudra.[9]

Dispossessing the Shudra of power was the genius of the caste system. It made the Shudras arrogant of their slightly superior status and keep others at bay. Mahatma Phule wrote,

Some members of the Shudra community proudly call themselves malis (gardeners), kunbis (peasants), goldsmiths, tailors, iron smiths, carpenters . . . on the basis of the vocation (trade) they pursued (practice). Little do they know that our ancestors and those of the so-called untouchables (Mahars, Mangs) were blood-brothers (traced their lineage to the same family stock).[10]

This calling on differences was a way of creating divisions among the depressed and downtrodden masses. For this reason it is all the more important for the subalterns and Dalits to identify common ideological grounds for strengthening solidarity. Mahatma Phule's vision was 'liberty for all'. This is what he wrote in his manifesto,

A little introspection will tell us that 'freedom' is imperative to man (*sic*! a person), and it is the duty of every gentleman to bestow this freedom on those who are deprived of it. When a man (*sic*! a person) is free, he is able to express his innermost thoughts orally or in writing to others. Even important beneficial thought cannot be communicated to others for want of freedom (of expression) and thus they evaporate in course of time. The Creator of this world, who is also omnipresent, has conferred some precious human rights upon mankind (all men and women). But selfish and cunning Brahmins have kept the people in the dark about their human rights. A truly liberated man (*sic*! person) will never hesitate to demand these human rights from his oppressors for himself (*sic*! herself). Due rights confer happiness on people.[11]

What emerges from this is an ideology for the emancipation of Dalits and Adivasis. This is where the relevance of Mahatma Phule's message for our times can be assessed. From what he wrote we can identify specific foundational themes to shape an ideology of emancipation. I have identified three such themes in his writings: *equality*, *truth* and *solidarity*.

A second awakening came in the twentieth century with Dr Ambedkar (1891-1957). In his endeavours for social equality he opposed the caste-system and untouchablility vociferously. Dr Ambedkar did so because he aimed to encounter the prevalent feeling of repulsion for Dalits that had reduced them to a state of *perpetual rejection* by a society laced with caste. Like Mahatma Phule he also took religion seriously. He worked out a standard: *utility* and *justice,* to assess a religion if it was beneficial for Dalits or not.[12] We can divide his journey in search of a good religion in three stages:

Stage One: 1927. Burning of *Manusmriti*. This was Dr Ambedkar's symbolic gesture for opposing and rejecting Hinduism.

Stage Two: 1935. Yeola Declaration. Here he declared his serious intention to convert to an egalitarian religion. This was Dr Ambedkar's assertion for freedom to choose.

Stage Three: 1951. Founding the Buddhist Society of India. This phase climaxed in 1956 when Dr Ambedkar converted to Buddhism. This was a positive step of accepting a new religion.

Dr Ambedkar strongly advocated conversion of Dalits to an egalitarian religion of their choice (towards the end of his life he advocated neo-Buddhism). In this way they will pave the way for radical cultural change. Dr Ambedkar pointed out the ineffectiveness of political freedom unless society was freed from the inequality of caste-system. For this one should not fear cultural change propelled by the tenets of an egalitarian religion. At the end of this life Dr Ambedkar offered his unique brand of neo-Buddhism to Dalits, just as Mahatma Phule had offered the *Universal Religion of Truth* for all people.

Attention must be drawn to the fundamental point in Dalit awakening. The point is: social liberty must be achieved before political freedom is acquired. This means forging an egalitarian society as a precursor for democratic political order. But true freedom does not descend to the people by merely adopting democracy; instead they have to rise up to appropriate it. Towards this end Dr Ambedkar's advice to Dalits 'to educate, to organize and to agitate' has become a liberative slogan too.

Adivasi Awakening

The Adivasi awakening was a result of factors affecting the social, economic, spiritual and political life of the Adivasis. The Sardar agitation (1875-95) which Birsa Munda (1875-1900) had joined was a landmark in this. The weak condition of the Adivasis under the Mughal rule[13] was adversely affected by internal strife and Maratha raids.[14] Clearly the British exploited the situation to their own advantage and got the *dewani* of Jharkhand in 1765. They captured the political power from the Rajas and their Adivasi chiefs. By 1771 Jharkhand was firmly under the control of the British East India Company.[15] The British completely disregarded the Adivasi democratic life by imposing feudal system in the tribal belt. Those who were given the ownership of the Adivasi land became their feudal lords. This was due to the inability of the Adivasi to produce adequate surplus with their primitive agricultural methods. Consequently the landholders or *ryots* were unable to pay the rent or tax imposed on the land they owned. Therefore lands of those who failed to foot the tax were acquired and auctioned to one ready to pay. So the title of ownership changed hands from Adivasi to an outsider or *dikku*.

One may recall that this rent in the Mughal rule was collected through the zamindars and the *rajas* of the area. The change was that under the Company the levy was higher. Defaulter's land, i.e. *zamindari* or *raj*, was settled on another person in payment of outstanding rent/tax.[16] Obviously the British did not understand the idea of the collective ownership of the lands by the tribes, and treated the zamindars, who were merely tax collectors of the Mughals, as owners. Consequently the Adivasi chiefs were made subservient to the zamindars. Their people were alienated from their land. The owners were reduced to farm labourers. Added to this humiliation was the declaration of the large territories as protected zones under the Forest Act of 1882. The activities of the Munda tribe were severely restricted in these zones who found it difficult to procure their traditional requirement of subsistence from the forests. It made them increasingly poor and dependent. This resulted in grave disaffection. The revolts against the zamindars, *mahajans*, British government and their officers started in 1796. The last in the series was the Birsa Munda movement. We can understand how under these conditions the young Birsa Munda became seriously anti-British and anti-missionary. His subversive activities were unacceptable to the British who finally arrested him. He died under mysterious circumstances in the Ranchi Jail aged barely 25 years. He has become an iconic figure among the Adivasi of the Jharkhand. The Adivasi movement reached its climax in the creation of the Jharkhand state on 15 November 2000 through affirmative political action.

It is clear from the above discussion that although the Adivasis were undeveloped as far as the latest technological know-how was concerned, they were not as isolated as they are often made out to be. Their isolation was due to their miserable position in society. This was deliberately done. The fact is that like the rest of the country they were affected by the rise and fall of governments and empires in India. They contributed to the economy of the country. Like the rest of India they too rebelled and revolted against those who ruled and dispossessed them. However, independence of India from foreign yoke did not sort out their sufferings. In more recent times, i.e. the late twentieth century, the exploitation of their land has been accelerated under the New Economic Policy of the government which unscrupulously acquires their land for mining minerals. These stretches of land have been handed over to multinational companies. It has resulted in increasingly dispossessing them of their land, forest and water. Their property rights are easily violated because they do not document anything in writing. Adivasi people have been internally displaced due to development projects without adequate rehabilitation. They were not compensated in terms of money and jobs in dams, power plants, mining industry, wildlife sanctuaries and army installations for which their lands were acquired. They were dispossessed of what they had.[17]

The resulting political powerlessness has dispossessed them of their ownership of *jal* (water), *jangal* (forest), *jameen* (land) and *zameer* (dignity). It needs to be highlighted that these four elements above are not merely material possessions for Adivasi communities, but these are their spiritual, cultural and ancestral heritages. The Adivasi people are awakened not merely in their awareness of the loss of their heritage but also that they need to repossess these. In this sense the Adivasi awakening is both a realization and a resolution which the ecumenical movement must make note of.

Some Common Challenges before the Dalits and Adivasis

History is the story of our civilization marked by tyranny, oppression, wars, destruction, decay and death. Life has become brutal, short, nasty, filled with violence and strife, unpredictable and unsafe (Thomas Hobbes). Paradoxically attempts of the right wing groups to liberate ourselves from this unfortunate situation have led further into serious life-threatening situations. Let us take some examples

(a) *Caste System*: The entire Indian society is culturally and religiously organized in line with the caste system. This results in extreme polarities in the distribution of socio-economic and political power. Some are very rich, over educated and politically powerful while the rest of the populace is extremely poor, illiterate and dependent. The other problem of a caste-based society is that unlike social classes, the people of one caste cannot move upwards or downwards into another caste. This results in social stagnation. Attached to it are the evils of untouchability and dowry.

(b) *Fatal Diseases*: Dalits and Adivasi are susceptible to diseases like tuberculosis, leprosy and HIV/AIDS. These diseases are either due to the prevalence of malnutrition or have lead to malnutrition. The prevention programmes carried out by the state and non-government organizations instead of strengthening the base communities by building economic and moral capacities of the people seems to dish out short-lived solutions, i.e. use of condoms. Emphasis on solutions which are based on scientific analysis of the situation using tools of psychology, sociology, and economics are lacking.

(c) *Adverse Effects of Nuclear Options*: China, India and Pakistan have clearly communicated their policy for using nuclear options when needed to defend their territory. This has reduced South Asia into an unsafe zone. No lasting peace can be gained under the mutual threat of nuclear power. The burden of nuclear research and maintenance of arsenals relegates state welfare towards Dalit and Adivasi to insignificance.

(d) *Instability caused by non-State Agencies*: Due to the crisis of political identity, non-state agencies take undue advantage of the situation. What seems to be offered by successive governments as an answer is military in nature. It is clear that a political problem needs a political solution and not military response. The consequence of this has been the menacing rise of non-state agencies, e.g. the Maoists.

(e) *Resistance in the Hinterland*: On the one hand, isolation of Dalits by society and on the other the political defeat of Adivasis has resulted in exploitation of their land resources, plundering of Adivasi lands and their displacement, and unjust financial compensation. This has in turn bitterly hardened the attitudes of many Dalit and Adivasi groups. Hatred, oppression and periodic spells of killing Dalits continue unabated. The resultant mistrust in the state protection machinery has strengthened the hands of armed outfits in the tribal belts. Here the role of education and conversion to egalitarian religions should be taken seriously. It is in these two areas that curbs are being imposed.

(f) *Hindutva*: The alternative ideology offering national unity by imposing Brahminic culture over and against the Shramanic is not new but it is now in a newly articulated form especially after the publication of Veer Damodar Savarkar's book *Hindutva* in 1923. The idea of forging unity by imposing religion and culture which is Sanskritic, saffron, singular and casteist will inevitably result in socio-political and economic inequality. Here the Dalit and Adivasi will be the worst affected.

(g) *Ecological Crisis*: Environmental degradation has reached alarming stages. The destruction caused by clearing forest, polluting the air and water by industrial plants, etc., has been going on since the Nehruvian era. To all this is added the havoc cause by the mega-hydro projects of dams which have made large bio-diverse regions of plants and animals to submerge into water reservoirs and displaced Adivasi population. It must be highlighted that such developmental projects treat certain regions and people as dispensable.

(h) *Infringement of Minority Rights*: The wisdom of the axiomatic truth that there can be no minority without democracy and no democracy without minority was never questioned up till now in India. In spite of communal tensions from time to time, people have lived together in a culturally pluralistic society for centuries. However, due to the government's indecisive attitude towards the incidences in Dangs region, killing of Graham Stains and his two sons, and arson in Khandmal district in Karnataka state has left the Christian community in a state of utter insecurity. Similar incidences are reported from the Muslim and Dalit front.

(i) *Social fragmentation of Dalit and Adivasi*: Though true, this is a tragic situation. This occurs due to many reasons which are imposed on the disadvantaged communities by the dominant people. For instance increased Sanskritization and Westernization of their culture. This means that either their society is broken up into castes like hierarchy or they are fragmented into economic classes. Christianity from West had earlier divided them into European denominations.

(j) *Persistent Poverty*: Due to their rejection and defeated position in society, the human rights of Dalits and Adivasis have been neglected. Consequently generation after generation they remain illiterate, unskilled in modern technology and ignorant of modern knowledge. Unable to get jobs and employment they are condemned to live in poverty.

So we see two things that emerge from the problems articulated above. The *first* is the position of Dalits and Adivasis at the extreme disadvantageous end of the social spectrum; and *second* is the subservience imposed on them. Consequently, the Dalit and Adivasi sufferings are not confined within the church but it has spread to all subaltern people. The need therefore is to reverse this by reinforcing egalitarianism and political participation. This will help the Dalits and Adivasis to be included in the mainstream of national life and enjoy civil liberties which is their rightful due as citizens of a free country. Clearly this sets the agenda for ecumenism in India.

Solidarity for Liberty

From what we have discussed above it is clear that social reform, possession of political power and moral commitment are the basic foundations for ecumenical movement in India. The first aims to strengthen egalitarianism, the second will enforce economic fairness and the third will ensure proper implementation of just legislations. However, without solidarity it is impossible to achieve these three goals. With this emphasis ecumenism will step into the next phase, i.e. people's unity. One expression of this is solidarity. Before we discuss solidarity as a significant dimension of socio-political movement of the Dalit and subalterns let us consider the trends in the ecumenical movement. In which groove can the Adivasi-Dalit awakening fit into in order to contribute to the unity of Christians.

It is well known that the ecumenical movement developed two fundamental approaches to Christian fellowship and mission. The first was *Life-and-Work* started by Archbishop Nathan Soderblom of Uppsala, and the second was *Faith-and-Order* which was associated with Bishop Charles Brent, a missionary in the Philippines. The first movement was born in 1925 at the *Universal Christian Conference on Life and Work* at Stockholm and the second at the *World Conference on Faith and Order* at Lausanne in 1927. Invariably, issues of doctrines and systems end up in disagreements among the partners simply because each church like a state zealously guards its identity and independence; whereas *Life-and-Work* results in unity. This is so because the churches have common interest to practically apply the gospel to solve the current social and global problems. This also applies to the Dalit and Adivasi problem.

Therefore the way forward is by forging solidarity. Solidarity reverses dehumanization. Attention should be drawn to the fact that economic exploitation and dispossession can only be sustained with its support. Dehumanization is a determined initiative which is systematically implemented. This makes a community feeble and its individuals drained of self-confidence.[18] Although such conditions exhibit psychosomatic symptoms of people, this should not be misjudged as a permanent trait of apathy and lethargy, instead the inner spirit to question and inquire, to resist and to rebel, to hope and to dream, to be courageous and be free can never be taken away from the defeated people. Keeping in view that solidarity is important for Adivasis and Dalits for their emancipation from their rejected and defeated conditions, the best slot for them to fit into will be the *Life-and-Work* groove of the ecumenical movement.

Way Forward with Fresh Theology for Ecumenism

As we have seen above ecumenism primarily has to do with unity of churches. Towards this end the World Council of Churches was organized and its first assembly was convened in 1948 in Amsterdam,[19] which in its self-perception is neither a super-church nor equivalent to Magisterium of the Roman Catholic church; rather it was a fellowship of churches that meet in a conciliar environment. In this way the ecumenical movement over the years has been crystallized in the WCC and its programmes. But it was detected that inadvertently the agenda of the WCC was dominated with northern interest.[20] For instance, the Special Fund to Combat Racism[21] which has been a predominant problem of the Western Christian countries. *Diakonia* and *Koinonia* were also seen more within the churches in dialogue under the umbrella of WCC. *Diakonia* took the form of addressing many contextual issues in Christian countries like racism, economic disparity, regimes of dictators, communism and poverty. But it did not take the problem of caste on board. Despite this observation the impact of ecumenism on the Indian church was such that it enhanced the organic union of churches in south and north India. We have already discussed this at the beginning of this paper.

Be this as it may, the point of this discussion is this: In what way the Dalit and Adivasi awakenings is giving a new perspective to ecumenism. In what we have discussed above, there are three things that emerge from this awakening which give a unique bend to the ecumenism in Indian context. The first is *egalitarianism*, the second is *gaining political power* and the third is *moral reawakening*. Egalitarianism will include developing a sense of kinship among equal people, political power means a democratic style of associated living of people and morality means to regard all that does not pertain equality, freedom and kinship as immoral. We have also pointed out in our discussion above that it requires solidarity among the Dalit and Adivasi to achieve these objectives. True unity cannot be constituted without these three considerations.

It must be admitted that the ecclesiologists have for long studied culture for hammering out unity among the diverse Christian groups. This has been in the form of inculturation, acculturation and inter-cultural studies. The motive of this has been either to encourage organic union or evangelization of people. But this has had a limited success. It may be that the idea of organic or institutional unity has no appeal anymore. For this reason we need a new theology for ecumenism in India. In this line of thinking I suggest the following:

In doing theology afresh we much move beyond culture and explore issues surrounding social equality in term of treatment, opportunity and sharing of power (including political power) among the people. Similarly, doctrinal differences have been for long a subject of discussion. Despite the publication of certain documents like Baptism, Eucharist and Ministry no one arrived at any definite concrete step. However, it is beyond the scope of this paper to say anything more than this.

In doing ecumenical theology from Dalit and Adivasi perspective we should go beyond the old ideas of federal and organic unity. Instead we must seek solidarity with Dalits, and Adivasis. This solidarity should also include all those who are vulnerable, rejected and isolated. Out of this will emerge the unity of faith and fellowship among those who are united with the Dalits and the Adivasis.

We need to theologically develop our understanding of the *divine choice* and *divine election* in our context of Dalit and Adivasi awakening. We need to see a relationship and also understand the difference between these two. In this case we will need to distinguish between God's election of Israelites as his people and God's choice of the rejected and isolated people. He elected the former to be His servant and a source of blessing to all people but He chose the latter to emancipate them from oppression and suffering. On the one hand God's choice of Israel demonstrates divine sovereignty, i.e. He will do what he wills. On the other hand, his concern for the rejected and isolated shows that God is a moral being who preferentially opts for the defenceless and broken people. A theology with this moral perspective will lead to three things: One, it will enhance the emancipation of Dalits and Adivasis. Two, it will enhance national integration. And three, it will produce ethical people. All this will be significant insights for nation building. This also means that we have to have a theology of politics. This will address the query: can a Dalit or Adivasi have power? The answer will be 'yes' if political action is pursued in unity. Here solidarity among the victims will be the expression of unity.

Will there be any relevant role or place for the ecumenical organization in all this? This leads us on to our next topic of discussion which is 'Towards a New Ecumenical Movement'.

Way Forward with New Insights for Ecumenical Movement

The relevance of an ecumenical organization will depend on its seriousness of taking up the Dalit and Adivasi issue on its agenda of services. It must be recognized that the mission of God in the context of a rejected and defeated people must take into consideration the following facts:

(a) Social rejection of Dalits and defeat of Adivasis is denial of human rights to a people of a free country.
(b) Rights have to be demanded and taken, they are not voluntarily given.
(c) Equality of rights can only be possible if human rights are enjoyed by each section of society and caste system is eliminated.

(d) Without political power no one can acquire their rights and resist oppression.
(e) This requires two fundamental initiatives: education and organization of people.

These considerations have also been identified by B.P. Keshari.[22] This means that we have to consider the ecumenical movement in India afresh with the aim of establishing a casteless and egalitarian society in India. I think of at least three things in this direction. First of all, the ecumenical movement in India has to go beyond the confines of the Church. It must seek solidarity with the larger human community of all *rejected* and *defeated* people including Dalits and Adivasis. Secondly, although Christians would share their faith and conviction with others, these will not constitute the pivot of the ecumenical movement. Instead the common factor for solidarity will be the *pain* and *sorrow* of the people. Thirdly, the struggle to remove the social, economic, political and religious impediments of Dalit and Adivasi will constitute the ground for unity of all people. To achieve this we will have to accept the political nature of the Dalit-Adivasi struggle. This will not only help to bring unity among the Christians but also unite them with others and in effect end social isolation of people and fragmentation of society arising out of religious and ideological differences and political inaction.

Admittedly, people suffering due to disadvantages of caste system and underdevelopment have come together on many platforms. Considering the divided nature of their society such unity in political and social sphere is remarkable. This coming together for action has been outside the orbit of the institutionalized church. The reason is simple. The church is a divided house on grounds of doctrines, denomination and caste. Achievement of union of CNI and CSI may not be repeated again. However, the churches and Christian agencies do continuously form ecumenical bodies and undertake ecumenical activities. In this endeavour the role of an ecumenical organization will be of an enabler, a facilitator and an accompanier of the people. It will offer its resources and share knowledge with people to strengthen their endeavour. Beside this it will also have to be the source of strengthening faith of the Christians involved in social movements and ensure that their level of inspiration is maintained. However, it cannot lead people's movements or organizations. Victims will have to lead their own movements for the emancipation of their people.

Therefore what Should be Done?

What comes out from our discussion is that the ecumenical movement in order to be relevant has to engage in God's mission. In the light of our above discussion the question before us is: Therefore what should we do? The answer is to build a humane community where justice, compassion, truth and solidarity will flourish, in other words to forge a just and equal society.

(a) *Professional Education to Eliminate Poverty:* Education, especially at the primary level, should be undertaken among the Dalits and Adivasis even to the remote parts of every district. Education should be double-pronged: *one prong* should be to establish good *professional education for living* or income. This will include formal stream, technical, professional and higher educational streams. It also entails raising scholarships to support the Dalit and Adivasi children and youth to complete their education and training. The aim should be to ensure that all children up to the age of 17 are in a school. This will help to abolish child labour among our people. Here the facilities of hostels should be considered and wherever possible the children should be made to live in hostels in discipline and prayer.

(b) *Value Education to Eliminate Caste System:* The *second prong* should be *value education for being*. This prong involves building awareness, leadership and intellectual capacities to help the growing Dalit and Adivasi boys and girls to harness rational, spiritual, ethical, ideological, theological and philosophical capacities. This will help us to raise a generation of people who will think critically and facilitate the social changes, organize advocacy for Dalit/Adivasi cause and resist extreme ideologies from making inroads into their consciousness and endeavour to forge a casteless egalitarian society. Value education leads on to two more things:

i. Rereading the Bible (including writing commentaries) for advocacy of Dalit and Adivasi cause.
ii. Rereading and writing commentary of religious texts of other faith communities especially Dr B.R. Ambedkar's *The Buddha and His Dhamma*.

(c) *Extend Health Facilities:* Health facilities have to be taken to the remotest parts of districts with a double-pronged approach. The *first prong* should be aimed at health education and preventive care programmes. This may include palliative care as well. The *second prong* should go for curative procedures. Health care has to be community-based by training community members to undertake as much as possible areas of health concerns. Special note should be taken to address the problem of alcoholism and substance abuse among the Dalit and Adivasi men.

(d) *Leadership Training for Mobilizing Dalits and the Adivasis:* This goes along with education and health concerns. This training could be given to the educators and health workers in the community. It involves organizing people, i.e. men, women, youth and children into groups, clubs, church, fellowships or organizations to help them progress with one another's cooperation. These basic organized groups will do two things: on the one hand, they will resist exploitation and oppression by the dominant groups or state machinery, and on the other they will resist inroads made by the non-state agencies. At the same time training for leadership will be continually taken up at all levels of organized life.

(e) *Clear Articulation of Agenda*: This has to be drawn up by Dalits and Adivasis. It will involve strategic programmes to eliminate caste system, remove caste-based discriminations, and restore to all Dalits their freedom, dignity and rights including the right to convert to any religion of their choice, the freedom to engage in any occupation for livelihood, strategic plans to eliminate poverty and equal treatment in society.

(f) *Preserve and Promote Adivasi Language, Culture and Rights*: This includes their demand to live with dignity and cultivate and preserve their identity, ancestral land, forests and water resources.

(g) *Preserve the National Culture of Plurality to Resist Hindutva Ideology*: This means that we must acknowledge, preserve and promote India's multi-cultural, multi-religious, multilingual, multi-racial diversity and heritage so that all people are included in the responsibility of national integration. Preserving local diversity is of key importance to promote national amalgamation.

(h) *Preserve Ecology and Environment*: This has to be especially done in and around the areas where Dalits reside. This will help them to rear their livestock and get provision to survive. The Adivasis need to preserve their geographical territories of forests with its environmental diversity not only to survive but also to preserve their cultural heritage. Here we still find that people's group will collide with agencies that try to impose the interest of the multinational companies in tribal areas.

(i) *Eliminate Gender Inequality*: Gender discrimination is also a part of caste system which has to be eliminated. For this women's organizations have to be strategically strengthened as well as education and training has to be imparted to women. This will empower them.

(j) *Replace Conflict with Dialogue*: Keeping in view that Dalits and Adivasi invariably become victims of social conflict, it is important that dialogue between different groups and communities should be undertaken systematically. Similarly, common programmes for the alleviation of Dalits and Adivasis should also be taken as joint programmes. This will help to secularize the society and resist religious fundamentalism.

(k) *Encourage Active Participation in National Politics*: The significance of this should be properly understood. Part of the leadership training should be to prepare good Dalit and Adivasi political leaders in the future. It must be underscored that political power is the key to emancipation of Dalits and Adivasi. The aim is to build a nation where egalitarian society would flourish.

(l) *Develop Political Theology*: Theological reflection in this line will do two things: on the one hand it will theologically develop politics, and on the other it will politically widen theology. This should not be confused with politicization of the church in a wrong way where caste exclusion is accepted and partisanship to the advantage of the privileged castes is tolerated. The full implication of this seminal thought will have to be further developed in detail.

(m) *Reviewing Ecclesiology*: Keeping in view that the Indian church largely comprises of Dalits and Adivasis, we will need to review our understanding of the church. Admittedly the church in obedience to her Lord in the twentieth century realized her ethical imperative to preferentially opt for the poor. In this way it became Church *for* the Poor yet it was far from being the Church *of* the Poor. Now it must step further and truly become the Church *of* the Dalits and Adivasis.

Adoption of strategic programmes on these lines will be important to forge a humane and just society. Therefore the aim of ecumenism will be to abolish the caste system and strengthen egalitarianism, freedom and kinship. What has been brought to fore in the above section is that education, health, training and leadership to enhance people's unity is a way of resisting dehumanization of Dalits and Adivasis. In other words, ecumenism cannot succeed in unity by merely doctrinal configuration, but it is possible for people to unite in mission convergence. This convergence can be brought about by adopting the above pointers for strategic programmes.

Conclusion

It is clear from our discussion that the Dalits and the Adivasis are the rejected and isolated people of India. They were reduced to this condition deliberately and intentionally. In this line of reasoning we can say that their emancipation and streamlining into the mainstream of Indian society also has to be deliberately designed. The design is solidarity. There could be other equally good designs too. We have already articulated that this has to be the agenda of the ecumenical movement in India. Despite their distinct socio-historical settings their issues are strikingly similar in nature, for example, social isolation, backwardness, inferiority complex, exclusion and so on. The basic clarity lies in realizing that the Dalits are the *rejected* people whereas the Adivasis are the *defeated* people. Consequently, both are socially isolated and suffer from perennial poverty and political powerlessness. This situation can be changed by none except the Dalits and Adivasis. This entails that Dalit and Adivasi Christians should pull away from their self-centerdness to the outward sphere seeking unity with all those people, movements and agencies that are involved in creating a just and equitable society. Ecumenical bodies within the church will have to move out in solidarity with people's movement. In this way their contribution will be to help the diverse sections of Dalits and Adivasis to unite for emancipation and to acquire civil liberty.

Unless the ecumenism takes this agenda up it will be under threat of becoming irrelevant. So the answer to our question that we raised at the beginning of this chapter: is Dalit and Adivasi awakening showing us a fresh way of doing ecumenical ministry? The answer is 'yes' because we see afresh the relevance of solidarity or people's unity for emancipation. Ecumenism will not be merely about the unity of institutional Churches or Christian organizations, but it will from now on have to work for the *unity of people* on all possible fronts.

NOTES

1. Bernard Lambert, *Ecumenism: Theology and History,* London: Burns & Oates, 1967, p. 29.
2. Ibid., p. 132.
3. Tony Lane, *Christian Thought,* Tring., England: Lion Publishing, 1984; Baker Academic, 2006, p. 28.
4. Stephen Neill, *Men of Unity,* London: SCM Press Ltd, 1960, p. 57.
5. Leonard Fernando and G. Gispert-Sauch, *Christianity in India: Two Thousand Years of Faith,* New Delhi: Penguin, 2004, pp. 175-7.
6. James Massey, 'Affirming Unity Proclaiming Justice: Exploring New Mission Agenda in a Fractured World', in *People of God for All God's People: Witnessing to Unity at the Service of Justice,* ed. Alwan Masih et al., New Delhi: ISPCK, 2011, p. 31.
7. R.W. Bryan, *Great Christians: Commemorated by the Indian Church,* Delhi: ISPCK, 1997, p. 62.
8. Robin Boyd, *An Introduction to Indian Christian Theology,* Delhi: ISPCK, 1989, p. 26.
9. Mahatma Jotirao Phule, *Slavery,* 1991, p. 1.
10. Ibid.
11. Ibid., p. xliii.
12. B.R. Ambedkar, 'Philosophy of Hinduism', in *Writings and Speeches* (vol. 3), Education Department of the Government of Maharashtra, 1987, p. 22.
13. B.P. Keshari, 'Development of Political Organizations in Chotanagpur', in *Cultural Chotanagpur: Unity in Diversity,* ed. S. Bosu, New Delhi: Uppal Publishing House, 1991, p. 126.

14. Ibid., p. 127.
15. Ibid., p. 128.
16. Ibid.
17. Stan Lourduswamy, *Jharkhandis Claim for Self-rule,* New Delhi: Indian Social Institute, 1997, p. vi.
18. Matthew Areeparampil, 'Development Versus Struggle for Human Rights', in *Cultural Chotanagpur: Unity in Diversity,* ed. S. Bosu, 1991, p. 155.
19. The World Council of Churches (WCC) was formed by a decision to combine the *Faith and Order* and *Life and Work* movements in 1937. The decision was acted upon in a meeting in 1938 in Utrecht where a provisional committee of the WCC was set up. Due to war the convening of its global Assembly had to be postponed till 1948. Barry Till, *The Churches Search for Unity,* Harmondsworth: Penguin Books, 1972, p. 229.
20. James Massey, 'Alternative Approaches to the Ecumenical Movement', in *Ecumenism in India Today,* Bangalore: BTESSC/SATHARI, 2008, p. 63.
21. Emilio Castro, *A Passion for Unity: Essays on Ecumenical Hopes and Challenges,* Geneva: WCC Publications, 1992, p. 59.
22. Keshari, op. cit., p. 154.

REFERENCES

Ambedkar, B.R., 'Philosophy of Hinduism', in *Writings and Speeches,* vol. 3, Education Department of the Government of Maharashtra, 1987.

Boyd, Robin, *An Introduction to Indian Christian Theology,* Delhi: ISPCK, 1989.

Bryan, R.W., *Great Christians: Commemorated by the Indian Church,* Delhi: ISPCK, 1997.

Castro, Emilio, *A Passion for Unity: Essays on Ecumenical Hopes and Challenges,* Geneva: WCC Publications, 1992.

Bosu, S. (ed.), '*Cultural Chotanagpur: Unity in Diversity,* New Delhi: Uppal Publishing House, 1991.

Massey, James, *Ecumenism in India Today,* Bangalore: BTESSC/SATHARI, 2008.

Fernando, Leonard and G. Gispert-Sauch, *Christianity in India: Two Thousand Years of Faith,* New Delhi: Penguin, 2004.

Lambert, Bernard, *Ecumenism: Theology and History,* London: Burns & Oates, 1967.

Lane, Tony, *Christian Thought,* Tring, England: Lion Publishing, 1984; Baker Academic, 2006.

Lourduswamy, Stan, *Jharkhandis Claim for Self-Rule,* New Delhi: Indian Social Institute, 1997.

Masih, Alwan et al. (eds.), *People of God for All God's People: Witnessing to Unity at the Service of Justice,* New Delhi: ISPCK, 2011.

Neill, Stephen, *Men of Unity,* London: SCM Press Ltd, 1960.

Phule, Mahatma Jotirao, *Slavery,* 1991.

Till, Barry, *The Churches Search for Unity,* Harmondsworth: Penguin Books, 1972.

8

Pentecostal and Charismatic Movements and the Social Demands of the Gospel

SIMON SAMUEL

Roots: The Pentecostal-like Christians from Christian Origins

The modern Pentecostal and Charismatic Christians trace their origin from the earliest tradition, teaching and the kergymatic and other spiritual experiences and practices of the first followers of Jesus in Jerusalem and Palestine.[1] The modern Pentecostals relate their name and identity to the first followers of Jesus who were filled with the promised Holy Spirit on the day of Pentecost (Acts 2). They believe that the Holy Spirit and His gifts which include also speaking in tongues (*glossolalia*) were not only available to all those who believed in Jesus then, but also to all those who believe in Him now.[2] The Christian Testament testifies that the first followers of Jesus, a small group of Jews (Hebrews and Hellenists[3]), Samaritans[4] and Gentiles (Greeks, Romans and other Asiatic natives) in the first century Greco-Roman world, after the resurrection of Jesus Christ, were filled with the Holy Spirit, some in Jerusalem (Acts 2), others in Samaria (Acts 8), and yet others among the Gentiles in Palestine

(Acts 10) and in the far flung location of Ephesus (Acts 19), in fulfilment of the promise of the risen Lord Jesus Christ (Acts 1.8).[5] Their infilling experience was expressed through certain spiritual gifts such as speaking in tongues, prophecy and healing and other manifestations including spontaneous charismatic worship, preaching, sharing and fellowship.[6] Subsequent to such experiences and manifestations, the first followers of Jesus ensued an expansive world-wide mission and ministry beginning from Jerusalem, Judea, Samaria to the ends of the earth.[7] According to Alan Anderson,

> The early church was a community of the Holy Spirit, and *the freedom of expression and spontaneity of its worship may not have been very different from that of many Pentecostal and Charismatic churches today*. Some of the characteristic features and ecstatic phenomena of Pentecostalism like prophecy, healing and speaking in tongues were common.[8]

The descent of the Holy Spirit and the Pentecostal-like experience of being clothed with the Holy Spirit with visible manifestations of speaking in tongues, prophecy, healing, etc., according to the Christian Testament, are the works of God in Christ among the first followers of Jesus Christ. Therefore it is ludicrous to think that these experiences and expressions of the Holy Spirit that began so vividly at the very outset of the Christian movement just ceased so suddenly after the early apostles and the composition of the Christian Testament;[9] and that they resurfaced only in the latter part of the nineteenth century among some weird, missed-line, sectarian, heretical Christians. Church historians who write the history of Christianity (in fact, histories of Christianities) from below[10] now argue that throughout the 2,000-year history of Christianity there have been recurrent reports and records of charismatic and other spiritual manifestations and expressions in the church that have resonance on the emergence of modern Pentecostalism in the latter part of the nineteenth and the early part of the twentieth century.[11]

Pentecostal-like Christians throughout the Histories of Christianity

The Charismatic strand and Pentecostal-like Christians have persisted and prevailed within Christianity and in the church always ever since its inception,[12] though at varying degrees they were treated and viewed in the Great Church and in its official history: sometimes with acceptance and tolerance, but other times with suspicion, hatred and even expulsion.[13] According to William W. Menzies,

> There is overwhelming evidence that the gifts of the Spirit never did cease entirely. The pages of church history are punctuated with isolated and limited outpourings of the Spirit. None of these eruptions survived. Certainly the main stream of the Christian church did not embrace such occurrences, but the evidence remains that there has been at least a sprinkling of gifts of the Spirit throughout the centuries.[14]

In order to illumine this point of the prevalence of the gifts of the Holy Spirit, including speaking in tongues, healing, etc., in the church all through the history of Christianity, we may glimpse through the pages of the history of Christianity. In the history of the post-apostolic times, Tertullian (the North African Bishop, *c.* 155-220) was an advocate of the gifts of the Holy Spirit such as prophecy, visions and ecstasy. Bishop Ignatius of Antioch speaks of an ability to understand heavenly things and his special gift, which he must restrain with humility. The *Didache* and the *Shepherd of Hermas* recognize prophets who spoke in the Spirit, and the author of *Hermas* was carried away in the Spirit when he saw visions.[15] Bishop Clement of Rome tells the Corinthian believers that a full outpouring of the Holy Spirit was upon them. Justin Martyr writes: 'Now it is possible to see among us women and men who possess gifts of the Spirit of God' and mentions of exorcism practised by Christians of his time. Bishop Irenaeus of Gaul (*c.* 130-202) wrote of prophecy, casting out demons, healing through the laying on of hands and even the raising of the dead. Clement of Alexandria stated that a perfect Christian is characterized by his or her reception of the charismata of 1 Corinthians 12. The Church Fathers never suggested that any of the gifts of the Spirit had ceased.[16] Throughout the first and second centuries, the gifts remained very important to the church. The church prior to AD 200 was charismatic.[17] But as the institutional structure and hierarchy slowly crept into the Christian movement towards AD 260, and a highly organized, well-educated, wealthy, socially-powerful segment increased in number in the church, the charismatic gifts came to be localized and formalized and ritualized in the offices of the bishops and priests,[18] and later on from their offices, these gifts were relegated to the verandas of the church.

After Origen (*c.* 184-254), most Western church writers of the Contstantinean and post-Contstantinean era began to think that charismatic gifts were for biblical times and had now ceased. For example, John Chrysostom (*c.* 347-407) said that spiritual gifts were no longer were needed. Augustine (354-430) was somewhat ambiguous on the subject. He said that occasions of speaking with tongues in the New Testament were 'signs adapted to the time' that had passed away. He posed a rhetorical question expecting a negative answer: 'For who expects in these days that those on whom hands are laid that they may receive the Holy Spirit should forthwith begin to speak with tongues?' Due to the influence of men like Augustine in the Western church and the church's imperial identification, status and ties, the subject of the Holy Spirit had become a closed chapter in this strand of the church.

But among the Eastern Christians we continue to hear of the practices of Pentecostal-like charismata. The Egyptian monk Pachomius reported to have spoken in tongues of angels. Gregory of Nizianzus mentions instances of divine healing in his family and of the diversity of the Spirit's gifts. According to Anderson, 'The Orthodox churches have always recognized, expected and controlled the charismata, including speaking in tongues, which has been a continuing experience throughout all the ages among them, though confined mainly to the monasteries.'[19]

Even in the middleages this was the case in eastern Christianity and churches. Pneumatology has always been at the centre of their theology. They have been open to the gifts of the Holy Spirit. Symeon, the New Theologian (AD 949-1022) was a mystic who has written much about his ecstatic experiences such as speaking in tongues and baptism in the Holy Spirit as a separate experience from water baptism. Gregory of Palamas (1296-1359) wrote of experiences of healing, tongues and interpretation of tongues.

In Western Europe the Catholic church continued to deny the possibility of spiritual gifts. By the eleventh century AD, the Western church regarded charismatic manifestations as demonic. In their place an elitist scholasticism and monarchism began to reign supreme in the church. However, even in those days of high scholasticism and monarchism also there were isolated reports of ecstatic experiences. The German Abbess Hildegard of Bingen (AD 1098-1179) was known for her fearless prophesies and miracles, oracles and speaking in tongues and interpretation.[20] Others with such experiences include Gertrude of Helfta, Brigitta of Sweden and Catherine of Siena.[21] Thomas Aquinas (AD 1224-74) made a distinction between ordinary gifts of language and the charismata of 1 Corinthians 12. The latter for him are revelatory gifts of God. Bonaventure (AD 1217-74), a disciple of Francis of Assisi wrote about Christian growth in the Spirit and healing miracles. Dante in the *Divine Comedy* spoke of his own experience of ecstatic and unintelligible speech. Missionaries Francis Xavier and Louis Bertrand are said to have spoken in foreign languages they had never learned, and Xavier had the language of angels and a ministry of healing. These were isolated and unusual events in the lives of saints and mystics and were not the 'normal' part of church life.[22] But it is important to note that these gifts existed and were practised at least by a minority in the church.

During the Protestant Reformation in the West, the gifts of the Spirit seem to have been unknown apart from occasional reports in the radical Anabaptist movement. Martin Luther believed that speaking in tongues is a sign to the Jews and it had ceased. Calvin taught that God had removed the gift of speaking in tongues from the church and miracles no longer happen.[23] In comparison the Reformers opposed the religious enthusiasm more than the Catholics. However, the spiritual gifts continued in the radical periphery of Protestantism (among the Anabaptists, the Quakers, the Cevenol revivalists, the Holiness and Pietist movements, some of the early Methodist and Scottish Presbyterian preachers, among the north American Shakers, Russian Pentecostals in the Black Sea area, the Moravian movement)[24] which was branded by the mainstream Protestants as sectarian tendencies.

Modern Pentecostalism: Beginnings and Background in the West

Modern Pentecostalism's immediate background in the West was in the nineteenth century Holiness movement[25] and German pietism. These movements in general and a few women belonging to such movements in particular (such as Phoebe Palmer[26] and others) emphasized the importance of a personal experience of God or a 'new birth' in the Holy Spirit over and above mere head-knowledge, as part of their argument for the ministry of women in the church. Pietism gave importance to emotion in Christian experience and worship. The Methodist-Holiness movement, the Reformed revivalism of Jonathan Edwards, and the Oberlin Perfectionism of revivalists like Charles Finney, the Keswick and Healing Movements of the nineteenth century England and America played an important influence in the rise of early modern Pentecostalism as a movement.[27] For instance during the Evangelical Revival of England in the late 1730s, John Wesley saw numerous 'outward signs' occur during his preaching. Similar occurrences are reported in Jonathan Edward's meetings.[28]

In 1894 a person by the name Frank Sandford, who was a Baptist pastor, experienced Spirit baptism through sanctification in the Holiness movement. He was, however, opposed to Pentecostalism. But his main impact was on Charles Parham of Topeka, Kansas and a few women[29] like Agnes Ozman, Mary Arthur, Anna Hall, Mabel Smith and Jessie Brown there who underwent a similar experience. He founded a Bible School in Houston, Texas where one of the odd attendees was William Joseph Seymour, a black African-American. He was permitted to sit outside the class room and listen to the lectures. After his training in Parham's School (Parham later on in his life turned out to be a strong advocate of white racism), Seymour went to Azusa Street in Los Angeles where modern Pentecostalism is believed to have its birth in the West.[30] Here various women, both black and white, also figured prominently.[31]

Pentecostalism in India: Apostolic and Historical Roots

In India Christianity began, according to tradition, with the mission and ministry of Apostle Thomas who was one among the twelve disciples of Jesus.[32] As a member of the Twelve, he was a participant of the Jerusalem Pentecost (of Acts 2) and a witness and practitioner of the Pentecost experience and expressions of the early Christian Charismatic and Pentecostal-like movement.

After the Jerusalem Pentecost and after being filled with the Holy Spirit, when the disciples of Jesus fanned out of Palestine, Thomas apparently chose to move to the east, to South Asia where there were settlements of Jews at various locations.[33] In Malankara (now Kerala) after his arrival, Thomas most definitely preached, professed, practised and presented a Christianity that he was familiar with and experienced along with the other apostles in Jerusalem. It is, therefore, unwise to think that he brought, preached, practised and presented a Christianity that is totally different from what the New Testament attests, and that the Malankara Thomas Christians at the outset in the first Christian century had a spiritual experience that is totally disconnected from the spiritual experiences of the earliest Christian believers of Jerusalem and Antioch, experiences so vividly attested in the Christian Testament.[34]

So I, as an historian of Christian Origins and a student of the Christian Testament, have no reason to suspect the possible charismatic and Pentecostal-like experiences of the Thomas Christians of Malankara in their earliest days. Subsequent to Thomas' charismatic Pentecostal-like missionary work, many Antiochean (Syrian) charismatic Christians apparently migrated to Malabar. These Antiochean Syrian charismatic Christians along with their eastern bishops and natives who converted into Christianity in India most probably believed and practised the gifts of the Holy Spirit including speaking in the tongues of angels and other ecstatic experiences just like some of their eastern bishops like Ignatius, Gregory and others.[35] This may be viewed as an argument from silence without any reliable historical evidence. But if we claim that the Thomas Christians in Malabar began their history from AD 52 and Thomas was a disciple of Jesus who came to Malabar, then his religious experiences that he practised, and the message that he propagated and preached in Malabar may not be different from that of what we read in the Christian Testament in general and in the Acts of the Apostles and in the earliest eastern church Fathers in particular. Therefore, there is no good enough reason to think that the apostle Thomas and the subsequent early immigrant eastern Syrian Christians and their bishops from Antioch and the native converts took a different course and pursued a totally disconnected experience from that of their fellow believers and bishops in Jerusalem, Antioch and Alexandria.

Perhaps the importance attributed to the Holy Spirit and spiritual gifts must have waned, if not vanished altogether, when the Malabar Christians got entangled initially into internal squabbles concerning the authenticity of the ecclesiastical offices and the ordination of their bishops. Later on they were forced into a relation with the colonial Western, mainly Portuguese Roman Catholic Christian tradition of the militant Jesuits, who vigorously opposed the Protestants in the West through a counter-Reformation movement and attempted to coerce and convert the Indian Syrian Christians into Western Roman colonial Catholicism.[36]

However, the importance attributed to the spirit and the practice of spiritual gifts prevailed within the eastern and Indian Christianity. This would be the reason why some suggest that the Oriental Orthodox churches do not believe in the cessation of Charismata and see continuity between their experiences with that of the modern Indian Pentecostal spiritual experiences.[37] According to Burgess and McGee, two important authorities on Indian Pentecostal and Charismatic movements,

> Pentecostal and Pentecostal-like movements in India preceded the development of 20th century pentecostalism in North America and Europe by at least 40 years. Apart from the revival under Edward Irving in the UK in the early 1830s, the most prominent revivals of the 19th century characterized by the charismatic gifts of the Holy Spirit occurred in India. When modern pentecostalism began there in 1906, it developed independently from the influence of similar revivals in the West.[38]

Preludes: Pentecostal-like Revival Movements in South India

Though we may establish an important link of modern Pentecostalism in India to the earliest followers of Jesus and to the Christian Testament and its roots in the Eastern Church's pneumatology, we do not underestimate the reforming effects of the works of Church Missionary Society (CMS) and other Protestant missionaries of holiness orientation in bringing reforms among the Malabar and other south Indian Christians. We know that some of the CMS missionaries like Thomas Norton, Benjamin Bailey, and Henry Baker worked closely with the Syrian church and taught at the Old Seminary in Kottayam founded by John Munroe (in 1813). Their cooperation and teaching paved the way for a revision of liturgy and removal of corruption and superstitions.[39] It sparked off the process of a revival and reformation in the Malankara Syrian Orthodox Church in 1837 especially under the leadership of a 'Malankara Martin Luther' by the name of Malpan Abraham (Malpan meaning Professor) of Maramon, who was a teacher at the Old Seminary at that time. This resulted in the very birth of a reformed church called the Mar Thoma Syrian Christian Church of Malabar.[40] The root of modern Pentecostal movement among the Syrian Christians in Kerala can be traced back to this and similar revival and reformation movements led by numerous native revival Christian preachers like Justus Joseph, Mahakavi K.V. Simon, Sadhu Kochukunju Upadesi, Punchamannil Mammen Upadesi and many other known and unknown revival preachers and wandering charismatics (men and women) of that time.

Similar revivals took place among the Christian converts in Tirunelveli and Travancore in the 1860s and 1870s as a result of the influence of missionaries from CMS and Pietistic background. These revivals marked the restoration of the charismatic gifts and other paranormal or 'pentecostal-like' phenomena. One such revival began at Tirunelveli in 1860 under the leadership of one John Aroolappan, a trained Anglican catechist. The charismatic phenomena in this revival included prophecy, glossolalia, interpretation of tongues, dreams, signs in heaven, falling down and vigorous evangelism, etc.[41]

According to McGee and Burgess, from the outset this revival took an indigenous turn. Missionaries and Western money had little or no influence in evangelistic outreach where men and women were involved. These revived Christians as a result moved out of the control of paternalistic missionary societies, churches and authoritarian clergy.[42] Through the influence of

Aroolappan family and their followers, the movement spread westward a decade later into nearby Travancore among CMS congregations and those of the Syrian Church of Malabar where it got considerable progress. Prominent among the two leaders who emerged within this movement were Kudarapallil Thommen and a Hindu covert Justus Joseph. Some of the highlight of this revival were the negation of caste, involvement of women in ministry, *glossolalia* and other related spiritual phenomena, setting aside of the Syriacal liturgical worship, challenging the meaningless rituals and festivals, and rejecting the monarchical and alienated episcopacy.

Preludes: Pentecostal-like Revival Movements in North-East and in North India

Towards the beginning of the twentieth century, independent of what was happening in Tirunelveli and Travencore (and in Topeka and Azusa Street in the USA), in the north-east of India in Khasia Hills revival broke out (in March 1905) among the tribal peoples of north-east at Welsh Presbyterian mission stations and at the Pandita Ramabai Mukti mission in Kedgaon, Pune[43] and the Zenana Bible and Medical orphanage at Manmad and CMS boarding school at Mumbai in Maharashtra with manifest gifts of the Holy Spirit such as *glossolalia* and other Pentecostal-like phenomena. This pushed aside the traditional Western order of worship and hierarchy.[44] In these revivals and experiences speaking in tongues was not seen as a primary evidence of the baptism of the Holy Spirit or a requirement of missionary preaching as in classical Pentecostalism later on.

The Holy Spirit led mission in north India especially in the north-west Punjab and frontier provinces is brought to light by James Massey in his article 'Holy Spirit Led Mission in North India'.[45] After suggesting the strong possibility of St. Thomas coming first to Punjab, then part of the Parthian Empire prior to his coming to Malabar in south India on the basis of the Apocryphal Acts of Thomas, Massey appears to make a passionate proposal of a Holy Spirit led Pentecostal-like mission and ministry of Thomas and the churches of Thomas Christians in the north-west of India which were later destroyed by the Indo-Kushan Mahayana Buddhist kings. Then it was the modern Protestant (Presbyterian) missionaries' turn to begin the Christian mission work in the north-west of Punjab. According to Massey these missionaries' works had little progress during the first fifty years (AD 1834-85) due to their exclusive focus of ministry among the upper castes. But from 1885 things began to change in terms of the number of Punjabis who turned to Christ which even surprised the Western missionaries. In the words of Massey, through this change

> we believe God's Spirit reveals its movement very clearly, and we see God's working and His option for the poor, lowly and downtrodden turning this whole affair into a movement of the Spirit. But in the beginning this 'Spirit Movement' (which church historians have labelled—'Christian Mass Movement') was not a happy sign for Christian missionaries in Punjab because there were very few so-called upper castes who accepted the Gospel. . . . In reality the Punjabi Christian community/church come from a Dalit background and it is because of the 'Spirit or Holy Spirit led Movement' among the Punjabi Dalits, in which an early Punjabi Dalit Christian, namely Ditt, played a major role.[46]

By 1900 half of the people of Ditt's caste (*chuhra* community) accepted Christ and by 1915 almost all the Dalits, known as *chuhras* of Sialkot district had become Christians. The Presbyterian missionaries in fact were, in the words of Massey 'troubled about the way God's Spirit was working'. He laments that the belittling of Dalit Christians by Western missionaries and the upper caste Sikhs and Hindus had a negative impact on them. He longs therefore for yet another Pentecostal outpouring of the Holy Spirit so that a holistic transformative mission and ministry may take place among the Punjabi Christians. The mission and ministry of Sadhu Sunder Singh can be characterized as a charismatic and Pentecostal-like one. He lived and ministered just like a first century wandering charismatic Christian preacher,[47] a fact which most Indian Christian theologians and mainstream historians of the history of Christianity in India would not recognize as Pentecostal-like.

Advent of Modern Classical Pentecostalism in India

In 1907 the Garrs (Alfred and Josephine) landed in Kolkata with their experience from Azusa Street revival which changed the direction of the Pentecostal movement in India. About the same time a Pentecostal-like revival broke out in the Elliot Road Orphanage in Kolkata under the ministry of Fannie Simpson, a Methodist missionary in whose leadership (after her expulsion from the Methodist Church), an orphanage for girls was established at Purulia. From then on in certain quarters of the Pentecostal movement it is asserted that speaking in tongues is the sole evidence of the baptism of the Holy Spirit [which is the stand taken by classical Pentecostals in the west (Parham) and in south India in the early days of the movement]. Thus speaking in tongues became the hallmark of a Pentecostal. Garrs travelled across the country and preached the classical Pentecostal doctrine. But this was questioned by Minnie Abrams and others who did not see speaking in tongues as the sole sign of Spirit baptism.

Despite this dispute, the largest number of veteran missionaries in any one country to embrace the pentecostal gifts including speaking in tongues lived in India by 1910, and among them a good number was women (Kate Knight of Christian and Missionary Alliance, Ramabai and Minnie Abrams of Mukti and many others[48]) who made notable contributions in theological and missiological reflections. Most of them remained Pentecostal-like within their own mission agencies and were unwilling to accept the classical Pentecostal view of speaking in tongues.

According to Burgess and McGee, mission publications carried stories of Pentecostal-like experiences across India among the Anglicans (CMS), Baptists, Danish Lutherans, members of the Christian and Missionary Alliance, LMS, Church of Scotland, Young Men's and Women's Christian Associations, Methodists, Presbyterians, Brethren and others. Along with confessions of sin and prayer storms, other wonders and charismatic phenomena captured attention: dreams, visions, signs in the heaven, accounts of visible 'tongues of fire', prophecies and miraculous provisions of food.[49] These Spirit-works across denominations and Pentecostal-like experiences and expressions need to be seen as a prelude to the later larger ecumenical gathering of foreign mission societies (International Mission Conference) in 1910 famously known as the Edinburgh 1910, a fact which did not receive much space within the mainstream of Christian historiography.

Spread of Classical Pentecostalism in South India and its Expansion to North India

It may be right to say that in comparison, south India was more responsive than north India to Pentecostalism. George Berg, an American missionary with Azusa Street revival experience came to Bangalore, in India in 1908. Another missionary who came to India, who later became the founder of Assemblies of God Pentecostal denomination was Mary Weems Chapman. She travelled extensively throughout India and settled in Madras in 1915. Later she moved to Kerala (Travancore) to help the flood victims. Along with a British AG missionary, Spencer May in 1922, she published the first Malayalam Pentecostal magazine called *Pentecostal Trumpet*. Robert Cook, another missionary touched by the Azusa Street Pentecostalism, came to India in 1913. Initially he worked with George Berg in Bangalore and visited various parts of Travencore. He later on left AG and moved to Chengannur in Kerala and founded the Mount Zion Bible Institute at Mulakuza in June 1927 with the help of two native school teachers turned charismatic preachers T.M. Varghese and

K.E. Abraham and a farmer turned charismatic preacher named K.C. Cherian from Kidangannur-Mezuveli. The former (T.M. Varghese) later on became the leader of the church of God (full Gospel) denomination of the Indian Pentecostal Church centred at Mulakuza and the latter two (K.E. Abraham and K.C. Cherian) in 1930s severed ties from Cook and Varghese and founded the Indian Pentecostal Church (IPC) centring their work at Kumbanad near Maramon.

John H. Burgess from the Assemblies of God (AG) came to Kerala in 1927 and founded the Bethel Bible Institute at Mavelikkara, which was later shifted to Punalur. This is the earliest Bible College of AG outside the US. Currently these three are the leading Pentecostal denominations in India with their own theological and ministerial training centres. At present the Indian Pentecostal Church of God (IPC) is the largest Pentecostal denomination in Kerala and also in India. In 1953 there was a split in IPC which led to the beginning of Sharon Fellowship Church under the leadership of Pastor P.J. Thomas. This church now has its headquarters at Thiruvalla and is currently led by Pastor T.G. Koshy, the founder president of Faith Theological Seminary, Manakkala, the first Pentecostal theological college in India affiliated to the Senate of Serampore College (University).

From the 1960s onwards we witness an upsurge and a quiet but rapid spread of Pentecostalism from Kerala to other states in India. The message of Pentecostalism especially the outpouring of the Holy Spirit with visible manifestation of speaking in tongues, signs and wonders, was taken to Andhra Pradesh by Pastor P.M. Samuel. He along with Pastor Paramjyoti, a native of Andhra Pradesh, was instrumental in spreading the Indian Pentecostal Church in Andhra Pradesh. It is from this strand that later on the Manna Church, a neo-charismatic church, originated under the leadership of Pastor Ernest Komanappali, son of pastor Paramjyoti and the New Testament Church of God and the Church on the Rock Theological College under the leadership of Pastor P.J. Titus at Bheemunipatanam in Andhra Pradesh.

Pastor Kurian Thomas took the message of Pentecost to Itarsi in Madhya Pradesh and founded the Central India Bible College and the Itarsi Fellowship of Churches which has branch churches in various parts of north India. This Fellowship of churches later spread to Rajasthan under the leadership of Pastor Thomas Mathews, to Surat and the surrounding tribal areas of Gujarat under the leadership of Pastor Raju Thomas. The Bible school that Pastor Thomas Mathews founded (Philadelphia Bible School) and the churches that began under its banner and the annual convention (Navapur Convention) they conduct, are well known among the Pentecostal Christians of north India.

Pioneers like Pastor P.S. Samuel took Pentecostalism to Raipur, Chhattisgarh. Pastor P.M. Thomas and his brother P.M. Philip took a Pentecostal-like church to Jammu & Kashmir which paved the way for the founding of Kashmir Evangelical Fellowship. Similar Pentecostal-like movements are led by Pastor P.G. Varghese (founder of Indian Evangelical Team and Bible College at Pippariya, Madhya Pradesh) and others to various parts of north India. One wandering charismatic named Sadhu Magdhulla and Pastor Harry Lydle and other pastors like T.J. Simon, Jacob Chacko and others are instrumental in spreading Pentecostalism in western Uttar Pradesh and Uttarakhand. The Doon Bible College which they led is one of the earliest Pentecostal Bible Colleges in north India and the Masih Mandali annual convention that takes place in the College ground is the earliest of its kind for Pentecostals in north India. Pastor Lanz was a leading Pentecostal pastor in Meerut and he was instrumental in pioneering the Pentecostal movement in the northwestern part of Uttar Pradesh.

The Operation Agape ministries started by Pastor C. George and a team of prayer partners during the violent Operation Blue Star days in Punjab had a tremendous impact in Punjab and its neighbouring states like Delhi, Himachal Pradesh and Jammu

& Kashmir since the 1980s. It began as a prayer initiative in Kottayam in Kerala praying specially for peace in Punjab in the violent Blue Star days which later led to a revival in the Christian Medical College at Ludhiana. A number of senior doctors like its Director Dr. Victor Chaudhari and other Professors like Dr. Alex Abraham and his wife left CMC for full-time Christian church ministry in the late 1980s. Dr. Chaudhari is now heading a popular house church movement in Madhya Pradesh and Dr. Abraham leads the Operation Agape Church planting movement centred in Delhi, Punjab and other north Indian states.

Others who are inspired by the Operation Agape prayer movement include Rev. George Chavanikamannil who founded the Bharat Susamachar Samiti, a charitable society that runs the New Theological College[50] and a number of schools and related socially empowering ministries in Uttarakhand and a church planting movement called the Christian Evangelistic Assemblies which currently has nearly 300 plus churches in many north Indian states. Squadron leader (retd.) Mohan Philip and Major (retd) Arun Kumar who were connected to Operation Agape ministries now lead independently the UP Mission which focuses on mission work in the rural villages of central and eastern Uttar Pradesh.

The *Yesu Darbar* under the leadership of R.B. Lal in Allahabad is yet another Pentecostal-like mission and church initiative which made huge inroads into the rural parts of Allahabad. These emerging charismatic and Pentecostal-like churches and socially and educationally empowering mission initiatives are in addition to the traditional classical Pentecostal churches such as the Indian Pentecostal Church, the Assemblies of God, Church of God and other established and known churches spread across the whole length and breadth of the country.

A number of these emerging church planting initiatives may identify themselves with neo-charismatic and neo-pentecostals. In addition to these there are also other Pentecostal-like charismatic and mega-church ministries such as the New Apostolic

Church (mainly in Tamil Nadu), the New Life Fellowship (in Mumbai), Missions India (in Nagpur, Maharashtra), Nagaland Christian Revival churches (in the north-eastern states), Christ Groups (in central India), the Omega Full Gospel Assembly and the Upper Room Ministries (in Karnataka). Such numerous named and innumerable unnamed charismatic and Pentecostal and Pentecostal-like churches, gatherings, mission initiatives and socially and missionally empowering organizations now constitute the largest Christian constituency in India.[51]

Most of these emerging churches and movements have not gained their deserved space in the academic limelight and in the acknowledged Christian scholarly (Pentecostal, Evangelical and Ecumenical) circles, publications and historiography. Some of them are initiated by charismatic Christian leaders who have the sense of divine call and their family members who pursued their call and passion. Their continuity and future leadership now appears to be more firmly family based than institutionally organized church structures despite having many churches and pastors. These missions and churches have their own publications which have a limited circulation mostly within their own mission organizations and churches. Perhaps it is time for researchers and church historians to examine this sphere of the growth of Christianity in India in order to assess their impact on church growth and on the socio-economic and cultural spheres of life of the nation in general and of the Indian Christians in particular.

The Pentecostal and Charismatic Movements and the Social Demands of the Gospel

There is a general prejudiced perception mainly among the main-line so called 'great tradition' Christians that the 'little tradition' Pentecostal and Charismatic Christians are other worldly sectarian 'sheep stealers' who seal and cement their spirituality solely within a private, personal level. They are so other-worldly and apocalyptic minded that they ignore the this-worldly life related issues of poverty, exploitation and injustice. Pentecostals are branded as advocates of a 'pie in the sky', life-after-death doctrine, as those who separate the sacred and the secular, who do not relate with or engage in wider social concerns.

But these are prejudiced perceptions. Such stereotyping can also be made on a wide range of Christians including many who belong to the 'great tradition' main-line churches, who have not resolved, and quiet rightly so, the insoluble 'promise-fulfilment', 'already-not yet' eschatological tension. I think that the aspiration and hope for an other-worldly life helps such main-line and Pentecostal and Charismatic Christians to be dissatisfied and even critical of this-worldly norms and oppressive status quos.[52] The Pentecostal longing for the other-worldly life is a dream that drives them towards the fuller realization of the new humanity (the new creation) which they experience inwardly in Christ here and now through the infilling of the Holy Spirit and outwardly in their festive worship and community life.[53] Pentecostals live in anticipation and strive for the advent of that new creation day. In the words of Harvey Cox, the volcanic eruption of the Pentecostal movement that relies on the direct experience of the Divine Spirit, rather than on archaic creeds and stately rituals, represents a dramatic example of a much larger development and a quieter revolution that is currently taking place in Christianity and in the world at large.[54]

The early Pentecostals were highly eschatological and apocalyptic dreamers who were keen on missionary and evangelistic work to save the least and the lost from eternal damnation.[55] In that sense they, like the post-biblical and early Christian apocalyptic visionaries, appear to be more other-worldly than this-worldly to an outside observer. But as the post-biblical and early Christian eschatology and apocalypticism had an inherent this-worldly political focus,[56] and that such writings were highly charged political (anti-colonial) writings in the first century context, the Pentecostal spirituality, theologically and experientially, is well-placed to engage the socio-political concerns of life. The socially marginalized persons attracted to Pentecostalism find in the Pentecostal experience the power to resist compliance with the *status quo* and struggle for a better life. The spiritual experiences of the Pentecostals create in them a 'symbolic world and meaning system' that question *status quo* and aspire for a better life.[57]

The Pentecostals' rejection of the world is symbolic and their spiritual expressions such as speaking in tongues, healing, etc., and the belief in the imminent end of the world with the return of Christ affirm their sense of personal worth and give them control over their lives and sustain them to cope with the insecurities of change and uncertainties of future. The theme expressed in Pentecostal meetings—radical conversion, sanctification in daily life, divine healing from all sicknesses and the powerful experienced presence of God through His Spirit in their midst, and the premillennial rapture—provide comfort in this life in dealing with disappointments and fears. The Pentecostal faith and expressions of festive worship and emotional outbursts, though they may appear like a 'feast of fools', they create a symbolic world for the faithful (fools for Christ) to live in and negotiate a life of meaning despite the uncertainties of present-day life.[58]

According to Alan Anderson, 'The history and theology of Pentecostalism certainly makes room for engagement with society, especially because of the freedom brought about by the Pentecostal experience'.[59] The Pentecostal experience of Spirit baptism is an experience of social empowerment. It gives the Pentecostals a new sense of certainty in terms of their vision for the future, boldness, confidence, determination and assertiveness at the individual level which can potentially be translated into public realms of life. The Pentecostal experience of speaking in tongues is an empowering experience of gaining voice by the voiceless within the community of believers. It is an experience of being baptized in the Logos (*sabda-nada*/primeval sound) of God and releasing the logos of the Logos.

Those who study the history of Pentecostalism and know its mission, ministry and theology from within would argue that modern Pentecostalism has its roots in the Jesus movement and therefore it has certain characteristics of that movement especially its focus on the alienated and the marginalized.[60] Just as the Jesus movement has its origin among the poor and the marginalized Galileans, who were living in the valley and shadow of death (Matt. 4.12ff), the modern Pentecostalism has its following predominantly from the socially and economically ostracized and dispossessed segments of society. Most of its pioneers in the United States of America and United Kingdom, for example, were from the racially segregated and oppressed black community.[61] Many were named and unnamed women[62] who were committed to speaking in the church and engaging socially in empowering ministries.[63] In recent years, this trend continues as we see the greatest quantitative growth of Pentecostalism in sub-Saharan Africa, South-East Asia, China, South Korea[64] and in Latin America[65] where its growth has been so phenomenal among the downtrodden that some would even think that the whole continent of Latin America may become Pentecostal.

In India too most of its early pioneers and believers were from the lower strata of society, both Syrian and Dalit.[66] In Kerala and elsewhere its reach is mainly among the lower segments of the Syrians, Catholics and other Protestant mainline Christians, though it is not exclusively limited to them. Many of the early leaders of Indian Pentecostalism in the post-Independent era were from the mainline Christianity because the Pentecostal movement in its initial days began as a reform movement within Christianity which later on emerged with its own denominational identity (similar to that of the Mar Thoma Church and for that matter any other Christian denominations that emerged in Indian Christianity). This led to an antagonistic stand between the mainstream Christians and the Pentecostal Christians. The former expelled those who took believers' baptism and those who show any sign of charismatic, festive expressions of joyful worship. The latter too viewed themselves as 'born again' 'saved' 'believers' and all others as nominal Christians, if not unbelievers. It took nearly 60 plus years for this antagonism to ease a little now even though it is not completely gone from the heart and mind of many on both sides of the divide.

Pentecostalism poses a severe criticism to the traditional churches for ignoring the marginated population of the world. It continues a vigorous critique to the abstract deity of Western and the classical Indian Christian theologies and philosophical systems. With its promise of an unmediated experience of God and of health and well being now, not just after death, it appeals to the millions of people the other churches failed to reach. This aspect of health and healing here and now reveals the this-worldly liberational focus of Pentecostalism. According to Anderson,

> the history and theology of Pentecostalism certainly makes room for engagement with society, especially because of the freedom brought about by the pentecostal experience. One of the results of the experience of the Spirit is what I term a 'Pentecostal theology of liberation'. On issues of discrimination or equality on the basis of race, class or gender, Pentecostals and Charismatics have sometimes led the way. . . .[67]

Pentecostalism began as a peoples' movement from 'below' away from the elite clergy, archaic rituals, and detached theologies and theologians. Therefore from early on it attracted people from ordinary walks of life, people who did not belong to the centres of ecclesiastical authority, who were neglected by the monarchic hierarchy. They faced ridicule, persecution and excommunication from established churches due to their experience of being filled with the Holy Spirit and speaking in tongues. The moment when they are filled with the Holy Spirit and profess their joyous experience in the fullness of the Spirit of Christ, they are exposed as heretical 'missed-line sectarians' and expelled from the mainline Christian churches.[68] But the newly-received experience and spiritual gifts give the excommunicated ones a confidence that enable them to withstand such experiences of ridicule, persecution and expulsion and assert an identity of their own just like the Johannine charismatic and Pentecostal-like Christians of the first century who were expelled from the Jewish synagogues and the churches of the Jewish cultural nationalist conservative Christians due to their high christology, realized eschatology, charismatic ecclesiology and parakeletic pneumatology (John 9.22; 12.42).[69]

The modern Pentecostalism began with a radical call to freedom from ecclesiastical oppressive structures, alienated episcopacy, unbiblical dogmas, traditions, beliefs and meaningless rituals, written down and antiquated liturgies and their emotionless, detached recitals, in a clergy-controlled ecclesial environment. In the place of a clergy controlled church life and worship, the Pentecostals introduced a wide variety of expressions of enthusiastic worship and prayer sessions where women and ordinary believers who are filled with the Holy Spirit too took leading positions. In the Pentecostal churches, their spirituality is expressed through songs, spontaneous prayers and outbursts, prophecies, a narrative theology and witness (testimonies). Though some of the Pentecostal churches are slowly turning to become institutional and hierarchical,[70] in their popular and informal gatherings, the ordinary members including women who are filled with the Holy Spirit and gifts of the Holy Spirit still take the lead.

Pentecostals maintain an ecumenical vision[71] and advocate a non-racial, caste-crossing and caste-erasing community life.[72] The Wesleyan and other holiness movements' roots of Pentecostalism give it a strong anchor to pose a social critique. They give a platform for a dialogue between Pentecostalism and liberation theology. For example, in Latin America the Pentecostals are playing an important political role for social transformation throughout the region.[73] Social transformation and empowerment of the downtrodden is a major focus of Pentecostal ministries in many part of India too at least in places where I am aware of the growth of Pentecostalism in north India.

From early on the Pentecostal churches did extensive mission work among the depressed castes and communities unlike the other main-line Christian churches. There was a great inflow of people from the dominated castes and communities to Pentecostalism and the baptism of the Holy Spirit brought an empowering experience to members coming from those communities.[74] The baptism in the Holy Spirit and speaking in tongues and other spiritual gifts challenged the caste barriers and other dehumanizing agencies and many entered into pastoral and other leading positions in the church and theological and ministerial training institutions from the marginal castes. This gave them opportunities to leadership within the churches and to assert their own identity and leadership in the church. It challenged the monarchical and ecclesiastical hierarchy and the family, social superiority of many in the mainline Christianity.[75] In the words of George Oommen (Biju),

> In the Pentecostal churches, there was no discrimination with regard to seating. All sat on the floor, no matter which caste they belonged to. It is also observed that unlike traditional churches, Pentecostal churches provided an opportunity to respond to the emotional nature of human beings. . . . Pentecostal preachers talked about equality, freedom in the Spirit and also criticised the traditional rituals of the church. These attracted the Dalits to Pentecostal churches. Moreover, Pentecostal worship was more akin to their pre-Christian religiosity (spirituality). Ecstatic forms of worship, use of drums in the church and opportunities to share testimonies as well as other experiences made the Dalits feel at home in the Pentecostal churches.[76]

Pentecostalism, as it matures in recent years in experience and theological reflection, is responding in an increasing level to the social demands of the gospel. Pentecostal theologians like Douglas Petersen,[77] Steven Land[78] and many others are inviting the Pentecostals to relate the Lukan experience of the power of the Spirit as expressed in the Acts of the Apostles to the Kingdom theology of Luke's Gospel. They sketch a wide theological programme which has to do with hermeneutics, trinitarian reflection and social and political ethics as much as with evangelization, church planting, prayer and praise. According to Miguez Bonino, the

> Pentecostal reflection on the Kingdom of God and the eschatological dimension of the Pentecostal experience to social responsibility can be best developed in a Trinitarian perspective in which the experiential unity of body and spirit, personalization and community and apocalyptic expectation of the Pentecostal spirituality and the emerging sense of the unity of Pentecost and Jubilee (Acts 2 and Luke 4)—the power of the Spirit and the peace and justice of the kingdom—are set in the context of the creative, redeeming and fulfilling purpose and action of the triune God.[79]

The Pentecostal belief, experience and expressions of the *pneuma* (spirit) may thus be seen as an alternative way of acquiring a liberative and liberated space in society. Their worship sessions are festive, freedom sessions where there is freedom of expression and emotions. The ideal heavenly life is experienced here and now; expressions of the Kingdom of God are seen in their worship sessions. It is from here that the Pentecostals move out into the world with a longing to strive for structures and institutions in the society to be changed. On the one hand, the Pentecostals live in a world practicality marked by experiential proofs and limits; on the other hand, they live in a world where individuals are not held captive to prevailing social and intellectual notions of rationality because God is establishing His new eschatological order.[80] Therefore, they demonstrate a desire to live peaceably within the existing order to the extent that it provided for their immediate needs but at the same time they demonstrate a capacity to critique the prevailing existing order as sinful in nature. The Pentecostals want to see tangible evidences of the working of the spirit in tongues and healing in historical life situations. Tongues signify the unity of diverse nations and peoples into the one body of Christ, and healings express recovery and restoration of that which is disturbed and distorted by the sinfulness of humankind.

The Pentecostal understanding of mission is grounded first and foremost in the conviction that the Holy Spirit is the motivating power behind this activity. The Pentecostal mission work is marked by signs and wonders and their evangelism is geared towards planting alternate Christ communities in society that will model the new creation lifestyles through their community life. Ever since the eruption of modern Pentecostalism, there is a tremendous church planting movement in many parts of India and around the globe which is not sufficiently documented. Most of these churches are house churches and they are mostly among the downtrodden classes, castes and tribals and other marginal communities. These ministries are initiated by the Holy Spirit-led individuals. Their activities are not limited to church planting. Wherever the Pentecostal churches emerged we can also see socially engaging and empowering ministries such as schools, orphanages and other socially engaging and transforming ministries.

Some of the early Pentecostals in India were keen to start schools, orphanages and dispensaries whereever they went as missionaries and church planters. For example, George Berg established five schools for children, each connected with a church and Robert Cook established four schools. But in comparison with other churches in this area of education, the Pentecostals did very little. In recent years this is slowly changing. Most of the unnamed emerging Pentecostal churches in north India are showing more interest in education-related mission activities. This may be because of the difficulties they face in evangelism in north India. Many mission organizations and churches, however, stayed in these difficult and unresponsive places through launching social and economically empowering ministries such as orphanages, schools, leper asylums and dispensaries to bring in a difference in the life of the disadvantaged and the under-privileged communities. The Assemblies of God has the most extensive system of institutional mission works in the Gangetic plain such as the Mission of Mercy founded by Mark and Huldah Buntain in Calcutta.[81] The Pentecostal Holiness church has begun a focused ministry among the tribal communities such as Paharia, Ho, Bihor, Munda, Oraon and Kharia tribes in addition to their church's works in West Bengal, Orissa and Uttar Pradesh.

Another area where the Pentecostals made significant contribution is in empowering and involving women in Christian mission and ministry.[82] The experience of baptism in the Holy Spirit and subsequent ministries such as preaching, prayer, etc., under the anointing of the Holy Spirit challenged to a great extent the gender differences in the church. This is not to suggest that the Pentecostal churches have many anointed women in higher realms of leadership and ordained ministries in the churches. But theologically and biblically a way is open for them to enter into leadership and play active roles in ministries. None can reject the fact that the Pentecostal movement grew and spread due to the direct involvement of a good number of known, unknown and nameless women in the ministry.[83] Wherever the Pentecostal movement grew, there women played very important leading roles. Some would even say that 'Pentecostalism globally has been framed by the ministry of spirit-empowered women'.[84] Over half the Pentecostal congregations functioning by 1930 were established and led by women. According to Harvey Cox,

> Pentecostalism is unthinkable without women. Seymour was touched in his youth by a woman with a gift, then recommended by a second woman to a third who actually provided him with a place to exercise his call. From Sister Hutchins and Aimee Semple McPherson to Kathryn Kuhlman . . . women have continued to play a disproportionately pro-minent place in the Pentecostal movement. . . . Pentecostals, who take the authority of the Bible very seriously but also believe in direct revelation through visions, have opened a wider space for women than most other Christian denominations'.[85]

In the words of Barbara Cavaness, women played vital roles of preaching and leadership at Azusa Street as well as receiving the blessing of the group as they carried the message across the continent and overseas. Of the first eleven elders of the Azusa Street Apostolic Faith Mission six were women.[86] The early Pentecostals used the theology of Spirit baptism as the sole means of empowering for ministry. They believed that whoever received this empowering baptism of the Holy Spirit had an extraordinary call to minister irrespective of gender difference.[87]

But as the movement transformed into established and formal structured churches, a male-dominated hierarchy developed within, and as a result women are relegated to the backseats to lead only auxiliary ministries and men occupied the prime places of leadership. The Pentecostal church now appears to be struggling between what Harvey Cox says a 'contest between the fundamentalist and the experientialist impulse',[88] that is 'the experience of equality in the spirit is confronted by conservative Bible reading and theologies that insist on male leadership in the home and church'.[89] Increasing institutionalization of the Pentecostal churches is leading to the suppression of the operation of the spirit and of women to minister and lead. In the words of David Roebuck, 'with the Church of God steeped in a tradition of separate spheres and a literal interpretation of scriptures that seemingly prohibit women from serving as bishops and from usurping authority over men, there remains continued resistance to the idea of women serving as bishops or in governmental roles in the denomination'.[90] Pamela Holmes laments: 'Pentecostalism, even with its denial of this world's ways and thinking, nevertheless has been enculturated to think within the modern world's value systems'.[91] A recent observation shows that other than the Roman Catholic Church, the classical Pentecostal churches appear to be emerging as the biggest male-dominated churches in the world.[92] The spirit may be empowering women to preach, but the fundamentalist elements in the church are aborting the ministries of the prophetically-called women.[93] This, to a large extent, is setting the stage for stagnation, even decline, of many classical Pentecostal churches.[94] Time has come for the classical Pentecostals to listen to and respond to what the spirit is saying to the churches.[95]

The entry of Pentecostal and Charismatic students and teachers to Union Evangelical and Ecumenical platforms is paving the way for a better understanding between mainline and Pentecostal-Charismatic churches and theological institutions. Now there is a certain recognition and acceptance among Christians that Pentecostalism might teach us about our common future.[96] Hence, there are calls for combined forums, centres and gatherings between Ecumenicals, Evangelicals, Pentecostals and Charismatics.[97] The inclusion of Pentecostals in Ecumenical and Evangelical forums has injected a certain level of enthusiasm in those segments of the Christian traditions and in return it helped the Pentecostals to balance their spirituality with social concerns in a much more accelerated and visible manner than before. The Pentecostals, at least some of them,[98] feel at home to hang on inconstantly in-between the Evangelical and Ecumenical divide and learn from both without losing their own essential Pentecostal identity and spirituality. Thus we are beginning to witness the early days of a wider ecumenism within and between the Christianities of India. The way forward for various Christian traditions and expressions in India and in the world at large is in pursuing a *koinonia* and forming an *oikoumene* (economy/household) of God in Christ where there will be respectful relationship, understanding and acceptance without pride and prejudice.

As the Pentecostal movements are turning increasingly to become denominational there are neo-charismatics and neo-Pentecostals who are emerging as reformers in the peripheries of classical Pentecostalism. They are now drawing quite a lot of believers from the established classical Pentecostal and other mainline Christian denominations.[99] It is time therefore now for classical Pentecostals to look at themselves critically and creatively to see the enormous contribution that they, along with the neo-charismatics and neo-Pentecostals, can make to world Christianity in particular and the world at large in general.[100]

NOTES

1. See Ronald A.N. Kydd, *Charismatic Gifts in the Early Church: An Exploration into the Gifts of the Spirit During the First Three Centuries of the Christian Church*, Peabody: Hendrickson, 1984. This book was originally written as a PhD thesis in the University of St. Andrews, UK. Also see Paulson Pulikottil, 'Emergence of Indian Pentecostalism', *Dharma Deepika* (July-December 2002), pp. 47-58.
2. Janet Everts Powers, 'Pentecostalism 101: Your Daughters Shall Prophesy', in *Philip's Daughters: Women in Pentecostal-Charismatic Leadership*, ed. Estrelda Alexander and Amos Yong, Oregon: Pickwick Publications, 2011, p. 133.
3. C.C. Hill, *Hellenists and Hebrews*, Minneapolis: Fortress Press, 1992; Todd Penner, *In Praise of Christian Origins: Stephen and the Hellenists in Lukan Apologetic Historiography*, New York: T&T Clark, 2004.
4. Scott Spencer, *The Portrait of Philip in Acts: A Study of Roles and Relations*, Sheffield: SAP, 1992.
5. Amos Yong, *Who is the Holy Spirit: A Walk with the Apostles*, Massachusetts: Paraclete Press, 2011.
6. Larry Hurtado, *At the Origins of Christian Worship: The Context and Character of Christian Devotion*, Grand Rapids, Eerdmans, 1999. For a cautious outsider's views on early Christian spiritual experiences see Luke Timothy Johnson, *Religious Experience in Earliest Christianity*, Minneapolis: Fortress, 1998.
7. Amos Yong, *Who is the Holy Spirit: A Walk with the Apostles*, Brewster: Paraclete Press, 2011. Also see Ben Meyers, *The Early Christians: Their World Mission and Self Discovery*, Wilmington, Delaware: Michael Glazier, 1986; E. Schnabel, *Early Christian Mission* (vols. 1-2), Illinois: IVP, 2004; Simon Samuel, 'The Acts of Philip and Certain men of Cyprus and Cyrene: A Remapping of Early Christian Mission Frontiers', in *Remapping Mission Discourse*, ed. Simon Samuel and P.V. Joseph, Dehradun, Delhi: NTC/ISPCK, 2008, pp. 42-73.
8. Alan Anderson, *An Introduction to Pentecostalism: Global Charismatic Christianity*, Cambridge: Cambridge University Press, 2004, p. 19 (italics mine). Also see Wonsuk Ma, 'Full Circle Mission: A Possibility of Pentecostal Missiology', in *Asian Journal of Pentecostal Studies* 8.1 (2005), pp. 5-27. For more on the charismatic nature of early Christian worship see Larry Hurtado, *At the Origins of*

Christian Worship. For the New Testament root of Pentecostalism see Dongsoo Kim, 'Johannine Root of Pentecostalism: Johannine Self-understanding as an Archetype of Pentecostal Self-Understanding', *Asian Journal of Pentecostal Studies* 9.1 (2006), pp. 5-16; Roger Stronstand, *The Charismatic Theology of St. Luke*, Peabody, MA: Hendrickson, 1984; Craig S. Keener, *The Spirit in the Gospels and Acts*, Peabody, MA: Hendrickson, 1997; Robert Menzies, *Empowered for Witness: The Spirit in Luke-Acts*, Sheffield: SAP, 1999; Gordon Fee, *God's Empowering Presence: The Holy Spirit in the Letters of Paul*, Peabody, MA: Hendrickson, 1994.

9. This is advocated by John Darby, Warfield and others; currently the advocates of this position (cessationism) are found in Dallas Theological Seminary and the churches that adhere to its position.
10. V.V. Thomas adopted this method in his *Dalit Pentecostalism: Spirituality of the Empowered Poor*, Bangalore: ATC, 2008 and Lee Hong Jung in understanding '*Minjung* Pentecostalism', see his '*Minjung* and Pentecostal Movements in Korea', in Anderson and Hollenweger (eds.), *Pentecostals after a Century*, Sheffield: SAP, 1999, pp 138-60; Deborah Kaye Cole, 'Historiographic Approaches to Asian Pentecostalism', *AJPS* 9.1 (2006), pp. 59-82. For more on 'history from below' see Felix Wilfred and Jose D. Maliekal (eds.), *The Struggle for the Past: Historiography Today*, Chennai: University of Madras, 2002; Roger Hedlund, 'Christian History from the Underside: Indian Instituted Churches and Indigenous Christianity' (Keynote address in a conference on Subaltern Perspectives on Seminary Training, Centre for Dalit Solidarity, Dharmaram College, Bangalore, 23 October 1998.
11. Anderson, *An Introduction*, p. 19, Kydd, *Charismatic Gifts in the Early Church*; Pulikottil, 'Emergence of Indian Pentecostalism', pp. 47-58.
12. Kydd, *Charismatic Gifts in the Early Church;* Cecil M. Robeck, Jr. (ed.), *Charismatic Experiences in History*, Peabody, Mass.: Hendrickson, 1985.
13. Tertullian in his challenge to Marcion affirmed that gifts of the Spirit such as prophecy, visions, ecstasy and interpretation of tongues were forthcoming from my side without any difficulty. He also says that healing, revelation and exorcism were among the joys available to Christians. See Morton Kelsey, *Tongues Speaking: The History and Meaning of Charismatic Experience*, New York: Crossroad, 1981; Ronald A.N. Kydd, *Healing through the*

Centuries: Models of Understanding. The Montanist movement in the second century believed and practised the gifts of the spirit in their worship, for which they were branded as heretics by the orthodox strand of Christians. Speaking in tongues and prophecy were common among Montanus and his disciples; and they believed in 'progressive revelation', so distasteful and destabilizing for the emerging orthodoxy that sought to establish itself. See Paul McKechnie, *The First Christian Centuries: Perspectives on the Early Church*, Secunderabad: Om Books, 2004, pp. 171ff.

14. William W. Menzies, 'The Reformed Roots of Pentecostalism', *AJPS* 9.2 (2006), p. 282 (262-82). Also see D.A. Carson, *Showing the Spirit*, Grand Rapids: Baker, 1987, p. 166; Jack Deere, *Surprised by the Power of the Spirit*, Eastbourne: Kingsway Publications, 1994, pp. 73-6.
15. See McKechnie, *The First Christian Centuries*, pp. 75-8.
16. Anderson, *An Introduction*, p. 20
17. Kydd, *Charismatic Gifts*, p. 87.
18. Cyprian of Carthage (*c.* 200-58) for example said that the Charismata were the sole prerogative of the Bishop.
19. Anderson, *An Introduction*, p. 21.
20. See Columba Hart and Jane Bishop (trans.), *Scivias (Know the Ways of the Lord)* by *Hildegard of Bingen*, New York: Paulist Press, 1990, pp. 17ff
21. For more on such men and women and their experiences see Elizabeth Ruth Obbard (intro. & ed.), *Medieval Women Mystics*, New York: New City Press, 2002; Emilie Zum Brunn and G. Epiney-Burgard, *Women Mystics in Medieval Europe*, New York: Paragon House, 1989; Monica Furlong, *Visions & Longings: Medieval Women Mystics*, Boston: Shambhala, 1997; Paul E. Szarmarch, *An Introduction to the Medieval Mystics of Europe*, Albany: State University of New York Press, 1984.
22. Anderson, *An Introduction*, pp. 22-3.
23. John Calvin recognized the manifest work of the Spirit in a pioneering church planting (unreached) context. See Menzies, 'The Reformed Roots of Pentecostalism', pp. 262-82. Calvin was less rigid about cessationism than many of his followers like Warfield in that he held to the tradition that in unevangelized areas, apostles and prophetic gifts could recur to confirm the Gospel (p. 280).

24. Donald Gee, *The Pentecostal Movement*, London: Elim Publishing Company, 1949; Vinson Synan, *The Century of the Holy Spirit*, Nashville, TN: Thomas Nelson, 2001; D. Dayton, *Theological Roots of Pentecostalism*, Grand Rapids, MI: Francis Asbury Press, 1987.
25. Susie C. Stanley, 'Wesleyan/Holiness and Pentecostal Women: Pentecost as the Pattern for Primitivism', in *Philip's Daughters*, pp. 19-37.
26. For Phoebe Palmer's contribution to the emergence of Pentecostalism in the west see Janet Everts Powers, 'Pentecostalism 101: Your Daughters Shall Prophesy', in *Philip's Daughters*, pp. 133-51.
27. For more on this see Anderson, *An Introduction*, pp. 28ff., Menzies, 'The Reformed Roots of Pentecostalism'; Deere, *Surprised by the Spirit*, pp. 88ff.
28. Deere, *Surprised by the Spirit*, pp. 89f.
29. For an excellent study on women charismatic leaders in the Pentecostal Movement see Estrelda Alexander and Amos Yong (eds.), *Philip's Daughters: Women in Pentecostal-Charismatic Leadership*, Princeton Theological Monograph Series 104, Eugene, Oregon: Pickwick Publications, 2009.
30. In the historiography of Pentecostalism also the women pioneers of Pentecostalism is sidelined. There were many women participants and leaders in the Azusa Street Revival who later on became evangelists and missionaries around the world. See Estrelda Alexander, *The Women of Azusa Street*, Cleveland: Pilgrim, 2006.
31. Harvey Cox, *Fire from Above*, pp. 58, 79.
32. A.C. George, *Trailblazers for God: A History of the Assemblies of God of India*, Bangalore: SABC Publications, 2004, pp. 25f. Most mainstream historians (Mundadan and others) also acknowledge this fact. See A.M. Mundadan, *From the Beginning up to the Middle of the Sixteenth Century* (*History of Christianity in India*, vol. I), Bangalore: Church History Association of India, 1989, p. 64.
33. The Thomas traditions (Eastern and Western) confirm this fact.
34. An increasing number of New Testament scholars (Gordon Fee, Robert Menzies, Stronstad, Keener, etc.) now argue that the earliest Christians were Charismatics and the early Christian movement was a charismatic Pentecostal-like movement which manifested the gifts of the Holy Spirit such as speaking in tongues, healing (signs and wonders), etc., in mission and ministry. But historians and theologians of the mainstream church traditions and Syrian

Christian traditions hesitate to say this though they are earnest in anchoring their roots to St. Thomas.

35 Pulikottil, 'Emergence of Indian Pentecostalism', pp. 47-58.

36. Anderson, *An Introduction*, p. 23; Pulikottil, 'Emergence', pp. 47-58; A.C. George, *Trailblazers*, p. 27.

37. Pulikottil, 'Emergence', pp. 47ff.

38. G.B. McGee and S.M. Burgess, 'India', in *The New International Dictionary of Pentecostal Charismatic Movements*, ed. Stanley M. Burgess, Zondervan, 2001, pp. 118-26.

39. For a fascinating reading of the kind of superstitions that the eastern Christians believed and practised early on and continued even in our times in Syria and Turkey see William Dalrymple, *From the Holy Mountain: A Journey in the Shadow of Byzantium*, London: Flamingo, 1998.

40. M.M. Thomas, *Towards an Evangelical Social Gospel: A New Look at the Reformation of Abraham Malpan*, Madras: CLS, 1977; V.C. George, *Christianity in India through the Ages*, Kottayam: Fr. Joseph Vadakkekara, 1972; Daniel Jeyaraj, 'The History of Christianity in India: An Overview from a Protestant Perspective', in *Missiology for the 21st Century*, pp. 195-211; George, *Trailblazers*, pp. 26f.; Burgess, 'India', p. 122; J.C. Dev, '*Keralathile Pentecosthinte Munnodikalum Samuhika Paschathalavum*' (Malayalam), *Maruppacha*, 15.10 (May 2011), pp. 3-6.

41. Gary B. McGee, '"Latter Rain" Falling in the East: Early-Twentieth-Century Pentecostalism in India and the Debate over Speaking in Tongues', in *Church History*, 68.3 (September 1999), pp. 648-65. He says: 'Pentecostalism had in Reality Become "full grown" in India before word of Azusa Reached the Subcontinent', p. 650.

42. This is evident in Pandita Ramabai's shift from the Anglican Church. See Ruth Vassar Burgess, 'Pandita Ramabai: A Woman for all Seasons: Pandita Ramabai Saraswati Mary Dongre Medhavi (1858-1922)', *AJPS* 9.2 (2006), pp. 183-98; Gauri Viswanathan, 'Silencing Heresy', in *Outside the Fold: Conversion, Modernity, and Belief*, Princeton: Princeton University Press, 1998, pp. 118-52.

43. According to several authorities, modern Pentecostalism in India began visibly at Ramabai Mukti Mission. See Ivan Satyavarta, 'Contextual Perspectives on Pentecostalism as Global Culture: A South Asian View', in *Globalization of Pentecostalism: A Religion Made to Travel*, ed. M.W. Dempster et al., Carlisle: Paternoster,

1999; J. Edwin Orr, *Evangelical Awakening in India*, New Delhi: Masihi Sahitya Sanstha, 1970; Jessie Mair, *Bungalows in Heaven: The Story of Pandita Ramabai*, Kedgaon: PRM Mission, 1993.

44. Burgess, 'Pandita Ramabai: A Woman of all Seasons . . .', pp. 183-98; McGee, 'Latter Rain', pp. 656ff.
45. James Massey, 'Holy Spirit Led Mission in North India', in *Missiology for the 21st Century: South Asian Perspective*, ed. Hedlund and Bhakiaraj, New Delhi: ISPCK, 2004, pp. 250-9. Also see for the history of Christianity in Pakistan John Rooney, *Shadows in the Dark: A History of Pakistan up to the 10th Century*, Pakistan Christian History Monograph No. 1, Rawalpindi, Christian Study Centre, 1984.
46. Massey, 'Holy Spirit Led Mission in North India', p. 254.
47. Gerd Theissen, *Sociology of Early Palestinian Christianity*, Philadelphia: Fortress Press, 1977.
48. Minnie Abrams, *The Baptism of the Holy Ghost & Fire*, Kedgaon: Pandita Ramabai Mukti Mission, 2nd edn., 1906, rpt. in 1999; Basi Miller, *Pandita Ramabai, India's Christian Pilgrim*, Pasadena: World-Wide Missions, n.d.
49 Burgess, 'India', p. 120; McGee, 'Latter Rain', pp. 652f. These publications were through Pengwern Jones, a Presbyterian and Minnie Abrams, a Methodist. Abrams later wrote 'Baptism of the Holy Ghost and Fire' in the *Bombay Guardian* (9 June 1906) which exhorts Christians to seek the baptism in the Holy Spirit. One could see this Pentecostal-like experiences across the denominations in the mission field as a prelude to the 1910 International Mission Conference (Edinburgh 1910), a fact ignored by the mainstream church historians.
50. www.ntcdoon.org. This college is perhaps the second charismatic, Pentecostal theological college that is affiliated to the Senate of Serampore College in India, after Faith Theological Seminary, Manakkala, Kerala.
51. For more on names and statistics of the emerging charismatic, Pentecostal and Pentecostal-like churches and mission initiatives see David B. Barrett, 'Annual Statistical Table on Global Mission 1997', *International Bulletin of Missionary Research* 21.1 (1997), pp. 24-5; Barrett and Todd M. Johnson, *World Christian Trends AD 30-AD 2200: Interpreting the Annual Christian Megacensus*, Pasadena: William Carey Library, 2001.

52. Critical theorists like Horkheimer and Adorno critiqued the traditional churches for capitulating to the *status quo* in their own attempt at institutional self-preservation, thereby often times muting their potentially liberating message. See their *Dialectic of Enlightenment* (tr. John Cumming, 1944 rpt., New York: Continuum, 1998.
53. See 'The Church as Experimental Community', 'Mystics and Militants', in Harvey Cox, *The Feast of Fools: A Theological Essay on Festivity and Fantasy*, Cambridge: Harvard University Press, 1969, pp. 93-7, 101-20. Also see his *Fire From Heaven: The Rise of Pentecostal Spirituality and the Reshaping of Religion in the Twenty-First Century*, London: Cassell, 1996. Cox thinks that his shift from his first books *The Secular City* (1965) and *The Feast of the Fools* (1969) to his new book *Fire from Heaven* (1996) is a 'natural development' of thinking in the same direction. See his 'Foreword', in *Pentecostals after a Century*, ed. Anderson and Hollenweger, Sheffield: SAP, 1999, p. 7.
54. Cox, 'Foreword', in *Pentecostals after a Century*, pp. 7f.
55. For more on Pentecostals in mission see Alan Anderson, 'Towards a Pentecostal Missiology for the Majority World', in *Asian Journal of Pentecostal Studies* 8.1 (2005), pp. 29-47; Paul A. Pomerville, *The Third Force in Missions*, Peabody: Hendrickson, 1985.
56. For apocalyptic writings as highly charged political combat writings see J.J. Collins, *Apocalyptic Vision of the Book of Daniel*, Missoula: Scholars Press, 1977; Richard Horsley, *Scribes, Visionaries, and the Politics of Second Temple Judea*, Louisville: WJK Press, 2007; Elizabeth S. Fiorenza, *The Vision of a Just World*, Minneapolis: Fortress, 1991; M.M. Thomas, *The Lamb Slain: The Inheritor of the Earth: Revelation 1-11* and *Behold, I Make All Things New: Revelation 12-22* (tr. T.M. Philip), Thiruvalla: CSS Books, 2010.
57. For more on the liberative potentials of aspiring for a symbolic universe and meaning system see the papers presented at the International Seminar on 'Symbolic Universe and Meaning Systems: A Probe into Dalit Consciousness' at the Centre for Dalit and Subaltern Studies, New Delhi (28 September-1 October 2011).
58. Petersen, *Not by Might*, pp. 31f. Also see Cox, *The Feast of Fools* and his *Fire from Heaven*.
59. Anderson, *An Introduction*, p. 261.
60. Yong, *Who Is the Holy Spirit*, pp. 33ff.

61. Hollenweger, 'The Black Roots of Pentecostalism', pp. 33-44; Beckford, 'Black Pentecostals and Black Politics', pp. 48-59; Roswith Gerloff, 'Pentecostals in the African Diaspora', in Alan Anderson and W. J. Hollenweger (eds.), *Pentecostals After a Century: Global Perspectives on a Movement in Transition*, Sheffield: SAP, 1999, pp. 67-86; Johns, *Pentecostal Formation: A Pedagogy Among the Oppressed*, Sheffield: SAP, 1998), pp. 65ff.
62. See David G. Roebuck, '"Cause He's My Chief Employer": Hearing Women's Voices in a Classical Pentecostal Denomination', in *Philip's Daughters*, pp. 38-60.
63. Karen Kossie-Chernyshev, 'Looking Beyond the Pulpit: Social Ministries and African American Pentecostal-Charismatic Women in Leadership', in *Philip's Daughters*, p. 63 (61-73).
64. Lee Hong Jung, '*Minjung* and the Pentecostal Movement in Korea', in *Pentecostals after a Century: Global Perspectives on a Movement in Transition*, pp. 138-60.
65. Juan Sepulveda, 'Indigenous Pentecostalism and the Chilean Experience', in *Pentecostals after a Century: Global Perspectives on a Movement in Transition*, pp. 111-34. Also see Petersen, *Not by Might*.
66. V.V. Thomas, *Dalit Pentecostalism*.
67. Anderson, *An Introduction*, p. 261. Also see Vincent Leoh, 'Toward Pentecostal Social Ethic', *Journal of Asian Mission*, vol. 7, no. 1, 2005, pp. 39-62.
68. My family and I have experienced this expulsion from the Mar Thoma Church in the early 1980s.
69. For a similar thought see Dongsoo Kim, 'Johannine Roots of Pentecostalism', *AJPS* 9.1 (2006), pp. 5-16.
70. For more on the phenomenon of institutionality and informality in Pentecostal/Charismatic ecclesiology see 'The Church in the Power of the Spirit: Pentecostal/Charismatic Ecclesiologies', in Veli-Matti Kärkkäinen, *An Introduction to Ecclesiology: Ecumenical, Historical & Global Perspectives*, Illinois: IVP Academic, 2002, pp. 68-78.
71. See Kilian McDonnell, *Charismatic Renewal and Ecumenism*, New York: Paulist, 1978; Kärkkäinen, *Pneumatology: The Holy Spirit in Ecumenical, International and Contextual Perspective*, Grand Rapids: Baker, 2002.
72. S.J. Land, *Pentecostal Spirituality: A Passion for the Kingdom*, Sheffield: SAP, 1993; Cheryl B. Johns, *Pentecostal Formation: A*

Pedagogy Among the Oppressed, Sheffield: SAP, 1993; Douglas Petersen, *Not By Might nor by Power: A Pentecostal Theology of Social Concern in Latin America*, Oxford: Regnum, 1996; Alan Anderson and W.J. Hollenweger (eds.), *Pentecostals after a Century: Global Perspectives on a Movement in Transition*, Sheffield: SAP, 1999.

73. This is taking place in the Latin American context. See Douglas Petersen, *Not by Might nor by Power.* This book engages in a scholarly dialogue with Latin American liberation theology and defends the fact that the Pentecostals are in no way behind in liberational front both in word and deed.
74. Thomas in his *Dalit Pentecostalism: Spirituality of the Empowered Poor* has elaborated on this aspect (Bangalore: ATC, 2008); George Oommen (Biju), 'Growth of Pentecostalism in Central Kerala from 1921-47: A Paradigm for Pentecostal Growth of Churches in North India', in *History of Christianity in India*, pp. 131-46.
75. Oommen (Biju), 'Growth', pp. 135ff. 'I grew up as a Mar Thomite in a Mar Thoma Church in central Kerala. In that church there were 400 families and till I was 25 years old I have not seen anybody from the lower caste coming to that church. There was one family. The head of the family was called 'Thoma' not 'Thomas' and his job was to dig graves in that church's graveyard. When his children grew up, they never came to this church, and now the whole family is not part of this church, though they live very near to the church. When I moved into the Pentecostal church I came across innumerable believers who are from the lower caste background and a good number of pastors also from that background. I know that there are problems in this area within the Pentecostal churches, but comparatively it is the Pentecostal churches that broke the caste barriers and the dominance of the Syrian-Christians in Kerala Christianity.'
76. Oommen, 'Growth', pp. 135f. Though he says this he recognizes the internal stress within the Syrian Christian dominated Pentecostal churches. He says: 'It should also be noted that in Pentecostal churches also the real integration of Dalits did not take place', p. 137.
77. Douglas Petersen, *Not by Might nor by Power*, op. cit.
78. Steven Land, *Pentecostal Spirituality*, op. cit.
79. Jose M. Bonino, 'Preface by Jose Miguez Bonino', in Petersen, *Not by Might nor by Power*, pp. xiii-xiv.
80. Petersen, *Not by Might*, p. 32.

81. McGee and Burgess, 'India', p. 124.
82. Shane Clifton, 'Empowering Pentecostal Women', *AJPS* 12.2 (2009), pp. 171-9. Women in Pentecostal church leadership see D.G. Roebuck, 'Cause He's My Chief Employer', in *Philip's Daughters*, pp. 43ff. For women pioneers like Ramabai in India, Gui-Im Park in Korea and KiyomaYumiyama in Japan see *AJPS* 9.2 (2006), McGee, 'Latter Rain', p. 664.
83. See Barbara L. Cavaness, 'Leadership Attitude and Ministry of Single Women in Assemblies of God Missions', in *Philip's Daughters*, pp. 112-30. She says: 'early Pentecostal women had great effect on their times. Many "called and anointed" women served as pastors, missionaries, evangelists, church planters, administrators, and founders of denominations' (p. 113).
84. Clifton, 'Empowering', p. 171. Also see S. Clifton and J. Grey, (eds.), *Raising Women Leaders: Perspectives on Liberating Women in Pentecostal and Charismatic Contexts*, Sydney: APS, 2009; E. Alexander and A. Yong (eds.), *Philip's Daughters: Women in Pentecostal-Charismatic Leadership*. In the Church of God (Anderson) by 1925 women served as pastors in one-third of all the congregations. The Assemblies of God (AG) has ordained women since its inception in 1914. The Church of God (Cleveland) is committed to developing the leadership of men and women, but it is not prepared to bring them to the level of leadership as bishops. See for more in Deidre Helen Crumbley, 'Sanctified Saints—Impure Prophetesses: A Cross-Cultural Reflection on Gender and Power in Two Afro-Christian Spirit-Privileging Churches', in *Philip's Daughters*, pp. 74-94.
85. Harvey Cox, *Fire from Heaven: The Rise of Pentecostal Spirituality and Reshaping of Religion in the Twenty-first Century*, New York: Addison-Wesley, 1995, pp. 121, 131.
86. Cavaness, 'Leadership Attitude . . .', in *Philip's Daughters*, p. 119.
87. Powers, 'Your Daughters Shall Prophesy', in *Philip's Daughters*, pp. 139f.
88. Harvey Cox, *Fire From Heaven*, p. 310.
89. Clifton, 'Empowering', p. 175. Also see Deidre Helen Crumbley who talks about the tension between 'biblical literalism' and 'valuing of divine revelation' in Spirit-privileging churches in 'Sanctified Saints—Impure Prophetesses', *Philip's Daughters*, pp. 92ff.

90. Roebuck, 'Cause He's My Chief Employer', in *Philip's Daughters*, p. 59.
91. Pamela Holmes, 'The Spirit, Nature, and Canadian Pentecostal Women: A Conversation with Critical Theory', in *Philip's Daughters*, p. 199.
92. Powers, 'Your Daughters Shall Prophesy', in *Philip's Daughters*, p. 135.
93. Ibid., p. 149.
94. Clifton, 'Empowering', p. 172. C. Catford, 'Women's Experiences: Challenges for Female Leaders in Pentecostal Contexts', in *Raising Women Leaders*.
95. One such voice is from Elizabeth Schüssler Fiorenza, in the form of a provocative question 'Should Women Aim for Ordination to the Lowest Rung of the Hierarchical Ladder?', in *Discipleship of Equals: A Critical Feminist Ekklesialogy of Liberation*, New York: Crossroad, 1994, pp. 23-38. Also one can hear of their concerns from within Pentecostalism through the articles in *Philip's Daughters*.
96. Harvey Cox, 'Foreword' in Anderson and Hollenweger (eds.), *Pentecostals after a Century*, p. 8.
97. This call is echoed in Dietrich Werner's paper presented in the Board of Theological Education of the Senate of Serampore College (BTESSC) at Clarke Theological Seminary, Mokokchung, Nagaland, India on 2 February 2011 with the title 'Challenges and Opportunities in Theological Education in the 21st Century: Pointers for a new international debate on Theological Education'. Initiative like this in a small way may be seen in the formation of Nav Jyoti Postgraduate and Research Center (NJPGRC), Delhi-Dehradun, affiliated to the Senate of Serampore College (in 2011). It is a unique initiative in India of three widely differing ecclesial traditions and theological persuasions—the Syrian Mar Thoma seminary called Dharma Jyoti Vidya Peeth, at Faridabad (Haryana), the Center for Dalit and Subaltern Studies, led by the CNI and Catholic Christians in New Delhi and the New Theological College, a pentecostal-cum-charismatic interdenominational evangelical seminary in Dehradun—coming together to launch, and work together to promote theological education and ministerial training at a higher level in the national capital.
98. I would include New Theological College, Dehradun, as one of such rare institutions in India.

99. Alan Anderson, *An Introduction*, pp. 144ff.
100. Anderson, 'Introduction: World Pentecostalism at a Crossroads' in *Pentecostals after a Century*, p. 21.

REFERENCES

Alexander, Estrelda and Amos Yong (eds.), *Philip's Daughters: Women in Pentecostal-Charismatic Leadership*, Princeton Theological Monograph Series 104, Eugene: Pickwick Publications, 2009.

Anderson, Alan, *An Introduction to Pentecostalism*, Cambridge: Cambridge University Press, 1994.

Anderson, Alan and W.J. Hollenweger (eds.), *Pentecostals after a Century: Global Perspectives on a Movement in Transition*, Sheffield: SAP, 1999.

Burgess, Stanley (ed.), *The New International Dictionary of Pentecostal Charismatic Movements*, Zondervan, 2002.

Cox, Harvey, *The Feast of Fools: A Theological Essay on Festivity and Fantasy*, Cambridge: Harvard University Press, 1969.

_____, *Fire From Heaven: The Rise of Pentecostal Spirituality and the Reshaping of Religion in the Twenty-First Century*, London: Cassell, 1996.

Deere, Jack, *Surprised by the Power of the Spirit*, Eastbourne: Kingsway Publications, 1993.

George, A.C., *Trailblazers for God: A History of the Assemblies of God of India*, Bangalore: SABC, 2004.

Hollenweger, Walter J., *The Pentecostals*, Peabody: Hendrickson, 1988, Zurich: Zwingli Verlag, 1969.

_____, *Pentecostalism: Origins and Development Worldwide*, Peabody: Hendrickson, 1997.

Johns, Cheryl Bridges, *Pentecostal Formation: A Pedagogy Among the Oppressed*, Sheffield: SAP, 1993.

Land, Steven J., *Pentecostal Spirituality: A Passion for the Kingdom*, Sheffield: SAP, 2001.

Petersen, Douglas, *Not by Might nor by Power: A Pentecostal Theology of Social Concern in Latin America*, Oxford: Regnum, 1996.

Philip, Finny, *The Origins of Pauline Pneumatology: The Eschatological Bestowal of the Spirit upon Gentiles in Judaism and the Early Development of Paul's Theology*, Tübingen: Mohr Siebeck, 2005.

Samuel, Simon and P.V. Joseph (eds.), *Remapping Mission Discourse*, Dehradun/Delhi: NTC Publications/ISPCK, 2008.

Thomas, V.V., *Dalit Pentecostalism: Spirituality of the Empowered Poor*, Bangalore: ATC, 2008.

Viswanathan, Gauri, *Outside the Fold: Conversion, Modernity, and Belief*, Princeton: Princeton University Press, 1998.

Yong, Amos, *Who is the Holy Spirit: A Walk with the Apostles*, Brewster: Paraclete Press, 2011.

9

Evangelical Movements and the Social Demands of the Gospel

RICHARD HOWELL

The Indian Christian evangelical reflection and action motivated by the call of God to bring wholeness and peace to the fragmentation and restlessness that runs through much of human life, has taken shape and evolved with increasing significance since the formation of the Evangelical Fellowship of India (EFI) in 1951. We are called to participate in the Triune God's vision of the reconciliation of humanity and the healing of all creation.

This article explores the theological basis of social demands of the Gospel and then explores some of the crucial and contextual issues.

Theological Basis for Praxis

The nature and activity of God embraces both the church and the world. A constructive engagement with the contextual issues which impact upon the transformational work of the church requires an understanding of the nature and work of the Triune God as Father, Son and Holy Spirit. It is through the trinitarian doctrine of God, we understand what God is doing in the mission of the church and what God is doing in movements and changes which are taking place everywhere in the events of history. This is possible through the presence of the Holy Spirit in the church and in the life of the believer, which causes him to trust the creative and providential power of the Father to direct all things towards the glorifying of the Son. Missional engagement is at the heart of the trinitarian life of God. 'Because God is triune, God can bless us. Because God blesses the other in God, God can bless the other without. Because God reaches out to another already within, God is not contained by the Trinity's inner life, but can reach out also to us.'[1]

Transformational mission is, ontologically, a defining characteristic of the church, for it expresses the inner impulse of the triune God to reveal himself through his church in the midst of the world. God delights to make himself known, and the church is both a sign of his kingdom, pointing to the reality of his rule of compassionate love, and a dynamic event of grace, in which he is present by his Spirit. The purpose of the church, as 'God's people and members of God's household' (Ephesians 2: 19), is to make peace (v. 6). To be a blessing for the nations (Gen. 12: 1-3; 15; 17; Isa. 42: 6). The church is called to exist for the sake of its Lord and for the sake of humankind (Matt 22: 32-40). The church must be visible in the world, living out the trinitarian faith as redemptive voice and presence.

The church as a called community of God's people has a special responsibility—to be a sign, a foretaste, and an instrument of God's reign. This means, that the community points beyond itself to the coming reign of God. As a Spirit-filled community, church is to manifest the coming reign of God in its common life and shared ministry. The church, as a messianic community, is to participate in the actualization of the coming reign of God in the world. God has called the church to proclaim the gospel (evangel) of the Kingdom of God in word and deed.

The historic Christian faith has insisted on the validity of revelation as the primary source of knowledge about God and emphasized the importance of the church and its traditions in rational discourse, legitimizing the validity of the Christian tradition of God as creator of humanity and the world. However, because something of God is known outside the Christian tradition, this offers the community an interpretative framework by which other traditions may be addressed on the common issues of existence, enabling the coherence and attractiveness of the Christian vision. We must realize that in addressing the role of the church and its proactive engagement in nation building, a biblical vision of society needs to be presented as the answer to the desperate communal tensions, economic disparity and human freedoms which continue to ravage the nation. Evangelical theology contributes in a dialogical process the insights of the gospel while attentively listening to plurality of voices. Believing in a dynamic and active triune God who is always present in the midst of changing circumstances, the church is called to be responsive, to learn, to grow, to change.

God's nature transcends all cultural variables and racial and caste prejudices and does not change. The churches belief in its core values and core purposes have their source in one and true God who revealed himself in history in the person of Jesus Christ. The teaching of Jesus communicated reliable information pertaining to normative principles regarding life. It also demonstrated that God's truth can be communicated in human, culturally influenced categories and languages. Like the message of Christ, the apostle's messages originated with God the Father, came through human concepts and words and were kept from error by the supernatural power of the Holy Spirit. It would be heretical to forfeit the timeless biblical message. The church should not adapt its core values in response to market changes, rather it should change markets to stay true to its core values. Beliefs define the enduring character of the church, a consistent identity that transcends the vacillations of the cultures and markets. But since the context keeps changing, it is imperative that the church engages itself with the contemporary perplexities and culturally rooted questions. We must enhance dialogue between the Scripture as a relevant and revealed Word of God and the contextual issues and needs of the post-modern secular society and a world of plurality of living religions. Indigenization of the Gospel is not a private or purely individual task. It is the responsibility of the local church and must be undertaken within the framework of the believing community.

The Holy Spirit illuminates the individual interpreter within the context of the church. The body of Christ has an historical dimension. The historical traditions of the church have great value in interpreting the realities of our contemporary existence. To participate in the mission of Christ is to enter into the reconciling ministry of the Spirit, who is continuously at work in the world in both hidden and incredible ways, with creative resourcefulness and with concern for the particularity of context.

We need a perspective that is wide-ranging in its scope rather than narrow and reductionist. We must reflect on the enormous breadth and range of the mission of the Creator Spirit. In order to participate in that mission, we need both the courage to look beyond our narrow evangelical and ecclesiological boundaries and also the wisdom to discern where the Spirit is at work, often in the unlikliest places and in the most unlikely ways.

Trinitarian unity is integrating and inclusive; its end is the full glorification of all creation in the triune God, healing what is sick, releasing what is captive, forgiving what transgresses divine relationship.

God Our Cosmic Host

Our Creator God is the cosmic Host (Genesis 1). As the first reality, God in love creates space for humans and the world to exist as a dependent reality upon him. As Polkinghorne suggests, when God created *ex nihilo* he brought into being 'a universe which is free to exist "on its own", in the ontological space made available to it by the divine kenotic act of allowing the existence of something wholly other'.[2] The distinction between God and His creation is characterized by the unlimited freedom of the being of the triune God, and the limited yet authentic freedom given to the whole universe. As Athanasius[3] made a distinction between the ontological dimension in God as Father and the cosmological dimension in God as Creator, arguing that God is always Father, but He is not always Creator. Torrance states, 'The creation of the world out of nothing is something new even for God. God was always Father, but He became Creator'.[4] The new, decisive acts of God in creation, incarnation and Pentecost are indicative of the absolute and unlimited freedom of God to be other than He always has been.

The Gospel of John tells us that it was the Word of God who had been with God from the beginning, who was the chief actor in all that was created (John 1: 3). The Word of God made room for creatures who became His guests and recipients of divine provision. The same Word of God who made room for humans, later became flesh and took on the name of Jesus. In the incarnation, the One who had made space for us came down to the world He had made (John 1: 14). But tragically, John's opening chapter narrates something else. 'The Word became flesh, became one of us, but when He came to His own people, His own people received Him not (John 1: 11-12)'. We were not at all hospitable to the One who is our ultimate Host. But isn't that just the nature of the very sin Jesus came to die for? Aren't we human beings constantly building walls, shutting people out, doing the spiritual equivalent of slamming our front door in the face of other people and other creatures?

Jesus came to remind us that hospitality is the universe's keynote and it has been so from the beginning. That is why it's so exciting to read in Matthew 21: 14 that Jesus clears space in the Temple. And then what is the very next thing we read? 'The blind and the lame came to Him and He healed them.' It was instantaneous! No sooner did Jesus make room that it filled right in with the people who had previously been shut out.

Jesus showed us that being on the inside of the Kingdom is not good because others are outside of it. The goodness of being an insider is always defined by the act of divine grace that brought us in to begin with. That grace is such a precious gift that if you really understand it, then the only thing in the whole wide world that you want is for this same grace to come to everybody. As a Kingdom insider, you do not define the goodness of that status by the fact that some are still outside. In fact, you are actually pained that any remain outside. You wish there were no outsiders.

The scripture describes hospitality as the way of life of the people of God. Hospitality is sharing our home, lives, personal space, and resources without communicating a need for show or an expectation of return. Hospitality should be done out of a grateful heart for all God has done for us, not out of obligation. We are to practice hospitality to one another without grudging (1 Peter 4: 9). To be a good steward of God's grace means we let our hospitality be an extension of God's hospitality to us. This hospitality is primarily the welcome we extend to outsiders, not to family and friends.

> In hospitality, the stranger is welcomed into a safe, personal, and comfortable place, a place of respect and acceptance and friendship. Even if only briefly, the stranger is included in a life-giving and life-sustaining network of relations. Such welcome involves attentive listening and a mutual sharing of lives and life stories. It requires an openness of heart, a willingness to make one's life visible to others, and a generosity of time and resources.[5]

In the New Testament, hospitality is considered a gift of the Holy Spirit. Hospitality ranks right up there with preaching, teaching, speaking in tongues, prophecy, and healing as a specific manifestation of the Spirit's work. All Christians are called to be hospitable towards one another and towards strangers. But some can become especially gifted in this area; hence the New Testament's speaks of hospitality as the Spirit's work.

The church's participation in reconciling service in the world is a costly one, as Anderson states: 'As Jesus exists in a community of relation with the Father characterized by self-emptying, so does the church exist as a community of self-emptying, or kenotic presence, in the world.'[6] This is best illustrated by the sacrificial death of Christ.

The cross of Christ is the greatest manifestation of the missional movement of God, so far as visible events are concerned, for in it God was crucified for humans. We know without a shadow of doubt that the cross is suffering in its greatest, most oppressive and unjust form.

> We must also sense that the cross is, so to speak, the beast of burden upon which God Almighty rode to descend from His dwelling place, where he had been veiled from all eternity, and come to us and take us by the hand. The cross is the supreme power of the dynamism of God, which brought God down to us and clearly revealed him.[7]

It is within the theology of the Incarnation that we understand the transformational mission orientation towards the world. The faith community's responsibility and commitment to and solidarity with the world is measured by incarnational solidarity and prophetic voice, which is the theological presupposition of all transformational engagement in the world.

Human beings are created for relationship. The first has to do with our relationship with God; the second is predicated on the first and is expressed as relationship with others in human community, on the one hand, and relationship with the non-personal world, on the other. The world created in the freedom of God's love, 'is not an impersonal process, a machine or a self-developing organism—a cosmic collective into which the particularity disappears—but that which itself has a destiny along with the human'.[8]

The nature of human beings living in community within the love of God is bound up intimately and necessarily with human responsibility for the world. To live responsibly as human beings within the created order embodies such concerns as the treatment of animal species in genetic technology, the environmental management of forests and waterways, and the allocation of resources for effective national/global stewardship. It also involves to move beyond a purely utilitarian ethic and to embrace a spirituality that acknowledges the wonder and mystery of creation. So our social engagement is the privilege of participation in Christ's reconciling work, 'in the company of beasts and plants and stones, accepting solidarity with them',[9] as well as with our fellow human beings.

This directs us to the values of contextual engagement with human experiences of life and the nature of the physical world in which human beings are privileged to live with our eyes wide open to the reality around us. We must practice the life as God has it for us. Right relationship in every sphere, according to that which God has ordained, all that brings human persons closer to the communion for which we were created, glorifies God.

The Need to Understand the Context

Only in understanding a given local context we can avoid the dogmatism that teaches us nothing. We do missions with a spirit of courteous listening and respect to people of different religious and ideological convictions and practices. We will never understand others until we are willing first to listen to people. Christain engagement focuses on the church as a servant community ready to listen to and identify with the world in its diversity and plurality.

In God's fallen world, history narrates a gory tale of pursuit and misuse of absolute power and control which dominates and decimates humans. The ruthless market economy celebrates accumulation of wealth as power, even by crushing its competitors, leaving behind a trail of causalities of crippled losers. The discourse of casteism has exploited and divided humans for thousands of years in the categories of purity and pollution. We must engage in a mission of justice, salvation and reconciliation for the peoples of all nations. So clearly exemplified, when God became involved with the whole world in Jesus Christ of Nazareth! He became involved in solidarity with the world he created at the most personal level possible. Our responsibility with regard to the world is measured by the faith community's commitment to and incarnational solidarity with the world. This highlights that all ministry is God's ministry and Christians are privileged to cooperate with God in his work of grace as they engage in the *praxis* of ministry. The gospel to be faithfully heard as the gospel of God must include the twin themes of transcendence and immanence.

Some Crucial Concerns

In this section of the paper we address a number of crucial concerns that relate to the local community of faith.

The 'Other India'

Who are these inhabitants of 'other India'? Nearly 90 per cent of all the poor people in India and 95 per cent of all the illiterate people in India are Dalits. Human rights abuses against Dalits are legion. Around 40 per cent of the Indian poor are landless labourers. Another 45 per cent are marginal farmers. Of the remaining, close to 10 per cent are marginal artisans. Their brothers and sisters who migrate to urban centres in search of employment make up the rest; they live in the midst of most dehumanizing conditions, e.g. 70 per cent of the residents of urban Mumbai lives in slums. Almost all of these people are Dalits, Adivasis, and Other Backward Classes.

The reflective action belongs where the triune God is redeeming his creation, among the poor and the threatened places of creation. There are millions of families in India and around the world whose financial resources—including their educational and occupational skills, the circumstances of their environment at home and at work, and their material belongings—fall dangerously below those controlled by the average person or family in society; they indeed are victims of poverty. Jesus was concerned about the poorest of the poor; the church needs to be concerned with them as well. In India the poor and the marginalized are exploited, disease and death are rampant, education and employment scarce, stinginess and sluggishness common, cheating and corruption epidemic, caste and colour discrimination abusive, and opportunity and realization of personal potential drastically limited.

Economic projects as such do not help poor people develop the crucial sense of self-worth. Rather the development of self-worth is the foundation for every other human growth. This makes the gospel so vital for change. The gospel transforms the perception of the poor from worthless failures to an appreciation that in Christ they have their own and other people worth. V.T. Rajshekar, a Dalit leader, suggests for the Dalits, 'Poverty is not the number one problem. People cannot live by bread alone. They want the self-respect which is denied under Hinduism. They will get it the moment they get out of Hinduism and convert to other religions.'[10]

In India nearly 300 million live in absolute poverty that their survival is daily in doubt. This indeed is offensive and heart breaking to God. The Bible speaks of the God who extends his loves to all. At the same time, Bible speaks of when the poor are oppressed, God is the 'defender of the poor' (Psalm 146: 7-9; cf. 14: 13. 'He who oppresses the poor man insults his maker, but he who is kind to the needy honours Him'). Indeed it is only when we right such injustices that God promises to hear our prayers and worship (Isaiah 58: 1-9). Poverty is not a necessary evil but often the result of social, economic, political, and religious systems marked by injustice, exploitation, and oppression. Evil is not in the human heart but also in social structures. Because God is just and merciful, hating evil and loving righteousness, there is an urgent need for Christians in the present circumstances to commit ourselves to acting in mercy and seeking justice.

Biblical justice means impartially rendering to everyone their due in conformity with standards of God's moral law. In Biblical passages which deal with the distribution of the benefits of social life in the context of social conflict and social wrong, justice is related particularly to what is due to groups such as poor, widows, orphans, resident aliens, wage earners and slaves. The common link among these groups is powerlessness by virtue of economic and social needs. Justice called forth is to restore these groups to the provision God intends for them. God's law express this justice and indicates its demands.

One of the dilemmas of the poor is the loss of community (Job 22: 35-6, Psalm 107: 4-9, 33-6). The responsibility of the community is stated as 'to make them strong' so that they can continue to take their place in the community. Justice requires conditions such that each person is able to participate in society in a way that is compatible with human dignity. Justice also requires socio-political actions that enable the poor to help themselves and be the subjects of their own development and the development of communities. Neglect of the poor often flows from greed. Further, the obsessive or careless pursuit of material goods is one of the most destructive idolatries in human history (Ephesians 5: 5). It distracts individuals from their duties before God, and corrupts personal and social relationships.

Caste Discrimination

The caste system is one of the most rigid and institutionalized brutality of Indian society. While the Gandhian agenda was achieved in 1947 with the attainment of political freedom! However, the agenda of Mahatma Jyotiba Phule, B.R. Ambedkar and E.V.R. Periyar which emphasized that a society divided by social oppression could not constitute a genuine nation remains unrealized.[11]

Reflecting on the opposition between 'the pure and the impure' in his classic exposition, *Homo Hierarchicus*, Louis Dumont has argued that this binary opposition is the ideological principal and the essence of the caste system.[12] Ideology as an instrument of domination, of ensuring that the common people thought and behaved as the ruling elite want them to, finds an archetypical expression in Brahminism. It stands for the aggregate of the sacerdotal literature, social structure and religio-political institutions that have been masterminded by the elite with the primary aim of keeping the masses ignorant, servile and disunited.

Brahaminism uses the ideology of caste as a crucial instrument to dehumanize, divide and dominate the productive majority. Different caste groups are separated from each other in matter of marriage, physical contact, food by rules of purity and pollution. Hierarchy—along with purity and power culminate in the Brahmin. Says Manu, the ancient lawgiver of Brahminical tradition, 'When a Brahman is born he springs to light above the world; he is the chief of all creatures, entitled by eminence of birth to the wealth of the world' (*Manusmriti* I.98-100).

Power politics is at the heart of Brahminism. The exercise of power necessarily involves conflict and resistance. The contest for economic, cultural, and intellectual resources between the powerful and the powerless involves both dominance and resistance. Despite resistance to caste and Brahminism, beginning with shramanic heterodoxies and Buddhism, followed by various streams of Bhakti movements, Sikhism, Sufism, similar lesser known campaigns and ideologies and anti-caste egalitarian movements in modern India, caste consciousness and Brahminic mindset persists in their modernized, metamorphosed *avatar*, defying and denying democratic ideals.

Caste thinking is in some of our churches. Many scholars have documented it. Anantha Krishna Iyer, outlining the caste- oriented manners and customs of Syrian Christians, writes, 'Each division among the Syrian Christians has become, as in Hindu caste, an endogamous sect, with no intermarriage between the members of one sect and those of another, though no objection is made to inter-dining'.[13] It is not uncommon that high caste

Christians demand separation, for fear of pollution, from the Christians of Dalit origin.

Reconciliation, Religious Liberty and Social Justice

Deeply concerned about the rapid degeneration of our social life; the hatred, often spread by religious leaders, caused incalculable suffering to families of the victims of riots, terrorism and religious persecution, in September 1998 in New Delhi EFI organized a national consultation on reconciliation, religious liberty and social justice in which about 150 leaders and heads of churches and Christian organizations drawn from 20 states gathered. EFI issued a statement some portions of which read as follows,

> We affirm that God's love as displayed in Jesus Christ compels us to commit ourselves to a ministry of reconciliation. We recognize that we need grace to learn to forgive instead of fighting for revenge. Reconciliation is impossible without spiritual resources to bear shame and humiliation and return good for evil, blessing for insult. Because inter and intra-communal harmony is a necessary prerequisite for nation building, we commit ourselves to fulfill the mandate for reconciliatory engagement as required by God's reconciling initiative in the death and resurrection of our Lord Jesus Christ.
>
> We affirm that human rights are inherent in our creation, they are not given by states, or by the majority to the minority. The state exists to protect the rights of the citizens. Human rights are equal rights—equal, in spite of our obvious differences of gender, creed, class, language or race. Freedom of conscience, thought and mind is the most fundamental aspect of human freedom. Securing other person's rights is our responsibility, because God has put us in the same family and so made us related to and responsible for one another. We commit ourselves to defend and strengthen these freedoms for all our citizens, using creative and constitutional means, even at the risk of our lives. Religious liberty and reconciliation have little meaning except in the context of a just social order. A just social order is characterized by dignity and respect for all human beings irrespective of their caste, creed, or gender. There has to be a special sensitivity towards those

who cannot compete equally because of special physical, medical, social, or economic disadvantages. We recognize that a multi-faceted battle against such all pervasive evils is beyond our human strength and ability. Therefore, we commit ourselves to pray for God's Holy Spirit to equip and enable us for the tasks He is entrusting to us.

The consultation was a noteworthy step forward to intentionally embrace issues of reconciliation, religious freedom and social justice as mission issues not in isolation but in cooperation with other ecumenical bodies and civil society.

Gender Discrimination

It is a universal fact that the human race exists as female and male, and humankind would not exist if there were either no women or no men. Most societies throughout human history openly or tacitly considered men superior to women. But are women deficient? Is there a reason to subjugate them?

The social world women inhabit is not constructed for their benefit; it is a world made for males in which females often feel pressurized to conform through discrimination and oppression. The violence against women on the streets, rape, eve teasing, acid attacks, love murders, honour killings, trafficking of girls, flesh trade, prostitution, sex tourism, rising rates of desertion of wives and children, feminization of poverty, teenage pregnancy, abortion, child marriage, permanent enforced widowhood, objectification of women, are all a sad commentary on how our society perceives and treats women. At times of war, riots, communal conflicts, and in prisons and police custody, women suffer unspeakable atrocities and exploitation. Depending on her context, a woman may suffer multiple layers of exclusion, e.g. in poverty, as a member of lower caste, apartheid, belonging to a less or least developed nation, as an AIDS victim, and so on. In a traditional, rural, agricultural society like India, caste and patriarchy combine to exercise severe domination of women by men, of lower castes by high castes, of the younger ones by the elders and of the poor by the rich. But this is not God's will for humanity.

The nature of God tells us nothing about what it means to live as a female in distinction to male and vice versa. We cannot use God-language to say what humans are like. God does model gender identity. Since God is beyond sexual differences, there is nothing specifically fatherly about relation that a man has toward his offspring. A human father can in no way read off his responsibilities as a father from God the Father. There is nothing in God that is specifically feminine, and nothing in God is specifically masculine. Therefore, nothing in our notions of God entails duties or prerogatives specific to one gender; all duties and prerogatives entailed in our notions of God are duties and prerogatives of both women and men. The different views of how men and women behave in different cultures show that gender difference and identity is given not only by our biology but also from the views of our society. It is the result of interaction between women and men within a given culture. Gender views change, while being male or female does not change.

We learn from the doctrine of Trinity that the three persons are not reduced to a common undifferentiated divine nature. Analogously, one gender should neither be transformed into another (say femininity into masculinity) nor melted into a new synthesis. As we emphasize the biological duality alongside changing social pictures of gender identities, it is crucial not to lose sight of the fundamental equality between women and men. While we uphold duality, we risk affirming inequality. Some say men and women are equal because they are the same. We reject both sameness and affirm equality between women and men. We seek to change the social practices in which the presumed inferiority of women is embodied and perpetuated —and even perpetuated when people say women and men are equal.

The Bible tells us that God created every human being in His own image. The Creation account in Genesis 1: 26-7 says: 'So

God created man in His own image, in the image of God He created them; Male and female He created them'. Both female and male are created equal, have equal worth and dignity. At the end of the every stage of Creation, God looked back at His own work and said, '. . . it was good', but at this last stage, He said, '. . . it was very good' vs. 31. In 2: 18, for the first time it is noted that something was not good: 'It is not good for a man to be alone. . . .' God gave a suitable companion to man. They are set in the garden as marital couple, lovers, and friends. Intimate love, partnership, and mutuality are the basis of relationship, reflecting the harmony and unity of the triune God of the Bible.

We must move towards an ecclesiology in which there is no permanent structure of subordination. Both females and males are redeemed equally and equally gifted by the Holy Spirit. Therefore leadership and service is determined by the giftedness of the Holy Spirit and is not based on gender. According to the scripture, every person who comes to faith receives from God spiritual gifts or abilities. These gifts are a manifestation of God's presence or power in our lives equipping us for service. Because the spiritual gifts come from God, they are supernatural. Since it is God who provides the spiritual gifts, we do not choose which gifts we receive. They are chosen for us by our all-knowing and loving Creator. And nowhere in the Scripture do we read that the spiritual gifts are given because of our personal merits, or because of our gender, ethnicity or class. Hence, in reading the three passages that address the spiritual gifts, we find no indication that the spiritual gifts are given according to human expectations. Therefore, you may in fact receive from God a spiritual gift which may prove to be unexpected and also challenging in the light of human prejudice. However, the scripture states clearly that our spiritual gifts are accompanied by an accountability or responsibility to God. The process of change based on the biblical values can transform humans, cultures and societies.

Transformation of Culture

What is the relation of churches to the cultures where they exist? We must develop an appropriate relation between leaving or distancing from and identification or uniting with the culture. The notion of culture is as wide as it is vague. It is the sum total of the values and worldview by which a particular human group lives. Cultures are not static but always undergoing change. Pannikar writes, 'Each culture begins with, or at least develops, a vision of reality. The principle enlivening this vision is what we call religion. The meeting of culture when it goes deep enough is always a religious encounter. Ultimate values are at stake.'[14]

Christianity, able to exist in many cultures, is transcultural. Christians believe the ground of their faith and conduct comes from outside any particular culture. God is outside of anyone culture. At the same time, because of the Incarnation of Jesus Christ, the second person of the Holy Trinity in a particular culture, Christians believe in the validity of all cultures. They believe no religion, not Hinduism, not Islam, not Buddhism, and not Christianity, can or should attempt to obliterate the cultural differences which lie at the core of identity. The ultimate allegiance of Christians cannot be to any culture, country or family with their local deities. The Christian belief in the oneness of God implies God's universality, and the universality implies transcendence with respect to any given culture. Christians can never be first of all Punjabi, Bihari, Tamil, Malayali, Naga, Manipuri, Mizo, Asians, Africans, or Europeans, then Christians. At the very foundation of Christian identity lies an all encompassing change of loyalty, from a given culture with its gods to the God of all cultures.

Both leaving and identification are essential. Identification without distance destroys: Can I affirm my exclusive identity as an Indian and want either to shape everyone in my own image or eliminate them from the world? But leaving without identification isolates; I deny my identity as an Indian and drawback from my own culture. Leaving a culture must never degenerate into flight from that culture but must be a way of living in a culture.

When the Spirit comes he creates openness in us to receive the other. Consider the transformation the Spirit brings when a person encounters Christ. Paul writes, 'Therefore if anyone is in Christ, he is a new creation, the old has gone the new has come' (2 Corinthians 5: 17). The Holy Spirit breaks through the self-enclosed world we dwell in and sets us on a journey with him and other members of the community of Christ. A transformed Christian identify with a particular culture, yet because of the openness created by the Spirit of God he is enriched by other cultures while contributing to the dynamic vitality of each culture. The openness created by the Spirit by making a new creation implies judgement against evil in every culture. If we cannot thoughtfully discriminate between right and wrong, we become monsters. There are evil deeds that cannot be tolerated by any religion or culture. We must retain our ability to judge, judging ourselves and our own culture first. Those who seek to overcome evil must fight it first of all in themselves. The Gospel does not presuppose the superiority of any culture to another, but evaluates all cultures according to its own criterion of truth and righteousness, and insists on moral absolutes in every culture.

The judgement must begin, however, 'with the household of God' (1 Peter 4: 17). Those who wish to overcome evil must fight it first of all in their own selves and their own culture. Leaving open our eyes to self-deception, injustice, and destructiveness, enables us to fight against them. A transformed Christian is brought to repentance, and, shaped by the Gospel of the Kingdom of God he/she is engaged in the transformation of the world. The struggle against falsehood, injustice, and violence both in the self and the other is impossible without leaving. Those who follow Christ have one foot planted in their own culture and the other in God's coming kingdom. Churches in mission must seek to transform and enrich all cultures for the glory of God thereby fulfilling their mandate to be the salt and light of the world.

In the battle against evil, in particular against evil in one's own culture, the openness created by the Spirit needs ecumenical community. The church has taken roots globally in many cultures, changing them as well as being profoundly shaped by them. Nevertheless all the churches in diverse cultures are one, just as the triune God is one. No church in a given culture must commit the sin of self-sufficiency thereby isolating itself. Every church must be open to all other churches. Every local church is indeed part of the worldwide church but the inverse is equally true that the worldwide church is also part of the local church. This makes every local church a truly worldwide community of the Spirit. This is evident in the life of Christians who overcome national and ethnic rivalries as a result of transformation in Christ. This position, the church as the multicultural community of the Spirit bound together by the power of the cross of Christ has been accepted. The moral and social transformation shapes the church as a transcultural community ordered toward purity of life and adoration of God. Our commitment to the Lordship of Jesus Christ and our commitment to the ecumenical community of Christ must go together. You cannot have Christ and reject his world-wide multicultural body.

Oppressive Market-oriented Models

In our process of transformation in this world, the household of Christ and market society are uncomfortable partners. The market society will not be able to absorb the church, for the presence and power of God is concretely and publicly manifested in the life of the community. The reality of market is all-encompassing as its channels flow into every nation, city, and village of the world. Market is changing the world. But the market will not redeem the world. Market has no power against sin, evil, and death despite its claims of universal spread and effectiveness. According to Robert Heilbroner, the nature of our society is accumulation of wealth as power and the logic of our society is exchange of commodities.[15] Everything hops around these realities. The modern man believes in them implicitly and shapes his life according to this logic. It is increasingly the reason through which people expect life, happiness, security, and future. No one can deny its awesome effect on modernity.

The proponents of competition never tire of repeating that their work has been done, and is still being done under the heading of altruism (unselfishness). For example, in agriculture, the constant slogan is 'serve agriculture' and 'feed the world'. These aims, as stated, are irreproachable, as pursued; they raise a number of doubts. Agriculture, it turns out, is to be served strictly according to the rules of competitive economics. The aim is to make farmers and Indian agriculture more competitive. With whom, we must ask, are our farmers, and our agriculture to be competitive against? And we must answer, because we know: against other farmers, at home and abroad. It is impossible to imagine that there can be any reconciliation between local and national competitiveness and global altruism. Strangest of all the doctrines of the cult of competition, in which admittedly there must be losers as well as winners, is the result of competition being inevitably good for everybody, that altruistic ends may be met by a system without altruistic motives or altruistic means.

The question that we finally come to is a practical one. Can a university, or a nation, afford this exclusive rule of competition, this purely economic economy? The great fault of this approach to things is that it is so drastically reductive; it does not permit us to live and work as human beings, as the best of our inheritance defines us. Rats live by competition under the law of supply and demand; it is the privilege of human beings to live under the laws of justice and compassion. It is impossible not to notice how little the proponents of the ideal of competition have to say about honesty, which is the fundamental economic virtue, and how very little they have to say about community, compassion and mutual help.

The damaging effect of the new global economy is visible with the increasing decline of traditional community-based life in the Indian society. In the information-based modern economic society, the individual comes up against an ever faster circulation of goods, images, money, ideas, and other human beings.[16] The shared meanings and healthy practices of community are emptied out in a process of isolation of the self. The rare product of modernity is the isolated individual in the midst of technological society, yet embedded in relationships which transcend time and space, via mobile phone and the worldwide web. The markets can be modified with communities that become the bearers of the values which define human beings beyond their possessions, their work, and their consumption. The challenge before the church is to be the genuine community of transformation.

The market-oriented models actively promote and impose their secular, materialistic and modern value systems on society. By doing this, are they not guilty of the proselytizing for which religious organizations are blamed? Secular approaches are not neutral. They have an agenda that the development of people and nation can take place without God and without an analysis of evil and sin.[17] Christians cannot be a party to this ideology. In the major religious traditions of South Asia the search for secular elements in the cultural traditions is a futile exercise. In these traditions the ideology of secularism is not only absent but also resisted.[18] The factor of religion has to be brought into discussion for the development of the community. Otherwise, human beings are being defined as necessarily and essentially secular.

The transformational theology refuses to let the world set the agenda by replacing theological imperatives with ideological causes. Christians can never take pragmatic approach to transformation that appears to be delivering results, for this would allow ideology to replace theology and the pursuit of power will eclipse truth. The church should never allow any ideology to eclipse its witness. However, the culprit is not the market *per se*, but what Karl Polanyi calls 'market society', that is, a society in which all the spheres in which social goods have to be distributed are controlled by the market logic itself.[19] There is a difference between Christian and secular approaches to transformation.

What cannot appear under the market is the reality of God's self-giving love, which is expressed in grace. The logic of the market, which is accumulation of wealth as power even by 'crushing competitors', gives no room for relationships and practices that are governed by obedience to the Lord, self-giving, righteousness, love, reconciliation, justice, cooperation, service, stewardship, love for neighbour, equality and empowerment by the Holy Spirit. Transformation is not just accelerating the process of change. God must be the source, the means, and the end for all we do in the transformation of communities—so that God is glorified, as individuals and communities experience the power and presence of God. The transformation of the market person, and the influence upon the market society with the above-mentioned values of the Kingdom of God, are the tasks of the transformational mission of the church.

Economy and Pleasure

Such is our human nature that we are active to the extent of being influenced by some affection. Our affections energize us to work in all affairs of life and inspire us in all our pursuits. In the economic arena, competition oozes pleasure for the triumphant, however, the victory over community or nature can be won only at everybody's cost. There are landscapes that have been defeated by clear cutting, by poisoning, by bad farming, by various styles of 'development' that have conquered their sites entirely to human purposes.

The holy affections beacon us to look beyond this all consuming 'hurry' of winning, to a realization in which use of creation is not synonymous with defeat. Such an appreciation emerges when we experientially know what gives pleasure or delight to God. This is best expressed in a four-line hymn of praise to God in the book of Revelation (4: 11) which is a celebration of God as creator of all things. 'You are worthy, O Lord, to receive glory and honour and power: for you have created all things, and for thy pleasure they were created' (Revelation 4: 11 KJV). The hymn begins with an ascription of worthiness to God based on the fact that he has created all things. The ascription of glory, honour, and power to God on the part of his worshippers is fully appropriate, because God is creator. That God created all things for His pleasure[20] is an awesome belief indeed, for it's a befitting reply to the environmentalist critics who falsely accuse the Bible of promoting utilitarian purposes. If we claim to fully comprehend God's pleasure, this will be sheer arrogance on our part. However, we certainly show reverence to God's pleasure in all things by our use of things that he has entrusted into our care. This means that we must not misuse or abuse anything, but also that by common agreement, some things and some places must not be used at all, but left wild.

Competitive economy is divorced from pleasure, which completely writes off the capacity of people to be affectionate towards what they do and what they use and where they live and the other people and creatures with whom they live. But, one can argue, isn't there an ever increasing pleasure industry that is thriving in our society today as never before? But isn't this also true that the pleasure industries are unashamedly exploiting our limitless inability to be pleased, which only proves our economy is divorced from pleasure and that pleasure has gone from our work and dwelling places? It's tragic that our workplaces are more and more exclusively given over to production, and our homes to consumption.

We assume work must be deprived of pleasure. And we long for the evening or the weekend, or vacation, or even retirement when the all elusive pleasure will satiate our hungry souls. The pleasure industries we turn to for relief from our defeat, betray us, for pleasure industries thrive and grow only upon our dissatisfaction with them. Pleasure should not be merely an extra or offshoot or reward; it is both an empowerment of our work and its essential assessment. God is delighted to see his people rejoice before his presence. The annual festivals of Israelite community, though primarily agricultural, established an orientation and lifestyle attitude: thanksgiving and joy. 'You shall rejoice before the Lord your God seven days' (Lev. 23: 40; cf. Deut. 16: 11, 14). Festivals, as ordered by Yahweh, were an expression of this joyful mood. The imperative to rejoice, like the imperative to love, indicates the basic posture of a transformed community. A major indicator of transformation is a change in the unholy affections of people in the society promoted by the pleasure industry and its accompanied vices with the holy affections and values of the kingdom as they are integrated into the daily rhythm of life.

Stewardship of Creation

The focus of an industrial, and now increasingly knowledge-based economy is to turn away from the land. However, there is no such thing as a post-agriculture society unless we learn to live without eating, drinking and breathing.

As farm land is taken over by agribusiness the goal is maximum profit at whatever cost, and their method is greedy exploitation. The fact of the matter is that agribusiness practices cannot be sustained over a long term because they depend on techniques that either produce a crop that often is equalled, even doubled, in weight by the soil lost to erosion, or kill the microbial, life-promoting soil structure with heavy pesticide use and deplete and contaminate groundwater systems—all predicated on a cheap and limitless supply of fossil fuel. In our rush to maximize profits, or simply to perpetuate cash flow, we violate the sources of life on which we depend. If our life is focused exclusively upon a humanly defined economy then we fail to cease to be attentive to the biological, extra-human conditions that are indispensable for life's flourishing. Transformation of cultures into consumerist, profit-driven organizations inevitably lead to the exploitation of the earth and its inhabitants.

The integrity of things, that they are of value in themselves and in terms of the roles they play in a larger whole, is eclipsed by our desire to turn them to our benefit. In fact, in many cases, human progress has been measured in terms of our ability to combat and control the land, and so to establish human flourishing in opposition to the well-being of the earth.

If we honour the Biblical account of the relationship between the Creator and creation, then we cannot deny the spiritual importance of our economic life. When we understand that we can only produce 'by reworking the works of creation, then we see that our work reveals what we think of the works of God'. How well we utilize the materials we use, and what we do with them after we have made use of them—all these are questions that have serious religious significance. In answering them, we practice, or do not practice, our faith. We need to understand the use of every skill or craft ultimately as a service to fellow creatures and to God. Our talents, materials, subjects, inspiration or vision are not personal properties with which we may do as we choose but as gifts of God, who must be honoured by the way we use them. The Bible teaches that we humans do not own the world or any part of it; 'The earth is the Lord's, and the fullness thereof, the world and they that dwell therein' (Psalm 24; 1-2). There is in our human law, undeniably, the concept and right of 'landownership'. But it's there merely to safeguard the mutual belonging of people and places without which there can be no lasting and conserving human communities.

The story of the giving of the Promised Land to the Israelites, 'I will give it to you for a possession' (Exodus 6: 8), has precious lessons for us, because the Promised Land is a divine gift[21] to a fallen people. God remains the donor because he was and remains the owner. People are not God. They must not act like God or assume godly authority. If they do, terrible retributions are in store. Moses warned: 'Justice and only justice you shall follow, that you may live and inherit the land which the Lord your God gives you'. Two regulations dealt with land use: Sabbath and the Jubilee (Lev. 25: 2; cf. 23: 10f). The practice of leaving the land fallow was not only for the purpose of rejuvenation but also to benefit the poor and wildlife.

A second ordinance that dealt specifically with land use is the jubilee, when the land was to revert to the family that originally claimed ownership. The jubilee aimed at the preservation of household units, ensuring their economic viability. With such agricultural practices as the Sabbath year and the jubilee year, a lifestyle characterized by non-exploitation of land and of people was inculcated. A considerate and caring attitude was encouraged.

Land is real. Earth is spatially definable. Life with Yahweh takes place here and now. The quality of life is all-embracing —it relates to Yahweh, to the neighbour and the environment. Life with Yahweh cannot be compartmentalized, as though his interests lie only within small areas. God's interests extend to the total humankind and to the total environment. He is misrepresented, and his people's life mis-shaped, if the wholeness of life is not emphasized. In the New Testament the concept of discipleship is equally all embracing.

How then should we live? First of all, we must be faithful, grateful, and humble, as we remember that the land is a gift. Our destruction of nature is not just bad stewardship, or stupid economics, or betrayal of family responsibility, it is flinging God's gift into His face, as if they were of no worth beyond that assigned to them by our destruction of them.

Second, we must be neighbourly. The land is described as an 'inheritance'. A neighbour is not just one who lives 'next door', but also the dead who have bequeathed the land to the living and of the unborn to whom the living in turn will bequeath it to. But we can have no direct behavioural connection to those who are not yet alive. The only neighbourly thing we can do for them is to preserve their inheritance: we must take care, among other things, the land, which is never a possession, but an inheritance to the living, as it will be to the unborn. It is a contradiction to love your neighbour and despise the great inheritance on which life depends.

Third, we need to practice good agriculture or husbandry and remember that we cannot use creation according to our purposes. The Bible does not teach stewardship of creation as a manipulation of the earth's resources purely for humanity's benefits. We cannot use creation according to the purposes we have for it, any more than we love one's neighbour in order to borrow his tools.

In the book of Job (39: 5-12) the wild ass and the wild ox are said to be free, precisely in the sense that they are not subject or serviceable to human purpose. 'Who let the wild donkey go free?' (v.5) 'Will the wild ox consent to serve you?' (v.9). Jesus made the same point in the Sermon on the Mount (Matthew 6: 26-8) regarding 'the birds of the air' and the 'lilies of the field'. The Creator's love for the creation is mysterious precisely because it does not conform to human purposes. The wild ass and the wild lilies are loved by God for their own sake and yet they are part of a pattern that humans can understand well enough to respect and preserve, though they cannot 'control' or hope to understand completely.

To the divine mandate to use the world justly and charitably we must respond with an appropriate discipline of stewardship. And stewardship involves long-term, courage, perseverance, devotion and skill. This skill has to do with the practical use and care of created things. Application of knowledge is the most important work, but also the most modest, complex, difficult and time-consuming. It also requires skills. For in the loss of skills we lose stewardship and become outcasts from the great neighbourhood of creation.

The dignity of being stewards, of being gardeners of creation is to those who are entrusted with resources to facilitate others becoming stewards as well. Transformational mission promotes just stewardship of resources, either by giving access to resources or through calling people to servanthood in using them. If 'the earth is the Lord's' and we are His stewards, then obviously some livelihoods are 'right' and some are not. What must be the design of a Christian transportation or sewer system? Does not Christianity imply limitations on the scale of technology and landholding? Is it Christian to seek profit or otherwise from violence? Is there not, in Christian ethics, an implied requirement of practical separation from a destructive or wasteful economy?

We cannot live harmlessly or strictly at our own expense; we depend upon other creatures and survive by their deaths. When we do this knowingly, lovingly, skilfully, as beggars with empty hands then we do it reverently as a prayer of thanksgiving in the presence of God. When we do it ignorantly, greedily, clumsily, destructively, it is desecration. In such desecration we condemn ourselves to spiritual and moral loneliness, and others to want. The goal of transformation must be one of fidelity to the land.

The Duties of a Christian Citizen

The importance Evangelicals and Pentecostals attach to evangelism and personal experience of God has led them by and large to lean towards a spirituality of detachment from crucial political concerns of society. Whereas Jesus' exhortation to 'Give back to Caesar what is Caesar's, and to God what is God's' (Matthew 22: 21) and Paul's requirement of submission to governing authorities, 'Let everyone be subject to the governing authorities, for there is no authority except that which God has established' (Romans 13: 1), prohibits such withdrawal. The Bible teaches that words of affirmation and praise encourage not only when they come from God (Romans 2: 29) and the church (2 Corinthians 8: 18) but also from the civil government (Romans 13: 3), since both the civil government and the church exist through divine ordination.

The affirmation that God is one has implications; the God of the Christians and of people of other faiths and ideologies is the same. All rule and authority comes from this one God who is the Lord of all. In practice, Christians should then be in the forefront of effectively reaffirming the transcendent basis of justice and law. God wills civil government as a framework in fallen human history for preserving justice and restraining disorder (Romans 13: 1 ff.). It is essential for our generation to recognize in civil law the will of God. This is vital because it is through civil law that God seeks to redirect fallen humankind's evil inclinations for insatiable wealth, power, pleasure, and privilege. Through civil order God seeks to reiterate His objective for humans' meaningful and creative life in the community.

If Christians focus purely on moral and spiritual freedom to the omission of legal freedoms, they will not only endanger themselves but also weaken love of neighbour. Do we hear God's call to serve one another and all our neighbours in the political arena as witnesses to Christ's lordship over all? Human rights are important in God's sight. Christians need to demonstrate the audacity and sacrifice understood in love as the public fulfilment of law by assisting in articulating the outcomes of justice and law in the life of the world. The state and kingdoms are part of the social body of humankind, and given the character of this age, it includes the ruler and the ruled. The transcendent task given to civil governments to restrain evil in society (Romans 13: 3-4) fulfils a divinely mandated mission within God's larger governance of the world.

Democracy is transforming India, as Ramachandra Guha in his *Makers of Modern India* comments:

> India was once a territory ruled over by Europeans; now, it is an independent nation-state. The political culture of India was once feudal and deferential; now, it is combative and participatory. The social system of India was once governed by community and patriarchy; now, it has had increasingly to make space for the assertion of individual rights as well as the rights of previously subordinated groups such as women and lower castes.[22]

Pavan K. Varma in his *Being Indian* argues that 'democracy has survived in India not because Indians are democratic, but because democracy has proved to be the most effective instrument for cherished pursuit of power'.[23] In fact, Varma builds a case that the Hindu society 'exalts the pursuit of material well-being, *artha*, as a principal goal of life'. A significant thought that he sums up is,

> Indians are extraordinarily sensitive to the calculus of power. They consider the pursuit of power a legitimate end in itself, and display great astuteness in adjusting to, and discovering, the focus of power. Those who renounce the lure of power are worshipped, not because their example is capable of emulation, but in sheer awe of their ability to transcend the irresistible.[24]

Answering the question why Gandhism failed in India, Varma states,

> Mahatma Gandhi believed that the means are as important as the end. His creed failed to attract followers because the concept was alien to Indian tradition. India's most well-known treatise on statecraft, the *Arthashastra*, written by Kautilya almost two thousand years ago, wastes little time on moral underpinnings of power. On the contrary, it advocates a compelling unsentimental recipe on how to seize power through means fair and foul. Kautilya's essential thesis is that expediency is far more important than conventional morality in conducting the affairs of the state.[25]

Democracy has flourished in India because most Indians perceived it to be a pragmatic and effective means to personal power by participating in the democratic process.[26] In the past, status was prescriptive, a consequence of one's birth. Today it can be acquired by other means, including greater avenues of upward mobility. But this has not made people more egalitarian in their outlook. In a country where resources are scarce and opportunities for upward mobility are limited, political power opens the gates to both.[27] The hierarchical frame of mind of the Hindu society has not been replaced by a new egalitarianism, rather democracy provides legitimacy to hierarchies, both old and new. Varma argues that, 'democracy did not adopt India. Indians usurped democracy because it could be moulded to fit earlier structures without threatening them. The miracle of India is that the practice of democracy has flourished within its boundaries for over five decades in the absence of a democratic temperament'.[28]

Given below are some of the basic components of responsible Christian citizenship.

(a) PRAYING FOR AUTHORITIES

Possibly, the key role Christian citizens can play is by engaging in prayer. Intercession for political rulers comes through in Jeremiah 29: 7: '. . . seek the peace and prosperity of the city to which I have carried you into exile. Pray to the LORD for it, because if it prospers, you too will prosper.' Several New Testament writers, but especially Paul and Peter, instruct Christians to be thankful for governments, to honour, obey, and respect governments, and to intercede on their behalf (Romans 13: 7; 1 Timothy 2: 1-4; Titus 3: 1; 1 Peter 2: 17). Prayers should be specific, reverentially brought to God, as well as courageous and thankful. They should be offered for all kinds of people without exception. Prayer for civil authorities has both an immediate and the ultimate goal. The immediate goal is a stable life, free of the disturbances and obstructions that civil strife, persecution, and suffering bring. The ultimate goal, for which the immediate is the setting, is godliness and holiness. Godliness means doing things God's way. Daily living of Christian faith in the power of the Holy Spirit is the standard of godliness which must come to full expression in holy living. Peter exhorts the believers to, 'Show proper respect to everyone, love your fellow believers, fear God, honour the emperor' (1 Peter 2: 17). Here, Peter simultaneously affirms responsibilities of believers to others, to each other, to God, and to the state. Under normal circumstances, loyalty to God and loyalty to the empire will not come into conflict. However, there remains the distinct possibility of situations in which the demands of God and the emperor will pull Christians in different directions and in which suffering will be the result.

(b) SUBMISSION TO AUTHORITIES

What is expected of a life transformed by Christ? Some enthusiastic believers' emphasis on the demand of the gospel not to conform to the sinful ways of the world led them to scorn the institution of the government. The Apostle Paul corrected this extremism by pointing out, that earthly authorities and institutions were appointed by God for the good of people. The injunction to be subject to government comes through clearly in Roman 13: 1, 5 and Titus 3: 1: 'Let everyone be subject to the governing authorities, for there is no authority except that which God has established' (Romans 13: 1). 'Remind the people to be subject to rulers and authorities, to be obedient, to be ready to do whatever is good, to slander no one, to be peaceable and considerate, and always to be gentle toward everyone' (Titus 3: 1-2). God wills civil government as a framework in human history for preserving justice and restraining disorder, and that Christians must accept this fact. Christians are counselled not to consider lawlessness but to acknowledge the propriety of governmental structures in the divine economy.

(c) PAYING YOUR TAX

Christians, in spite of the common misuse by government of monies collected, are plainly taught to pay taxes.

> Then the Pharisees went out and laid plans to trap him in his words. They sent their disciples to him along with the Herodians. 'Teacher,' they said, 'we know that you are a man of integrity and that you teach the way of God in accordance with the truth. You aren't swayed by others, because you pay no attention to who they are. Tell us then, what is your opinion? Is it right to pay the imperial tax to Caesar or

not?' But Jesus, knowing their evil intent, said, 'You hypocrites, why are you trying to trap me? Show me the coin used for paying the tax.' They brought him a denarius, and he asked them, 'Whose image is this? And whose inscription?' 'Caesar's,' they replied. Then he said to them, 'Give back to Caesar what is Caesar's, and to God what is God's.' When they heard this, they were amazed. So they left him and went away. (Matthew 22: 15-22)

The plan of the Pharisees was to entrap Jesus by getting Him to say something that might be used against Him in their attempt to get rid of Him. If Jesus was no respecter of the wealth, position, or power of a person, He might as well speak critically of the emperor's taxation of the Jews. Their plan failed because Jesus was able to transcend the dilemma they forced on Him. If Jesus was willing to pay the temple tax (17: 4), he was equally willing to pay the tax to the Romans. Jesus at the same time articulated a fundamental principle by which the disciples can chart their existence as the people of God's kingdom living in a yet imperfect world governed by civil authorities. We must render to God the totality of our being and substance in obedience and service, and give government its due in taxes. Loyalty to government must always be set in the larger context of the full submission of the self to God. The later New Testament writers regard the ruling powers as instituted by God and as worthy of honour, faithfulness, support, and intercession (Romans 13: 1–17; 1 Peter 2: 13–17).

(d) BEING A PEACEMAKER

Another essential duty of a Christian citizen is to be a peacemaker. Such an emphasis is to characterize all aspects of a believer's life and therefore also the citizenship role. 'Blessed are the peacemakers,' we read in Matthew 5: 9, 'for they will be called sons of God.' Christ shapes his followers by a new set of values with the vision to create just, truthful, and peaceful societies. Humans are not in the world as products of chance or necessity. God of love created each of us, together with our world. We are not in the world to fend for ourselves while pursuing lives filled with as little pain and as much pleasure as possible; God has created us to live with Him and one another in a communion of justice and love.

The gospel teaches that humanity has not been left to itself to deal with the divisive results of our deadly failures to love God and neighbour—a fracture of rivalry and suffering that taints all human history and scares individual lives; in Christ, God entered human history and, through His death on the cross, unalterably reconciled human beings to God and one another. There is hope that the plundering time will not swallow us into nothingness; at the end of history, God, who took on our finitude in Jesus Christ, will make our fragile flesh imperishable and restore true life to the redeemed, so that forever we may enjoy God, and each other in God. The irreversibility of time will not chisel the wrongs we have suffered into unchangeable reality of our past; the evil done will not ultimately triumph over the victim; and suffering will not have the final word. God will expose the truth about wrongs, condemn each evil deed, and redeem both the repentant perpetrators and their victim, thus reconciling them to God and to each other forever.

(e) EMBRACING THE OTHER

Jesus illumined hope in the hearts of the oppressed when He proclaimed that God's unconditional love was available to those who repent. For example, the Samaritan woman's life was transformed when she met Jesus at the well (John 4). She had suffered from double oppression, first gender, for she was a woman, and also racial, for she was a Samaritan, the outcaste of her times. Although she was much sinned against, she also needed to repent for she too had committed sin. Jesus established a connection between the hope he provides to the oppressed and the complete change of life he demands of them. The new set of values in the Kingdom of God cannot take place without a change of heart and conduct. People from all castes and races need transformation. Be it Samaritans or Jews, Dalits or Brahmins, Blacks or Whites, all need to repent, forgive, and reconcile. Conversion to Christ ushers in a reconciled community serving and reconciling in society.

Miroslav Volf writes,

> For a victim to repent means not to allow the oppressors to determine the terms under which social conflict is carried out, the values around which the conflict is raging, and the means by which it is fought. Repentance thus empowers victims and disempowers the oppressors. Repentance creates a haven of God's new world in the midst of the old and so makes the transformation of the old possible.[29]

(f) DISOBEDIENCE TO CIVIL LAW

At least one additional Christian duty must be mentioned. While Christians are to be submissive to government, all citizenship obligations are subordinate to the requirements of consistent Christian living. Daniel (Daniel 5: 23-8), and various other Old Testament saints, send us a clear signal that godly people should not hesitate to practice civil disobedience when warranted. This thread runs throughout the scripture. Thus we read, for example, in Acts 3: 18-20 and Acts 5: 27-9 that the disciples disobeyed the civic authorities when the authorities forbade them to preach the good news. As was the case when Jesus was instructed by Pilate to speak, but He refused to do so (Matthew 27: 12-14), so also followers will encounter times when the civil law must be disobeyed. Two problems confront Christians in articulating the divine law and the constitutional guarantees into laws of the land: first, that of avoiding coercive imposition of religious beliefs in a secular state, and second, that of challenging the secular state when it would require what God prohibits. Christians serve the providential realm of God's kingdom by taking a responsible role as citizens—by caring for their neighbours and the nation. Transformational mission indeed brings biblical perspective to bear on social ills and influences society by the values of the kingdom of God.

Service: A Celebration and Promotion of Life

When we submit to the biblical understanding that our lives are inextricably bound with the lives of others, then service takes on a completely different meaning. Rather than service being a demeaning activity, it is a willingness to enter into life with others on earth and seek the flourishing of all. Service is indeed the ultimate act of celebration and promotion of life. This was exemplified by the Lord of all, Jesus Christ when He washed the feet of His disciples (John 13). The example of Jesus' limitless love calls for love in action that expresses itself in limitless ways. So also the mutual service of love between the followers of the servant is rooted in His redemptive service, and is the source, inspiration, and pattern of our service as well. Service stands in contrast with the reductive, instrumental tendencies implicit in the desire to explain and control, and seeks to expand our vision and make it more faithful to the mystery and grace that comprehends and sustains all. The prerequisite for service is the taming of our desire to the scale of the Creator and His creation. The goal of human life, and therefore also its inspiration, must be the peace and rest that marked the climax of creation. Our desire, our knowledge and our work must finally end in the celebration of joy and delight that mirrors the creator's pleasure in the goodness of creation. We must labour for the transformation of all work, in the light of the interdependence of creation.

The church is the actual historical bearer of transformation. The disciples are creative catalysts; they are the preserving and illuminating elements in the world. As Jesus said: 'You are the salt of the earth', 'You are the light of the world' (Mathew 5: 13-14). The disciples are called for the accomplishment of God's purpose in the world. Their mission is accomplished not only in word but in the deeds of their daily existence. The church is expected to be indeed the conscience of the culture it lives in. Churches that are to be 'the salt' of the culture are too often as insipid as everything around them. 'If the salt has lost its saltiness, how can you season with it?' asked Jesus rhetorically (Mark 9: 50). A sense of tragedy hangs over the question. If Christians make no effort to affect the culture around them, they are of little value to God. Since you cannot season it, tasteless salt 'is no longer good for anything, but is thrown out and trampled underfoot' (Matthew 5: 13). The warning about being thrown should lead us to repentance from captivity to our own culture which is accompanied so often with blind self-righteousness.

The transformation that Christ brings creates reconciled people who work for justice in the midst of injustice, for truthfulness in the middle of deception, and for peace in the centre of a violent society, as stewards of creation in the hurting environmental degradation. The church must be engaged in the transformation of the world. God is the source and power of transformation.

NOTES

1. Eugene F. Rogers Jr., 'The Stranger as Blessings', in James Joseph Buckley and Stuart Yeago (eds.), *Knowing the Triune God,* Williams and Everdman Publishing Company, 2001, p. 271.
2. John Polkinghorne, *Science and Christian Belief,* London: SPCK, 1994, p. 167.
3. Athanasius of Alexandria (b. *c.* 296-298 – d. 373), a Church Father and the chief defender of the Trinitarian faith against Arianism. See *St. Athanasius on the Incarnation,* tr. and ed. a religious of C.S.M.V., Crestwood: St Valdimir's Orthodox Seminary, 1993, p. 41.
4. Thomas F. Torrance, *Divine and Contingent Order,* Oxford: Oxford University Press, 1981, p. 208.
5. Christine Pohl, *Making Room: Recovering Hospitality as a Christian Tradition,* Grand Rapids: Eerdmans, 1999.
6. Ray S. Anderson, *The Shape of Practical Theology: Empowering Ministry with Theological Praxis,* Downers Grove: IVP, 2001, p. 116.

7. Fr. Mata El-Menken, *The Passion of Jesus Christ in Our Life*, Cairo: The Monastery of St Macarius, 2002, p. 17.
8. Colin E. Gunton, *The Promise of Trinitarian Theology*, Edinburgh: T&T Clarke, 1991, p. 13.
9. Karl Barth, *Church Dogmatics*, Edinburgh: T&T Clarke, 1960, p. 242.
10. V.T. Rajshekar in *The Gospel among our Hindu Neighbours* ed. Vinay Samuel and Chris Sugden, Bangalore, 1982, pp. 131-2.
11. Gail Omvedit, *Dalit and the Democratic Revolution: Dr Ambedkar and the Dalit Movement in Colonial India*, Delhi: Sage, 1994.
12. Louis Dumont, *Homo Hierarchieus*, Delhi: Vikas, 1970, pp. 33-64.
13. A.K. Iyer, *Anthropology of Syrian Christians*, 1926, p. 218, cf. Louis Dumont in his classic *Homo Hierarchious* (English tr.), points out, 'even Catholics of more recent origin are divided into four distinct groups or castes. Christians originating from untouchables seem to have their own churches'.
14. Raimundo Pannikar, 'Indic Christian Theology of Religious Pluralism from the Perspective of Interculturation', in *Religious Pluralism*, ed. K. Pathil, Delhi: ISPCK, 1991, p. 20.
15. Robert Heilbroner, *The Nature and Logic of Capitalism*, New York: W.W. Norton, 1985, pp. 31-2, 141-8.
16. Scott Lash and John Urry, *Economies of Signs and Spaces*, London: Sage, 1994, pp. 314ff.
17. Chris Sugden, *Gospel, Culture and Transformation*, Oxford: Regnum, 1997 & 2000, pp. 15f.
18. T.N. Madan (ed.), 'Secularism in its Place', in *Religion in India*, Delhi: Oxford University Press, 1992, p. 400.
19. Karl Polanyi. *The Livelihood of Man*, New York: Academic Press, 1977, p. 9.
20. The Hebrew word (rason) carries three major shades of meaning. The primary is 'favour' or 'goodwill' of God (Deut. 33: 16; Isa. 60: 10; Ps. 5: 12). The second shade of meaning is the 'delight' or 'acceptance' of an individual (Ex 28: 38). The third shade of meaning which attaches to this word is 'desire', 'pleasure' in the specific sense of 'will', as the 'will' of God. (Ezra 10: 11 Ps 40: 9 et al.). In prayer the formula 'May it be pleasing in thy sight is used. This corresponds exactly with the expression used by Jesus in Matt. 11: 26. (cf. Lk. 12: 32; Heb. 10: 6, 8).
21. 'There are eighteen explicit references in all parts of the book (Deuteronomy) to Yahweh's promise of the land to the patriarchs,

all but three of which speak also of his giving it', Patrick D. Miller, 'The Gift of God: The Deuteronomic Theology of Land', *Interpretation* 23 (1969), pp. 451-65.

22. Ramachandra Guha, *Makers of Modern India,* New Delhi: Penguin Books India, 2010, pp. 4-5.
23. Pavan K. Varma, *Being Indian,* Viking Penguin Books India, 2004, p. 55.
24. Ibid., p. 7.
25. Ibid., p. 26.
26. Ibid.
27. Ibid., p. 22.
28. Ibid., p. 23.
29. Miroslav Volf, *Exclusion and Embrace,* Nashville: Abingdon Press, 1996, p. 116.

PART IV

THEOLOGICAL AND ECCLESIOLOGICAL PERSPECTIVES

10

Rethinking Theology in India for the Twenty-first Century: Ecclesiastical Perspectives

ROGER GAIKWAD

In the past, external forces, namely Syrian Christianity, Roman Catholic Christianity and Western Protestant Christianity have to a large extent shaped the Christianity that has evolved in India. In recent times Pentecostal Christianity and Charismatic Christianity have also been impacting the existing churches and forming new ones in India. So also, particularly during the twentieth century, we have witnessed the rise of indigenous expressions of Christianity, as a kind of reaction to, or offshoot of, the forms of Christianity that have struck roots in Indian soil from outside.[1] However, in general, Christian faith expressions in the different traditions have been influenced by what we have received from outside.

Christian Expressions in India: Mirror Images of Their Founding Missions

While it has been taught in theological institutions in India that Scripture, Tradition, the Church, Revelation, Reason and Experience are the formative factors of theology, for the majority of the Christians these formative factors have been those which shaped Christianity outside and the products of those factors have been almost imposed upon churches in India as 'givens'. As Roger Hedlund observes in his presentation entitled, 'The Witness of Christian Movements in India':

> Despite this early sensitivity to social customs and culture, the churches arising from the missionary presence were inevitably European in form—German Lutheran in Tranquebar, English Baptist in Bengal, Church of England in Tirunelvelli and Calcutta, American Presbyterian in Punjab, Welsh Presbyterian in Shillong, American Methodist in Bareilly, American Baptist in North East India and Andhra, Salvation Army, Quaker, Alliance—each according to the image of its missionary creator.
>
> Ziegenbalg in South India, Carey in Bengal, and other pioneers, certainly carried a number of 'indigenous' ideals. But, like the Roman Catholics, they too were bearers of their own cultural traditions so that the churches arising on Indian soil nevertheless were molded in the shape of the Catholic and Protestant missions.[2]

In general, Christian creeds, statements of faith, etc., of churches in India have been systematic theological articulations of the confessions which they have inherited. Along with the forms of faith affirmation, we have to a great extent also adopted the forms of church administration, manner of worship, style of celebrating festivals, and eating and dressing culture from the bringers of the gospel to us. At the same time they presented a model of Christian service in terms of establishing educational and medical institutions, orphanages, old people's homes, meditational or retreat centres, and actions of relief and rehabilitation in the event of any natural or other calamities. A pattern of evangelism was also handed over to us, in which Indian religions and cultures were in most cases looked down upon as unhelpful for salvation, or at best precursors to the gospel of Jesus Christ.

It is significant that an emphasis was laid on the gospel as good news for the weak, the discriminated and the downtrodden. A good number of Dalits therefore embraced the gospel, as did many tribals in India. P. Surya Prakash writes:

It is this new message of social justice and equality and alleviation of poverty and illiteracy with a spiritual vehemence that eventually awoke an impressive response among Indian masses. Consequently, by the end of the 19th century, there were significant group conversions among tribals and untouchables in many parts of the country. Almost all the late 19th and early 20th century Christian converts are from the Dalit communities.[3]

The Structures and Boundaries of Indian Christian Faith Expressions

Most of the outsiders also gave the churches they founded their concepts of biblically based and theologically sound Christian faith (from their respective confessional perspectives) and therefore termed any expression not agreeable to them as heresy.[4] Since this stricture was present all the time, most Indian Christian leaders, when they sought to express their faith indigenously, still used the given conceptual or dogmatic framework from outside. Therefore in most cases, the confessions of faith of Indian churches are translations of the Apostles Creed, the Nicene Creed, and various church confessional creeds or statements of faith in Indian regional languages. Given the pervading influence of Hinduism, theological articulations have been largely done using Hindu philosophical and religious terms and concepts. Robin Boyd's well-known book *Introduction to Indian Christian Theology* clearly highlights these theological endeavours.[5]

When tribal scholars first started articulating Christian theology they too were inclined to present the Christian faith in systematic theological concepts, such as explaining the understanding of God, interpreting the significance of Jesus Christ's life and work, and so on, expressing them, however, in suitable indigenous terms. While Dalit theologians have taken the context of suffering under the caste system as their starting point of theologizing, the articles of faith in the churches that Dalits are members of, still are the traditional outsider-given affirmations.

Similar is the case with work of recent Tribal theologians. While they have spoken of the context of discrimination and neglect and emphasized the significance of land, integrity with nature, and the importance of the community, the churches of which they are members still hold on to the theologies that were given to them by the founders. Even the indigenous church movements which have sprung within the country have not stirred the so-called mainline churches to rethink and rearticulate their Christian faith and practice.

The Gospel Converted to a Religion

What has happened to Christianity in India? In general it has transformed the gospel into a religion, just as it has happened elsewhere. While in some villages, towns, cities and states, Christians may be living in communities, in general Christians tend to be a scattered people. Even in many of those places where they dwell together within a locality, the church is not seen as a gospel movement because Christians are faced with the struggles of day-to-day living, problems of interpersonal relationship, etc., though there could be some expressions of unity during festive occasions, or shows of solidarity when faced with some oppressive situations. In other words, Christianity is generally presented and seen as a religion of people who have opted for it as their *ishta dharma* (religion of their choice).

Not only has the gospel become a religion for many Christians, it has also been reduced to largely a weekly Sunday exercise. This kind of coming together gives them a sense of identity, a bond of togetherness, an experience of catharsis when they pour out their problems in prayer (usually silently) while sitting or kneeling inside the church building, the 'pat on the back' experience that they have given something to God (they have done their Christian duty!) through their offerings and other services which they render, a sense of hope that God would answer their supplications, and a feeling of assurance that God is with them as they go about their life at home and in the society. As far as sermons are concerned, the congregations like to listen to some good orations. The listeners may discern some answer from God in the sermon to their own respective contexts, hopes and desires, but usually even good sermons are eventually forgotten.

This kind of a Sunday religion is strengthened by special programmes which are conducted from time to time such as retreats/conventions, picnics, charitable services, etc. So also celebrations/observations of births, weddings, funerals, baptisms, the eucharist, etc., provide opportunities for Christian religious practices. However in every congregation one may come across a number of dedicated or religiously active persons who play an important role in the administration and activities of the church. There are others who attend the worship services, regularly give their offerings, seek solace and strength from God, pray for others, etc., but they do not play any big role in church activities and are not interested in or disturbed about any problems in the church.

Churches in India have further become religious organizations with their constitutions, their ecclesial meetings (from the local church level to the highest organizational level), their polity (Episcopal, Presbyterian, Congregational, etc.), their various institutions and related administration responsibilities, etc. In all such matters social, cultural, ethnic, economic and political factors interact with one another. Churches are therefore confronted with problems arising out of difference of opinion, group tensions, conflicts and court cases, etc., which affect the life and witness of the church in India. For example, commenting on the problems of episcopal governance, Samartha writes,

> At the moment far too much power, authority and privileges are concentrated in the office of the bishop. The assumption that episcopacy would provide stability, continuity and a point of unity for a church living among different communities of faith has proved to be incorrect. . . . A visible point of unity, in the person of a president or moderator or bishop, is indeed necessary for the identity of the church in a pluralistic society, but the exaggerated importance which the

episcopal office has . . . is disturbing developments. A disproportionate amount of time, energy and money is spent in electing and maintaining the office of the bishop. A radical transformation of the character of episcopacy, to emphasize simplicity, nonviolence, renunciation, loyalty, cooperation and the gift of human friendship, is necessary. This could lead to a new kind of participatory leadership, infused by the Spirit, in place of the authoritarian model.[6]

Since the gospel has been converted into a religion, churches tend to relate to neighbours of other faiths, not as people to people, but as one religion with another religion. Therefore evangelism gets interpreted as convincing the other about the validity of one's theological perspectives, equating them almost with scientific or philosophical truth. Evangelism in such cases is more a matter of the mind, followed by an act of the heart when the recipient of the evangelistic activity is convinced that he/she is a sinner, repents, and accepts Jesus Christ as his/her Saviour and Lord. In some other cases evangelism becomes a power display when Christianity is presented to individuals as the sickness-healing and problem-solving religion.

One does not deny that any movement does evolve its structure with a creed, code and *cultus*. In fact, such religious formulations and practices are important in the life and growth of any movement. The danger arises when the movement loses its movement character and the structure, creed, code and *cultus* become a rigid religion; succeeding generations are forced to abide by that religion. A movement should always have a dynamic, flexible structure. It must keep on adapting itself according to the changing context. The message or objective of the religious movement will need to be rearticulated in different contexts, and in the process deeper or newer dimensions of the message/objective would also be discovered. For example, during Paul's time, while slavery was accepted as a part of the structure of society, in later times, Christians realized that the Christian gospel and the institution of slavery were incompatible. Similarly, apartheid was justified in South Africa by White clerics who interpreted certain passages of the Bible to mean that the Black people were only meant for hewing wood and performing manual labour for their White masters, and also on the basis of biological theories of racial superiority.[7] Several decades of struggle ultimately resulted in overthrowing apartheid in the South African Christian society.

Faith Affirmations Articulated in the Christian Religion

Where is the issue of rethinking their faith or theological articulations in all this? In general Christians are happy to recite the Apostles Creed or Nicene Creed during Sunday worship. The Lord's Prayer also constitutes some sort of a faith expression for many. The beliefs they have internalized during their Sunday school days as children, the lessons they learnt during their confirmation classes, and the popular beliefs that Christians generally hold regarding creation, the Bible, the life and work of Jesus Christ, the status of other religions, the end of the world, etc., form the content of their faith. There are occasions when that faith gets challenged: when scientific studies or claims disturb their understanding about creation, miracles, etc., when communal forces question their beliefs; when they experience authentic spirituality or power among adherents of other faiths; when incidents happen for which their faith cannot give a satisfactory answer, etc.

The Christian Religious Tradition Goes On

This kind of Christianity which has become a religion however continues to exist throughout history. Human nature is such that it generally holds on to the faith and traditions of the fathers and mothers. There is inertia for change. People are satisfied with their individual spiritualities or religiosities. Though they are aware of problems in the church and society, many Christians in general have neither the time nor the inclination to become actively engaged in movements for change, unless something very calamitous happens. There are occasions when some Christians may change church memberships for different reasons: change of residence leading them to become members of the church that is in, or close to their vicinity; they may like to have a more emotionally satisfying worship service including the sermon; they are not happy with what is going in the church where they are presently members; there are certain benefits they could avail of in another church, etc. In general, however, the different church traditions continue to go on, with periods of ups and downs.

The kind of Christianity with its several confessions, and each confession having its constitution, orders or kinds of ministry, its educational, medical, engineering, agricultural ministries, its orphanages, old people's homes, shelters, rehabilitation centres, etc., goes on! Some of these ministries in certain places have become rather weak and are unable to maintain their earlier quality of service. Some of the churches have also seen a decline in their membership, while newer churches have arisen. In certain places Christian worship places and institutions as well as the houses and personal property of Christians have been vandalized. In some states laws prohibiting conversion (particularly to Christianity) have been passed. Time and again, churches come together to register their protest against such atrocities and injustices. There are occasions when churches stand up publicly for their minority community rights when they experience or fear infringement of those rights. But by and large, Christians are content if they are allowed to practise their religion without much disturbance.

The Gospel Blunted in Christian Religion

As a result of having become a religion, Christianity in India has not prophetically addressed the ills of Indian society. One such problem is the caste system. While churches continue to affirm in line with Gal. 3: 28 that in Christ all discriminatory distinctions disappear, caste system remains a bane of the church, though one may not explicitly acknowledge it. Some churches and church-related organizations are caste-based, marriage alliances are made on caste basis; elections are fought on caste lines; inter-personal relationships are determined by caste, etc. When caste considerations still play an important role inside churches, how can Christians effectively address the caste injustices in society?

Another problem which Indian Christianity did not address, but rather accepted as the culture of society was the institution of patriarchy. As we are all aware patriarchy is a system of social structures and practices, in which men dominate, oppress and exploit women and children. It is based on a system of power relations which are hierarchical and unequal. Rather than being a gospel of just and loving relationships in the society, Christianity appropriated patriarchy as the governing system even of the churches in India. While in some regions in the country, the coming of Christianity did lighten the burden that women and children experienced in their pre-Christian society, the basic principles of patriarchy, however, have continued in Christian communities.[8]

A third important issue which the church has been addressing only on the surface without rooting out the evil is poverty in India. The church has been engaged in ministries of charity: providing food, clothing, and shelter to the needy; giving alms to the poor, providing for their medical treatment, running hostels, orphanages, old age homes, etc. The challenge which the gospel should have addressed, in line with the Nazareth Manifesto of Jesus (Luke 4: 18-19), was the causes of poverty in India, the systems, structures, and culture that perpetuate poverty, and giving expression to the reign of God in the society.

A fourth important issue which the church for long did not care about is ecology. Tim Cooper, himself an evangelical Christian, writes:

Most Christians still envisage leaving the earth when they die and going "up" to heaven. This 'otherworldly' strand in Christian teaching leads many to understand salvation in terms of deliverance from the physical, material, bodily world. To them the Earth is like a huge airport terminal where we spend what seems to be an unduly lengthy period, overcrowded and a little bored, waiting for the plane to heaven to take us away.[9]

Traditional Christianity has been more obsessed about saving human souls than with saving the planet. The first Christians expected the earth to be destroyed and replaced by a new earth. Later Christians believed their ultimate destiny to be far away from this planet. Moreover popular hermeneutics of scripture led humans to see themselves as being called to have dominion over the earth and all living things upon it. Such a policy of failing to care for this earth is now endangering the future of succeeding generations, and may be judged very self-centred. Thus the 'other-worldly' hopes, so treasured in the traditional Christian world, are now becoming a threat to earth's planetary future.[10]

Even the educational and medical services for which the church in India has been known have become notorious in many urban places in India for their commercial ideology. For instance regarding educational services, Soroj Mullick, an ordained member of the Salesian Society, and founder of the Mission Educare in Bengal makes this critical comment:

Christian urban schools and colleges are corporately following the line of corruption by commercializing education. With the soft coated 'donation' over the high capitation fees, admission fees to new section within the same schools and colleges, are only few signs to prove this point. The market economy with cut throat competition and hedonic consumerism has found headway into the Christian schools which are meant to serve the poor and the neediest. This proves the moral vacuum and value deterioration that the school management extend to the students and parents, breaking down the educative cultural ethos of the society. Money making game has crept into the Christian education system, poisoning the minds of the students and adults in the society, encouraging creating prejudices and hatred against the

Churches. This is a war being waged between the rich, including the school management and the poor *dalits, adivasis*, minorities and backward classes who get all the more marginalized.[11]

Mullick further comments:

Education is a pastoral ministry, an evangelization process that teaches the Gospel values and promotes the culture of love and justice through counter-culture move in ushering God's Kingdom. We need to distinguish the Church's educative mission to teach the Gospel values, giving a religious view of the person and the reality that is essential from the strictly development work. It cannot be seen in reductive terms, as something merely material.[12]

Alleged corruption in the church especially with regard to property matters and church body elections is another major blot in the life and witness of churches. It is publicly alleged that some of the church leaders are more of businessmen rather than religious dignitaries, cutting shady deals on church property, taking donations for school admissions and the like. When the leaders are corrupt, people down the line in church governance and administration are also made to follow suit; thus their silence is purchased.[13]

Challenges Faced by Churches and Christians

While the church is beset with its internal problems, it has to face external ones too. In a country where concerns of economic prosperity are becoming predominant, there are forces which fan the flames of religious communalism, thereby attacking and destroying the livelihood and commercial enterprises of another community. In a country where acquiring of political power have become very important, there are forces which politicize religion, and so elections are fought on the basis of religious loyalties and sentimental attachments. Therefore Christians have been subject to persecution: Christian programmes are disturbed, church buildings are destroyed, Christians are killed, anti-conversion laws are passed, Christian institutions are sought to be brought under government control, Christian establishments are forced to abide by strictures and directives of right-wing forces, attempts are made to take over church property, Christian dalits are denied rights and privileges, etc.[14]

Spirituality in the Indian Christian Religion

In the context of what has been discussed above, Christianity for a significant number of its adherents has become a matter of cultivating individual spirituality within the given socio-economic political *status quo*. Consciously or unconsciously the theology or faith affirmation which most Christians seem to be living by is a dichotomous sacred-secular perspective in which they are concerned about the welfare of the soul, a perspective in which they are not anxious about the happenings in the world but rather are more obsessed about going to heaven. It is a reflection in general of popular Indian spirituality in which the goal of one's existence is the attainment of individual *moksha, nirvana*, or salvation. This individualistic spirituality among Christians is further strengthened by a martyr complex spirituality in the context of the persecutions that Christians face from time to time. Attacks on Christians are considered to be the works of Satan to draw Christian individuals away from their devotion to Jesus Christ.

It is not that churches have totally ignored social earthly concerns. Consultations and seminars have been conducted on issues relating to injustice in society, liberation theologies of the poor, of women, of Dalits and Adivasis have been advocated, and commissions and task forces have been formed to address matters of justice, peace and creation. So also there are several Christian NGOs committed to relief and transformation. However, all these discussions, projects, programmes and activities lie on the periphery of the faith of most Christians in the country. The church is physically in the earth but is spiritually not relating to the earth, regarding which Jesus taught us to pray,

'Your kingdom come, Your will be done on earth as it is in heaven'.

There are other Christians who are content with a spirituality that justifies their consumeristic and possessions-oriented lifestyle. They are attracted to miracle ministries and prosperity theologies. The ideology of globalization strengthens such spiritualities. As we reflect on the theme, 'Rethinking Theology in India for the Twenty-First Century', there is one temptation to continue as we have done in the centuries gone by. The content of the faith which sustains the church remains the same, only its form is suitably changed. The following invitation to join a particular church makes it very evident

> I would like to personally invite you to come and worship with our church family this Sunday morning. We have a loving, vibrant, diverse congregation that is full of His Spirit. New Millennium Community Church is more than just a place or a people, it is so much more!
>
> It's a life-giving tapestry of relationships, ministries, dreams, hope, help, faith, and the kind of love that is genuine and real. It's a family that believes that Jesus Christ is Lord and that miracles still happen today.
>
> Family is an important word in our congregation. But it's not just a word; it is a feeling of belonging. We hope that you will soon feel it too! Our church family includes babes in arms, children, active teenagers, adults who juggle many different responsibilities both in and out of the church, and older adults who provide stability and the wisdom of age.
>
> We welcome you with open arms. Come as you are and be a part of this exciting, Old Message in a new package church. I look forward to connecting with you.[15]

Rethinking Theology in India

In the light of the above discussion, the theology of the church in India has to be thought of afresh. While not denying the value of systematic theologizing which we have inherited and continue to practice, what is required is emphasis on contextual theologies which make sense to the people in their respective contexts. In other words, the gospel would have to be discovered afresh by the people in relation to challenges and needs of the people in their respective situations. Jesus and the Gospel should come alive to us in our context.

The implication of the above statement is clear: Theology should not be merely an academic exercise. Let discussions about creation *versus* evolution, the scientific proof of the miracles in the Bible, the appropriateness or inappropriateness of the infant baptism, sprinkling baptism, etc., the superiority of one religion over another, and so on not distract Christians from living out the gospel meaningfully in their own situations. Theologies should therefore arise from the midst of the people; theological institutions should be with the people and facilitate those processes of theologizing.

While human beings tend to articulate their spirituality in some form of religion, and such articulation also has its importance, we need to remember that spirituality goes beyond religion. Religion by itself does not save; at best it is an instrument in helping humans to find fulfilment in life. The form of religion should lead us to realize the essence of religion. There is bound to be disharmony in society when people identify their particular religious way of life with spirituality, and therefore look down upon other religious expressions as unspiritual or inadequate.

If religion should facilitate spirituality that is just, loving, edifying and leading to fulfilment and God-realization along with others, then theology would have to rediscover and encourage relevant ecclesiologies. Churches should not have buildings as their primary symbol. Churches should make their governance structures democratic and participatory. The church in India would have to look at the significance of house fellowships or neighbourhood or grassroots fellowships. But these fellowships should not be cloistered gatherings. Rather they should serve as nuclei for movements of justice, peace and love.

Living in a pluralistic society, let us be reminded that, as Samartha says, the problem is not of one religion against another.

Rather the issue is of the good and responsible people in all religions and ideologies having to relate to the bad and irresponsible people in all religions.

What is therefore required is theologies that are human friendly and eco-friendly. What is therefore required is theologies that give expression to relevant, just and empowering spiritualities, while at the same time are open to recognizing that there could be other expressions of dynamic and relevant spirituality.

NOTES

1. Examples of indigenous church movements are: The National Church of India, founded in Chennai in 1886, and 'Christo Samaj' which was formed in Kolkata in 1887. Cf. J.W. Gladstone, 'Indigenisation of Christianity' (http://www.ichenetwork.net/Mission_3.pdf; accessed on 1 September 2011). The Ceylon Pentecostal Mission could also be said to be an indigenous movement in the 1920s. The movement which Bakht Singh started in the 1930s, and that of K. Subba Rao are some other expressions of indigenous movements.
2. http://www.missionstudies.org/archive/conference/1papers/fp/Roger_Hedlund_Full_Paper.pd; accessed on 1 September 2011).
3. P. Surya Prakash, 'Christianity in India: A Promised Land for Dalits?' (http://www.ev-akademie-boll.de/typo3conf/ext/naw_securedl/secure.php?u=0&file=fileadmin/res/otg/doku/641010-Prakash.pdf&t=1286117305&hash=9d1b149718eb52599bd12ea5f993f785; accessed on 7 September 2011).
4. An Indian Christian, G.V. Job, writing in 1938, said. 'The Christian movement in India has no theology, not even an indigenous heresy to show that serious thoughts are simmering in its mind'. Winburn Thomas, writing in the mid-1950s, remarked that 'thus far, most of the theological contributions of Asian Christian scholars have been rewrites of Western theology' (http://www.reformedreflections.ca/articles/th-theological-trends-asia.html; accessed on 3 September 2011).
5. Robin Boyd, *An Introduction to Indian Christian Theology*, rev. edn. 1975, Delhi: ISPCK and Trivandrum: Indian Theological Library (1st pub. 1969).

6. Stanley J. Samartha, 'Vision and Reality: Personal Reflections on the Church of South India, 1947-1997' (cf. http://findarticles.com/p/articles/mi_m2065/is_n4_v49/ai_20150891/pg_4/; accessed on 5 September 2011).
7. Cf. Saul Dubow, 'Afrikaner Nationalism, Apartheid and the Conceptualization of "Race"', *Journal of African History*, 33 (1992), pp. 209-37.
8. Cf. Views of Nazareth Sister Shalini D'souza (http://www.religiousindia.org/2010/07/21/%E2%80%98empowerment-of-the-weak-will-check-patriarchy%E2%80%99/; accessed on 9 September 2011).
9. 'Economy, Ecology, Ethics: Making the Connections Theologically or Christianity for the Ecological Age' (http://www.sofn.org.uk/conferences/lg96conf.html; accessed on 11 September 2011).
10. Ibid.
11. http://sorojmullick.blogspot.com/2009/12/commercialized-christian-education-with.html (accessed on 11 September 2011).
12. Ibid.
13. Cf. http://www.savecsi.net/2010/06/is-too-much-financial-power-of-csi.html (accessed on 11 September 2011); http://geoconger.wordpress.com/category/anglican-church-news/church-of-north-india/(accessed on 11 September 2011).
14. Cf. http://en.wikipedia.org/wiki/Anti-Christian_violence_in_India (accessed on 12 September 2011); http://www.milligazette.com/dailyupdate/2006/20060908_Anti_Christian_Violence_India_terrorism.htm (accessed on 12 September 2011).
15. http://newmillenniumchurch.org.

11

Towards a Critical Theology of Risk-taking: The Changing Landscape and Discourse

INDUKURI JOHN MOHAN RAZU

Sifting the Rubble

Theological enterprise in India for decades is being ventured by those who belong to the dominant caste categories. Theologies that had emerged and dominated the Indian canvas right from the beginning and until the mid-seventies of the twentieth century were by and large articulated by the so-called 'high castes'. Theologies that revolved around and premised on philosophical, conceptual, doctrinal and creedal abstractions by and large have been questioned, critiqued, and subsequently rejected. Likewise, theologies that have condoned the system of caste and used the dominant Hindu philosophical frameworks and tenets are under intense scrutiny. Similarly, theologies that remained silent about discrimination, oppression, exclusion and exploit-ation of the Dalits, the indigenous peoples, and other excluded communities are scathingly reviewed and put aside as supporters of life-negating forces. But the survival of these types of theologies remain in the ventilators of the theological institutions and certainly are invalidated by base ecclesial communities. Likewise, theologies with the middle axiom that fails to state its purpose and position by playing 'safe games' and 'opportunistic politics' have been sidelined by victims of societal, economic, political, cultural and religious forces.

The other side of the canvas portrays that those even after their theological education and ordination do believe and practice caste and thus are entrenched in the human-made divides and barriers. So, when it comes to power-sharing and representations to committees and positions in the ecclesial bodies they rather work subtly in favour of their castes. As the years passed by, theologies of those types have lost its favour, significance and relevance. The shift from the centre to the periphery has taken in radical ways. It is indeed a historical shift. The theologies from the margins have broken new grounds. The theologies from the *cherries*, i.e. where the Dalits and the vulnerable live, delved into the unexplored terrains that the so-called 'high castes' deliberately thwarted and concealed. They are the ones who are involved in venturing new ways and developing relevant and authentic theologies from their own contexts. This shift is of course hard to accept and even be digested by the so-called 'high castes', but is indeed a fact.

This shift has ushered radical reversals in the arena of Indian Christian theologies. India is changing. However, as it changes it is also posing a number of challenges to those who have been isolated from the forces of globalization. In such a fluid and complex scenario only those who are fit could survive. And those who are fit have been integrated and accommodated by the laws of social Darwinism. In the process, it has intensified and escalated the suffering of those who live on the margins. If this scenario is not altered, in due course of time, people on the margins would resort to new ways of engaging in struggles. The communities that are caught up in hopeless and agonizing situations tend to ask: what is God doing and where is that God who is our Servant-Savior? This is where critical theologies from the margins play the crucial roles.

Theologies emerging from the underside are supposed to enliven the hopes and extend new meanings and interpretations for the struggles that the people on the margins undergo. If the theologies from the margins, by the margins and to the margins do not offer or cater to the needs and expectations of the people and communities, then those theologies and theologizing will have no value, relevance and authenticity. Theological enterprise in India ought to have an impact or bearing on the lives of people/communities. If there is no bearing or impact on the lives of people/communities, then, that type of theology is dead because the God who is talked about automatically is mutilated. In such an event the best place for that type of theology to remain is within the boundaries of theological institutions and be kept in the shelves of the libraries. Out of those, a few seemed to be good for casual reading, but are read only when compelled as required by subjects. The theologies that are prescribed as something compulsory or required will have its existence till the completion of the course, and then they become redundant and subsequently forgotten.

The contextual theologies are living theologies because they respond to the challenges and take the readers to the real life situations. The contextual theologies unfold the text and integrate the context where the faith communities live. This is where the victims who live on the margins find their God of the Bible who constantly interacts and intervenes in their affairs. They are given the assurance that their God of history and of the living Bible is with them and participates actively in their struggles. At this point of juncture, we are once again reminded by communities on the margins that the theologies constructed and produced by the so-called 'arm-chair theologians' are no more entertained because their God-talk is bundled with sheer abstractions and do not reflect the life-situations of people who strive for meaning in their existence. Therefore, any theology, in order to be relevant and authentic, is to respond to the changing contexts (micro and macro) of those who live on the margins and are excluded. Accordingly, it has to change and cater to the dimensions of materiality and spirituality. So,

> We want theology to be a service to life and to human wholeness. It should be service to life at all levels—from the tiny blade of grass to the singing bird, to the growing baby, to the height of rigorous thought and warm friendships, to the depths of mystic joy and divine darkness. We want a theology that will be at the service of life with its many needs and spiraling possibilities as well as its transcendence and its endlessly expanding quest and onward thrust. Our theology will be at the service of those who work, suffer, and hope, those who struggle for justice and human dignity for all women and men.[1]

In conjunction with the above quotation a few questions surface. Do theologies that we propound and articulate take along with them the people's hopes and yearnings seriously as part of its content and essence? What should then be the aim and purpose of theology that we want to venture and articulate? From where do we take the materials for our theologizing? Does it have any bearing for the people who they are theologizing? Do they address to the context and extend hope to the people to who they are theologizing? Therefore,

> A theology capable of serving the wholeness of life will be ever springing force at the meeting point of faith and the reality. . . . The experience of faith and the experience of human existence meet in tension, love, and suffering; they illumine each other's depths, question and challenge each other, and enable each other to new self-understanding, to fresh interpretations of human hope, to committed action and profounder silence.[2]

It is this scenario that warrants the organic intellectuals and organic *pujaris* to take seriously the excluded communities of our society who undergo all types of risks in their day-do-day existence.

It is at this juncture, let me state, that barring a few, a majority of 'cerebral' theologians and 'professionals' of theology have deliberately ignored the nauseating terrains where about 200 million Dalits live and survive in abject and sub-human conditions. The dominant theologies, including the Indian Christian theology, deliberately concealed and camouflaged their topography and constructed its theologies on 'India Shining under the System of Caste' (Appendix 1 comprehensively explains the genealogy of caste) by opting in favour of the so-called 'pure people' who enjoy all sorts of privileges and powers. The raw materials and frameworks that have been used resonate and revolve around the classical/systematic theologies and philosophical methods and dominant frameworks. As against this background, I intend to unpack the latent motives of the Indian Christian theology. Only then, constructing a critical theology of risk-taking is possible. It is unfortunate that seldom we enter into the terrains of the excluded communities. At this stage, the abundant materials available in the field need to be retrieved and located from where our theological mandates come from. It is of course a historical necessity because the context where the Dalits live is impregnated with heart rendering metaphors and narratives. Hence, the confluence between contextuality and inter-contextuality are the primary locus and reality. If these are not taken seriously and undermined, then those who enter into any form of theologizing or theological enterprise in India becomes a futile exercise.

On the canvass of theologies in India the names that are projected as 'friends', 'comrades', and 'sympathizers' who articulate and theologize for the Dalits come from the so-called 'high caste' rungs. Under their patronage, some of the young 'Christian pseudo-Dalit theologians' are lured and co-opted for petty gains. The strategies, plots and ploys devised and executed are detrimental to the Dalit communities in the long run. The so-called 'high caste' Christian theologians in collusion with the pseudo-Dalit brokers want to institutionalize the contextual theology *vis-à-vis* Dalit theology. For them, the raw materials that are unravelled from the context posit potent volatility and are therefore covertly ignored. The rationale they give is that the materials that are found are crude, filthy, raw, and close to their life and death mirroring their past and present. The materials that come out while digging are from the volatile terrains and bound to create more ripples, disturbance and irruption. Precisely because of these reasons, they prefer to enter into discourses on any dogmatic themes or areas that obviously lead to sheer abstractions. Further, they conveniently and shrewdly enter into subject matters that are speculative and other-worldly that would lead to superficial effect and psychedelics promoting false consciousness. In the process, the real and impending issues and problems, contradictions and conflicts being faced by the excluded communities are neutralized and blunted.

Within the Christian domain there are some Dalits who by using Dalit identity have climbed up to the top echelon as theological educators, pastors and church leaders. The same identity users when it comes to struggle and solidarity remain silent. And others living overseas who act as interlocutors, intermediaries, brokers and spokespersons for Dalits' cause, state that 'there is no Dalit theology as such, but only International Theology'. For them, 'Dalit Theology has brought about divisions and fragmentation amongst communities'. It has destroyed the 'peace', 'tranquillity', and 'harmony' amongst communities who once lived without any 'caste prejudices, biases, distinctions and divisions'. There are others who claim that the 'classical theologies from Barth down to Bultmann to Moltmann to Kaufman to all sorts of Manns gave us the theological grounding, showed us the theological horizons to understand and articulate God and thus enabled us to construct global and transnational theological frameworks and perspectives cognitively and logically'. According to them, Dalit theology has created a clear wedge within and between people and communities. Therefore, Dalit theology or any other brand of contextual theologies will have to be shelved or if need be aborted. For them, the raw materials that are unearthed from the context are crude, stinking, filthy, and volatile, and therefore should as far as possible be not accommodated nor be considered.

In addition, there are a good number of educated Christian Dalits who are engaged in the profession of teaching in the theological institutions and serving as Pastors and Bishops in the churches yet prefer to renounce their Dalit identity because of the basic assumption that the moment they embraced Christianity everything has changed by quoting 'there is neither a Dalit nor a non-Dalit, and all are one in the Lord and before the God'. In principle their assumption could be right, but in reality it is just an illusion, a *maya*. While others use the Dalit identity that brings individual benefits (economic and personal) for aggrandizement, they tend to vacillate and oscillate by changing their perspectives and standpoints depending upon the situations that would suit their agenda. These are the pseudo-Dalits who are the enemies of the Dalits and also betrayers of the Dalit cause. For want of power and position this segment could go to any extent. Knowing their weaknesses, the so-called 'high-caste people' throw crumbs and they are easily co-opted. For the sake of petty gains and incentives this category betrays their fellow Dalits.

This phenomenon prevails mostly in the middle-rung who have hardly encountered problems or lived and experienced with the Dalits either in the rural or urban settings or participated or shown solidarity in the Dalit struggles. So what we see is that their Dalit consciousness is not shaped by their Dalitness, but rather clouded by their pseudo-imitation of the dominant values and ethos. In sum, this category tends to be over-ambitious, self-seeking, individualistic, slimy and naïve. Their presence and participation for the Dalit cause are by all means counter-productive and hence are the renegades of the Dalits' emancipation and freedom. A web of issues that are connected with these individuals manifests their state of consciousness that is being shaped by their false contextualization with which they exist. False contextualization and false consciousness thwart critical

Dalit consciousness. The moment false consciousness seeps in, it blunts the Dalit consciousness, leading to uncritical accommodation. Authentic contextualization and Dalit consciousness are always connected and pave way for prophetic vocation arising out of genuine encounters between God's world and Dalits' world involved in challenging and changing the situations availing the opportune time, namely, the kairos.

Constructing the Risks

Dalits are the original inhabitants of this land. They constitute almost one-fourth of the total population. Their contributions to the nation both mental and physical labour for the progress and prosperity of India have been noteworthy. But it is a paradox that their 'domicile' is under threat and their 'personhood' is under question. Dalits as persons and as people do matter to the Indian society. Indian society enjoys the fruits of the labour of the Dalits, but has failed to treat them on par with them. Likewise, the Dalits are numerically more both in the Protestant and Roman Catholic churches. Like the secular world even in the Christian world for decades the Dalits have been denied of their dignity, personhood, and self-esteem and are treated as untouchable people with no human face or value. In the name of caste, Dalits have been excluded and shown all kinds of difference. Precisely because of these reasons the Dalits have moved beyond the pains and are determined to struggle against the casteist forces with grit and are determination, resolve and resilience. These are the factors that ignite the Dalits both mentally and physically to come to terms and to struggle and strive against all odds that the system of caste and Indian Christianity inflicted on them.

The Christian Dalits who live in the villages and slums in their own ways ask: can there be an Indian Christian theology or any contextual theology without us? What then will be our part in evolving or developing or constructing this theology? Who would choose or determine its focus, its method, and guiding principles for its future? Would the Dalits be at centre or on the periphery? Would their role be simple or complex? Would their life experience of all sorts be the method in the construction of theology? In what way is this theology going to make their life, destiny, and history better or different? Would the change be radically different? The challenge of theology comes from the depth of the Dalitness entrenched in their hope for a co-human persistence of their unshakable faith as well as varying strategies and emphases as they manoeuvered and moved across the difficult paths of their terrains. The spirituality of the Dalits evokes them to ask: what role did the non-Dalits play in history, in their struggles, and in their sufferings?

Have the non-Dalits genuinely come to terms or are convinced that without the Dalits there is no meaningful word about God that can be spoken or undertaken in India? Don't they understand or apply their common sense that no theological enterprise be mooted or conceived or even envisioned for any contextual theologies or even contemplate of any change in Indian society? Maria Arul Raja, SJ, while elaborating this aspect, reiterates,

> . . . every attempt at doing theology begins with questions. These are raised neither from the textual world of the tradition nor from the rhetorical field of the theologians. They emerge from the particular human community, in context of the awakening of Dalits, endeavouring to become a better one upon the actual historical plane amidst the existing conflicts. That is why it gets itself rooted in the on-going dialectical interaction between cognitive structures (cultural symbolism) and social structures (power relations). This conversation is sought to generate new energies in transforming the present disorder into a new order in future.[3]

The ingredients and the basic materials needed for theologizing comes from the questions that are raised by the victims of the caste system. Based on these questions one can enter into the activity of theologizing or from this point one's theologizing starts. One cannot construct theology particularly Dalit theology without the live materials that are hidden in the terrains. A.P. Nirmal succinctly elaborates '. . . theology is a human activity. It is written neither by God nor for God to read. It is written for the benefit of the humans. It is not a study of God but of the concept of God . . . the primary datum for doing theology is human life.'[4] The locus of theology revolves around human life that is to be respected with dignity and esteem. Each individual is endowed with personhood that should be promoted and protected. Hence, 'The primary task of theology, therefore, is to make sense of human life and give it a certain direction and goal. The criteria of theology to them must be derived from human life and not from some other 'givens'.[5] The so-called 'high caste people' do not give value to Dalits in the Indian society. For them cows occupy a better status than Dalits. Being called by different names, the existence of Dalits is one of a lesser human being. The sites of the Dalits are filled with horrifying events and episodes. One should wrestle with the *cherries* or Dalit habitations and probe seriously the dynamic potential and vibrant tenor they hold within them.

One of the country's leading dailies carried out an article in its magazine section entitled 'Night-soil Workers . . . Head-loads and Heartbreak' written by well-known journalist P. Sainath. He graphically narrates a live story of people who are destined to do this job because they are the Dalits. Patasi Bai, a Dalit woman collects a *roti* (made out either from jowar or wheat) from each of the 25 households in Sikar, Rajasthan. Once a month, some of them give her a few rupees. Those who give her the *rotis* would not eat with her. But the job she does is indispensable for them. But they are careful not to have any sort of contact with her. Who is she? She is a manual scavenger who cleans their dry toilets or to put it simply their shit. When asked: 'Yes, I carry night soil. The payment is one roti a household daily and may be Rs.10 a house each month. I clean around 25 homes every day. We do have to carry the night soil in baskets on our heads to the dumping place which could be half a kilometer from the latrine she cleans.'[6] She is one among many thousands of women forced to earn here living this way. As scavengers the name that is given by the casteist society, who clean out dry latrines by hand and who carry excreta which the so-called 'India's civilized society' calls 'night soil' in baskets on their heads. The women use *parethas* (metal pans) to scoop up the night soil with short brooms in their hands. The work she does earns her no more than Rs. 250 a month. Some houses pay nothing because they consider the work they rend as *karma* since they were born as Untouchables and by doing this job at least in the next cycle of birth they would be born in a better way.

Manual scavenging is a caste-based occupation and in many families it is almost hereditary. In the year 1993, the government at the centre passed the Employment of Manual Scavengers and Construction of Dry Latrines (Prohibition) Act. The execution of this Act vests with the local governments' subject and therefore the central government sought and gained the support of West Bengal, Tripura, Karnataka, Maharashtra and Goa for its legislation. Kerala ended this practice much earlier. A little later, Madhya Pradesh, and Andhra Pradesh joined the fold. However, almost all the states barring one or two is continuing with this practice. For instance, the girls cleaning night soil in Sikar in Rajasthan are often young. For example, Shakuntala 16, Lachchi and Reena both 14 years are just three among many. 'For months, we abandoned this work. Nothing happened. No one came to our aid. We were given no other options. So we resumed, though we hate. Only women do this job.'[7] They keep demanding trolleys or wheelbarrows and also longer brooms, but of no anvil. Since they are given short brooms as they bend to sweep they get into direct contact with the mouth leading to all sorts of health hazards. There are many different statements the casteist Indian society uses to humiliate and shame the Dalits and this is one among the many.

In conjunction to this, Susan E. Chaplin from her research

points out that 'action on the law has been mostly confined to States that first supported the Act'. Since most of the States did not act on the act, the act remained as a toothless tiger which ensured that the dehumanizing practice continues in no less than 2,500 towns across India. It was found that as early as 1956-7 the Commissioner for Scheduled Castes and Scheduled Tribes made an open appeal that the practice be stopped such as the head-loading of night soil. He also reiterated that as thinking people we are responsible 'for the spread of evil of untouchability'.[8] The system of caste has given a tag and monopoly to the Valmiki community because no one can do it. It is ironic that the so-called 'high castes' do not want to or hesitate to clear their own shit, but expects others to carry their night soil. Throughout the states of south India barring Kerala, dry toilets still exist. Nonetheless, like all other states Kerala practices the system of caste and all forms of discrimination. Manual scavenging is being carried out only by a particular category of people and this category of people is involved in this job for centuries. This is how castes work. As we have entered into the second decade of the twenty-first century, has there been any drastic change for the Dalits who are designated by the system of caste to collect the shit of others?

The cases that were presented happened almost at the end of the twentieth century and exactly a decade after the dawn of the twenty-first century and at the end of the first decade in one of the captivating write-ups in *The Hindu* titled 'Enslaved by Tradition: The Manual Scavengers of Vidisha'. Vidisha, known for the thriving trade of ancient India being mentioned by Emperor Ashoka and also features in Pali scriptures and Kalidasa's romantic epic *Meghdootam,* a premier tourist destination in the glossy brochures of Madhya Pradesh Tourism, and also the Parliamentary Constituency of Sushma Swaraj, the leader of opposition in the Lok Sabha, continues the banned practice of manual scavenging and is still a forced occupation for several Dalit families. About 200 families in this district continue to bear the brunt of caste discrimination primarily through the practice of manual scavenging. 'Every morning, I go to eight to ten households, collect the garbage of night soil in a straw basket and dump it a mile away from the village. When it rains, the waste oozes through the basket over to my hair', says Guddi Bai (38) of Neteran tahsil.[9] While the practice was banned by law in 1993 with the passage of Employment of Manual Scavengers and Construction of Dry Latrines (Prohibition) Act, it still continues in several parts of India. The deadline for the eradication of manual scavenging from the country, after having been revised thrice (December 2007, March 2009 and March 2010) was recently set for 2012-end by the National Advisory Council, headed by UPA Chairperson Sonia Gandhi. NAC noted that it was 'deeply distressed to observe that the shameful practice of manual scavenging persists in India, despite being outlawed'.[10]

Even after 63 years of Independence and 17 years after a law was passed by the Indian parliament banning manual scavenging the practice continues. The so-called 'high castes' justify that they are destined to do by fulfilling their karmic duties. What do they get in return? Those who are involved in cleaning night soil get an average 20 to 50 kg of grain annually and a few old clothes on occasions, says Basanti Bai (40), who has been scavenging ever since she was handed the job by her sister-in-law after her marriage.[11] Contradicting the statement of the Collector, she said, 'If we quit, the upper caste women ridicule us ... (you seem to act like a Brahmin woman), they say. Moreover, that is the way it has always been going on.'[12]

The next striking and unbelievable narrative comes from Bangalore, the so-called Silicon Valley of India, the premier outsourcing hub and cosmopolitan mega-city, plagued with manual scavenging which I consider is a crime against humanity. Under its very nose of Electronic City, sewerage disposal is being practised in medieval forms. For instance, in Rammurthy Nagar, night soil is manually removed from publicly maintained cesspools. The waste is transported on busy roads and is dumped at a convenient spot, usually in one of the city's lakes. Those who are involved, over 600 of them engaged in scavenging work in Rammurthy Nagar, use simple methods, and their only tools are a few drums, buckets and pick-up vans used to transport the filth. Residents of the area, which lacks basic sanitation and sewerage facilities have to make phone calls to have their cesspits cleaned, says Vincent, a 28 years old who has been cleaning cesspits for over five years.[13]

In view of the perennial sewerage problem, 'Most of the residents of this area have our mobile numbers. So whenever their sewage tanks are full, they call us. We get calls every day from the residents.'[14] He added further, 'we work in batches of three. One of us get into the pit and hand over a filled bucket to another standing on the edge of the pit. He relays it to a person on the pickup van who empties it into one of the drums on the van.'[15] For the work they do, they charge between Rs. 700 and 900 to clean a single pit, but the residents feel it is reasonable for a messy job. A resident J.P. John (58), confesses that 'It is a horrifying job and we engage them with a lot of guilt, but we have no choice. The BBMP has not provided us with proper drainage facilities, so what do we do?'[16] But the then BBMP Special Commissioner K.R. Niranjan blatantly denied the practice and prevalence of manual scavenging in the city of Bangalore. 'Today laborers engaged in other activities earn Rs. 400-500 a day. So why should anyone do this scavenging job? As far as I know, manual scavenging does not exist in Bangalore'.[17] All these clearly manifest and testify that 5000 years of institutionalized social inequality has not ensured the Dalits of their freedom and offered a solution to go beyond from that of being shit collectors.

Atrocities against the Dalits in diverse modes are unleashed by casteist forces in a systematic manner across the country. One such gruesome incident that portrays the sad state is that of a 38 year old Dalit woman forced by a mob to drink human excreta mixed with water in front of her husband and children. She had to undergo this punishment because she resisted the advances of a so-called 'upper caste' man towards her in Keela Urappanuar village in Thirumangalam block of Madurai district, in Tamil Nadu. Shocked and bewildered by the treatment, Muthumari, wife of a labourer, Pitchai narrated that a group of so-called 'high caste people' had also splashed human excreta on her family. It all started when she was returning home around 2.30 in the afternoon after cutting grass. Raju, son of a Sellathevar of the village, who had been making advances towards her for some time waylaid her on that day and grabbed her hand. She managed to wrench herself free, and ran home saying that she would bring this incident to the notice of the village panchayat. Her husband Pitchai came home the same evening at about 7.30 and found her wife profusely weeping. When asked what had happened she narrated the incident and he had assured her to take up this matter to the village panchayat the next morning. In the meantime, as Pitchai was having his super, a group of 15 persons barged into their house, abused her using all sorts of names, attacked her, and even tore her blouse. Raju's wife Vijaya accused her of trying to insinuate her husband and threw a bucket full of human faeces at the family. She then forced Muthumari to drink excreta-mixed with water.[18] And this incident took many twists and turns. Nevertheless, the whole family for no fault of theirs had to suffer because they are Dalits and she being a woman and a Dalit woman!

An equally horrifying incident occurred on 22 May 2002 at Thinniyam village in Tiruchi district in Tamil Nadu. Thinniyam is a tiny village located near Lalgudi where 100 Dalit families live. Apart from the other castes, Kallars numerically dominated the village. Two Dalits, namely Murugesan and Ramaswami, were forced to 'feed each other's human excreta. The 'crime' they committed was that they supported Karuppiah, a Dalit, who was engaged in a prolonged struggle against a former Panchayat president who belong to a so-called 'high caste', i.e. Kallar caste, to recover an amount of money paid to him to get a house for his sister. When the husband of the panchayat president Rajalakshmi flatly denied having received the money, Karuppiah told him that he would lodge a complaint in the police station. Enraged by this, Subramanian along with his son, abused and assaulted him with footwear. Then, the following morning Subramanian and his relatives assaulted Murugesan and Ramaswami with footwear and hot iron rods for helping Karuppiah for making this problem public which damaged their 'caste honour'. It was at that time that the two were reportedly forced to feed each other with human excreta.[19] The Indian Christians are no exception. There are exclusive caste-based cemeteries for caste Christians and separate burial ground for the Dalit Christians. In some of the traditions there are separate churches. Discriminatory practices are commonly found both in the life and witness of the Indian church. Some of the sites of exclusion and discrimination of Dalits are described comprehensively in Appendix 2.

Theologizing on the 'Risks'

The locus of theological conversations and discourses about God has shifted. It has shifted from the centre to the margins; from the casteist to the casteless; from the septic tanks/western commodes to dry toilets/ cesspools; from the *oorrus*/villages to *cherries*/Dalit *wadas*, and from classical to contextual. This is one of the most important, significant and historic shift that ever happened in the whole gamut of the Indian Christian theology. It is a radical reversal that happened in the centre of gravity of the Indian theological systems. Most of the so-called 'high castes Christians' are aware of these changes that include the best informed mind, but deliberately pretend as if this shift has not happened or never taken place. This shift is not only from the west to the south, but certainly from 'main streets' to *cherries*, from 'main roads' to 'by lanes' 'urban' to 'rural' and from the 'centre' to 'underside'. The shift that has taken place in India is certainly from the casteist-centres to the world of the Dalits.

This shift cannot be construed as just demographic, but also theological, socio-economic, politico-cultural and certainly in terms of power equations. For instance, some time ago, in one of my casual conversations with some well-informed Christian leaders and theological educators who continue to subscribe to their caste tags blurted out that theological endeavour or enterprise in India has always emerged from their land. Therefore, any theological activity will have to emerge from their locale and thus considered it as their prerogative and pre-occupation. What they implied by this was theologizing and theological enterprise *per se* in India is their monopoly. I thought to myself that they lived in a fool's paradise. Nevertheless, I retorted back saying that shift has already taken place in India and they should come to terms with the changing scenario. Hence, caste is a state of mind. It is visible and invisible, covert and overt, subtle and direct.

The use of 'shift' here basically connotes the context. Therefore, critical theology of risk-taking takes the context of the Dalits more seriously. Further, it takes the contemporary context more seriously for theological reflection and action. In the case of theology of risk-taking contextual reinterpretation of text plays the vital role. Therefore, context here is described as 'locale' which is essential to the 'contextuality' of social interaction or structural knowledge. As seen in the previous section the social context of the excluded communities, particularly that of the Dalits, presents both the objects as well as subjects involved in the rugged situations that are always volatile. It is here the critical theology rips open the underside of the scripture and tradition not just as sources of reflection, but as the basis. Hence, more emphasis is given to the context which is increasingly visible in recent decades. For a critical theology of risk-taking the social context forms the basis and acts as an episteme. The social context of the Dalits is filled with human experience and thus ignited by Christian faith and perennial struggles that the Dalits face in their day-to-day existence for centuries. In such a scenario, contextualization is nothing but an inherent dynamic of Christian faith and critical-praxis. So, a critical theology of risk-taking is rooted in concrete Dalit experience of a particular culture of a caste-ridden social setting.

The experience of the Dalits in India cannot be exclusive as their unique social context emerged as a result of their descent and occupation in the caste hierarchy that pre-supposed the existence of so-called 'high castes' in a hierarchical order. Their cumulative experience is an outcome of their sufferings and struggles emanating from an asymmetrical context in which more than 200 million Dalits live. It is grounded on and propelled by both the internal and external factors. Therefore, a theology of risk-taking is a critical theology which is not something optional, but a Christian mandate and a categorical imperative. A critical theology of risk-taking embarks by removing the theological blinkers so that the raw brutalized body and the Dalit mind will be seen. It is in such a context a critical theology of risk-taking emerges to articulate the raw and rugged experience of the Dalits. It provides the required language and basic materials for theologizing. It is their raw flesh and blood that thus acts as the anchor and foundational stone of the very nature of theology of risk-taking. In this sense, risk-taking theology is a radical critique of classical/systematic and Indian Christian theology. Peeling the social context of the Dalits layer by layer and as the layers gets cracked off, the materials that come out forms the constitutive element for a theology of risk-taking.

A theology of risk-taking emerges from this inter-subjective world of the Dalits. It is important to affirm their Dalit identity is not an individual identity but cumulative as being members of the shared subjective world. In that, their existential experience is mediated by a language that the Dalits speak which should be the language of the theology of risk-taking. The language that is used does constitute multiple meanings arising out of diverse context-specificities. The context is engulfed by a set of circumstances and conditions that determine their ideas, theories, theologies, propositions or concepts, thought processes and frameworks. These circumstances could be spatial, temporal, situational, social, economic, political, cultural, and religious. Since the Dalits' terrains are impregnated with anger, dejection, resolve and resilience their language and actions can only be understood when their social context is understood comprehensively. Only then, the interaction with text is plausible and meaningful. However, the nature of the context of the Dalits is dynamic and vibrant. It is influenced by both the internal and external factors. Therefore, context is necessary which really determines everything.

In such a ruptured, devastated, ravaged and besieged context where the Dalits have been living for centuries opens up a number of possibilities. Some have totally wilted and succumbed to the forces of domination, while the others went all out defying, resisting and annihilating the life-negating forces. In such a context, modes of resistance, defiance and annihilation involve risk-taking. Succumbing or avoiding or remaining passive or being silent in the long run is counter-productive and will further strengthen the casteist forces to align and unleash their venom. Most of the Dalits do not have security and safety and lead a life filled with all sorts of insecurity and risks. Security in the context of Dalits is a myth, a Maya. For them avoiding dangers is no safer in the long run than outright combat. Faith involves risk and courage. In my own life many a times I have been challenged and opted to take risks. This is where the theology of risk-taking emerges. Risk-taking theology involves disappointments, failures, betrayal, insecurity and loneliness, desperation, exclusion and dejection. Dalits have been living in precarious conditions for centuries by risking their lives. It is their deep-rooted faith in God and total dependence on Him which gave them the courage and resilience. If not for their unflinching faith and pragmatic spirituality, the Dalits would have perished from the face of this earth long ago.

For many, theology is something which is beyond their understanding and comprehension. They tend to think that it is for those who are professionally qualified and should get engaged in theologizing. This is what the systematic/classical theologies that include the Indian Christian theology did by defining and elaborating about God within a complex system of ideas over centuries. On the other, God is not something relatively fixed and untenable to be studied as a pre-formed and pre-fabricated body of knowledge. Critically commenting on the modes of these theologies such as Karl Barth's Trinitarian Christology and Christological Trinity, A.P. Nirmal said, 'If Barth were to be alive, I would have argued with him that his understanding of the richly diverse and inexhaustible nature of God and the sovereign and free love of God necessarily implies that God in his freedom is free to save men and women in more ways than one.'[20] For him, 'although theology is in pursuit of the Transcendent Truth, its conceptual and heuristic tools have to be derived from empiric and immanent realities'.[21] Theology is, in the final analysis, what we mean and regard God in our lives. Anyone can reflect upon God with God given sense that is common. Therefore,

> The 'given' in theology is neither some creed or doctrine handed down from the past nor a theology imported from outside, but our life. The 'original' and the 'given' in our context is our own situation, our own history, our own struggles, our own aspirations, our own fears and our own hopes. God is dynamically present in these. He is savingly active in these.[22]

Out of these encounters has emerged a critical theology of risk taking.

Theology of Risk-taking

The Dalits live in a world of risk-prone society. Since they live in a caste-ridden risk society, they are bound to take risks. Their risks arise as a consequence to the system of caste. The risks the

Dalits face, in this sense, is absolutely theirs, and is not shared by others. As they continue to engage in countering the institutions of caste, its instruments and its processes, the risks keep multiplying, aggravating, and intensifying. Etymologically, the term 'risk' is derived from the Italian 'risco' or 'rischio' meaning 'danger'. Knowing the impending 'danger', if someone jumps into it by succumbing to or venturing into or embarking upon for a cause is said as 'risk'. So, 'risk' is something which has to do for progress, change or advancement. Therefore, risks are 'human-made constructs' that combines politics, economics, socio-cultural, religio-ethical and technological dimensions. In this way, 'risk' has to do with social relations and political arrangement. Risks are thus inseparable from the 'abject realities' of hazard or danger. Risks are varying in dimensions and degrees, and so can never be uniform or the same. The degree, veracity, intensity and alacrity of 'risk' keep changing from one context to another. Hence, one should not jump to drastic conclusions till the context is analysed and thoroughly probed.

Dalits face enormous risks because of the system of caste. For centuries they have been living in captivity, exclusion, volatility, oppression and exploitation. This is why Dalits venture into multiple-risks. As seen in the previous sections, they are bound to take risks because there is no other way and no option. When they are surrounded by the life-negating forces there is only one way out, i.e. taking risk. Because the world of the Dalits does not reflect God's mandated values of equality, human dignity and freedom, the Dalits continue their struggles for these for centuries. God's created order has always been contingent, based on clear-cut principles. It ought to reflect not 'domination', but 'dominion'; not 'feudalism', but 'relational responsibility', and not 'a select few', but all the humans.

God's creation exemplifies wholeness of all people. It underscores the basic tenet of trusteeship between God and humans with clear covenantal relationships. The base and the superstructures reflect this in its essence and quality. Despite knowing the unpredictable, complex and conflicting nature of the human beings, God has taken the 'risk' by elevating 'humans' to such an extent that we shall have dominion over creation not by our domination but by our servitude and stewardship. God indeed has taken risks despite knowing human nature. Nonetheless, the world in which we live and all its resources are indeed the gifts from God. It is unfortunate that the core principles of which the whole created order hangs on has been trampled with. The rich and the powerful have appropriated and exercised their monopoly over it, and in the process pushed the majority to the margins. Humans have forfeited their right to have dominion over God's created order. Those who exercise their authority based on their socio-economic status show their domination over the Dalits and the vulnerable, and also ruthless involvement in ravaging the natural resources for maximizing their profits. They will have to face grave consequences because of violating the core values of creation *vis-à-vis* 'imago dei' (Gen. 1: 26-7), 'not domination, but dominion' (Gen: 1: 31). In both the cases God creates and accepts what could be termed as risks of highest order.

Knowing the fallible nature of humans and their tainted institutions, organizations, systems, processes, instruments and principles of governance, God went ahead by taking risks. God is aware of the constraints and limitations of the humans that by nature are complex, conflictual and sinful. However, God went ahead in delegating the supreme responsibility by brushing aside knowing fully well that He would be morally held responsible for His actions later. If God is all-knowing and all-powerful, can God be held in such a state of vulnerability to His creation? If this is the scenario, how could God be in control of everything? Having raised all these, it should be borne in mind that this does not mean that God is primarily the initiator of risks. Being aware of the sinful nature of humans and their institutions of governance, Creator-God went ahead giving dominion over creation who would act responsibly as stewards of creation. On the contrary, humans failed to dispense justice and behaved not fairly to the fellow human-beings and nature.

God continues to absorb the pain being inflicted on fellow human beings who are vulnerable and hapless. In this sense, God is both actively participating in the affairs of those who live on the margins and involved in humanizing the de-humanized world. The image of God is fractured the moment the so-called 'high castes' treat others as sub-humans. Nonetheless, God continues to be the co-participant by being and showing solidarity with the victims of the system of caste and those who are countering the life-negating forces. These are rays of hope. In its entirety God is the prime source of risk. In tune to this John Sanders[23] has thus argued that the idea of a risk-taking God is consonant with several biblical traditions. These materials form the basis for a theology of risk.

Further, the Christian idea of incarnation elucidates that God is not only taking risks but also accepting the risks implied by the openness of creation. This is again a radical reversal. For example, throughout the Christian era, the dominant view of God has been that he is all-determining and all-controlling. The Christian traditions and conventions underscore God's sovereignty and control. They imply that God's will is final and supreme and human will at all costs and by all means have to be surrendered/subordinated before God's infinite power. But this understanding has been challenged and countered by the understanding that God is the prime-mover of risk-taking. In such a dynamic, the dimensions of creation and redemption come into play as twofold dialectic. Understood in this way, the principle of risk claims its validity and relevancy at this historical juncture in every case of the Dalits. It is this theological principle which is the core of the riskiness in risk-taking theology. A critical theology of risk-taking has reached a new phase in history that the principle of risk as the surer way for freedom and emancipation, since God being the prime-mover of risk-taking.

Throughout the Biblical narrative we come across people of

God both women and men in faith who have taken risks not for themselves but for the sake of others to establish a quality of life for all. In Genesis, we see degrees of risks involved in the divine creation of human beings. In the Old Testament when Abraham was asked to leave Ur and leave everything, i.e. all his possessions including his family (Gen 12), he had to take risks to edify his faith before God cf. Heb: 18-19. Abraham was a risk-taker. Moses represents a long list of risks who heeded to God's call in leading the people. In Exodus Moses had to confront Pharaoh on numerous occasions and safely led the Hebrew people out of Egypt and into the 'Promised Land'. His risks were significant and daring. Likewise, Joshua and others in Maccabees had taken great risks for the people. Prophets spoke against the oppressive empires, admonished the rich and the powerful, and daringly preached that 'another way was possible'. Standing upright before the Kings or Emperors and looking straight into their eyes and on the face uttered that their ways and modes were unjust and righteous God does not like and certainly they be punished. They went all-out and edified daringness and boldness to speak before the emperors, kings, powers and principalities without fear and favour for the poor and the needy. In this sense, they had taken risks at the cost of their lives. Truly they were the risk-takers.

In a similar vein, in the New Testament, although Peter at the first instance hesitated to walk on water eventually jumped from the boat the moment he saw Jesus. Further, Peter denied Jesus three times, but instantaneously took the risk of going to the courtyard. He did edify his faith by taking risks. Likewise in the New Testament we come across a number of personalities who have taken risks. Therefore, risk-taking is an instrument and God's sign that characterizes God's covenant and our response representing the larger cause of God's care and human continuum. The list culminates in Jesus Christ who is the last Adam, the first born of the new creation. The ultimate risk-taker is God's Messiah who came to proclaim the Kingdom of

God which is at hand. Jesus was the paradigm knowing well what would happen and yet took risks throughout his life and ministry. Jesus is the risk-taker for the last and least (Lk 4:16-21; Mt 9: 31-38; Jn 8: 2-11). The very life of Jesus was the clear manifestation of taking risks for the sake of humanity. His life, works, teachings and actions clearly vivify this. Jesus took the ultimate risk and came out the other side.

The kind of risk-taking will have to be qualified and also be seen within the context-specifics. Without contextualization it is not possible to qualify the levels of risks people take. Therefore, we should exercise caution and prudence by not equating or simplifying 'risk-taking' with 'just trust in God'. Could risk-taking be synonymous with 'just trust in God' or does it involve much more than simple equations? Of course, it presupposes 'trust in God'. Nonetheless, trust and Christian praxis should go together. Risk-taking is obviously the demonstration of that trust in whom we affirm our faith. In other words, unless and until Dalits take risks, their talk of trusting or having faith in God will be just empty rhetoric. As Dalits and as people of the crucified and risen Messiah, Dalits are expected to take risks. The organic intellectuals among Dalits who claim to provide an alternative or bring about changes to the way things that the Dalits experience should get involved in taking risks. In doing so, we will live out the story that shapes.

Those who have risked suffered the most in their personal, familial and professional life for seeking and speaking 'truth'. There are a number of Dalits within the Christian and secular domains in India who keep striving for fairness, justice, truth, equality; equity and quality of life and suffer because they did take all types of risks. The questions that arise here are: Why would a search for truth involve great risk? What motivates their personal or communitarian sacrifice? How have they suffered as a result? Taking a position against the dominant belief, caste oppression and exploitation calls for risks of sacrificing one's profession and sometimes even life. As Christians the implications of risk-taking should be affirmed with full theological confidence that we are striving for a 'New Heaven' and a 'New Earth'. In Jesus' incarnation as human in flesh and blood who confessed to be the Christ, something historically happened. It is the birth of 'New Humanity' in which everyone without any distinction and divide live in harmony with self-esteem, human dignity and mutual respect. And this 'New Humanity' shall strive for realizing and establishing a new humane and just order reflecting God's righteousness through a casteless society. Its aim is to establish 'wholeness' devoid of narrow, parochial, divisionary and nefarious tendencies. Towards this end a critical theology of risk-taking revolves around and aims toward bringing together the fractured, fragmented, segmented, divided caste-ridden Indian society. The 'New Humanity' in its effort will strive relentlessly dismantling the shackles of caste and thus build an inclusive society.

As I conclude let me reify a critical theology of risk-taking. Risks are not something that exists out there so that we can grab or enter into, but risks always exist for somebody in a given situation. As posited, for the Dalits the context itself is filled with all sorts of risks. So the Dalits can never escape/avoid risks but ought to take risks, because their terrains are engulfed with volatility prior to the risk. For the Dalits, risks are part of life and nothing abnormal. Therefore, risks for the Dalits are existential and inevitable, and cannot simply be replaced either with *karma* or fatalism or even insecurity. In similar ways, the risks of God take place within the ambience of creation-restoration. When God takes risks, these are always subordinated within the rubric of incarnation-resurrection. Within this dialectic dynamic risk critical theology of risk-taking is grounded.

God in creation and redemption has taken numerous risks and continues to take risks even now in restoring the created order. The more risks God in Jesus takes, the more God is able to absorb the risks while restoring the lost and least, the hapless and the vulnerable. It is this saving activity that restores the fractured and tormented creatures. If not for this, the divine risk-taking and human venturing into a critical theology of risk taking loses its meaning, value and essence. It is this divine-human confluence that makes a critical theology of risk-taking more vibrant and dynamic. It is apparent that God often bears and endures the risks whenever humans out of greed and other compulsions abuse free choice and responsible freedom.

In Jesus, Dalits are free and set free, because for Dalits Jesus means freedom. In Dalits' tradition God is also taking the brunt of a victim by identifying and showing solidarity with the Dalits. The story of the cross *vis-à-vis* death and resurrection of Jesus Christ is the embodiment and assurance of abundant life for all. For the Dalits they symbolize the wholistic restoration of humanity. The events leading to the cross are filled with all sorts of risks that culminate in Jesus' death on the cross. On the cross Jesus exposed and de-mystified the importance and significance of risk-taking. The sequence of events leading to death and resurrection vividly expose the locus of risk-taking God in Jesus. God in Jesus, while suffering on the cross as a political revolutionary, socio-economic critic, religio-cultural transformer and a rebel against the state, risked himself by exposing and challenging the powers and principalities, so that all shall have fullness of life. Therefore, cross and resurrection symbolize an ongoing life-affirming continuum for a theology of risk-taking. Jesus Christ is the unifier who represents the victims of risks, signifying that God in Jesus is actively involved in transforming those who lose while taking risks. We are reminded time and time again that we should be prepared or willing to lose life, then only we shall gain it. Therefore, a critical theology of risk-taking is clearly grounded on the dictum that 'unless the seed dies it cannot bear fruits' meaning 'fullness of life is not possible'.

NOTES

1. Samuel Rayan, 'Reconceiving Theology in the Asian Context', in Virgina Fabella et al., *Doing Theology in a Divided World*, Maryknoll, New York: Orbis Books, 1985, p. 124.

2. Ibid.
3. A. Maria Arul Raja, SJ, 'Dalit Concerns and Theological Education in India', presented at a workshop on Critical Pedagogy at Gurukul Lutheran Theological College and Research Institute, Chennai.
4. Cited by J. Russell Chandran, 'A.P. Nirmal: A Tribute', in *Voices From the Third World*, vol. XX, no. 1, June 1997, p. 142.
5. Ibid.
6. See the Weekly Edition 2 of *The Hindu*, 3 October 1999.
7. Ibid.
8. Ibid.
9. Mahendra Pratap Singh, 'Enslaved by Tradition: The Manual Scavengers of Vidisha', in *The Hindu*, 16 December 2010.
10. Ibid.
11. Ibid.
12. Ibid.
13. T.S. Srinivasa Raghavan, 'Shit, Scavenging, is Big Business', in *Bangalore Times*, 3 September 2010, pp. 1 and 4.
14. Ibid.
15. Ibid.
16. Ibid.
17. Ibid.
18. P. Krishnaswamy, 'Dalit Woman Forced to Drink "excreta" for Spurning Advances', in *Indian Express*, 30 September 2009.
19. For the complete incident see http:/www.fribtkube.com/fil 921/ stories /20021050051039OO/Lton.
20. J. Russell Chandran, 'A.P. Nirmal: A Tribute', op. cit., p. 144.
21. Ibid., p. 143.
22. Ibid.
23. Careful, profound theological queries and challenging arguments are expounded in John Sanders, *The God Who Risks: A Theology of Providence*, Downers Grove: Intervarsity, 1998.

APPENDIX 1

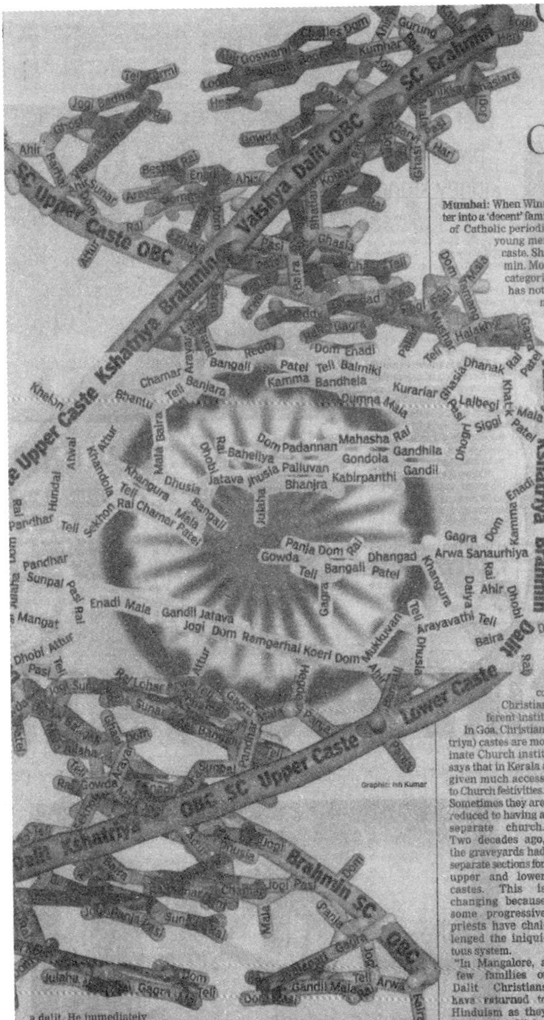

Only in India: A Brahmin groom for a Catholic bride

Ashley D'Mello | TNN

Mumbai: When Winnie D'Souza wanted to marry her daughter into a 'decent' family, she scanned the matrimonial columns of Catholic periodicals in Panaji. After shortlisting a few young men, D'Souza made inquiries about their caste. She wanted her daughter to marry a Brahmin. Most Catholic publications do not list caste categories as they did 20 years ago, but casteism has not disappeared among Christians. It has merely become more subtle.

Unlike Bihar, Orissa and the North-East, which have large tribal Christian populations, the Christians of Goa, Kerala and Tamil Nadu remain in thrall to the caste categories of their Hindu ancestors.

Father Augustine Kanjamala, a theologian in Mumbai, has researched caste among Christians. Caste exists in different forms in various Christian communities, he says. In Kerala the Christians admitted to the faith almost 2,000 years ago are called Syrian Christians. They are better off than Latin Christians, who are mainly from poorer communities. Syrian Christians and Latin Christians do not inter-marry. They even have different institutions to train their priests.

> "Caste will not die out in the Church easily, but in cities like Mumbai, the urban situation has led to the breaking down of barriers of caste" says Father Augustine Kanjamala, a theoligian

In Goa, Christians belonging to Brahmin or Charado (Kshatriya) castes are more privileged than the others. They dominate Church institutions and activities. Father Augustine says that in Kerala and Tamil Nadu, Dalit Christians are not given much access to Church festivities. Sometimes they are reduced to having a separate church. Two decades ago, the graveyards had separate sections for upper and lower castes. This is changing because some progressive priests have challenged the iniquitous system.

"In Mangalore, a few families of Dalit Christians have returned to Hinduism as they felt humiliated living among Christians who discriminated against them," says Father Augustine. "Caste will not die out in the Church easily, but in cities like Mumbai, the ur-

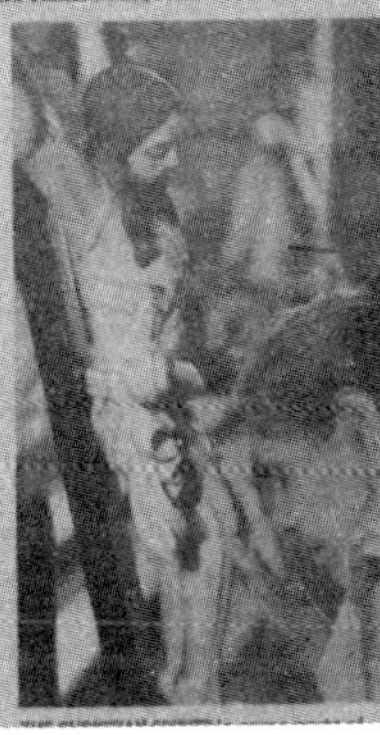

a dalit. He immediately
ned the advance and said I couldn't have
ouse."
at it is the inter-caste marriage — the ac-
vent and its aftermath — that often re-
the caste gene most starkly. Psychologist
na says that even families that allow such
as, generally consider the new (out of
member of the family "the outsider and
she has to make extra effort to mix

Perhaps. But Javeed Alam, Chairman, Indian Council of Social Science Research, says there is reason to hope Indians' caste gene won't be a chromosomal cancer for the country. "Caste today is no longer what it was a few decades ago. Even though caste discrimination is present, the caste system has died out. In fact, the struggles of the lower castes have led to the expansion of

APPENDIX 2A

At Cherumittampalayam village in Namakkal district, memorial stones in the burial ground of Arunthathiyars.

At Koozhaiyanur village in Theni district, a Dalit man points to the place where his brother, S. Raju, was buried in his own field after caste Hindus refused access to the common burial ground.

APPENDIX 2B

The Cemetery in the church compound. All along, 'upper-caste' Christians have resisted Dalit Christians' attempts to bury their dead here.

The site in the cemetery where Velankanni, brother of a Dalit priest, was buried overcoming 'upper-caste' opposition.

The Cemetery of the Adi Dravidar (Dalit) Christians on the outskirts of the village.

PART V

RELEVANCE OF RELIGION IN THE TWENTY-FIRST CENTURY

12

Multi-Faith Response to the Dalit Movement in India

RAVI TIWARI AND ASHISH KUMAR

Introduction

The Indian social system is a very complex system which often perplexes people who are not familiar with it. It is often considered to be an omnipresent system which has even penetrated into other systems which have never been part of it. The tribes and people who migrated to the Indian subcontinent from other geographical areas from time immemorial, slowly and steadily got sucked into it and became very much a part of it. An introductory discourse will be helpful in understanding the context of the discourse of the paper, though some details may be found elsewhere in this volume.

(a) *Indian Social Structure of Caste: Varnasrama System*

The caste system functions as a system of social stratification and social restriction to determine the destiny of those who are within, and also those who are outside, this system. It bestows privileges to some, and deprives others, benefits, based upon the person's birth in a particular group. The one who is born in a higher caste family, by the privilege of his birth, is entitled to various privileges while the one who is born in a lower caste family is deprived of various social benefits. However, the caste system does not directly determine the class of the person. To be specific, the caste system is not a direct determinant of the economic status of the person. However, the privileges which come with the caste system can be used to uplift the economic status. There are poor people both in the higher caste and also among the lower caste groups.

There are thousands of sub-castes existing in India which determines the dependence and interdependence of various groups. Each caste/sub-caste determines the occupational specialization of a person and thus link one group with other groups through a complex network stretching across regions. Caste/sub-caste also plays their role in marriages. Maintaining caste/sub-caste purity was considered mandatory and violation of this in marriage would result in excommunication of the family from the caste system.

The caste system also determines the lifestyle of the people. Generally, the higher caste people would have a prosperous living where as people of the lower class would be directed to have a lifestyle different and often less affluent. The caste system also defines the level of purity. The purer caste is ranked on top while the impure caste is ranked at the bottom. For instance, Brahmins are expected to conduct rituals and impart teaching which is considered the purest occupation while the Shudras whose occupation is scavenging is defined as impure and thus put at the bottom rung of the level of hierarchy.

One should not fail to notice the racial aspect of caste, not only through the obvious social practices, but through the very fact of using the term. *Varna* means both colour (of the skin) as well as the sequence of words in the alphabet, signifying the relative colour of the skin of the people as well their standing in the social hierarchy.

(b) *Religious Foundation of Caste*

The history of the religious foundation of caste goes back to as long as 3,000 years ago. Some consider that it was the Vedic literature which first provoked the crisis of culture.[1] James Massey too, while tracing the historical roots of Dalits, shows it began with *Rigveda*.[2] In the vast body of literatures, commonly known as the Vedas, we find the expression of caste system. Though the written expression of caste system appears 3,000 years ago, it is possible that there must have been considerably long period of time where the norms of caste system was transmitted orally. The *Rigveda* first attempts to define the caste system by the following sukta: 'The Brahmin was his mouth, his two arms were made the Rajanya [Kshatriya, king and warrior], his two thighs [loins] the Vaishya, from his feet the Sudra [servile class] was born.'[3]

It is interesting to note that the *Rigveda* defines not only the four categories based upon the qualities, but also determines their respective functions. Such an intelligent demarcation of groups, and also determination of their functions, enabled the caste system to survive for such a long period of time. Another interesting point, which Ekta Singh has also noted, is that, Vedas never mention the concept of untouchability.[4] It was the later development within the society itself.

It was the *Manusmriti* which defined in detail the caste system. The law of Manu elaborately dealt with the rules pertaining to various social castes (2.25-11.266). The *Manusmriti* almost made Brahmins a divine class while making the life of the lowest class as difficult as possible through prescribing the severest punishment if they violate the law of Manu. *Manusmriti* has been constantly used to justify the caste system, and also validate the Brahmin's supremacy. The following points may be noted:

(i) The origin of the caste system can be traced to oral tradition which must have continued for a long period of time before being written in the Vedas 3,000 years ago. The *Rigveda* therefore becomes the first written document describing the nature of the caste system.

(ii) Further, *Rigveda* does not seem to be as harsh as *Manusmriti* towards Dalits. In other words, the *Rigveda* makes a division of labour and does nothing to determine the social exclusion of Dalits. It was *Manusmriti* which brings this into practice.

(iii) The concept of untouchability did not exist during the time of Veda. It was later development in Hinduism which did not receive religious sanction from the sruti literatures.

Response to Dalit Movement from the Majority Religion of Hinduism

Among the majority of religions there are multiple factions which retain varied degrees of reactions towards the Dalit movement. These multiple factions can broadly be categorized under two groups, viz., the conservative groups and the liberal groups. The conservative groups comprise orthodox and conservative Hindu sects, RSS, VHP, Bajrang Dal and the like. The liberal groups are diversely represented that includes Bhakti and reform movements, such as Ramakrishna Mission, Sri Sri Ravishankar Movement, Satya Shodhak Samaj, etc.

(a) *Response from Conservative Groups*

RSS is a Hindu socio-religio-cultural volunteer association, often alleged as a Hindu militant organization. It claims to be founded upon the principles of selfless service to the nation. In understanding the response of RSS towards Dalit movement, some caution needs to be taken; this organization constantly keeps its intention concealed towards the Dalits. Moreover, there is also some ambiguity in its response. This ambiguity is displayed by their varied reactions. For instance, RSS suggested that Dalits and Other Backward Classes be trained, and appointed, as head priests at major temples in the country which raised general eyebrows in the country. [5] Further, RSS severely condemned the barring of Dalits from Jagannath Temple in Kerdagarh in Orissa.[6] Though, the above attitude of the RSS may portray them as the messiah of the Dalits, Raj Kumar would consider this as one of the strategies of Hindutva forces to co-opt Dalits into the Hindu fold.[7] Making his point clear, he writes:

> The Hinduisation of Dalits by BJP, ABVP and RSS combine operates at two levels: at the theoretical level, BJP is trying to misinterpret. Ambedkar mode of thinking and argues that his act of conversion was in conformity with Hinduism rather than its subversion. Also these neo-Hindu forces are attempting the comparison of Ambedkar with Hedgewar and Savarkar and are showing how all these tried to create common Hindu identity by overcoming the bad practices of caste and untouchability. In the recent times, BJP is appealing to dalits to overcome their secondary differences based on Caste and untouchability and assimilate a common Hindu identity for fighting against the common enemy.[8]

Not only Raj Kumar, other writers like Prem Kumar Shinde, were also found attesting similar attitude of RSS. Shinde considers that the reconversion of Dalits to Hinduism is a part of RSS strategy to absorb Dalits into the Hindu fold.[9] This is done with the intention to consolidate Hindu vote bank which has political implications.

Now the question is, does RSS intend to retain the caste system or has a plan to annihilate it for the common good? Truly speaking, RSS does not seem to have a strategy to abolish the caste system, it is simply trying to absorb Dalits into the Hindu fold and attribute them an identity within the caste system. In that case, the caste system would simply survive, and will be transported into new forms. Thus the exploitation of Dalits will continue further through the emergence of newer forms.

(b) *Response from Liberal Groups*

Liberal groups of Hinduism adopt a different approach towards Dalits. The conservative groups may appear to be sympathetic towards Dalits whereas the Liberal groups are empathetic to the sufferings of Dalits. However, this is not to say that they have done enough for the upliftment of the same. One such liberal group is ISKCON. In the assessment of ISKCON movement, Graham Dwyer and Richard J. Cole comments that ISKCON is in total opposition to many aspects of modern Hinduism and in particular to caste Brahmanism.[10] Moreover, they mention that ISKCON is also against the principle of untouchability. Another organization which is actively involved in the emancipation of Dalits right from their inception is Ramakrishna Mission founded by Sri Ramakrishna Paramahamsa.[11] Sanjay Paswan notes the contribution of Ramkrishna Mission commenting that it tried to uplift socio-economic conditions on the basis of individual freedom and equality.[12]

Response to Dalit Movement from Minority Religion

The response from minority religion is truly blurred and ambiguous. On the one hand the minority religion condemns Manu's code, on the other hand, they also play a role in the oppression of Dalits. For instance, in Christian hierarchy we can evidently see the domination of caste groups as against Dalits. This is also true for other faiths like Sikhism and Islam. Further, a Dalit's opinion is not regarded at par with a caste person, is another evidence of the oppression which a Dalit faces within minority religion.

However, particularly speaking about their attitude towards the Dalit movement, the minority religions are more open to Dalits in comparison to the majority religion. Along with this, the minority religions are generating more funds for the support of the Dalit movement. The following are to be noted with regard to the response of minority religion towards the Dalit movement that recognizes the ambiguous nature of their response towards Dalits.

(a) *Minority Religion Identifies Dalit Oppression*

Be it Islam, Christianity, Neo-Buddhism or Sikhism, all identify the plight of Dalits. They well comprehend the injustice Dalits have undergone throughout the centuries in the name of caste. Further, the minority religions not only recognize the agony of the Dalits, but, to a certain extent, they are either sympathetic or empathetic to them. This has led many Dalits to embrace one of the minority religions in order to escape the social stigma attached to them by the caste hierarchy. However, this, in reality, has done little good to Dalits. P. Surya Prakash, as a matter of fact, observed, in case of Christian converts, that Dalit Christians are Dalit first and then Christians.[13] James Massey terms this as 'Christian faith has become a kind of appendix to their old faith'.[14] Further, he also mentions that Dalit Christians continue to be exploited, discriminated and their rights are being ignored. This observation is again attested by the report presented to the National Commission for Minority, Government of India. This report suggests that 'whatever the nature and extent of the disabilities imposed by caste on Muslims and Christians, it is beyond debate that such disabilities are imposed most severely on Dalit Muslims and Dalit Christians'.[15] This might be true not only for Christianity but for Dalit converts to other minority religion as well. Thus to say that a Dalit's suffering though well recognized by the minority religion is not well addressed by the minority religion within itself. One more thing which comes clear is that minority religion shows seriousness in identifying a Dalit's oppression but does not show any seriousness in going beyond it.

(b) *Minority Religion Creates Awareness about Dalit Oppression*

Dalit oppression has continued in Indian history from centuries unnoticed. It was thought of as a natural phenomenon which need not be addressed. However, from the time caste system came under criticism, Dalit oppression became a point of issue. In the twentieth century when rapid Dalit conversions to minority religions took place, the minority religion felt encouraged to highlight Dalit sufferings. As a result, there was flood of literature highlighting Dalit suffering under the caste system. Majority of the scholars who talked about this issue belonged to the minority religion. Further, minority religion also organized Dalit solidarity programmes in order to support Dalits in their struggle for liberation. This also helped in creating awareness about the Dalit issues, their situation and circumstances and the prevailing caste system. Further, such an attitude generated Dalit solidarity among caste siblings too. In this regard, it can be said that the minority religion worked steadily to empower Dalits with the tools which were needed to make their lives better. Minority religion also addressed the issues of caste and untouchability, and stood strongly to favour the cause of the oppressed masses. Dalit solidarity programmes run by the minority religion created awareness regarding the social injustice Dalits face in the modern and contemporary India. Such an act promoted and encouraged Dalit movements and created means to generate resources to fight for their cause.

Now the question which puzzles most is: when minority religions are so actively involved in generating awareness towards the injustice done to the Dalits, why do we still see Dalit oppression not only among caste Hindus but even within minority religion? This depicts the discrepancy. In fact, the minority religions, as a whole, do not seem to be working for the cause of the Dalit. There are segments within the minority religions who are devoted to the cause of Dalits whereas the majority are unconcerned about them. This is to say that, within Neo-Buddhism, Islam or Christianity, there are a few registered or unregistered organizations which are active to favour of the Dalit cause, while the large masses are either unaware, or tend to remain unaware about the plight of Dalits. If every segment of the minority religion becomes proactive to further the cause of Dalit, the change will be more evident, and inevitable.

(c) *Minority Religion Attempts to Empower Dalits to Eliminate Oppression*

In the Indian scenario, particularly in the context of Dalits, empowerment need not be understood as something where we stand with power to protect Dalits, but it is to provide power to Dalits so that they can protect themselves. In the past, many segments within the minority religion took the task to uplift Dalits without realizing the fact that uplifting Dalits is not possible until the Dalits posses the power to uplift themselves. However, in recent times, strategies to uplift Dalits have changed. Now organizations standing for the cause of Dalits are empowering them with the tools with which they can uplift themselves and their community. Education is one of the major tools which can radically change the Indian scenario launching a tidal wave of Cultural Revolution in favour of Dalits.

In the past, the Brahmin class was understood as the teacher class. Since the caste system excluded Dalits to be in contact with Brahmins, the Dalits remained uneducated. In the present, when quality education became a costly affair, the socio-economic condition of the Dalits did not permit them to opt for education. Chinna Rao Yagati notes this dynamics in context of Dalit education, as he notes, 'In addition to caste Hindu prejudices and non-cooperation with colonial policies, the socio-economic conditions of the Dalits were also responsible for the fall of their educational growth along with fear of oppression by the caste Hindus'.[16] Thus, the educational growth among the Dalit masses remained very low in spite of the various efforts made to improve it.

One of the major contributions of minority religion is education. Several educational institutes were opened up in various parts of the country. Moreover, promotions for Dalit education were also taken up aggressively in the past decades. This has not only helped Dalits to be educated but also brought up revolutionary and visionary Dalit leaders with potential to change the Dalit situation in India.

We see an ambiguity in educational endeavour of the minority religions, particularly in relation to Dalit. The educational institute of minority religions have educated more upper caste people (which outnumbers Dalits several times) some of whom are now opposing the cause to favour Dalits.[17] Further, the minority religions have also failed to recognize the right target group among Dalits. To be specific, the education facilities provided by the minority religion have been distributed unevenly among the subalterns.[18] Few well-to-do groups within Dalits are consuming the benefits which are meant for all Dalits particularly the not-so-privileged. This creates a Brahmin class within Dalits who are there to grab the benefits meant for all.[19] In this regard the minority religions have failed to identify the target group and missed their goal in empowering the weak. This has resulted in what we can call as empowering the powerful.

(d) *Minority Religion and Dalit Movement*

There are two dimensions of the ongoing Dalit movement. One is social and another is political. The social Dalit movement attempts to uplift Dalits by attempting to eradicate the social stigma attached to them. It seeks to see Dalits at par with caste people at the social level, whereas the political Dalit movement attempts to keep political powers within the Dalit fold. Minority religions play hide and seek between these two dimensions of Dalit movements. They tend to support the social Dalit movement so as to uplift Dalits at social levels and project themselves as apolitical. However, at other occasions the minority religions tend to support political Dalit movement though not apparently in order to get political benefits. This jumping off between two dimensions of Dalit movement makes the response of minority religions more ambiguous. There are various reasons for this response towards Dalit movement. First, the minority religion supports Dalit movement because the Dalit movement apparently are unsatisfied with the dominant religious system. This gives the opportunity to minority religions to gain adherents from Dalit community which serves both the religious and political purpose of the minority religion. Second, the minority religions support Dalit movement in order to project that their religious system does not support untouchability and casteism. Such a projection helps minority religions to establish themselves as distinct from Hinduism. This can have positive implications as well. Around sixth century BC when Buddhism established itself as a distinct religious tradition from Hinduism, it could impact the social situation in India. Similarly, the minority religion which intends to impact the social situation aims to project itself as distinct from Hinduism. Thirdly, minority religion supports Dalit movement because it feels empathetic to the sufferings of Dalit. The religious ethos of the minority religion gives room to them so as to work in favour of Dalits. Hinduism, on the other hand, restricts the welfare of Dalits simply because it believes that Dalits are suffering due to their sins, committed in the previous birth (theory of karma).

An Assessment of the General Attitude of Indian Society at Large Towards the Dalit Movement

The general public in India are an easygoing class. It includes farmer, labourers, unskilled workers, business person, housewives, working women, school or college goers, scientists, engineers, doctors, nurses, other professional workers, and a large number of unemployed people. Majority of the general public are concerned with their own survival in the midst of the rapid changing globalized world. In light of this, it is often evident that the general public tends to remain introvert and shows little or no awareness of the Dalit Movement.

(a) *Assessment from a Religious Perspective*

Majority of the Indian masses are considered to be religious/spiritual. However, their religious orientation is not society-centred; it is rather individual/family centred. Indian spirituality does not encourage people to form inter-personal relationship, but motivates them to move towards intra-personal relationships.[20] Intra-personalism of Indian spirituality orients people with other worldly attitude. Therefore, everything that goes on in the world is either considered to be vanity or perceived as *maya* (illusion or unreal). This may be the reason for the majority of Indian masses to remain unconcerned about the Dalit movement. Further, the general public are ritual-centred. Rituals lead people to a routine and monotonous way of life where everything is predetermined by the religious functionaries. Though rituals are monotonous and routine, they are considered an essential part of life. The life of public, in general, is occupied with a number of rituals. For majority of people, adhering to Hinduism, there are different opinions as *Gautamsmriti*[21] prescribes 40 rituals, whereas the liberal Puranas mentions 16 as main rituals.[22] An ordinary Hindu, however, still remains entangled with these rituals, leaving hardly any time for them to concentrate on the movements meant for the welfare of Dalits.

The Indian people, though unconcerned towards the Dalit movement, are not ignorant about the religious laws which determine the social status of the people under the caste system. They are aware of the clear demarcation of the social status of the people based upon the religious code. This demarcation involves the social, cultural and economic rights of the members, based upon their birth in a particular family (*jati*). These rights and privileges are hereditary. They are also aware of the unequal distribution of the power and privileges across caste groups. The lower caste groups, though unhappy, are forced to remain silent on the ground that these divisions are religiously sanctioned (*vidhi-lekha*) and culturally practiced through time immemorial (*samaj-dharma*).

(b) *Assessment from a Political and Economic Perspective*

As mentioned earlier, the majority of the Indian public comprises those groups who aspire to see political and economic growth.

They are the people who struggle for their daily survival. In such a context, where their total concentration is on their own survival, it is obvious that they would not tend to bother about the Dalit movement. Largely, Dalit community too comprises people who are politically and economically deprived. At a time when inflation, unemployment and lack of opportunities confront most of them, how can groups of people who themselves are poor (like majority of the Indian masses) contribute towards eradicating the suffering of another group (the Dalits)?

From a political and economic perspective, the issue of reservation becomes significant both for larger Indian masses and Dalit community. A significant group of Indians also face similar deprivation. As Dalit community is given the privilege of reservation, it becomes a matter of envy for the general public who also wish to share the same privilege. In such a context, where resentment born out of jealousy prevails, many among various Indian communities do not feel motivated to participate proactively in the Dalit movement. Further, this only contributes to create a chasm and rift between the communities who also aspire to share the fruits of political and economic growth.

Moreover, there is a prevailing and increasing feeling among many that the Dalit movement does not intend to do any good to the suffering Dalit community, but is for the benefit of the selected few. Such a perception tends some to keep a distance from the movement for the empowerment of the Dalit community. Moreover, the Indian public has an impression that the leaders of the Dalit movement are not working for the common welfare; they are there for their own self-interest. Such an impression yet again demotivates the general public to participate in the Dalit movement.

Conclusion

This paper has attempted to sketch a general view about the varied and complex responses of multi-faith communities in India towards the Dalit movement. The following points can be stated as tentative conclusions. First, the response of multi-faith people towards the Dalit movement is ambiguous. On the one hand, there are several programmes which are in operation for the welfare of Dalits, yet, on the other hand, they seem to show little commitment on essentially uplifting the Dalit community as a whole. Secondly, the response of multi-faith people towards the Dalit movement is complex. It is complex primarily because it is not devoid of self-interest. In the context of minority and missionary religion, they tend to support the cause of the Dalit movement so as to attract adherents from Dalits. The majority religion also tends to support Dalit movement so as to co-opt/keep the Dalits among its fold. However, when the self-interest is taken care of, the Dalits continue to remain Dalits. It is the inter-play between the self-interest and the religious ethos of common good that makes their response complex. Third, the multi-faith response to Dalit movement is determined by social, economic and political factors. The majority of Indian public who are adherents of various faiths are primarily poor and politically deprived. They are therefore concerned for their own survival than to be bothered about the Dalit movement. Finally, the multi-faith response to Dalit movement is determined by their respective religious ethos. The theory of *karma* in Hinduism restricts operations meant for the welfare of Dalits. It would consider that the Dalits will continue to suffer till the effect of accumulated sins of their previous birth is exhausted. However, other religious traditions which would disagree with the theory of *karma* may still find their own religious theory which could prevent their involvement in the Dalit movement. For instance, the other-worldly attitude which is found in many religious traditions, including Christianity, would claim the present suffering as momentary, and would, therefore, exhort people to wait for the heavenly intervention which would resolve all sufferings and problems.

NOTES

1. Himansu Charan Sadangi, *Dalit: The Downtrodden of India*, Delhi: Gyan Publishing House, 2008, p. 42.
2. See James Massey, *Dalits in India: Religion as a Source of Bondage or Liberation with Special Reference to Christians* (rpt.), New Delhi: Manohar, 2009, pp. 24-30.
3. *Rigveda* X.90.12, This, though, is considered by some, a later interpolation, does not take the validity of the charge.
4. Ekta Singh, *Caste System in India: A Historical Perspective*, Delhi: Gyan Books, 2005, p. 22.
5. *Times of India*, 30 October 2006.
6. Ibid., 3 January 2007.
7. Raj Kumar, *Essays on Dalits*, Delhi: Discovery Publishing House, 2003, p. 153.
8. Ibid.
9. Prem Kumar Shinde, *Dalits and Human Rights: Dalits and Racial Justice*, Delhi: Isha Books, 2005, p. 142.
10. Graham Dwyer and Richard J. Cole, *The Hare Krishna Movement: Forty Years of Chant and Change*, London: I.B. Tauris, 2007, p. 201.
11. Cf. Himansu Charan Sadangi, *Dalit*, p. 147.
12. Sanjay Paswan, *Encyclopaedia of Dalits in India: Emancipation and Empowerment*, ed. Sanjay Paswan and Pramanshi Jaideva, Delhi: Gyan Publishing House, 2002, p. 200.
13. P. Surya Prakash, 'Christianity in India: A Promised Land for Dalits?' *Online-Texte der Evangelischen Akademie Bad Boll*, http://www.ev-akademie-boll.de/typo3conf/ext/naw_securedl/secure.php?u=0&file=fileadmin/res/otg/ doku/641010-Prakash.pdf&t=1286117305&hash=9d1b149718eb52599bd12ea5f993f785 (22 March, 2012).
14. Massey, *Dalits in India*, op. cit., p. 108.
15. Satish Deshpande, 'Dalits in the Muslim and Christian Communities: A Status Report on Current Social Scientific Knowledge', *National Commission for Minorities Government of India*, http://ncm.nic.in/pdf/report%20dalit% 20%20 reservation.pdf (22 March 2012), 12.
16. Chinna Rao Yagati, 'Education and Identity Formation Among Dalits in Colonial Andhra', in *Education and the Disprivileged: Nineteenth and Twentieth Century India*, ed. Sabyasachi Bhattacharya, Hyderabad: Orient Blackswan, 2002, p. 102.

17. Cf. Vishal Mangalwadi, 'An Indian Constantine?', *International Journal of Frontier Mission* 18/1 (Spring, 2001), p. 21.
18. Cf. Bharat Singh, *Dalit Education*, New Delhi: Anmol Publications, 2004, p. 11.
19. Cf. Himansu Charan Sadangi, *Dalit*, p. 200.
20. A generalization of this may seems to be exaggeration. However, an observation of this phenomenon may reveal that Indian spirituality prefers mysticism than community centrism.
21. See, 8: 2.
22. For further exposition and details, see, Raj Bali Pandey, *Hindu Samskar*, Delhi: Motilal Banarsidass, 1969.

13

Demands for Social Change: A Multicultural Response

ATOLA LONGKUMER

There seems to prevail a mood of confidence in the nation as an emerging economy with unprecedented wealth, but the Tribals and Adivasis continue to be isolated, neglected and without basic human rights. It is over a century since the abolishment of caste discrimination was enacted as a legal Act, and over half a century since B.R. Ambedkar's conversion to Buddhism in protest against caste structure derived from Hindu sacred texts, but little seem to have changed for the Dalits and the Tribals.[1] The persistent suffering and marginalization of the communities outside the so-called caste structure in India calls for consistent, creative and persuasive engagement from every possible location and perspective. Among these the understanding of the development of sacred texts and their institutionalized religion is vital. In the case of Dalits and the Tribals and their marginalization, it is Hinduism that needs to be scrutinized in order to locate the root cause and legitimization of the oppressive worldview. The category of multiculturalism can be a helpful analytical tool in the critical evaluation of a homogeneous and reified Hinduism whose history and cosmology has marginalized the subalterns[2] of the nation.

The concept and practice of multiculturalism is challenged at different quarters, not least in contexts where it is pursued as a political instrument to ensure equality and recognition of identity differences derived from cultures and religions. It has become imperative to assert the significance and relevance of multicultural reality of religio-cultural history of Indian society. Insistence upon homogeneity and demands to accommodate to a mono-reading of culture strike at the root of identity of diverse religio-cultural history of people, consequently, leaving unquestioned the fact that there was a dominant historical process of constructing a social reality by the dominant group that negated the history and cultures of the marginalized and the powerless. Multicultural conversation poses the questions: who reified history and culture; who canonized religious sacred texts, and to whose advantage? Multicultural conversation brings the reality of plurality and diversity to bear upon the lopsided discourse of homogeneity with its selected representation and marginalization of certain groups. Hence drawing from the discourse of multiculturalism of religion and culture, the following discussion will argue that demands for social change from disadvantaged groups such as Dalits and the Tribals in India need to be addressed in the light of historical reality where the dominant group of people have suppressed and silenced the voice, perspective and location of the Dalits and the Tribals. The following are some questions that will undergird the discussion: whose version of sacred texts and history has been the authority to dictate, organize and create the present oppressive hierarchical structures? Who had been the representatives and codifiers of the so-called caste system that negates the basic human dignity of the Dalits and the Tribals? What are the other sources of religio-cultural tradition of the people in constructing their own identities? The discussion will also, briefly address the challenge to the concept of multicultural conversation posed by gender and internal hierarchies existing within marginalized groups.

The Vulnerables

As the country goes through tremendous changes rapidly in every possible area of society as a result of globalization and the unprecedented explosion of technology, the marginalized people and communities continue to be victims and vulnerable. The fruits of economic progress and technological advancement of the country are enjoyed by the dominant few and the communities that have been marginalized and dominated have remained more or less in the same structures and socio-economic conditions that have exploited and excluded them for centuries. India is still far from being an egalitarian society, wherein all citizens are guaranteed the right and opportunity to enjoy equal access to resources, equal respect and dignity of common humanity. There are communities that continue to languish in the age-old discrimination of caste hierarchy and patriarchy. These communities are made vulnerable by the constructed discourse based on categories such as ethnicity, caste, religion, sexuality, and gender. While these categories may be related to one another in the experience of discrimination and exclusion at the hands of the dominant group and discourse, the communities of the Dalits, and the Tribals and their experience of exploitation and victimization are highlighted to assert that these communities are the vulnerable and violated ones, whose demands for social justice cannot be ignored or appeased with token measures.

The tribal people of north-east are among the most neglected and isolated communities from the centres of power and development. India is claimed as an emerging economic power with nuclear capability, yet there are villages in north-east India, which do not even have a motorable road, electricity or basic medical facilities. Accessing the international borders seems to be easier than reaching the urban areas of the country. Apart from district level government hospitals which are ill-equipped for sophisticated medical facilities, there are no advance medical facilities. The same dismal situation exists for education. Therefore for educational purposes, many young people from the region migrate to urban areas in the mainland in search of higher education and employment. This migration to the cities is not without its woes and sacrifices. There is a growing number of incidents of harassment and exploitation of the people from the region at the hands of the locals in the urban areas, sexual harassment of women not the least. While the socio-political movements of the region has more complex history, the negligence by the state and attitudes of the mainland population, certainly feed into the people's movements for self-determination and empowerment.

Admittedly, there are measures introduced to ameliorate the discrimination and exploitation of the subaltern people in the country, however, data and reality of people's experience indicate the persistent discrimination against the subaltern people. Indeed, there are indications that violence against Dalits is on the increase. For instance, Ghanshyam Shah and others report the following statistics to underscore the continuing discrimination of Dalits:

> The official statistics for the decade 1990-2000 indicate that a total of 285,871 cases of various crimes against Dalits were registered countrywide, of which 14,030 were registered under the Anti-Untouchability Act and 81,796 under the Prevention of Atrocities Act. This means that an average of 28,587 cases of caste discrimination and atrocities against Dalits were registered every year during the 1990s. These include 553 cases of murder, 2,990 cases of grievous hurt, 919 rapes, 184 kidnapping/abductions, 47 dacoities, 127 robberies, 456 cases of arson, 1,403 cases of caste discrimination and 8,179 cases of atrocities.[3]

Hence Felix Wilfred surmises that every hour more than three cases of atrocities against Dalits are registered, and everyday three cases of rape, and at least one murder are reported. Violence against the Dalits continues unabated. Dalits continue to experience violence not just derived from the traditional caste structure which entails the discriminating purity-pollution practice but Dalits have become victims of violence as a result of modernity. According to Wilfred, the first type of violence against the Dalits takes place when the so-called traditional caste codes are transgressed, such as romantic relationship between a Dalit and another caste, the refusal by the Dalits to remove dead carcasses of cows, drawing water from the well 'meant' for the upper castes, drinking water or tea from the same cups with the upper caste, refusal to seek 'permission' for religious rites, entry into temples, etc.[4] Another form of violence against Dalits arises from the intolerance of Dalits empowerment and assertion of their rights. As part of their empowerment the Dalits' demand for increase in wages by agricultural labourers, legal justice which contribute to the seemingly improved condition of the Dalits and this 'perceived prosperity and political empowerment of the Dalits are difficult for the so-called upper caste'.[5] The growing assertiveness and relative empowerment that are products of modernization of the society irk the so-called upper caste. The so-called upper caste people's intolerance of Dalit empowerment and growing consciousness of their rights provoke violence against the Dalit in different forms: agricultural, social ostracization, deprivation, and humiliation. Here's another example of violence against Dalits when their rights are asserted:

> In the month of January 2006, a Dalit by name Bant Singh from Mansa district of Punjab was attacked by a mob of upper-caste people. He was so badly beaten up that his limbs had to be amputated. The reason is that in 2004 when his eldest daughter was raped by an upper-caste Jat, he went to seek justice in the courts which resulted in the conviction of several high-caste people. This legal victory was the source of anger and violence on the part of the upper-caste mob.[6]

Communalism is another source from which stem violence against Dalits in the country, as Wilfred explicitly states, 'the assertion of the traditional values by Hindutva has meant in practice the re-assertion of caste ideology, and the practice of discrimination against Dalits'.[7] The idea of a Hinduness or a Hindu consciousness is derived from the sacred texts of the Brahminical religion, which obviously have constructed the discriminating caste hierarchy and privileged their so-called superior position. Ironically, the Dalits are mobilized as the mob to carry out the fundamentalist agenda of violating the rights of other community group members. In addition, the Hindutva movement is also working relentlessly among the Dalits and the Tribals/Adivasis to recruit the foot soldiers with the ideological assertion that the Dalits and the Adivasis are Hindus.[8]

Discrimination, violence, exclusion and exploitation are a persistent reality of the subalterns in the country. Marginalization at every dimension of the society is a certainty of the subalterns. Economically they are excluded, socially they are denied their basic rights, religiously they are either targeted as pawns or manipulated for communal ends. Despite the Constitutional rights and legal mechanism developed to empower and liberate the subaltern communities, and despite the claim of social mobility, and empowerment, marginalization and discrimination continue unabated against the communities that have been victimized for centuries. What is the underlying source that a society negates and marginalizes certain members of its own society to such inhumane degree? The following section will enumerate the constructed hegemonic discourse that need to be laid bare in claiming the rights of the marginalized and the vulnerable.

Subjugated by Constructed History

A primary source of the marginalization of the subaltern people in the country is the construct history and culture that have remained dominant and hegemonic, a reified history linked with the sacred. Canonization of religious sacred texts by the dominant group of people contributes significantly to the discriminatory social hierarchy. A certain version of sacred texts and history has legitimized the oppressive hierarchy and claimed the authority to dictate, organize and create the present oppressive hierarchical structures. The discrimination and exploitation of the subaltern peoples in India need to be addressed in the light of historical reality where the dominant group of people have suppressed and silenced the voice, perspective and location of the people. The pursuit and assertion of a mono-reading of culture and homogenization of society undergirds a society that is hegemonic wherein the constructed social reality by the dominant group negates the history and cultures of the marginalized. It is imperative to lay bare the dominant historical process of 'inventing a [hegemonic] tradition' by the Brahmins.

This process of dominant history contributed to the emergence of traditions, evolution of communities and reified practices. The renowned Indian historian R. Champakalakshmi, identifies four dimensions in the process of making communities,

> The first is the notion of tradition, particularly textual or canonical, which is central to community consciousness and identity. Tradition is not immutable, it is often fluid and dynamic and hence, subject to interpretations, re-interpretations and re-construction by those who seek to control it. This is linked with access to various forms of power. The second major concern is to show what kinds of institutional structures were evolved to disseminate and control tradition. The third aspect relates to the kind of religious authority relationships that emerged between society and religious leadership; between religious leadership and political authority and how they were mediated. The fourth, what their social base was and which segment of the community was responsible for creating and perpetuating their identities.[9]

These four aspects: textual, institutional structures, religious authority and social base are essential forces in the making of the tradition and history as we know them today. Religion and its sacred texts have served as the repository for the social structure and worldview as evidenced in the context of Indian religious history. While religious worldview has directed social realities and hierarchy, even the category religion held as source of all that is sacred and pure is a 'manufactured' category.[10] Even so, it is interesting to note that the term 'Hinduism' is itself a construct of a context and not inherent to the culture it represents. It was not until the nineteenth century that the term 'Hinduism' as we know today became the term to represent and describe the religiosity of the people. Richard King in his discussion of making of modern Hinduism presents lucidly the thesis that modern Hinduism is a construct of the Orientalists within the colonial structure and aided by the 'crucial role played by indigenous brahmanical ideology in the formation of early Orientalist representations of Hindu religiosity'.[11] King continues, 'the notion of "Hinduism" is itself a Western-inspired abstraction, which until the nineteenth century bore little or no resemblance to the diversity of Indian religious belief and practice'.[12] The term 'hindu' is a Persian term for the Sanskrit word 'sindhu' which refers to the Indus River, and therefore used by the Persians to describe the people living by the Indus River. The West in its search for comparative category for religion and textualized sacred texts akin to Christianity in a non-Western context contributed to the construction of Hinduism as it is known today. One of the primary steps was the identification of a perceived sacred text, which serve as the core of the religion. This identification was the act of 'locating the core of Indian religiosity in certain Sanskrit texts (the textualization of Indian religion)'.[13] In locating, identifying, recording, and translating the selected Sanskrit texts, the Orientalists began the process of obliteration and suppression of the non-Sanskrit version of history. A religious text in Sanskrit which was representative only of a small percentage of the population was only of the Brahminical worldview, not relevant and applicable to the non-Brahminic people and religions. The process of textualization of religion in the country produced the lopsided monolithic 'Hindu' religion directed by the sacred texts, and produced an imagined homogeneity that had no semblance to the reality which was a myriad of languages, diverse groups of people, different religious adherence and multiple cultural practices.

The construction of the 'myth of homogeneity' and a monolithic Hindu religious tradition was initiated and reified during the colonial context as Champakalakshmi writes,

> Perceptions of a monolithic Hindu tradition were first projected by colonial reconstructions of the past to which colonial and imperial historians made a major contribution . . . based on the ways in which a 'Hindu' past was presented to colonial administrators by native interpreters from specific social and religious backgrounds intent on privileging their understanding on the development of a Hindu religious community.[14]

Apart from the misrepresentation by one component of the region's religion and social culture for the diversity and plurality in existence, thereby creating the hegemonic social structures which guaranteed privilege to some and complete subjugation to some, another dimension necessary to be reckoned is the fact that even the misrepresented hegemonic tradition has evolved through a process of interactions and encounters. There has been multiple traditions and complex processes of their evolution. This process of evolution has not been without power dynamics, wherein the domination of a specific tradition has been intertwined with the ideologies of power. Those with power and authority dictated the terms and perspective of the traditions. Hence Champakalakshmi states,

> Traditions are constructed through a process of transformation. Confrontation, interaction, accommodation, and marginalization lead to such transformation and the fashioning of dominant traditions. Alternative traditions, opposition, and non-conformism are often accommodated or subordinated, the study of which is crucial to the discourse of domination and power.[15]

If sacred texts have been the source of legitimization of practices and creation of social hierarchies, then there was creation of consensus with power and authority and force such as the collaboration between the Western Orientalists and the native informants, who happened to be Brahmins, and hence in effect reified a sacred history privileging the Brahmins.

Another significant perspective on the discussion of construct of hegemonic social hierarchy is the lucid argument presented by Nicholas Dirks in his book *Caste of Mind: Colonialism and the Making of Modern India,* wherein he persuasively argues the historicity and contextuality of caste as a category of identity in modern India. The core thesis of the book is that caste is practised and employed in modern India for dominance, and political mobilization is 'a product of an historical encounter between India and Western colonial rule'.[16] To be sure, Dirks does not say that social hierarchy of the caste is a creation or an invention of the British colonials out of an *ex nihilo*. The point is that there was a time when caste was more fluid and without canonized religious legitimization. The pre-colonial social context and social identity had more multiple, complex and constantly changing world without having a monolithic categorization such as caste known today.[17] The identification of *Manusmriti* as the sacred text and law of the land with the translation of it by the prodigious orientalist William Jones in 1794 launched the reification of social stratification in the form of caste for modern India. A text confined and relevant to a small group of Brahmins became a uniform social code and was canonized as the religious source for the hegemonic social order, which would prove a bane in modern India.[18]

The dynamics of colonial power, orientalists' production of knowledge, and textualization of religion with willing collaborators such as the Brahmins who stood to gain with the process produced a constructed history that privileged the dominant and subjugated the subalterns. The subaltern communities in the country, as a result has endured centuries of subjugation and victimization, however, today they are being empowered and are voicing their demands for rights and asserting their cultural identity distinct from the Brahminical structure. In this process of empowerment and movement for demands of their rights, the role of modern education and modern liberal democratic values have been crucial, ironically the modern administrative and legal governing apparatus introduced by the agents of the West, such as the colonials and the Christian missions. It cannot be denied that there are programmes and mechanism to enable the subaltern people to claim equal status and dignity. Nonetheless, legal and bureaucratic measures will not be sufficient without an awareness, commitment and deliberate espousal of multicultural vision of society as opposed to a homogeneous one. Multiculturalism ensures the minorities and historical and religio-cultural others are accommodated and given their rights.

A Multicultural Response

In his remarkable book *Why I am Not a Hindu*, Kancha Ilaiah makes it clear that growing up in his community, the Kuruma, he did not know about Hindu gods, 'we knew nothing of Brahma, Vishnu or Eswara until we entered school. When we first heard about these figures they were as strange to us as Allah or Jehova or Jesus were.'[19] The Tribal communities of north-east India can echo the same, it is not Shiva or Ram but Tsungrem or Pathian who are part of their religious cosmology. It is not caste but clan structure that is more a social identity rather than a religiously sanctioned social order, which provides the members their identity. Hence, it is preposterous to impose the social structure derived from the Brahminical sacred texts that had nothing do to with the subalterns. A multicultural vision of society is open to the diverse traditions and identity of the members and guarantee equal status to all the members of the society.

The concept and practice of multiculturalism is a term associated with the development of liberal democracies in the West during the last quarter of the twentieth century. The migration of labour from the global south to the global north occasioned the need for a policy that guaranteed rights, protection and assimilation of 'the other' either ethnic or religious. In Euro-American societies where the conventional culture and power was in the hands of the Euro-Christian descendants, the concept and practice of multiculturalism was introduced as a policy to ensure the ethnic minorities and the traditionally excluded groups such as the indigenous people in North America, the descendants of the slaves from Africa and the religious other—Jews, Hindus, Muslims, Sikhs, Buddhists, Jains, their cultural identities and the affirmation of the cultural values. Put alternatively, the concept and practice of multiculturalism is antidote to a homogeneous and monolithic vision and worldview. In the context of the West, multiculturalism is

> the radical idea that people in other cultures, foreign and domestic, are human beings too—moral equals, entitled to equal respect and concern, not to be discounted or treated as a subordinate caste. Thus understood, multiculturalism condemns intolerance of other ways of life, finds the human in what might seem Other, and encourages cultural diversity.[20]

Multiculturalism accepts cultural differences, recognizes the rights of individuals and minorities, protects plurality of identities, it ensures that every member of the society has equal status and rights. Ironically, if multiculturalism is relatively a late twentieth century development in the West, in India multiculturalism has been the practice for millennia, until the colonial apparatus and its native collaborators invented a uniform, homogeneous Indian tradition, which has been inherited by the Hindu right group pronouncing a Hindutva vision for the nation, that espouses an equation of India as equal to Hindu.

Pluralism and diversity of cultures and ways of life has been a way of life in pre-colonial India. Religiously, India is a multi-religious country from its antiquity, as annals of history bear witness. The phenomenon of multi-religions and the many by-products of such a context is not a modern phenomenon for India unlike the European and American societies of the late twentieth century, where immigration from different parts of the world has occasioned multiculturalism in these societies, which not long ago were known as Christian countries populated predominantly by Europeans and descendants. It is not however, to deny the existence, struggle and the impact of the African cultures via the former slaves and their descendants.

For India multi-religiosity is part of its heritage from antiquity. Historians of religions inform us about this fact, for instance, Wendy Doniger of University of Chicago in her book, *The Hindus: An Alternative History* (2009) narrates the interactions of many religions in India, as she writes, 'Hinduism interacted creatively with, first, Buddhism, Jainism, then Judaism, Christianity, then Islam and Sikhism, as well as with tribal religions and other imports (such as Zoroastrianism).'[21]

The fact that many so called 'world religions'—Hinduism, Buddhism, Jainism and Sikhism have their origins in India bears witness to a context that is fecund to diverse, creative and new expressions of religiosity. Zoroastrianism, Judaism, Christianity, and Islam have significant impact upon the people and cultures of modern India, tracing back to the earliest advent of these religions. According to tradition, Christianity took roots in India in the state of Kerala as early as the first century with the arrival of St. Thomas, one of the twelve disciples of Jesus along with the spice merchants from Arabia. Zoroastrians found a safe haven in India and flourished producing a rich legacy for the nation. The Jewish community, albeit declining, both in Kochi and Mumbai provide another example from history of yet another religion that flourish in the region. Buddhism from India became a missionary religion under the patronage of King Ashoka and it has flourished in Asia, if not in its home country. It is important to note, however, there is a resurgent Buddhism in the country associated with B.R. Ambedkar's conversion to Buddhism along with thousands of Mahars, in protest against the caste practice derived from the Brahminical sacred texts. Islam, although, began as a 'conquering religion' has given unique cultural heritage, for instance, the world famous Taj Mahal and the poetic language Urdu is a child of two great cultures. There are also recent studies on the plausible interaction with cultures and philosophies of Greece.[22] These historical facts bespeak of an open, tolerant society, accommodating of different religions and thereby engendering plurality of religion in this part of the world. That multiculturalism that embraced plurality and diversity was a practice and worldview in the region can be ascertained confidently.

The practice of modern Hinduism is itself so diverse that it indicates the accommodation of many local cultures and rituals; the influence of another religion is evident. Hinduism of today is different from the Rigvedic religiosity, e.g. women's role in the religiosity, which bespeaks of the adaptability of the Hindu religion. The evolution of Hindu religion as a construct of modernity, which has been reified at a certain historical period is itself one that has seen a complex process of interaction and absorption as stated by historian R. Champakalakshmi,

> The making of India's religious traditions has been one of the most complex processes in the development of its culture and civilization. Hinduism, as this religious tradition is known, defies definition as a religion, nor can it be described as a way of life. It certainly is more than both. It is the result of a complex interaction between Vedic and Puranic Brahmanism and innumerable indigenous cults, that is, regional and local beliefs, practices, cult forms and ethnic associations, many of which are still unexplored, ultimately contributing to the emergence of a pan-Indian tradition, with interesting regional manifestations and variations.[23]

At different historical periods in different contexts the practice of multiculturalism was employed resulting in lasting influences and most interesting syncretistic religiosity. The introduction of the Brahmanical philosophical texts such as the Upanishads beyond the land of origin has also a most interesting inter-religious, multi-cultural link. There is interesting narration being developed of the influence of the Upanishads upon Western philosophers. And this was due to the patronage of the Islamic king Akbar to the Jesuits in the sixteenth century. The Upanishads were translated to Persian which was the conduit to other Western languages, beginning with Latin, so the German philosopher Schopenhauer read the Upanishads via the Persian that was translated in Akbar's court.[24]

Another illustration that points to the tolerant and creative religious interaction is observed in the phenomenon of *bhakti* spirituality in the medieval period. While it is not without contention, the area of research on the interaction between Hindu *bhakti* spirituality and the Islamic *sufi* spirituality is most promising for a study on cultural influences and local adaptations on a common denominator like human spirituality. The devotional songs (*padas*) of *bhakti* mystics Kabir and Mirabai show influence of *sufi* spirituality.[25]

An outlook of multiculturalism apparently is the undergirding principle in these creative interactions, relative tolerance of other, and diversity. Multicultural practice which is made evident in the history that India has been a region of creative interactions between diverse religions and home to many world religions, producing a context of tolerance and deep religiosity simultaneously. Hence, Doniger notes an 'eclectic pluralism', which entails freedom to the individual's freedom and choice of religious practice.[26]

A word of clarity is necessary in relation to the above perspective of tolerance and plausible creative interactions. The point to note is the general tendency of receptive and harmonious encounters, but it would be like the proverbial ostrich to ignore the particular incidences and religious policy of different rulers at different periods in history. There are perspectives that reveal not-so-creative encounters and not-so-tolerant attitudes, particularly in micro-history. And we can surmise that not one perspective is the final word for the colossal reality that is India.

Within this backdrop of plausible multiculturalism of precolonial India how do we explain the antagonism towards certain religions, the assertion of a homogenous identity, the intolerance of difference that have been a constant phenomenon of modern India?

The assertion of a homogeneous culture with a lopsided perception of India as a monolithic culture emerged during the colonial period, with events such as founding of the Hindu right movement such as the Rashtriya Swayamsevak Sangh (RSS) in 1925. The founders and ideologues, Keshav Baliram Hedgewar, M.S. Golwalkar, and V.D. Savarker launched the vision of a homogenous nation derived from religion which had no tolerance and room for the perceived other, as the following statement of Golwalkar indicates:

> There are only two courses open to the foreign elements: either to merge themselves in the national race and adopt its culture or to live at the sweet will of the national race. That is the only logical and correct solution. That alone keeps the national life healthy and undisturbed. That alone keeps the Nation safe from the danger of a cancer developing into its body politics of the creation of a state within the state. From this standpoint, sanctioned by the experiences of shrewd old nations, the non-Hindu peoples in Hindustan must either adopt the Hindu culture and language, must learn to respect and hold in reverence Hindu religion, must entertain no idea but those of glorification of the Hindu race and culture, i.e. they must not only give up their attitude of intolerance and ungratefulness towards this land and its agelong traditions but must also cultivate the positive attitude of love and devotion instead—in one word they must cease to be foreigners, or may stay in the country, wholly subordinated to the Hindu nation, claiming nothing, deserving no privileges, far less any preferential treatment—not even citizen's rights. There is, at least should be, no other course for them to adopt.[27]

It is clear that for Golwalkar, India is a homogeneous country with no space, rights and privileges for those religious others. This vision of Golwalkar continues in the Hindu right group today. Consequently, in modern India there is a section of the population who perceive a homogeneous culture of the region. This group of the population adheres to a vision of one country, one religion, while negating the many 'others' and the diverse traditions. The logical step of such a position is homogenization, resulting in curtailment of rights and freedom, and moreover 'abuse of history' as Doniger would describe.

The notion of a homogeneous people negates peoples' history and imposition of a dominant history takes place. Further, such a homogenizing project in turn creates a 'clash within' as described by Martha C. Nussbaum in her book *The Clash Within: Democracy, Religious Violence and India's Future* (2007). The 'clash within' that exists in modern India as described by Nussbaum, is quite different from Samuel Huntington's thesis of *Clash of Civilization*, wherein it is generally the democratic West and an anti-democratic Islam which is at odds with each other. In India it is a clash within a nation itself between two categories of people, wherein, one civilization cannot tolerate people who look different, the other, who 'feels safe only when homogeneity reigns and the different are at the margins', and the other 'civilization delights in its diversity and has no fear of people who come from different backgrounds. These latter are those who affirm a moral political democratic principle.'[28]

This 'clash within' where there is fear of the different, has produced such legal measures that curb individual's right and freedom to choose religions of their own free will and the violence committed against those perceived as violating these laws. Furthermore, the intolerance of the other history and culture has produced mechanism to subjugate and oppress a large section of the people, making them victims of the dominant group. In such a context of oppressive, homogeneous vision of society, the concept and practice of multiculturalism need to be asserted and pursued that will ensure equality for all its members as Bhikhu Parekh states

> from a multiculturalist perspective the good society cherishes the diversity of and encourages a creative dialogue between its different cultures and their moral visions. Such a society not only respects its members' rights to their culture and increases their range of choices but also cultivates their powers of self-criticism, self-determination, imagination, intellectual and moral sympathy, and contributes to their development and well-being.[29]

While multiculturalism when put into practice, ensures the demands of minorities, subalterns and the marginalized ones, there are inherent limitations especially in the context of inherent social hierarchies of any given community. For instance, in the name of multiculturalism certain cultural practices and attitudes of a group that may be unjust and oppressive to members of its own members need not be tolerated, such as women's inferior status, and rights of children. Multiculturalism need to be measured by the vision of a good society that ensures equality and protection and development of all members of the society. Multiculturalism also has the perils of producing isolated communities with diverse and conflicting goals, therefore a common vision which benefits mutually all the sections of the society should undergird the practice of multiculturalism as Parekh proposes:

> A multicultural society cannot be stable and last long without developing a common sense of belonging among its citizens . . . through their mediating membership of a shared community, and they are committed to each other because they are all in their own different ways committed to a common historical community.[30]

While history can be a two-edged sword, it is the history of the land in all its diversities that need to be reckoned along with the constitutional rights affirmed by the most powerful and binding document of the land in responding to repressive laws and violence in the name of religion and exploitation in the name of sacred traditions. The 'eclectic pluralism' as observed by Doniger should direct the spirit of tolerance and engender a context of freedom as guaranteed by the Constitution, without different religio-cultural group abusing the fundamental right, either by fraud, exploitation, coercion or hegemonic dominance.

The state and the communities in modern India should ensure the spirit of creative tolerance and mutual equal status of all the citizens of the nation. In a simplified way, the post-modern concept of hybridity, a by-product of multiculturalism wherein difference are accommodated, respected and celebrated, need to be pursued with commitment to a common vision of equal quality of life to all. The practice of multiculturalism tempered with justice can direct towards this goal of equal quality of life for all.

NOTES

1. A word of clarification on the terms, Dalits, Adivasis and Tribals; while these terms are employed to describe the group of people that share certain similar experience in relation to the dominant people of being exploited, and dehumanized, it is important to underline the distinction in culture, language and religiosity underlying these constructed categories.
2. The term 'subaltern' is used advisedly for the Dalits, Tribals and Adivasis to state the common experience of being perceived as 'inferior' according to the Brahminical caste structure, and the shared history of struggle for liberation and common demands of their rights. The commonality of being subjugated undergirds the usage of the general term 'subaltern' keeping in mind the differences and the irrationality of 'homogenization of the subaltern'. For more discussion of the term in relation to the Dalits see, Sathianathan Clark, *Dalits and Christianity: Subaltern Religion and Liberation Theology in India*, New Delhi: Oxford University Press, 1998, pp. 6-7.
3. As quoted in Felix Wilfred, *Dalit Empowerment*, New Delhi: ISPCK, 2007, p. 20.
4. Ibid., pp. 18, 21.
5. Ibid., p. 22.
6. Ibid., p. 23.
7. Ibid., p. 25.
8. Ibid., See also, Dharmendra Kumar and Yemuna Sunny (eds.), *Proselytisation in India: The Process of Hinduisation in Tribal Societies*, Delhi: Aakar Books, 2009.
9. R. Champakalakshmi, *Religion, Tradition and Ideology: Pre-colonial South India*, New Delhi: Oxford University Press, 2001, p. 248.
10. See, Russell McCutcheon, *Manufacturing Religion*, Oxford University Press, 2003.
11. Richard King, *Orientalism and Religion: Postcolonial Theory, India and 'The Mystic East'*, London/New York: Routledge, 1999, p. 98.
12. Ibid., p. 98.
13. Ibid., p. 101.
14. Champakalakshmi, *Religion, Tradition and Ideology*, p. 247.
15. Ibid., p. 3.
16. Nicholas Dirks, *Castes of Mind: Colonialism and the Making of Modern India*, Delhi: Permanent Black, 2002; Princeton: Princeton University Press, 2001, p. 5.

17. Ibid., p. 13.
18. Ibid., p. 35.
19. Kancha Ilaiah, *Why I Am Not a Hindu: A Sudra Critique to Hindutva Philosophy, Culture and Political Economy,* Calcutta: Samya Press, 1996, p. 7.
20. Susan Moller Okin, *Is Multiculturalism Bad for Women?*, Princeton: Princeton University Press, 1999, p. 4.
21. Wendy Doniger, *The Hindus: Alternative History,* New Delhi: Penguin/Viking, 2009, p. 45
22. See, Demetrios Th. Vassiliades, *The Greeks in India: A Survey in Philosophical Understanding,* New Delhi: Munshiram Manoharlal, 2000.
23. Champakalakshmi, *Religion, Tradition, and Ideology*, p. 2.
24. King, *Orientalism*, p. 119.
25. Doniger, *The Hindus,* p. 566, See also, Saiyid Athar Abbas Rizvi, *A History of Sufism in India,* New Delhi: Munshiram Manoharlal, 2003.
26. Doniger, *The Hindus,* p. 44.
27. Quoted in Martha C. Nussbaum, *The Clash Within: Democracy, Religious Violence, and India's Future,* Ranikhet: Permanent Black, 2007; first published by Harvard University Press, 2007, p. 162.
28. Ibid., p. 332.
29. Bhikhu Parekh, 'What is Multiculturalism?' in http://www.indiaseminar.com/1999/484/484%20parekh.htm accessed on 15 October 2011.
30. Ibid.

14

Rethinking Theology in India: Secular Ideologies and Theologies of Religions

T. K. JOHN

Introduction

Full and integral development and blossoming of the human being is the aim of the following pages. Ideologies, religions, social, economic or political processes that promote it need to be affirmed. On the contrary, anything that impedes it, is to be held as reprehensible. Affirmation of the origin, nature, dignity, rights and freedom of the human person as well as the ultimate destiny is fundamental to such a development.

The child just born into the world, male or female till his/her death, is the supreme concern—of God, of the life-system. He has set in motion, the dynamics of the health care culture and systems, of the parents, of religions and ideologies, of ethics and morality, of the society and the community, of the governance machinery that is the state. The child is expected to be provided with all that are required to grow as a healthy adolescent, reach manhood/womanhood, allow transition to old age and move to the next life happily. The required food, shelter, protection and care, social acceptance, stimulants for intellectual moral-religious-aesthetic development and space for creativity, should be available to the new entrant into the world. Before her/his cessation from this life one should serve the society to her/his full capability and satisfaction from which she/he has received all these.

A Flower! Let us contemplate the miracle in the garden, in the dale, atop trees, in the field! The blossoming of a flower is a mini theophany, a silent explosion, a gentle weaving together of the beauty and splendour, of elegance and harmony, all dipped in fragrance. This pinnacle of grandeur for the blossoming of which the slow and silent life process was at work for months or years in the plant are climaxed with that miracle. There is satisfaction writ on the plant. The flowering of the plant is almost the goal of the gardener, of the farmer. Similarly, the full flowering of the human person is the plan and will of the Creator. Everything in the created order is geared to the realization of this divine plan.

The full flowering of the human person, of every person without exception, has to be the universal concern, the concern of everyone. It is based on the growing esteem for the origin, nature, dignity and destiny of the human person. It had been, has been and will be the concern of all ideologies, philosophies and religions in their origin. The organization of the society with its laws, prescriptions, prohibitions and strivings at promotion of knowledge, are guided by the same objective. Medical and health care systems and all forms of governance are geared to the development of the human person. Education claims the development of the human person as its over-arching goal. And, theological education, the concern in these pages, is geared to the task of enabling the candidates to acquire the required knowledge and skill to facilitate the blossoming and flowering of those committed to their care. It is a sacred trust invested in the discipline. Definitely it is so of theologies and their spiritualities.

But alas! Such a piece of marvel and splendour that is the

human person 'is everywhere in chains'—such was the lament of Rousseau who ignited the French Revolution. Countless and subtle are the blocks that retard the growth and development.

But gradual detection and elimination of all that blocks the development and restoration of the diminished dignity rights and freedoms have been the goal of authentic religions and some ideologies. The concern and focus of these ideologies is certainly upon the human person and her/his life in the society.

Need of Our Times

A noble culture of collaboration and convergence of all agencies and pooling together of the best humanizing resources is the need of the hour. This is to facilitate that process that will enable the full flowering of the citizen. This can be evolved given the facilities, resources and consciousness of our times. This collaboration is also for a similar concerted task: for evolving a collective contract of all humanity to leave behind customs, traditions, perceptions, values, prohibitions that were discriminatory and inhibitive for the healthy growth of the child of today. Top in the exhaustive list of outdated stuff weighing heavily on the human caravan struggling to forge ahead should be: gender, caste, racial, colour, and religious discrimination. The baggage has to be dumped if we wish to move ahead.

The Dream for a Better Tomorrow

We should dream and strive for gradual evolution of a true community consciousness—at the regional, national and international level. A global consciousness is evolving, true, but unfortunately it is tainted by the wolfish instinct of one human being feeding upon the other. We will have an authentic global human and humanizing culture when this wolfish culture is replaced by the more humanizing value and practice. In what does it consist? It consists in the difficult and rare disposition, conviction and virtue of affirming the other, being in the service of the other and every heart becoming capable of holding the other in one's bosom. The degrading pursuit and worship of the god of profit, as the ultimate goal of all economic commercial and consumerist culture of the day, has to be corrected by the god of love—of all. An inclusive perception is what we need to develop to save our civilization that is heading towards breakdown and ruin. *I Am Thou: Meditations on the Truth of India* (1984) is the title of the great work of the late Ramchandra Gandhi, grandson of Mohandas Karamchand Gandhi. The very title of the book thunders and creates tremors in the mind. It invites the attention of humanity to restore and reunite all that remains fragmented.

Humanism and Formation of Cultures

The glory, dignity, rights, and freedom of the human person being dimmed, distorted, and swallowed by sorrow, pain, suffering and, alas, eventual death—has been the puzzle as well as dismay of all thinking men and women of all times. Extortion, exploitation, discriminatory perceptions and practices, injustice, inequality—have been degrading the human community for centuries and millennia. Fundamental questions were raised by philosophies and religions as to why there is such an instinct in human beings? Can it be detected and treated? The origin, nature, dignity and destiny of the human person—had been, have been and will be the brooding and probing occupation of religions, philosophies and ideologies.

An ideology of great appeal in modern times and one that often replaced religion in the hearts many a scholar has been 'humanism'. Advocacy of the human person was the exclusive concern of all forms of humanism. Universal recognition of specific human endowments and properties like freedom, reason, liberty, equality constituted the essentials of any humanism. These are found to be covered over by layers of blocks and chains. Religion, rituals and doctrines were ignored since these were seen as lacking in the affirmation and promotion of these precious properties that constitute the human person.

Standing firmly for a culture based on and guided by reason over against credulity superstition conformism and many an unhealthy values and practices in the name of religion was Ramasamy Naickar popularly known as 'Periyar', the great innovator from Salem in Tamil Nadu. Holding the torch of reason aloft, he believed that, to dispel the darkness that marks human conduct and human relationship, sound use of reason was the only way for the actual liberation of the human person. His was a pro-human stand critical of the many misconceptions current in the society about caste, gender, sterile ritualism, superstition, and other forms of values, customs, and practices.

Among the contributions of Marxian ideology has been his advocacy of the human person and establishment of a just and equitable social order. In the wake of the Industrial Revolution the majority of the population became subject to the inhuman and degrading condition of the new category called by him as the working class. His critique of the capitalist ideology is being restated in the wake of globalization. Soviet experiment may have failed. But his call for the liberation of the human person from iniquitous systems structures values and practices and his rejection of religions that are callous bystanders along with unjust and exploitative systems, still resound the world over.

Marxian ideology's role for promoting self-criticism in religions is recognized by critics today. Religion in Europe was a callous bystander when workers in the factories of industrial Europe, including children, were exploited in the most inhuman way. He rejected religion because of the neglect of its duty to uphold the human person with all her/his dignity and worth.

Most religions after the primal days of their origin in pursuit of the fundamental need and their realization translated these experiences and sentiments into rituals, doctrines and celebrations. Some extended these into a phase now known as life-beyond. In that process elaborate and highly ornate systems of philosophy/theology also were built up. The primary task was lost sight of. Ideologies were generated by visionaries interested in the well-being of the human person to continue the search, to secure appropriate remedy, apply them and help the suffering humanity to regain the lost form of peace and happiness. Some of these ideologies were seen more focused on the here and now of life. On that count ideologies were also critics of religions.

Early Phase and Subsequent Fate of Theology

A new 'fire was cast upon earth' (Lk 12: 49), by Jesus of Nazareth, born in a poor stable to burn and melt down all chains that bind, block and retard the full development of every child born 'in the image and likeness of God, both male and female' (Gen. 1: 27). Him and His sacred project in history, in creation, to interpret was the task and vocation of theology. Theology was expected to contain that fire in the process of interpretation and elaboration. It seems that fire is not in the present-day theology. That necessitated the current project: Rethinking Theology in India. To explore the role of ideologies and theologies of religions to rekindle that fire in theology is the discourse in this paper.

The term 'theology', is a late comer on the scene. The word originated during the time of the Greeks, but later was appropriated and given specific and perhaps unique content, during the era succeeding the Christ-event and related events both before and after. Community fellowship and bond in all matters was central to the Bible, both in the Old Testament and the New (Ex 24: 3-8; Lev 23-5; Acts 2: 42-7). The era of Patristic theology elaborated the vision and the praxis and succeeded in developing an integral vision of Christian life where the living out of the thinking was taking place.

It grew as a beautiful edifice, with the assistance of Hellenist philosophy, quite comprehensive according to the criterion of those times. It was given the title 'Queen of Sciences'. The monasteries of those days played a major role in shaping theology. But the equality of the monastic community could not prevent the emergence of communities marked by hierarchy. Feudalism was the name of that incipient capitalism.

But much of the liberative and humanizing treasures of the Bible did not enter into the make up of that theology. Nor were the pathos of the struggling humanity registered by theology. The empirical consequences of sin, the depth of the misery of enslavement and exploitation, the exodus dynamics, the vision of the Leviticus community and the vision of the Jubilee instructions (Lev. 23-5), the nature and significance of prophetism are central to the Old Testament.

In a similar strain it can be said that the fascinating story of the Incarnation life teaching and the immeasurable depth of the paschal event make the life of Jesus Christ truly appealing. It became a true and unique 'light of the world' (Jo 8: 12). But scholastic theology could not embody the poignancy and pathos portrayed in the Letter to the Hebrews. It abstracted the essentials of Christ-experience as filtered through the strainer of Aristotelian philosophy through the selective exercise of Aquinas. Theology could not resonate with the suffering and degraded humanity all over the world. It is only in recent centuries that an effort at recovery of the God of history was attempted, quite successfully. But at what cost!

And so it is that soon other secular disciplines grew up rapidly, bypassed theology and sped ahead. It was an indication that theology was not incarnate and inclusive enough to deal with many a question raised by a thinking and struggling humanity in the wake of colonialism, Industrial Revolution, rise and consequences of capitalism, as well as encounter with other cultures and religions. The encounter with world religions did force substantial revision of theology that had shrunk and become very narrow. The devastation of modern civilization by the two world wars betrayed the moral bankruptcy to which that era sank.

Proliferation of Ideologies/Philosophies and Theologies of Religions

Production of knowledge, followed by organization and dissemination of learning came out of the control of monasteries and of Schoolmen. The world has been virtually flooded with philosophies and ideologies. Thinking and articulating became as free and diverse as there were visionaries of life and of meaning systems. Just as fireworks fill the sky with marvellous display of myriads of forms and flames, so was the world of ideas. Revolutionary ideas exposed the layers of petrified social systems, structures, values and traditions. Just as discovery of new colonies opened up opportunities for conquests trade and related activities in the new world, so did the worlds of philosophies, of science, medicine, etc., become multipliers of further ideas and developments. Re-visiting existing social institutions, transmitted philosophies, belief systems, customs and traditions as well as venturing into new mode of thinking made the era in many ways memorable. The human spirit began to burst forth and assert.

Under the umbrella of 'modern philosophy' proliferation of schools of philosophies originated and flourished. Equally impressive was the arrival of ideologies. Enlightenment, rationalism, personalism, existentialism, agnosticism, modernity, and a host of philosophies and ideologies showed the fertility of the human mind that put forth newer and fresher ideas. The exploitation and dehumanization of the working class consequent upon Industrial Revolution generated massive ferment in Europe. Theology was not sufficiently on the scene. Marx was on the other hand. The rest is history in the West.

Similarly, if rivalry among colonizers led to the disastrous First World War, humiliation of the loser, Germany, led to the Second World War. The weakness of theological systems became further manifest there in so far as resistance to the Holocaust could not come sufficiently from religions in Europe. Europe saw the rise of three powerful ideologies: Nazism, Fascism and Marxism. With the failure of religion to withstand these totalitarian ideologies and regimes there was chaos and bewilderment in the society. Three movements that were born to alleviate the feelings of humiliation and restore national pride and integrity, soon degenerated and became worse than evil which the originators wanted to combat. It looked as though 'Enlightenment' is followed by Dark Age!

Again, enchantment with and espousal of 'secularity' had become one of the striking consequences of the miracle of Science. With the arrival of science and its by-products like technology, industry, the world of consumer goods and the many wonders these worked, many momentous developments had been taking place in that part of the globe that had been witnessing this rising tide of new ideas.

The 'here and now' struck the prophets of modernity. Life here on earth required more attention than was granted till then.

The world of religions had assigned more space and time, as well as prominence, to life beyond. Hence quality of life on earth received less attention than what was needed. Verifiable truths became more important than truths received and transmitted by faith. Inherited social organizations, structures, values and traditions failed to be subjected to the demands of reason. Evidently the new world of science and critical thinking gained ascendancy over that of faith and authority. Many were the predictable consequences.

One was the slow but steady receding of the religious phenomenon. Religion had been part and parcel of the human phenomenon from its very history. It was being replaced by the sudden ascent to considerable heights of secularity. Religions and their manifold manifestations seemed to be on the way out. It was like the disappearance of stars and other celestial luminaries with the arrival of the Sun. The apparent evanescence of religion in the wake of science and its myriad marvels dismayed the believers. But scientists know that stars do not disappear. They are there. Their splendour and luminosity are only dimmed by those of the sun, when that part of the earth is under the domain of the earth. The upstart secularity cannot for ever take over the domain of the religious permanently. The latter belongs to the constitutive dimensions of the human phenomenon.

As with Religion so with Theology too: The Decline

Impact of the new developments on religion seemed to have happened to theology far more decisively. Has it not become an esoteric discipline—people began to wonder, useful for and intelligible to, the initiates, namely, the clergy. Since the clergy lived a life far removed from the smoke and fire of a struggling humanity, the difference was not noticed, the relevance was not questioned. Its language is largely internal, and is intelligible to initiates only, as the market of books and related publications seem to tell us. Has it not become a discipline for internal consumption only? Its content appeared a-historical, in so far as concerns and issues of the human life-struggle in the modern society, controlled by the market malls and avid consumerism, seemed to figure minimally only in theology. Why is theology not capable of generating the fire to burn away accumulated garbage in the Indian society?

Secularity, born of protest against lopsided religiosity and theology, has become an ideology but it has to be recognized for the contribution to authentic religiosity. It is an invitation to revisit the authentic religious phenomenon and vindicate its claims: healer of the wounds, and provider of ways to reduce or minimize or handle suffering and affliction, and path-maker to the life after cessation. Religiosity and theology are called upon to recover and assume their true identity and form fully. For religion is counted as the meaning dimension of the human life. Yet why is it that theology cannot ignite the imagination of its adherents and inflame their will to decisive action to renew a moribund society laden with many social evils? The question has been raised repeatedly.

Enfeebled Theology in India and Upsurge of Ideologies

Theology in India lived with strange paradoxes. First, theology largely co-existed with colonial subjugation of the Indian people. Second, decades-long India's struggle to rid the country of colonialism was only partially registered by theology and institutions. The events of freedom struggle did not shake theology in India. Third, caste system in the Christian community and in the open society was not a concern for theology. Both co-existed, as people some time continue sleeping even when the cobra has fallen on the bed from the thatched roof! Amnesia had seized theology, clergy and the community, that of Caste! Fourth, gender discrimination and inequality were not yet something theology took note of seriously. Fifth, poverty and illiteracy that have been plaguing the Indian society, was not systematically studied by theology. Sixth, economic exploitation rampant in urban situation and the elephantine culture of landlord-landless rural sectors was only mildly attended to in theology. Seventh, social domination and over all apathy and callousness of which the historian Kosambi deplores (1956) had made social living an inhospitable exercise. Some of the earlier books of the Nobel Laureate V.S. Naipaul [*India: A Wounded Civilization* (1977); *An Area of Darkness* (1964)] have had morbid titles. That is because of the shock and dismay one registers on close observation of the social mores: layers upon layers of countless stagnant customs/rituals and superstitious practices that benumb the mind, and yet are transmitted across, from one generation to the next. The discovery did prove shocking to the sensitive observer of social mores. Eighth, the most entrenched and obnoxious of these negative parasitical perceptions and practices in the Indian social system has been caste system with 'untouchability' for its sign board! Even Christians practised 'untouchability', even at the bones level! Separate cemeteries! Finally, these seem surpassed by the stench of decline of values, breeding maggots that crawl around of which the common title is 'corrupt practices'. In spite of powerful means at our disposal like education—battling against corrupt practice could not become the seal of 'Christian education'. Laudable exceptions excluded.

Theology in India is now called upon to give an explanation for the lapses and attend to them.

Theology in India began to wake up when people from the civil society began to knock at the doors of theological and other institutions when some ideologies were already in India. A variety of initiatives, inspired by different ideologies, offered new paths to the seekers.

Civilization worth the name is achieved when the finest expression of the human spirit is manifested by enriching and elevating the very concept and reality of the human person and human relationship. Inclusive culture, acceptance of every member as an equal, recognition and honouring of the rights dignity and freedom of every one, and absence of any kind discriminatory practices, should constitute the very foundation of social organization, and social structures. Ethics and morality derived from these should stabilize social behaviour and practice. But this may not be the actual reality in the history of societies. Many a revolution that has taken place in history did try to upset existing unjust systems.

Bible's Transformative Power

We have to recall the inspiring and transformative potential of the Bible. The Bible is a universally revered book. It is reportedly the most translated book in the world. One of the chief reasons for its universal grip over minds might be that it raises eternal questions of vital interest to all humanity, and, offers answers that are satisfying. Besides, the transformative potential of the Bible is unrivalled. This cannot and need not be expatiated within the limited space of this paper.

And, theology is primarily its explanation. The inspiring and transformative potential of the Bible is expected to be passed on to theology. Since theology is expected to have a direct bearing on the times and places of its exercise, it is expected to share the features of the Bible. But it looks as though the transformative potential of the Bible was not transmitted to theology. Theology remained at theoretical heights and did not come to the grounds where life-battle has been raging.

The contribution of the Bible to India through the many services of the personnel and institutions of the Christian community in India is acknowledged. Christianity's contribution to India has been recognized by all. India has acknowledged it freely and frankly (although the tenor of dissident voices of late has been changing primarily because of the orchestration by the Hindutva agents!). The momentous challenge the Bible gave to India through Christianity in general, and through its manifold services, resulted in the 'Hindu renaissance', as acknowledged by many scholars. But it looks as though theology could not elicit the interests of the affected.

It is almost like the silence of theology in Europe when European Christianity for nearly two centuries played with 'Negro' purchase-sale-use culture and the infamous slave trade. Slave trade seemed to have co-existed with theological instructions in seminaries! We have its modern replay when *Hitler's Willing Executioners: Ordinary Germans and the Holocaust* (Daniel Jonah Goldhagen, 1996) ravaged German sanity when millions of ancestors of European Christianity, namely the Jews, were hunted down and exterminated. Theology co-existed with the poisonous gas of the gas chambers! Goldhagen, in the book referred to says:

> Throughout the period of Nazi rule, as the government and people of Germany were subjecting the Jews of Germany and those of the conquered countries to an increasingly severe persecution that culminated in their physical annihilation, the German protestant and

Catholic churches, their governing bodies, their bishops, and most of their theologians watched the sufferings inflicted on the Jews in silence. No explicit public word of sympathy for the Jews, no explicit public condemnation or protest against their persecution issued from any of the authoritative figures within the churches or from any of their ecclesiastical offices. Only a few lowly pastors and priests spoke out, or rather cried out forlornly their sympathy with the Jews, and with it, their bitter reproach of the Church authorities for their silence. (pp. 436-7)

The growing 'contextual theological method' in India is to correct the mistakes and enable theology to travel with the social processes of the living context. If theology is loaded with the burden of past thoughts only, the danger cannot be averted. Theology is expected to focus on the present in view of the future.

One of the objectives of the 'Rethinking Theology in India' is to develop this contextual theological method. The living God, speaking though the living context of the struggling people can be obeyed only if theology also is a living discipline. Constant monitoring of and travelling with the struggling peoples of the country has to be part of the new theological method.

In India in spite of the enormous investment in theology in terms of finance, personnel, institutions and time, there are not many voluntary takers for theology inside the Christian community, still less outside. Very few takers there are even inside the community. There is some interest among the religious, but that too may be because the consumption is internal, like dispatching the theologically initiated to the task of 'formation'. Again, that is an internal discourse through deployment of the initiates.

I have heard of some university students learning French to read French radical authors or poets, or Russian to study Russian revolutionary thinkers and poets like Pushkin, or German language to get in touch with philosophers like Marx and others who offer an alternate vision for humanity with an alternate philosophy of human history and interpretation of political economy. But only rarely have I come across social activists intent on system change or advocating emancipation of still 'unfree' people in India rushing to theological bookstalls or libraries. Why—is it a valid question? Yes, theology needs rethinking.

Theology, although its source is scripture, on the contrary, can in no way come close to the Bible in its reach and appeal to people. Why? It might be a worthwhile exercise to examine whether books in theology are translated and disseminated, with some exceptions most certainly. The translation of the Bible goes on. But not that of theology! Why?

Though Christianity in India is under attack of late, not theology (except perhaps when some doctrinal issues are at stake, but that emanates from internal quarters where orthodoxy is the dominant concern!). Antagonists of the Bible have burned or destroyed the Bible. But no book on theology is yet burned or destroyed. Again the question is why?

Role of Ideologies

Ideologies, on the contrary, seem to have more takers than theology in the open world of advocacies and among those engaged in the task of building up of the nation. Some of the known NGOs are inspired by certain ideologies. Greater part of peninsular India seems under the grip of Maoists. A particular ideology is beckoning the youth to turn that way. Why that ideology attracts many in the intelligentsia or the youth? Even NGOs and activists in the Christian community seem interested in such ideologies, not perhaps in theology. What makes the difference?

It is presumed that Rethinking Theology is aimed at investigating reasons for this challenging contrast! May be restoration of the authentic continuity of the biblical vision of things in theology can revive theology. And when theology in its turn penetrates and percolates into the Christian community, it can play a significant role in the service of the people of India. To emancipate the deprived, the excluded and the degraded sections of the Indian people, such a revitalizing and re-animating process is required. Far too long has it been coexisting with iniquitous social and economic systems structures and values in India. It is desirable that we return to the primordial times as we have in the central source for theology, namely, the Bible. Some trends among these ideologies can be cited.

(a) *Striving for a Classless Society*

When industrialized Europe was deeply divided into the exploited and greatly impoverished working class and the profit-making capitalists, the vision of a classless society hoisted by sociologists and economists like Marx had been supplying fuel for a series of revolutions in Europe. That vision brought under one banner the workers of the world, irrespective of colour, culture or profession. It had kindled the working class in England, Belgium, Germany, Czarist Russia and some other countries in Europe at a time when the industrial revolution had just begun to affect the condition of the society. The social divide between the exploited class and the profit accumulating beneficiaries had widened. Deep discontent had been brewing in the hearts of millions of impoverished and exploited workers leading to revolts and disruption of the social peace and order. It is then that the vision of a classless society where the economic resources are held in common by legislation and the authority of the state constituted entirely of the working class was articulated and placed before the society.

Of course, in the process of theorizing by Marx the idea of God, of religion, of private ownership of land, etc., were rejected. But the idea of a re-organization of the society as one without class distinction appealed to many in the society. Deep prejudice has been preventing recognition of the truth that much of these rather innovative ideas were drawn from the Bible. May be theology was slow to extract the vision from the Bible and save the society from the violence and bloodshed that marked the Russian experiment following the October Revolution.

The collapse of Soviet Russia controlled by atheistic communist party has led to the failure of the experiment in Russia and its satellite countries in Europe. And the rise of global capitalism has been trying to erase the very idea from the minds of modern man and woman. The downward trend of modern culture is further compounded by the protagonists pushing for a moral values-free culture in Europe (Marguerite A. Peters 2009). But the balloon blown full size and sent up in the sky has been hurtling earthwards in the wake of the recent economic collapse.

(b) *For a Caste-less Society*

If the idea of a classless reorganization of the unjust unequal and distorted society had fired the imagination of Karl Marx, the vision of a casteless society and sufferings—free human life did move the brain of another reflective mind brooding for decades over the inequity of the Indian society and sufferings—marked human life. That was the brain and mind of Siddharth of Kapilavastu of earlier times. For both, Marx and Siddharth, God and religions appeared irrelevant and peripheral to the burning issues affecting everyone. The inequality and injustice in the system were seen as co-existing with religion and God. The societies in their times seemed not to get much benefit from 'God' or 'religion'. Although the god of the Brahminic class, in league with political and caste power, eventually succeeded in banishing the once-flourishing Buddhism from the country, yet his insight is still flourishing in greater part of Asia.

The goal of a casteless society was resuscitated by another experiment in India by B.R. Ambedkar. *Annihilation of Caste* (Ambedkar) was a project for Ambedkar. The ideology grew to become a project leading to the mass exodus of millions of

Dalits from the confines caste-ridden Hinduism. Though he too partially only succeeded at that time, the hot wind generated by his creative mind is still blowing over the subcontinent in the form of many splinter movements. They are valiantly campaigning for a social order that will cast away the hideous caste system. Remember, theology was innocently being imparted in the classrooms when these momentous agitations were creating tremors in the Indian society. A caste-stained Christian community could not engage in a critical soul-searching at that time. Theology was unable to campaign for a caste-free Christian community in India in those days.

(c) *Drive for a Welfare Society*

From Nepal in the Himalayas to the southern tip of the Indian peninsula an alternate ideology and way of life of attending to the basic needs of people is under way. The initiative came from the people. The inspiration came largely from the Leftist ideology, as is popularly termed. They are known in the society as Maoists.

The estranged people, having experienced for decades neglect from the state and rejection and exploitation from the powerful landlords, have come to the conviction that to establish a just society coercion and physical force are needed. It is impossible to breakdown resistance from the vested interests. Persuasion and legislation after legislation came in quick succession. But they felt the rural roads, bridges, schools, hospitals and health centres, ration shops, electricity, etc., existed and functioned mostly on documents and files only. They were minimally only available in reality to the people. People remained deprived of the benefits of planning and development by the nation. Virtually these failed the people. The officers designated for the task lacked the will to deliver the goods.

So the people lost their faith in the governments that ruled over them for decades after decades. Neither do they have faith in the existing social system that denies them their due rights.

Anger and discontent generated by decades of neglect of the basic needs of the people have driven them away. Desperation has driven them to take up arms. Many of them get killed in the bargain. Many security men also get killed. Disruption of normal life takes place at all levels. Both Maoists and 'security men' are Indian citizens, therefore it is our own people that are destroying our own people. We all have mutual responsibility for our common well-being, directly or indirectly. But this contradiction stares us at our face.

At this juncture we should remember that it was a famine that drove the Patriarch Jacob's children to Egypt to go and procure wheat. Land was held out by Moses as the promise to mobilize the enslaved descendants of Joseph. The basis for the Palestinian settlement of the 12 tribes was, again, land. In other words livelihood was the chief concern. It is full livelihood that is decent and becoming the human person, that the agitating people of these vast regions in central India are clamouring for.

The question at this juncture is: to what extent these get full attention of theology in India? If theology were to be penetrated by and shot through by living issues of the Indian peoples, that would to some extent influence and shape the consciousness of the Christian community, which could in its turn contribute to mitigating the situation. For it is the belief that theology should help shape the Christian community. And the Christian community is expected to contribute to the reshaping of the human community that at present is seen distorted and not in conformity with the plan of God. The ultimate question is: to what extent theology has mediated God's soothing, reconciling, and justice-imparting message to the disturbed sections of the Indian people, since the Good News is for all of human family.

(d) *The Move for a Secular Society and Theologies of Religions*

The following considerations are worth recalling for theology in the context of the growing acceptance of plurality of religions. On the one hand, we can be happy at our acceptance of secularism of the Indian version. India has no state religion. All religions, big or small, are equal before law, holds the Indian Constitution. And, every Indian is free to believe practice and propagate a religion of his/her choice.

This has placed before Christianity a new challenge. It lived for centuries as the religion of the state in greater part of Europe. In India it continued to live with the centuries-old conviction that Christianity is the true religion for all peoples of the world. Now it is called upon to be one among many in India. Redefining of its universal mission is thus demanded of it by a new historical situation. A new culture of interacting creatively with the plurality of religions in India has to be evolved. Inter-religious dialogue has been gradually growing. Dialogue becomes a new window. But such interaction presupposes a mature theology of religions. Religions have to shed mono-cultural mindset that was inherent to each tradition.

Dialogue today has its demands. It will grow when inter-scriptural exegesis is initiated. From inter-scriptural we may have to move towards inter-sacramental or inter-ritual exchanges. Multi-religious celebration of festivals hitherto proper to each tradition may be the next step. Interreligious marriages have been taking place cautiously. Multi-religious institutions, ministries and such ventures may be the future of ministries. In other words true implications and demands of the prayer 'Our Father' need to be prudentially and judiciously explored. Much more systematic and honest efforts are needed to make the dialogue move forward.

The new situation has been inviting theology to generate that culture that will promote collaboration with all religions for the wider service of the nation. Most religions had their origins in response to the problems of life. To attend to the sorrows and afflictions that marked human life was a major objective. Keeping in mind this pristine phase of religions, it is time for all religions to revisit the early times, to restore the original call and together to contribute to the removal of problems that beset life.

Authentic religion is a guide to practical life also, like a small torch while travelling through unknown and dark terrain. Organization of both individual and collective life to secure welfare is one of the growing concerns of civil administration. Religions could contribute to this national objective by healthy collaboration. Rituals and celebrations that are part of religiosity could be balanced by service of the community in the secular field. A major block to the development of the nation is corrupt practices that have become almost universal.

The will to do good, to serve the other, to be truthful and honest, is provided largely by sound religiosity. It is an opportunity for the many religions of the land to contribute to this religious perspective. This presupposes that we need to strive together to evolve a new spirituality.

Revisit to Biblical Presentation of God's Plan

Ideologies do exercise certain fascination for the human mind ever in search of new vistas. But they have their limitations. Chief among them is the silence of these ideologies about future life, revelation, scripture and other essentials of religion. In spite of such limitations creative interaction with the core vision of religions is becoming increasingly necessary for the health of humanity. Here the core of Judeo-Christian heritage is introduced.

Biblical Vision for the Human Family

God's dream and plan for the human family was His people living a full life enjoying all-round welfare and happiness, and consequent peace (shalom). The Garden of Eden (Gn 2: 8), the symbol of fabulous prosperity and well-being, is the announcer of that vision for the human family. The biblical designation for that situation is the Reign of God or the Kingdom of God. To live in complete harmony with God and His plan was expected of the humankind. But a fundamental rupture between God and the first couple, according to Pentateuch, brought upon the human species a disastrous fate: alienation. History of the humankind is the record of its manifold fragmentation consequent upon that primordial alienation: gender, racial, caste, class fragmentation and its continuity in the economic, the social, and the political realms. But God's love pursued the humankind in the form of mercy, justice, patience and announced the Restoration. Prophets mediated this divine pursuit of the recalcitrant race. Finally, to announce and inaugurate this restoration God sent His only Son. Kingdom of God is the name of that project (Mk. 4.).

The goal of the Indian nation, as announced by the Founding Fathers/Mothers is an equitable social order supported by economic opportunities for all. That meant social transformation accompanied by economic opportunities for all (Ambedkar, Nehru). The mission of the church is serving this divine project, the Reign of God, in and through the service of the people of India. There is convergence of both these dreams. Christian community, admittedly a small community, is expected to be in solidarity with this task in India.

Convergence of an Ideology and Theology: An Equitable Social Order

Both the demands of the theology of the Kingdom of God and the vision of the founding Fathers/Mothers of the Indian nation converge on one idea: that of a social order befitting the human person and economic opportunity for all, a society that eventually enjoys welfare. An economic and social order that will facilitate its emergence has been part of that commitment to the nation.

The Deuteronomic injunctions after the liberative journey of Israel out of Egyptian domination and exploitation had a number of prescriptions that ensured that no form of slavery entered and distorted the community: both economic and social. Thus Deuteronomy 15: forbids that there be any poor (economic slavery) in the land, and that human slavery (social slavery) should not be promoted. Slavery was commonly practised by the neighbouring societies. The criterion is given: Israelites were subject to multiple forms of slavery in Egypt. It is Yahweh's mighty hand that freed them and brought to the land of freedom and prosperity (Deut. 15: 12-18).

Jesus Christ in the new dispensation emphasized and re-enforced this vital injunction (Lk 4: 18-19). His three-year long ministry was devoted to restoration of the distorted human society. The early phase of the Christian community was in consonance with this his will (Acts 2: 44-7).

The early phase of Christianity in India is now seen as inattentive to these divine injunctions. Caste discrimination prevalent in the Hindu society at that time entered into the Christian community too. The consequence is now staring at the face of the church in India. Presence and practice of caste in the church, with its twofold economic and social slavery, has been proving to be counter-witness to the efforts at proclamation.

Theological institutions that have been existing and functioning in India need to revert their attention to these cardinal divine injunctions. One of the demands of 'Rethinking Theology in India' is this revisit to the primordial plan of God. An equitable human social order needs to be kept before the students while expatiating on the scripture.

Religion and Social Living

How does 'Religion' fare in the world culture today, a world culture that is seen steadily moving towards stark secularism, almost like its Greek ancestry? Greek culture had thrown up two counter-cultural developments, known as Hedonism and Epicureanism. India's trend towards spirituality was counter-checked by its opposite, namely, Charvaka philosophy. These three sprouts in the map of world religions had a short span of life, though silent adherents of these were there all through the ages.

On the one hand, some have rejected religion in essence and manifestation. Some have just ignored it. There are some who affirm religion but do hold its role is in the private domain. It should have no say in matters public. Shunned in public, religion can have life in isolation from the society, they argued.

At the same time there are many who swear by religion and that it should have absolute domain in private as well as in public or state domains. Where could be the truth—is a valid question.

Most religions also supervise behaviour of their adherents. Livelihood is the concern of everyone. Livelihood is earned by a complex of activities: economic, social, and political. The ethical, moral and religious fields will provide norms and guidelines in order to ensure that correct values and principles are invoked to provide guidance for correct actions worthy of the human person's nature and destiny. For instance the Mosaic Law and the minute prescriptions covering every aspect of the life of the Jew were available to the members of the Israelite community.

Today, for reasons worth exploring, this comprehensive assistance of religion has ceased to be availed of. For example, one critique of the current economic process is that market is the ultimate authority. But markets, however, have norms derived from sources internal to the domains of economics. Ethics and morality, derived from human reason, may or may not play supervisory role. Hence it is termed as an ethicsless, hence heartless system and process.

It is part of the task of theology to assist the Christian community to perform this task satisfactorily. 'Rethinking theology' is to help the Christian community to rethink its identity and service in this land in the new situation.

Secular ideologies and theologies of religions do contribute to renewal in theology by re-opening ignored windows of religiosity. This they do by challenging it to enlarge its scope and incorporate their wider human historical essentials. Also these disciplines compel established perceptions and practices to revisit them.

One reason why theology could not assist the church substantially in these critical decades and travelled in isolation is due to its inability to regularly monitor and respond to the social and economic processes of a rapidly changing society and the issues they raised up. Human issues propped up regularly and were clamouring for listening ears and caring hearts. For instance a major post-Independence movement that swept through the country decades ago was what was then known as *sampoorna kranti* (total revolution) launched by Jayaprakash Narayan. Although due to practical reasons the movement fizzled out, yet it did influence the countrymen and women to incorporate key insights into their own thinking. Some political ideologies even now are under its sway.

Wisdom in Rethinking Theology

Lions are known to halt on their gallops through the forests, and raise their heads and look back and around. The purpose: to survey the track covered and the route ahead and to ensure safety and security. Submarines in mid-ocean periodically raise their telescopes above surface: for spotting possible warships ahead or around and to ensure safety and security.

Scripture is the word of God, ever new, ever living. Theology is time-bound and obviously ever in need of updating because cultural context is ever in transition, always subject to change.

Time seems to have come for theology in India of the third millennium to halt, to assess the terrain and plan for the next decades. The Christian community faces hitherto unseen situations. Old answers to new problems would be inadequate. The widespread restlessness in the heart of the church in India is calling for a short halt before further proceeding. Certainly many do share this widely-felt need for rethinking Christianity in India. In the light of the assessment of the context current theology in India is seen as inadequate for the church to meet the prevailing apostolic challenges.

Why the Need for such a Rethinking?

Fresh understanding of the church as the people of God inserted and immersed in the life-struggle of the people emerged. The fundamental values derived from the Gospel and associated with Christ began to receive more attention.

A new realization dawned on the communities that the rather impressive organizational structure and resulting social and institutional power, have been dimming the glow of authentic church in the midst of nations. 'Christ is the Light of the Nations' (Lumen Gentium), for instance, is one of the documents of the Roman Catholic Church after the marathon sessions of the Second Vatican Council. The following significant passage is taken from it:

> Christ is the light of the nations. Hence this most sacred Synod, which has been gathered in the light of the Holy Spirit, eagerly desires to shed on all men that radiance of His which brightens the countenance of the Church. (LG 1)

Shedding of this radiance of Christ is primarily by its members living their lives in the midst of the secular world that has been becoming increasingly secular devoid of ethical-moral values that are closely related to the very identity dignity and destiny of the humankind. Specifically Gospel values and virtues need to be made visible. Some of these are recalled.

Love is the knitting and animating power of the human community known as the church. This love is of God, nay God is love (I Jo 4: 8). This love is expressed through many forms: forgiveness, compassion, service, patience, kindness, mercy, self-control, self-sacrifice—all this manifested in true humility.

But systems structures and institutions at the local, regional, national and international level often are seen as not embodying these universal human/Christian values. For instance, if life is precious how can war as an institution be still maintained? How can life-eliminating and planet-destroying practices like nuclear bombing, nuclear-weapons stockpiling, etc., be still considered? How can anti-life steps like abortion, euthanasia, starvation-deaths promoting economic or political systems be permitted? How can torture of the incarcerated and captive victims be permitted even if it is with the motive of extracting truth? How can death penalty be accepted as a way of meting out justice in a civilized society? How can the present mode of functioning of capitalism, with its goal that appropriates natural resources, governed by its unethical and highly exploitative methods go unchecked?

Again, equality, dignity, fellowship, freedom are non-negotiable and distinctive ideals and values the Gospel stands for. The church's conviction is that every Christian, every Indian should enjoy these values and characteristics of being a human full person. Through the manifold services she is committed to live by these convictions and promote them.

Here again the economic, the social, the political, structures institutions and their operations are seen often functioning devoid of these fundamental endowments of the human nature as held by the Gospel. Attempts are made that through a variety of ministries or services the above virtues and values are expressed in concrete terms and incorporated into the systems and structures.

However, over recent decades self-critiquing has been found and accepted as a redeeming exercise. The Christian community began to feel, with Shakespeare, that many of these golden norms are observed more in the breach than in practice. Take for instance the virtue and value of equality. Practice of caste inequality has been rampant in all sectors of the Christian community, although equality of all, male and female, Jew and gentile, is proclaimed!

Because of that another supreme value, 'dignity' has been another casualty. Dignity of every human person is accepted as a great value and jealously to be guarded by the individual as well as the society. But the dignity of the Christian, belonging to apparently so-called low caste, is breached, tarnished and diminished!

Further, the 'freedom' of the individual is taught as non-negotiable. But the freedom of the caste-bound is restricted in its exercise in many areas: in the family, in the neighbourhood, in the public domain, in institutions whether public or private, in the church and other areas.

Theology had been imparted for decades in India without seriously challenging the members of the Christian community. Now the time has come to do that. Theology has to be reconceptualized. Only then can one engage in creative thinking for the growth of the community.

Truth has to be practised before preached/taught.

The Sharpening Contextual Edges

Rethinking theology in India is needed also because of the rapid changes in the global and consequently in the Indian situation. The colour of the context is turning hot! A few of the new situations are cited.

(a) *First, the two-faced challenges from Indian religions*: One is the ever-increasing hostility of rightwing Hindu organizations to Christianity and to Islam. Close study of these organizations show that they seek to establish an exclusive identity, rejecting even the right to exist in the land to Muslims and Christians. The publicly expressed and owned goal is establishing a Hindu Rashtra. Direct action using extreme forms of cruelty and violence has become the means. Contemporary history shows that what happened in Kandhamal in Orissa, Dangs district in Gujarat, and innumerable instances of attack on Christian shrines, prayer groups, small institutions, is verification and validation of the declared objective. Capture of political power to attain this goal is their national goal.

However, the pace of recently initiated dialogue of religions has been maintained, along with the offensive directed at Christian personnel and institutions.

(b) Second, global capitalism is being pursued by Indian upper classes relentlessly through new forms of networking of financial institutions, corporates, industrial and agricultural policies. This has been leading to accumulation of fabulous amounts of wealth in the hands of a few families. And the result? Steadily increasing pauperization of the great majority of the world population. Sudden spurt in unemployment, suicide of farmers and industrial workers, increase in organized violence, universal corruption, etc., has been on the increase.

Exclusive and relentless pursuit of wealth without due regard for the ethical-moral principles and norms contributes to the decline of civilizational values. How to prevent the breakdown has to be the concern of the guardians of conscience.

(c) Third, although dictatorship of the proletariat, state totalitarianism as experimented unsuccessfully in Russia, Germany, Italy, China, etc., have been successfully encountered and democracy re-established and confirmed by the Universal Declaration of Human Rights, yet a more subtle form of dictatorship in the form of a faceless and heartless market economy has taken control of the comity of nations. Among the consequences will be the decline of participative culture, people's planning, grassroots democracy, and increasing constraints imposed on peoples' movements.

(d) Faced with pluralism of religions in many a Western country, some nations begin to keep the public domain free of any symbols of religion. For example, symbols like the cross, the sword, the 'parda' and symbols of particular religions are being declared as illegal. With such steps along with the maximal erosion of ethical and moral values, modern civilization is heading towards a dismal future. India is steadily moving along the track.

(e) The tribals, the earliest inhabitants of the land, once enjoyed legal and cultural protection. The practice continued till recently. A variety of schemes, supported by legislations, have been assisting the massive entry and operation of industrialists, national and international corporations, which gravely threaten the identity security and continuity of the tribals. Millions of tribals are being force-evicted, their habitats destroyed, legitimate resistance and protests silenced or key leaders hoodwinked by seductive offers and promises and bought off. The damage to ecology, to agriculture, tribal heritages, etc., is devalued and trivialized by compliant states and their national and international allies and accomplices. Short-term benefits eagerly calculated and pursued have been replacing long-term values of the land, of the people, of the mode of governance and especially of religion and morality.

(f) Six, there has been powerful awakening among sections of the people these decades, especially during the freedom struggle. It had raised hope in them. But gradually the situation has been changing. Democratic experiment seems to be corroding due to two movements and their impact, namely, the dictating culture of the globalized world that has affected the sovereignty of the nation and also because of the internal developments due to globalization.

(g) Finally, in spite of certain forms of spirituality, both popular and yogic, there has been a colossal decline of ethical and moral values. An instinctive drive towards acquiring wealth by any means has imperiled the moral imperative. This has weakened the human incline towards honesty, uprightness, rectitude of behaviour, feel for the needy and the afflicted and similar sublime values. Wealth and pleasure have taken the place of deities in worship.

Fresh Dreaming

'India of my Dream' has been a vision-setting exercise by many visionaries in the land. Our national leaders who plunged into the freedom struggle at great cost were motivated by a vision: a free nation with its people enjoying all-round welfare. The great revolutions of history were motivated by a vision: of a society free of the restricting and enslaving conditions. Some of the religions were originally driven by dream of a suffering-free life on earth. They do hold aloft a vision: an affliction-free life on earth and happy life beyond.

The Dalits and subaltern sections of the Indian people do entertain a vision, a dream: emergence of a human community rid of the many humiliating, degrading, and enslaving practices, customs, laws, perceptions, prejudices and even religious myths and their interpretations, and to live as non-graded but equal citizens in a society where there is space for all for exercising the inborn rights, duties and responsibilities.

Such a vision for an alternate society, held aloft by the 'visionaries', needs to fire the imagination of the masses. Then they need to get organized and launch the campaign. That means the vision needs to be shared by many. Only then will a stagnant society get awakened, and become agitated. The restlessness and discontent have to become widespread so as to become a movement fuelled by the desire for a distortion-free life in a society marked with equity. Significant social changes take place only after intense and prolonged campaign. The sustaining power for the movement has to come from the vigour and fire of the ideas through which the vision has been articulated and reaches far and wide.

If the evil of caste system has been holding its sway even now in the church and in the civil society at large, one reason could be absence of such dreamers and revolutionary ideas. It is here that we turn our attention to theology. The Gospel's revolutionary potential has not yet sufficiently been tapped and disseminated in the Christian community at large, not to speak of the open society. We may be put to shame by rare individuals like Mahatma Jyotirao and Savitri Phule who did discover that power in the Gospel paraphrased it in terms categories of social dynamics, and made the Satyashodhak Samaj virtually a revolutionary movement. There are many instances of such breakthroughs in India.

Ambedkar, the framer of the Indian Constitution, while introducing the finalized version of the constitution, had drawn the attention of the nation that if social transformation and economic opportunity do not go hand in hand the dissatisfied masses that constitute the majority of the Indian population will revolt and throw overboard the well-crafted framework for governance.

Now social transformation in India has already proven to be a difficult task. Current global, national and regional trends have only been aggravating the situation.

While entertaining such enthusiasm-generating hope Dalit intellectuals are dismayed by the question: does the existing theological education facilitate the emergence of such a community. They feel that both the prevailing education, available in the secular institutions like the universities and theological education pursued in existing and functioning institutions do not offer much hope either. 'Educate, organize and agitate' has been the integral method evolved proposed and experimented by the great national leader, B.R. Ambedkar. The great educationist of our times Paolo Freire would advice caution. He has stated long ago that it is not education that shapes the society, but on the contrary it is the society that shapes education. Ambedkar suggested that it is critical use of education that needs to be promoted. Current trends will illustrate the point. The trend is clear: it is the cyber world and its promises that greatly set the curriculum for educational institutions, at all levels. The technological world has dwarfed the world of humanities in the universities. The elites of old, led by Brahminic worldview, wanted a hierarchical social order. For that they invented myths and stories that would seal the fate of such ordering of society. India is still struggling to get out of its clutches. Dalits are at it. The feminist movements are at it. So are other subaltern movements.

Therefore the pertinent question is: what kind of Indian society do we envisage or dream after. Many answers can come from many sectors. We pursue here the dream of the 'losers of history', namely the Dalits, the tribals, the women, all the dispossessed and marginalized, all the deprived of India.

It is to facilitate group thinking, debate, sharing and such exercises that would generate a common vision conformable to the vision ingrained in the Bible, namely, the vision of the Kingdom/Reign of God that the title of the common project, Rethinking Theology for India, is initiated.

The Indian society is being rattled by many issues that affect the life of the commoner. Should not theology be closely following these developments and infuse new ideas among the large number of young pursuers—people affected by these issues ask. Many therefore ask: Is Christian discourse within the campus of theological education out of tune with the contemporary phase of the society, especially from the Dalits' and subalterns' perspective?

Emerging Method in Dalit Theology

Here is one consideration to understand the present-day theological discourse in contemporary Dalit communities about the need of rethinking theology.

Let us invoke a golden principle from the history. Integral development of persons and communities depend on the critical co-relationship between religious experience and social processes of the contemporary society. The axiom seeks to hold as a golden principle that sound religious experience, because it is rooted in God, should lead to socially transformative dynamics to bring about positive change in the society in favour of the 'community' that is in greater and urgent need.

The best example is that of the Bible. Experience of the

deplorable human experience in Egypt drove Moses to the wilderness of the mountain where he was met with the profound God experience. This twofold experience filled Moses with the dynamics of social transformation in so far as an enslaved oppressed and persecuted community was liberated and settled down in Palestine. Once settled, normative prescriptions were introduced by the enlightened leadership so that a community culture emerged in which the individual's integrity was assured by the collectivity and the collectivity ensured the individual's integral growth and development.

Similarly, Jesus Christ's experience of the human community of his times and His Abba experience led to liberative movement in His lifetime as we have in the Gospels and later on in the historic Christian movement of the apostolic times.

These historical events tell us: Dalit theological method will emerge when Dalit human experience, and not an existing metaphysical edifice, is the starting point of the faith-reflection.

The chief contention in these pages is that critical use of secular ideologies and theologies of religions can rekindle the fire in theology. The anchorage of the exercise is on the Bible. The contention is that 'secular' as well as 'religious' ideologies and perspectives, can have their impact on Christian theology to animate it. Tracing the nature of their interaction promises to be a wholesome exercise.

Close scrutiny of the Bible can show that secular ideologies and theologies of religions are at work in the Bible. All that people seek is all round welfare.

One can find the foundations Marx's idea of economy and organization of one's life and society in the Book of Leviticus. Moses insisted on the following. Every family should have its own land. It should be cultivated by human labour and maintain one's life. Labour is for human maintenance not for exploitation and excessive profit seeking. None should be enslaved. In case by one's own folly either land or oneself is mortgaged, such a one should be helped to free from that situation. If one is in irredeemable debt, it should be written off. This should happen periodically, for instance, every 49th year. Fiftieth year is Holy Year, the Jubilee year. The year of God's and peoples' holiness. Holiness of God AND THE PEOPLE OF God is established when the agreed covenantal commitments to God and to one another are flawlessly observed. The social contract and the covenant with God become the pillars of a new human and humane community.

Bhim Rao Ambedkar had a vision of India. He stood for a caste-free India where people are provided with economic opportunities and social space for creativity and freedom. Social transformation is the first step before one moves towards redistribution of the sources of livelihood like land, capital, etc. Rule of law should guide the life of the citizens. The society or community should be entitled to all rights that are proper of the human person. The citizens should have the freedom to critique and discard whatever is seen as superstitious.

Gandhi entertained the idea of *swaraj*. What did he mean by *swaraj*? 'Gandhi wants Indians to be well fed, well housed, well-clothed, well-governed, well read, and cognizant of the place and function of aesthetics and art of life' (A. Parel, *Hind Swaraj*, p. lvii).

There is also the incipient political economy and Christian version of 'capitalism' as envisioned by Pope Leo XIII in his *rerum novarum*. Essentials of 'community' and of pluralism as Ambedkar envisaged, and self-reliance through self-investment and labour for earning one's bread, are held pillars of a future community. Every family should have land. Everyone must labour and produce for each one's livelihood. But production is not profit and accumulation-oriented, and for feeding one's unlimited and unquenchable greed and consumption. Here is community with diversity and pluralism. The 12 tribes in Israel were maintaining their separate identity but all together constitute one community, that of Israel, the covenant community. The key insight that is worked into the system *in perpetuum* is: revisit and check every 49th year. In case idleness of one or greed of another has led to enslavement of some or over-fattening of another, be human and return to the original vision. All are equal. None should be slave. All should have land or economic resources. All should labour and sustain their livelihood. The underlying principle is: (1) land belongs to God, (2) all are God's people and hence equal, (3) none should be enslaved and exploited, (4) periodic self-examination should ensure the pristine status. The much-abused word, jubilee, these days is an exercise in consumption, but was central to the Levitical thrust. It reminds all believers of this task and responsibility.

A vision for another way of living as humans should be placed before us and guide us as a pole star. We get suffocated by the ugliness constraints and inadequacies of our present society. Only those who work in deep dark dusty coal-mines will appreciate the fresh air and space of Mogul Gardens of India's Rashtrapati Bhavan. To dream of genuine human community in India we should contemplate the first dawn of creation as we have in Genesis, the first dawn of the Resurrection and the first dawn of the New Creation heralded by Jesus at His Resurrection.

We recall the basics: 'God is love' (IJO 4: 8). Christ is the incarnation (IJO: 14) and the sacrament of God (LG. 1) and His love. The church is the body of Christ (I Cor. 12: 27). The mission of the church is to raise all humanity as the body of Christ, as a community of love. That is the Kingdom of God, Christ came to inaugurate (Mk 1: 14-15).

Conclusion

'You are the light of the world . . . let you light shine before others' (Mt 5: 14); 'You are the salt of the earth' (Mt 5: 13). So if God is love, and if Christ is God's love incarnate in human history, and if the church is that body of Christ and is mandated to be the light of the world and the salt of the earth, theology has to be in the service of that church. Theology has to highlight, promote, and vindicate these properties as necessarily inbuilt into community. Love (of God and His people), service (of God and His people), sharing (of time, goods, sentiments . . .), sacrifice (of one's interests, priorities, selfishness, etc., for the other), forgiveness and such virtues have to be the distinguishing mark and expression of the church in the world. Fellowship and equality have to be experienced exercised and verified in practice, in day-to-day relationship. Conviviality, commensality, connubiality, etc., have to be actualities. But they are not yet. Caste practice is still rampant. When confronted there is the experience of pain and resistance as well as reluctance to move away from caste-dominated living to real social egalitarianism. Theology has to facilitate their emergence in the church. The community has to embody these dimensions/virtues poured out by the Spirit of Christ at Pentecost.

15

Common Task for Tomorrow

JAMES MASSEY AND T.K. JOHN

The First Stage

The endeavour at the Dalit front so far had been focused on the Dalit-subaltern groups, rather exclusively, so that available energy is not dispersed and attention too widely scattered. The trends had been towards generation of a Dalit theology which was, and continues to be so, engaged in that task. It had been quite effective and successful. In concrete:

- Here the effort has been to deepen the awareness of the present deplorable situation generated and disseminated by a variety of agencies and strategies.
- That awareness has been generating awakening among them to wake up and organize actions in order to rid themselves of the unjust, unequal and degrading social human situation which has been inflicted on them by the upper castes in India.
- This was intended to empower themselves to regain their lost status, dignity, power, rights and responsibilities and become an empowered, liberated human community.

This seems to have been the first stage of journeying with

the Dalits of India. Time came for moving forward to the next stage.

The Second Stage

Then it was felt we should move on to the next phase of societal change. Efforts were extended towards this goal.

At this stage the social space and our conspectus was widened to include the other subaltern groups equally at a disadvantageous position in the social ladder. In this process the other subaltern groups like Tribals, Adivasis, Women, etc., were included, so that what had been happening to the Dalit groups, namely awakening—leading to empowerment and liberation—could happen to these latter groups as well.

In other words, all deprived human groups should come together to eventually acquire a new status, and achieve a transformed human social situation free of constraints created by caste, racial or gender discrimination. The networking proved fruitful.

The Third Stage

Our perception moves further. The Gospel's transforming power affects all, generating new cultural expressions through the medium of local cultures purified and enriched by the Gospel. Gospel values of equality, sharing, collaboration, interrelatedness, find expression through existing village or urban cultures, varying from place to place, from state to state. The new theology that is thus emerging is due to the transforming power of the gospel. A new ethos emerges, that of a new community consciousness, leaving behind barriers and walls created by caste. The earlier dominant-dominated relationship is now replaced by a certain fellowship.

In other words, the goal of the new theology should be for the emergence of a society free from these inequalities and a new co-equation has to grow. 'Together we should strive for a community-culture'. New relationship is established between the once-dominated groups and the dominant societies leading to mutual collaboration for riddance of the unequal relationship. The dominant groups of all cultures and communities should be invited to collaborate. This new initiative could have the following objectives:

- Penetrated by the power of the Gospel, through the new consciousness, the dominant community engages in a self-critiquing exercise so that their new convictions are expressed through their own cultural modes.
- The dominant castes/classes own up their role in the perpetration of the evil of domination and oppression.
- A consciousness and willingness is generated in them to own up their role for this unequal situation.
- This could lead to gradual discarding of the mindset responsible for the unjust system and social structure and recasting of all human relationships marked hereto by disequilibrium.
- Both the groups could take active and effective steps for creation of a genuine human community where a new ethos is generated and prevails.

This new change is concretely expressed through a new culture of participation, collaboration, sharing, fellowship, togetherness, etc. It is the beginning of a new community; veritable anticipations of the reign of God on this earth is inaugurated (Matt 4).

It is a new human and humane community.

Contributors

FR. A. MARIA ARUL RAJA SJ is a Jesuit Priest and Professor of Biblical Studies in Arul Kadal Regional Theologate at Chennai.

FR. MONODEEP DANIEL BAC is a member of the Brotherhood of the Ascended Christ, Delhi, and is an ordained Presbyter (Priest) in the Church of North India, Delhi Diocese.

REV ROGER GAIKWAD is the General Secretary of National Council of Churches in India and also a professor of Religion.

REV RICHARD HOWELL is the General Secretary of the Evangelical Fellowship of India, New Delhi.

FR. T.K. JOHN SJ is Emeritus Professor of Vidyajyoti College of Theology, Delhi and Chairperson of Centre for Dalit/Subaltern Studies, New Delhi.

Ashish Kumar is Administrative Assistant, Senate of Serampore College, West Bengal.

REV WATI LONGCHAR is Professor of Christian Theology and Dean of SCEPTRE, Kolkata.

ATOLA LONGKUMER is Associate Professor of Religion at Leonard Theological College, Jabalpur, MP.

FR. S. LOURDUSWAMY is Associate Director, Centre for Dalit/Subaltern Studies, New Delhi and Correspondent, St. Joseph's Matric, Hr. Sec. School, Vellore.

REV JAMES MASSEY is Director of the Centre for Dalit/Subaltern Studies, New Delhi; Member, Assessment & Monitoring Authority & Planning Commission of India, Govt. of India.

BP. NIRMAL MINZ is the (retired) Founder-Principal of Gossner Theological College and (retired) Bishop of the NWGEL Church, Ranchi.

SR. SHALINI MULACKAL is a Presentation Sister and Professor of Systematic Theology at Vidyajyoti College of Theology, Delhi.

INDUKURI JOHN MOHAN RAZU was Professor of Christian Social Ethics at the United Theological College, Bangalore. He is presently associated with ACTS Academy of Higher Education in Doctoral programmes in Bangalore.

REV. SIMON SAMUEL is Professor of New Testament Studies and History of Christian Origins, Principal, New Theological College, Dehradun.

REV. RAVI TIWARI is the Registrar of the Senate of Serampore College (University), West Bengal. He has been teaching Philosophy and Religion in different theological colleges since 1979.

Index